THE
MURCHISONS

The Rise and
Fall of a
Texas Dynasty

JANE WOLFE

ST. MARTIN'S PAPERBACKS

THE MURCHISONS: THE RISE AND FALL OF A TEXAS DYNASTY

Copyright © 1989 by Jane Wolfe.

Photo illustration on cover by Marc Tauss.

Library of Congress Catalog Card Number: 89-35328

ISBN: 0-312-92418-6

Printed in the United States of America

St. Martin's Press hardcover edition published 1989
St. Martin's Paperbacks edition/March 1991

10 9 8 7 6 5 4 3 2 1

*This book is for
Leon Harris,
who has brought endless joy and
excitement to my career and to my life.*

Acknowledgments

Although the members of the Murchison family collectively spent nearly one hundred hours being interviewed by me for this book, this is not an authorized biography. I have checked facts with individual members of the family, but no member has seen any part of this book prior to publication and no member of the family is in any way responsible for what I have written. If there are errors of fact or judgment contained within this book, I alone am responsible.

As is the fate of every biographer, there were instances when I was given somewhat differing versions of the same anecdote, as well as conflicting opinions. Therefore, I have had, like a juror in a trial, to select the one that seemed to me the more accurate and the more likely. On matters of unresolved controversy, I have tried to show the differing points of view. In some instances the sources are listed in the story; in other instances, they are named in the Notes at the back of the book. To promote clarity, portions of certain interviews and other quoted passages have been condensed or refined, and some correspondence has been reconstructed from interviews. In the course of my research I studied numerous family scrapbooks, photographs, and letters, and read hundreds of newspaper and magazine articles, but I have relied primarily on firsthand witnesses.

This book could not have been written without the help and unwavering cooperation of all three generations of the Murchison family. I am eternally grateful for the many hours they spent being interviewed by me and for their extraordinary candor. By revealing their faults and failures, as well as their successes, the Murchisons made it possible for me to write a more accurate and ultimately more compelling history than would otherwise have been possible.

Virginia Murchison Linthicum devoted hours of her time to interviews, provided me with hundreds of letters, photographs, and news clippings, and permitted me to visit Acuña in Mexico and Gladoaks in East Texas in order that I could see at firsthand the places where Clint Sr. spent so much of his time. Lupe Murchison and Jane Murchison Haber also were generous with their time, opened their homes to me, and recalled with clarity the events that helped shape their family's history. Also valuable in a different way were the third-generation Murchisons who had only vague recollections of their grandfather, but who contributed the most in explaining the events of the last ten years, since John Murchison's death. They are Clint Murchison III, Judy Rice Murchison, Robert Murchison, John Dabney Murchison Jr., and Barbara Jeanne Murchison Coffman.

I also conducted more than 250 interviews with friends, business associates, and competitors of the family. While almost every person I interviewed provided me with some new fact or insight for the book, those to whom I am most grateful are Burch Ault, Phil Bee, Annette Besser, John Black, Malcolm Brachman, Bill Carey, Louis Carroll, Ellie Caulkins, George Caulkins, James Clark Jr., Governor William P. Clements, Bill Dunagan, Andre Emmerich, Lou Farris, Bernard Fulton, Broughton Gauntt, Henry Gilchrist, Marcus Ginsburg, Robert Ginsburg, Bobby Goldman, Reverend Olen Griffing, Ebby Halliday, Walter Hagan, Golden Hale, Darrell Hamric, Dr. John Jenkins, Lee Roy Jordan, Truman Kemper, Pete Kriendler, Tom Landry, Frank LaRue, Janie C. Lee, Nancy Lemmon, John Lunsford, Gerald Mann, Stanley Marcus, Susan Marcus, DeLoach Martin, Spencer Martin, Mary Lynn Aldredge McEntire, Kenneth McGee, Kenneth Murchison, Kenneth Noland, Enslie Oglesby, Albert Oldham, Harry S. Parker III, Mary Ann Perryman, Howard Reed, Roy Reed, John Rogers, Steve Rooth, Lucy Morris Runge, Tex Schramm, Blackie Sherrod, Frank Schultz, James Speer, Taz Speer, Walter Spradley, Jim Stroman, John Taylor, Eula

Mae Tilley, Dr. Raymond Thomasson, Tom Webb, and Ruth Woodard.

A rich source of detailed information about Clint Murchison Sr. is *Clint,* a book written by his private secretary, Ernestine Van Buren, who in our several interviews provided additional fascinating information.

Like all historians, I am greatly indebted to a number of librarians, most particularly those at the Clint W. Murchison Henderson County Memorial Library and the Henderson County Historical Commission, both in Athens, Texas; and the Texas/Dallas History and Archives department of the Dallas Public Library. The many profitable hours I spent in these institutions would not have been possible were it not for the dedicated, careful, unsung librarians who over the years collect the materials that record our history.

I also want to thank particularly Carr and Estelle Pritchett, with whom I stayed many times in Athens and who taught me about East Texas, as well as so much about the Murchisons.

I am grateful to Marvin Wise and Ron Vassallo who helped me sort through hundreds of legal documents that were essential to understanding this story.

My special thanks go to Thomas Dunne, my editor at St. Martin's Press, who showed faith in this project from the start and never gave up hope that it would be completed, and to David Hirschfeld, my Assistant Editor, who provided many thoughtful and helpful ideas. I also thank Julian Bach, my agent, for believing that I had a fascinating story to tell in the Murchisons. Finally, I express my deepest appreciation to my mentor and friend Leon Harris, without whose constant support and love this book would never have been written.

PART
ONE

1

"Cash makes a man careless."

The winter storm that blew in on February 1, 1985, lashed violently at the twenty-five-acre Clint Murchison Jr. estate in North Dallas. Icy wind gusting up to thirty miles an hour destroyed trees that had been nurtured as carefully as the valuable limbs of Murchison's Dallas Cowboys. Tree branches snapped under the weight of ice and crashed to the ground.

The blizzard, with a windchill of ten degrees below zero, was the worst to hit Dallas in years and brought the city to a halt. Schools closed and citizens were repeatedly warned not to leave their houses. But despite the warnings, on that Friday morning more than twenty lawyers representing top banks from around the world slowly made their way on perilously icy streets and bridges to the estate eleven miles north of downtown Dallas. They represented Clint Murchison Jr.'s largest creditors, and they had come at his request.

In the last year these and other creditors had filed claims against Murchison for repayment of loans totaling more than $175 million. Despite his repeated promises to make good on these notes that he had personally guaranteed, he had not done so—nor could he. What he knew and these visitors did not know was that he owed more than half a billion dollars. For months quiet, gentlemanly requests for payment had gone unanswered. But unlike the howling blizzard, these creditors came to the estate reluctantly and with no great enthusiasm for their task.

Creditors who had long been obsequious to the name of Murchison now were wary of it. Clint Jr. had already sold his beloved Dallas Cowboys for $80 million, and he was scrambling to convert his family's holdings into cash. At this very moment two anxious creditors were threatening an immediate courthouse auction of the twenty-four acres surrounding Clint's home, an indication of just how serious things had become.

Exacerbating Clint's financial situation was his rapidly failing health. He suffered from cerebellar degenerative disease, a loss of nerve cells in the part of the brain that controls balance and motor functions. Although his mind had not been affected and he was still very alert, his ability to speak and walk had deteriorated in recent months until he was now confined to a wheelchair. He depended on his associates to speak in his behalf. The most ordinary tasks were now a struggle for him.

But the stony-faced visitors to the family compound at 6200 Forest Lane found a man still surrounded by evidences of extraordinary wealth. Clint had spared no cost in 1963 when he designed the 43,500-square-foot mansion and directed the planting of each tree, the building of ponds, the sculpting of shrubbery, on virtually every foot of the estate's rolling, wooded acres. He also built a football field where he and his children played touch football.

The seven-bedroom house itself covered more than an acre. It was run by computer, with a state-of-the-art electronics system designed and built by the owner himself. Curtains opened and closed with the flick of a switch, an electronic bar made drinks to order. A complex intercom system brought servants from one end of the U-shaped home to the other. The house cooled quickly during hot Texas summers—it had a power source that could have provided electricity for a thirty-story office building.

Clint Jr. designed the home's two industrial kitchens with walk-in freezers, supervised the laying of Italian travertine floors throughout the house, and the construction of two swimming pools. One, according to *Time* magazine, "could float the *Queen Mary*," and had one side made of glass so that the owner, in his adjoining sunken playroom, could study the swimming bodies.

Clint Jr. and his brother, John Dabney Murchison, who died in 1979, were still in their twenties when they were given a fortune by their oil-rich wildcatter father, Clint Murchison Sr. Clint Jr. and John quickly increased the fortune, and for many years the father and sons were thought to be among the half dozen richest families in America. What made the three Murchisons remarkable was that in addition to being rich, they were active investors, unlike some Rockefellers and Mellons who had turned their fortunes over to others to manage.

A 1961 *Time* magazine cover story on John and Clint Jr. described the brothers' capture of the giant New York holding company, Allegheny Corporation, as "a coup that outdealt even the feats of their wheeler-dealer father." The article said, "In the biggest and bitterest proxy fight in U.S. history, the Murchisons snatched Allegheny out of the hands of Woolworth heir Allan P. Kirby, 68, a Wall Street titan with a fortune far bigger than theirs. More impressive yet, they won by rallying more Wall Street support than Kirby himself."

What surprised *Time* and most of the Eastern Establishment was that these yokels from the boonies could outsmart one of Wall Street's shrewdest entrepreneurs and his lawyers and advisers. The idea that the Murchisons were "just simple country boys" was one that they worked very hard to maintain.

Clint Murchison Jr.'s signature alone was once all that was needed to borrow millions of dollars. So great was his business reputation and so confident was he in his success that he personally guaranteed hundreds of loans not only for his own businesses but for those of any friend who asked. There were no limits to his arrogantly casual disregard in signing notes and pledging collateral. The Texas Homestead Act established that a person's home and land could not be seized by creditors. But Clint foolishly signed away part of that protection when, desperate for collateral, he pledged the acreage around his home.

Clint Jr. had a genius I.Q. and was educated at Lawrenceville and MIT, where he received a master's degree in mathematics. From his very start in business, he was a formidable competitor. He built the Dallas Cowboys from scratch, beginning in 1960 when, against the advice of his father, he obtained a National Football League franchise for Dallas. Not

only was it tough for the new team to prevail against older
NFL teams, but Clint Jr. had an additional problem. Lamar
Hunt, of the rich H. L. Hunt clan, had established an American Football League team, the Dallas Texans, and the two
were competing for fans. Shrewdly, inventively, relentlessly,
in only a few years, Clint Jr. drove Hunt's team out of town.

When Dallas's city fathers refused to allow him to build a
new stadium downtown, Clint Jr. took his ball club eleven
miles north to the dusty town of Irving, Texas. There he masterminded the innovative design and financing of a $25 million
space-age stadium whose seats and luxury suites would become the most expensive in American sports. From his fifty-
yard-line owner's box, Clint Jr. watched his Cowboys develop
into a world-renowned organization that would be dubbed
"America's Team."

Selling the team to pay off debts had been the most emotionally wrenching experience of his life. But not everyone felt
sorry for Clint Jr. Painfully shy and constantly preoccupied
with his plans and his desires, Clint Jr. snubbed people everywhere he went. Acquaintances who greeted him on the street,
in elevators, at downtown men's clubs, were offended when he
looked straight past them. Many times he even refused to say
hello to men in the same boardroom or involved with the same
business deal. After the downfall the mention of Clint Jr.'s
name often brought the reply, "He was a rich, arrogant son of
a bitch. He probably deserved what he got."

Equally unmoved by Clint Jr.'s financial crisis were those
who disapproved of his constant philandering. The mystique
of Clint Jr.'s mythic wealth did not mask from his friends and
associates a severe psychological problem. He was sexually
obsessed, priapic. The brilliant mind that had impressed his
teachers at MIT was, for most of his adult life, focused largely
on the tactics and strategies of serial seduction. Every young,
pretty woman he met was a potential bedmate. His was a sexual hunger that could not be satisfied, a thirst that could not be
slaked. The more he got, the greater his need.

A Dallas arts philanthropist asked one of Clint Jr.'s best
friends why Clint Jr. cared nothing about any of the arts. "Be-

cause he cares about only two things," came the laughing reply. "One is business and the other is not art."

For years Dallas society sympathized with Clint Jr.'s beautiful first wife, Jane, who finally divorced him in 1973 when the evidence of Clint's assiduous adultery became unbearable. But when things turned sour for Clint Jr., many found it difficult to pity the second Mrs. Clint Murchison Jr., who had been married three times previously and constantly proselytized as a born-again Christian. "I still sin but I confess and ask for forgiveness," said Anne Murchison, adding that she relied on Jesus to help her find a parking place at the supermarket.

The enigma of Clint Jr. was that outsiders saw only the dark side of him. They recognized the arrogant egotist but ignored the brilliant and inventive businessman. They condemned the flagrant adulterer, unaware that he was also a loving and sensitive father. They saw only his distant side and never the immense wit and charm he reserved for making a deal or a woman.

Only those who worked closely with him knew of his extreme loyalty to friends and business associates. During the Dallas Cowboys' formative years, the team had one losing season after another, and fans were demanding that coach Tom Landry be fired. Instead, Murchison called a press conference and announced a new ten-year contract for Landry, a commitment then unequaled in professional sports. So intense was his loyalty that it often overcame his better judgment and eventually was instrumental in his downfall.

"There were very few people that Clint associated with who were of good character," said his ex-wife, Jane Murchison Haber. "A lot of people used him, and many times he knew it, but he would never cut off an associate, ever. Every friend of Clint's was a friend for life."

The creditors that came to the house on February 1, 1985, were distressed by Clint's appearance. He still had his crewcut hair and his trademark clothes—very narrow ties and white short-sleeve shirts, even in the dead of winter—but gone were the impish grin and the famous twinkle in his piercing blue eyes.

Like his father, Clint Jr. was a very small man, only five feet six inches tall. Both Clint Jr. and his brother, John Dabney Murchison, inherited their father's looks, but their even more obvious similarities to Clint Sr. were in the way they conducted business. Though the brothers were the antithesis of one another, each clearly represented one of two opposing forces within their father. John was smart and careful, and surrounded himself with able advisers. Clint Jr. shot from the hip and preferred to make deals secretly, relying almost exclusively on his own brilliance and instinct. Clint Sr., at times a careful planner, at other times a carefree plunger, recognized himself in both his sons, whom he laughingly called "Vice and Versa."

The business characteristic that the brothers shared with one another was their father's devotion to making one highly leveraged business deal after another. Big Clint, beginning in the twenties, built his oil fortune on credit, swapping a share of one oil lease for money to buy a second. "Financin' by finaglin'," was the way he described it. Associates said the elder Clint had an uncanny ability to add $1 million and $1 million and come up with $11 million. In a series of ingenious parlays in the 1930s and 1940s, he created an intricate, multimillion-dollar empire that ranged from a pipeline in Canada to a silver mine in Mexico.

In the late 1950s Big Clint's worth was estimated at more than half a billion dollars, but he always liked to talk down his wealth. "After the first hundred million," he said, "what the hell."

His sons started in business with a Texas-size bloc of their father's immense interests. Big Clint also gave them some advice: "Money is like manure. Pile it in one place and it stinks like hell. Spread it around and it does some good."

The sons listened and amassed their own fortune, once estimated to equal their father's net worth. Buying, selling, borrowing, and investing, John and Clint Jr. diversified until their partnership, Murchison Brothers, had interests in some 120 companies, including residential and commercial real estate and construction firms, insurance companies, banks, hotels, pipeline companies, oil and gas properties, a water utility, an airline. To spread the risk, or the so-called manure, their portfolio also included a candy company, an amusement park, and the New York book publisher Henry Holt & Company. To the contemptuous question, "What are those Texans doing sticking their noses in New York publishing?" came the reply, "Making money."

It was a tenet of Big Clint's business philosophy that "Cash makes a man careless," and he prided himself on the vast sums that he owed. "I figure," the elder Murchison said, "a man is worth about twice what he owes."

Ironically, it was Clint Jr.'s devotion to his father's faith in using the maximum possible credit that led first to his phenomenal success but finally to his downfall. Clint Sr.'s sons operated as their father had, and the practice was highly successful for years. But the collapse of oil and real estate prices in the eighties, coupled with high interest rates on their debt and the end of rampant inflation, outmoded this longtime Murchison *modus operandi.*

If the meeting during that winter storm on February 1, 1985, had been inevitable, it was a long time coming. Creditors' worries had suddenly intensified months earlier, on March 16, 1984, the eve of the Cowboys sale. On that night Murchison was honored by the Boys' Clubs of America at a black-tie dinner for seven hundred guests in Dallas's grandest ballroom. Former Texas Governor John Connally, Senator John Tower, Texas Governor Mark White, the mayor of Dallas, NFL Commissioner Pete Rozelle, as well as hundreds of bankers and powerful businessmen from New York to California had come to pay tribute to the diminutive Texas millionaire. But Clint surprised most of the people in the ballroom when he arrived, for the first time at a large public gathering, in a wheelchair. Many of the guests were stunned at the sight, and even more shocked to learn that he was barely able to speak.

When Clint was presented the Boys' Clubs' Herbert Hoover Humanitarian Award and an associate pushed him in his wheelchair onto the dais and accepted the award on Clint's behalf, panic set in. Many of the men in the ballroom were officers or directors of banks that held Clint's promissory notes for millions of dollars, on which they had not been receiving payments. For months rumors had been circulating that the sixty-year-old Murchison was seriously ill, suffering from a degenerative nerve disease. Now suddenly the gossip that Murchison was a sick man was no longer just gossip.

The evening, which had been orchestrated by the head of Dallas's biggest bank and one of the Murchison family's biggest creditors, was intended to boost Clint's image. But it had the opposite effect. When his creditors saw him in person, they immediately feared that his illness would make recovery of their already overdue loans increasingly difficult. "That's when people really got scared," recalls one of Clint Jr.'s closest associates. "Suddenly they thought, 'What happens if this old guy dies and we're left holding the bag?' "

The sale of the Cowboys the next day failed to relieve Murchison of the huge claims. Instead, it triggered a rush for payment. He was being sued by some of the biggest names in finance. The Continental Illinois National Bank and Trust Company (soon to face its own reorganization) was suing for $75 million. Merrill Lynch Private Capital, Inc., was seeking $26 million; Citicorp Real Estate of New York, $17 million; the Arab Banking Corporation and European American Bank, $18 million each. He owed money to banks where he was a director or major stockholder, including a Nevada bank where he was the second-largest stockholder. The bank sued when he failed to make an interest payment.

The meeting on February 1 was Murchison's final effort to plead for more time for an out-of-court settlement. Through his lawyers Clint suggested that the creditors form a committee to work together in bringing about a reorganization of his ailing empire. That very day plans were in the works, he said, for Fort Worth's Bass brothers to take over some troubled Murchison real estate projects. Ironically, the Bass fortune, which had grown into the billions, began with Clint Murchison Sr.'s lifelong partner Sid Richardson, dubbed by the press "The first billionaire west of the Mississippi."

Like the elder Murchison, Richardson was proud of the money he owed. "I'm a bigger success than you are," Sid bragged to Clint. "Some of my paper is held in London." When Murchison once talked of getting out of debt, Richardson retorted, "Don't do it. The day you do you'll be dead and I haven't got time for a funeral."

But Clint Jr.'s creditors were unmoved by the alleged interest of the Bass brothers. Despite his estimated net worth of $250 million in 1984, his creditors knew Murchison was long on nonliquid assets, such as real estate and oil wells, and short on cash. Many rich Texans were hurt by a slump in the energy and real estate markets in the early 1980s, but for Clint Jr., who was always heavily leveraged, the prognosis was particularly grim. He reportedly had $400 million invested in noncash-flow real estate projects that simply could not generate enough cash to pay his $80 million a year interest payments, let alone principal payments.

The combination of recession, high interest rates, and a soft housing market left many of his real estate projects standing half-completed: a townhouse project in Washington; condominiums in Richmond, Virginia, and Palm Springs, California; a resort complex in Key West, Florida; and major development projects in New Orleans and Hawaii.

But even as his big projects were failing, he continued to borrow huge sums to finance new—and often bigger—ones. In business as in football, he was a man who hated short yardage plays. Instead, he liked to go for the long bomb, the "Hail Mary" pass.

When things began to turn sour, he became defiant, resentful of the banks and attorneys who imposed their laws and strictures on his casual, freewheeling business style. In 1981 he sold a downtown Dallas building which the purchaser then imploded. After a picture of the dynamiting ran in a Dallas newspaper, Clint received an angry letter from the Southwestern Life Insurance Company pointing out that they had a lien on the building that had been destroyed. The company charged that the act constituted misuse of its collateral and demanded immediate payment. Clint dashed off a one-sentence reply: "Picky, picky, picky."

According to a Murchison associate, Clint knew that the mortgage had been paid off and the insurance company was in error. But the letter exemplified his mischievous sense of humor, and his talent for pithy one-liners.

Clint was being sued, and was repeatedly threatened with suits not only from banks and corporations but from his own family. Hostilities within the family began after John Sr.'s death in 1979, when his only son, John Dabney Murchison Jr., demanded that his trust, which was established by his grandfather, Clint Sr., and was years overdue, be delivered.

John became viewed as the family villain, threatening to divide an empire that had long been known for its cohesiveness. Angered by the trouble her son was causing, his mother, Lupe Murchison, filed suit to have John Jr. removed as co-executor (with her) of his father's estate. John resigned on the eve of a trial that would have brought Richard "Racehorse" Haynes, representing John Jr., head to head with Lupe's attorney and close friend, former Texas Attorney General John Hill. Texans were disappointed that the courtroom scene, which would have revealed the intimate secrets and intricate business dealings of one of Texas's richest families, was avoided. But John Jr. was not easily quieted. In 1981 he filed a $30 million lawsuit against Clint, claiming that his uncle had mismanaged his assets, specifically his trust fund, which was still tied up. John Jr. charged that the assets in his trust, estimated to be at least $30 million, were being used to finance Clint Jr.'s own shaky business deals.

By 1985 internecine battles were overshadowed by Clint Jr.'s deepening financial crisis. For a long time, Dallas society could not believe the television and newspaper reports. "Murchison: A Fortune Lost," claimed *The New York Times* on March 5, 1985. Five days later *The Dallas Morning News* explained, "How Murchison's Empire Was Shaken."

Murchisons in money trouble seemed impossible. Clint Jr. and John were the Texas golden boys of the sixties and seventies. Their uninhibited and unembarrassed enjoyment of their constantly growing fortune were part of the Texas myth. John and Lupe spent their millions like modern Medicis, buying homes around the world, collecting contemporary art, commissioning Salvador Dali to design Lupe a 29-karat diamond ring. But what suddenly was threatening the fortunes of both branches of the family was not extravagant living but Clint

Jr.'s business mismanagement and his inability to adapt to changing economic conditions in America and the world.

The meeting on February 1 at his home did not turn out the way Clint had hoped. Instead of the usual servile bankers and their lawyers to whom he had always been accustomed, he was now faced with men who clearly had grave doubts about whether they should continue the loans they had already given him. In fact, many were ashamed of their past deferential conduct and regretted that they had never demanded a proper balance sheet.

Six days later, on February 7, 1985, three of Clint's creditors filed a petition forcing him into bankruptcy. Their petition was converted to Chapter 11, and Clint began what he hoped would be an orderly reorganization of his assets. But it was a tragic and bitter end. In the coming months, an army of lawyers for banks, corporations, and individuals around the world would begin to dismember one of America's greatest personal fortunes.

"It was like a death in the family," said Clint Jr.'s daughter-in-law Judy Murchison, unable to control her tears. "You wondered and you asked yourself, 'How did we ever fall so far from where we were? How could this ever have happened?' "

2

"If I owned Texas and Hell, I would rent
out Texas and live in Hell."

For generation, after generation, after generation, Clint Murchison Sr.'s ancestors were poor.

His great, great, great grandfather, Kenneth Murchison, left Inverness, Scotland, for America in 1773, hoping to make his fortune. Consistent lack of success followed Kenneth and his son Murdoch and his son Daniel from North Carolina to Tennessee to Mississippi to Texas. There were many who doubted that Texas offered much chance of success, including General Philip H. Sheridan, military governor of the state after the Civil War, who declared before the war, "If I owned Texas and Hell, I would rent out Texas and live in Hell."

Texas had never been rich. It had only won independence from Mexico in 1836, because, not discounting the courage of its American-born revolutionaries, the Mexicans thought it too poor a province to spend more blood and money to keep. From 1836 until 1845, it had been the Republic of Texas, admittedly a grand title, but it seemed so unlikely to survive on its own that after only nine years it sought admission as the 28th state in the Union.

In 1855, the same year that Sheridan offered his appraisal, Daniel Murchison's twenty-seven-year-old son Thomas Frank Murchison left Crockett, in Houston County, for the tiny hamlet of Athens. The village was fifty miles southeast of Dallas, which had been settled only fourteen years earlier. Athens was carved out of a stand of virgin East Texas forest, located on the backbone ridge between the Trinity and Neches rivers.

When Thomas Frank (called "T. F.") arrived at the red oak

14

tree that marked the center of Athens, he had with him only his horse and a wagon full of dreams. He and his father had been lured to the state a few years earlier with the same hopes as thousands of other southerners who hung "Gone to Texas" signs on their doors. Although many of those who came pouring into the state were bankrupts seeking protection under the Texas Homestead Act, many others were merely poor and hoped for a chance to begin again. Despite some of the later pretensions of descendants of these early settlers, very few men and women set out to the frontier's edge if they were leaving something better behind.

When the Republic of Texas joined the United States in 1845, it retained ownership of all its public land, making the state the largest land promoter in the country. Much of the real estate was turned over to private promoters. Early settlers in Henderson County soon learned that they had been victims of these public relations men, who promised that the soil near Athens was "rich and capable of growing all manner of crops."

The land was, in fact, almost pure sand, forty feet deep in areas, and instead of the easily plowed wide-open spaces that had been promised in advertisements, the land was abundantly cursed with trees. The sandy soil, little more than pulverized silica, rejected most crops. The one crop that could survive in the soil was cotton, but first the land had to be cleared for planting, and pulling up tough brush oak and scrub oak stumps with the help of only a few slaves and mules was back-breaking work.

Henderson County offered none of the lush greenery found in the piney woods to the east near Tyler. Its soil bore no resemblance to the rich blacklands in the counties to the north, nor did it have the strong, natural nutrients found in the prairie grasslands two hundred miles to the west. Not until nearly a century later would anyone realize that under this barren, hardscrabble, sandy land of East Texas was one of the richest pools of oil on the planet. The great East Texas field—a two-hundred-square-mile sweep of sandbar covering five counties—lay buried deep beneath the soil these farmers cursed.

The first settlers came to Henderson County in the 1840s

and 1850s from Alabama, Georgia, Tennessee, and the Carolinas. They crossed rugged terrain in wagons, risking the often fatal dangers of disease, summer heat or winter storms, and despair. The strength they displayed during the trip west continued to be needed long after they arrived. Lesser men and women would have turned back long before reaching the red oak tree at the center of town. Even after they arrived, the land continued to be their enemy. Henderson County abounded with creek beds, which made cross-country travel even slower and more treacherous. The closer to town, the sandier the terrain. Wagons got stuck and horses lost their footing. From the start it was clear that the very land that brought these settlers would be their greatest hardship.

The town, optimistically named Athens, was founded only five years before T. F. Murchison arrived. Because it was located near the center of Henderson County, it was chosen as the county seat, then called the "seat of justice," for the county court was held there. The designation of county seat assured its survival if little else did.

T. F. Murchison built his first home with his own hands, chopping down trees with an ax and using mules to hoist logs into place. Most of the one hundred and fifty Athenians who arrived before him had built themselves dog-run cabins with an open "dog run" (breezeway) through the center to make hot summers more bearable. T. F.'s house was even simpler—one room with a dirt floor and a bed made of wood slats supported by tree trunks.

At this same moment, in San Francisco, it was not the many thousands of miners searching for gold who were getting rich. It was the few storekeepers, who sold the miners trousers and shovels and salt pork, who made their fortunes. Likewise in Athens, T. F. saw that farming was not the way to make a fortune. Instead, he clerked in a mercantile store for a few years and then opened his own.

At first T. F. sold mostly groceries, feed and grain. But soon he was ordering stock from New York, shipped by sea to Galveston and then transported to Athens by ox or mule cart. The stock grew to include clothes, household tools, and farm implements. Barrels of coffin nails, along with the coffins, were cheek by jowl with baby bonnets and barrels of whiskey—the later separation between "dry goods" and "wet goods" as yet unknown. A merchant's stock was expected to include everything from a sewing needle to a shotgun.

If the store saw as many as a dozen customers, it was a good business day. But T. F. found ways to lure farmers into the store. As was the practice before running water, T. F. kept a barrel of water and a tin cup in the store's back room, with a washtub where men could take a weekly bath. Merchants of the day employed only male clerks.

Like most small-town merchants, T. F. offered credit to his customers, by necessity rather than choice. Because there were no banks in Athens until the last decade of the century, farmers bought their supplies on credit. In the fall, after their crops were sold, they paid the storekeeper what they had borrowed plus 10 percent interest. Murchison was fair to the point of generosity, providing farmers with the necessities of life until the crop came in and often longer if the crop failed. Only a handful of farmers could afford to buy their tools and seeds outright, and even they often preferred to keep what little money they had earned buried in a sack in the ground.

The cotton farms in Henderson County were mostly small-scale, but farmers managed to pull a meager living from their fields, then bartered with Murchison, who took their pounds of cotton in exchange for shoes, hats, flour, and other essentials. By 1857 thirty-year-old T. F. had saved enough money to marry, to build a new house and begin a family. In the next twelve years he fathered six children, three boys and three girls. Perhaps as a testimony to their parents' strong genes, all six children survived childhood, a percentage uncommon in those days.

Murchison looked like a man on the rise. He had a close-cropped gray beard and wore a wool suit to work at the store. He spoke proper English, unlike many of his customers. Many of the men and women who came to his store could neither read nor write. In 1862 a Confederate regiment was formed in Henderson County, and 600 of the county's 3,400 white citizens rode off to war. Murchison was not among them, although he later took the title "Colonel Murchison" for his efforts back home. During the war he commanded the Patty-riders in the county, who were in charge of overseeing the area's slaves. With the landowners at war, Murchison saw to it that the crops were gathered and that there were no slave revolts. His was a big responsibility, as many in Athens feared that what had happened in Dallas two years earlier, on the eve of the Civil War, might happen in their county.

On a July day in 1860 with temperatures in the 100s, most of the business buildings of the town of Dallas went up in flames, including stores, stables, saloons, and whorehouses. Damage was estimated at more than $250,000. Although newspapers reported that the fire was probably ignited by a careless workman's match, a vigilante committee of fifty-two men appointed itself to investigate the cause. They uncovered what they said was a plot by slaves and northern abolitionists to burn the town. As a result, three black men were hanged and the vigilante group ordered that all the slaves in the county be whipped to teach them a lesson.

After the war, when the Confederate soldiers marched back to Henderson County, they found themselves even poorer than before. East Texas was a forlorn land of dilapidated homes, deserted plantations, idle industries, and poor means of travel. Farmers returning from the war struggled to raise corn, wheat, and oats, but the land yielded only the most meager crops. Cotton was still one of the only viable crops, but the soil was exhausted from wartime production. And methods to keep the now-freed slaves working in the fields had to be worked out. The new systems of sharecropping and tenantry, which dominated the South and Southwest, had many flaws. Clearly, much of the hope and optimism that had settled Henderson County died with the Confederacy.

But T. F.'s store had prospered during the Civil War years when he had also helped found the First Presbyterian Church and served as postmaster. He continued to do well after the war when large numbers of new settlers eager to leave the depleted states of the Old South arrived, bringing with them new capital. But despite the population growth, the town remained stagnant. Still, Murchison was optimistic that progress would come, but he knew that a railroad was vital to the town's survival.

Westward expansion of the railroads had been delayed during the Civil War, but during Reconstruction the track burst ferociously through Texas towns, linking East with West and North with South. In 1874 the first train of the Texas & Pacific railroad moved through Dallas, giving the town a direct connection with the East. Large wholesale concerns sprang up, and almost overnight Dallas became a shipping point for raw materials to the large consumer markets in the Northeast. Cotton buyers swarmed in, and by the end of 1877 the town's population had reached an astounding 7,054.

Athens had been bypassed by the T. & P. railroad in 1874, and witnessed Dallas's growth with increasing resentment. Feeling cheated and angry, Murchison and three other leading Athenians traveled to nearby Tyler to meet with Richard Hubbard, an attorney for New York railroad magnate Jay Gould. The leaders of Athens saw an opportunity to link up with another railroad, a narrow gauge line of Gould's that was pushing west from Tyler.

When the men arrived at Hubbard's home, they found the former Texas governor ailing and fearful of death. Murchison did not profess to be a doctor, or even a faith healer, but he shrewdly opened the meeting by explaining that although the governor must feel uncomfortable, he knew enough about the disease to know it was not fatal. Hubbard was so elated with the news that he quickly accepted the town's offer to deed land they owned to the railroad. A few years later, in 1880, the railhead reached Athens, and within two years the tracks were changed to standard gauge. The line became the St. Louis Southwestern Railroad, known as the "Cotton Belt."

Texas eventually made gifts to the railroads amounting to over 32 million acres, more than one-sixth of the area of the state. The land grants made to the railroad companies included not only right-of-way for the tracks, but also alternate sections that were a minimum of ten miles on either side of the track. The railroad determined the life or death of towns in the West, long after the tracks had been laid. Often they discriminated against farmers in fixing freight rates, charging higher

rates for farm than for other shipments and higher rates in the
South and West than in the more competitive Northeast.

Tracks were laid quickly and with no fences along them to
keep animals and humans out of danger's way. When the track
reached a new town, railroad owners shrewdly hired the best
local attorneys—and often judges—to represent their interests. So the small-town farmer was out of luck if a train collided with his cow, his son or daughter. Still, there was no real
alternative for shipping goods from land-locked Athens, and
at the turn of the century the town fought another battle to
connect with the north-south Texas & New Orleans line.
When the T.& N.O. pushed through town in 1900, Athens had
made the crucial step into the next century.

At the turn of the century the small-town farmer had a long
list of enemies—banks, worn-out land, the cotton-destroying
boll weevil, droughts. But at the very top of this list of villains
was the almighty railroad. Hatred of the North in East Texas
was as much a product of extortion by the Yankee-owned railroads and the Eastern banks as of the Civil War itself, and
much of Clint Murchison Sr.'s dislike of the Eastern Establishment he learned from his grandfather T. F.'s struggles. If
the railroads could extract every possible penny from the citizens, why shouldn't the oil industry? If the railroads could
own senators and congressmen and governors, state legisla-
tors and local judges, why shouldn't the oil industry buy such
powerful friends for itself as Senator Lyndon Baines Johnson,
Senator Joseph McCarthy and other powerful political allies?
If the railroad industry could manage to avoid lowering its
profits by avoiding competitive freight rates, why shouldn't
the oil industry fix prices? Ironically, the government body
that limited oil production—thereby enabling the oil industry
to fix prices—was the Texas Railroad Commission.

As more customers came to T. F.'s general store by way of
the Cotton Belt, the contents of the steel safe he kept in the
back room grew. He had bought the safe for his own use, but as
farmers and other merchants came to know and trust him,
they asked him to lock up their cash and valuables too. Eventually he gave written receipts, but by 1885 the population of
Athens had grown to six hundred, and the number of citizens

wanting to deposit their valuables at the store soon exceeded the capacity of the safe.

By the late 1880s banks had already been organized in Tyler, then the largest town in East Texas, and in Palestine, the next town south of Athens. Having for years sold his wares on credit, T. F. saw the need for a bank where farmers and merchants could borrow money. At the moment the cotton-rich Moody family of Galveston was investing in new banks around the state. W. L. Moody Jr. had earlier sent representatives to Henderson County hoping to invest capital, but they saw little chance of profit in the poor farm community. Murchison, however, convinced Moody otherwise, and in 1890, with Moody's help, $12,500 in U.S. Treasury Bonds and $40,192.54 in cash and exchange, the sixty-two-year-old Murchison established Athens' first bank.

The First National Bank, a two-story red-brick building next door to T. F.'s mercantile store, opened for business on April 17, 1890. Visitors came from all over Henderson and even neighboring counties, arriving in their Sunday best in buggies and wagons or on horseback to celebrate this rite of passage from village to city. They tied their horses to the hitching posts in front, and entered under a large brush oak tree that shaded the building.

While many of the visitors came from miles away just to look, others came to do business. On its first day the bank received $4,710.73 in deposits and made loans totaling $228.39. The town had gotten off to a slow start, and the street in front of the bank was not only unpaved; it was still full of tree stumps. Athens was a long way from resembling its namesake in ancient Greece, but at last it had something to brag about.

3

"If that dunce can make so much money, we'll go too!"

Clint Murchison made his first pennies trapping raccoons and selling the pelts to Henderson County fur traders. At three o'clock each morning, while his brothers and sisters slept, seven-year-old Clint climbed out of bed, raced to the nearby woods, and collected the coons and other animals that had fallen into his traps during the night. He skinned the animals in the dark, then carried the pelts to town, where he sold them for a few cents each. The pelts were put on a train for Sears & Roebuck in Chicago, and Clint was back home before his family awoke.

Young Clint covered the floors and walls of his bedroom with all kinds of skins, which, because they were untreated, produced a terrible stench. But the smell did not seem to bother him, and he brought more and more skins up to his room. The smelly collection was one of many early signs that Clint did not share the social formalities of the county's leading banking family.

John Weldon Murchison, vice president of the First National Bank, his wife Clara, and their eight children lived on Tyler Street, a few blocks from the courthouse square. Tyler Street grandly called itself "the street of plantation homes." Although the homes were made of wood and were Victorian in style, rather than the traditional plantation brick with white columns, many were indeed grand.

The white house at 407 Tyler Street sat alone on an entire city block, shaded by one post oak tree. Behind the house stood a barn and stables, a carriage house and three small frame houses for the black servants, as well as a vegetable garden and chicken yard. The large home, with its tall eaves and broad porch, made clear to local citizens that the Murchison name would continue to be an important one into the next generation.

When T. F. Murchison died in 1902, he left control of the bank to his eldest son, D. R. Murchison, and his second son, John, who shared responsibility. Although T. F. had three daughters and another son, it was John Murchison's heirs who would keep control of the bank through its first century.

John had married Clara Williams, of Tyler, and as newlyweds they moved to Tyler, where John worked in his father-in-law's saddle business. They began their family in 1893 with their first child, named Thomas Franklin Murchison for John's father, followed by a second child, named Kate for Clara's mother.

On April 11, 1895, in Tyler, Clara Murchison gave birth to a third child, another son. John and Clara named him for Clara's father, Ethelbert Clinton Williams. He was christened Clinton Williams Murchison, "Clint" for short.

A depression wiped out Ethelbert Williams' saddle business, and John and Clara and their children returned to Athens. By now the town had grown to 3,000, boasted seventeen attorneys and eight physicians. Wooden stores were being converted to brick, and land in some sections of the county sold for as much as thirty dollars an acre.

Still, the Athens where Clint grew up was not vastly changed from the area his grandfather helped settle four decades earlier. Despite the progress that came with the railroads and the First National Bank, turn-of-the-century Athens was still a struggling agrarian community dependent on its cotton production. Not only was cotton the only major money crop of Henderson County, its value had dropped steeply in the decades after 1860. Throughout the United States huge new areas of land were put under cultivation. Because production had increased at a much faster rate than the population, the supply of cotton, grain, and wheat soon exceeded demand. The result was that a pound of cotton, which brought 31 cents in 1866, was worth only a meager 6 cents on the market in 1893. The figure was a bitter reward for Henderson County planters who, by the 1890s, had spent years tilling, shaping, and struggling with their land to make it right for cotton.

Although most of the state's biggest cattle ranches were in West Texas, when Clint was a young boy, livestock traders constantly passed through Henderson County. At the age of nine, he would race directly from the school yard to Athens' wagon yards and livestock sales, listening and watching closely as one cow or horse was swapped for another. Clint idolized the savvy horse and cattle traders who made their money from other men's ignorance. It was a game whose excitement was his chief pleasure all his life.

His first trade he remembered always. "A professional horse trader came to Athens and traded his snide to me," Clint recalled. (A snide in horse trading parlance is a defective horse that looks fine.) "I gave a fairly good horse, eight dollars, and a calf for that snide. It sure taught me to look things over more carefully after that."

Clint became friends with another local boy who was equally fascinated with the tactics of livestock swapping. His name was Sid Richardson. Four years older than Clint, Sid taught his younger friend many of his earliest business lessons.

Sid's ancestors were also among the earliest settlers in Henderson County, and he and Clint shared the same middle name, although they were not related. Nannie and John Isidore Richardson were devout Baptists—as well as saloon keepers—and named their son for Sid Williams, an itinerant evangelist.

Sid was only eight years old when he made his first trade. His father had given him a lot on the square, then offered to trade him a bull for the lot. Sid agreed and ended up with a bull but no cows to go with it and no lot to keep it on. "My daddy taught me a hard lesson with that first trade," Sid loved to explain. "But he started me tradin' for life."

When Sid was fifteen, a wagon rolled over and crushed his left leg. Sid's older sister, Anne Richardson, was dating a doctor, Perry Bass from Mineral Wells, Texas, who operated on the leg. Perry and Anne later married and had a son, Perry Jr., father of Fort Worth's billionaire Bass brothers. "Doc Bass had to remove two inches of bone and build a trough to put the leg in," explains Perry Jr. "People kidded Uncle Sid that if Doc Bass hadn't been going with Anne Richardson, Sid would have had his leg amputated."

A year later Sid was fired from his dollar-a-day job at the Athens Cotton Compress because his boss said he was lazy. In fact, he was exhausted at his job. Instead of sleeping during his off hours, he was trading cattle. The same year that he was fired from the compress, he made $3,500 trading cattle, and he was just getting started.

Sid made his first big coup in the cattle business in Louisiana. Because of a drought and tick infestation in Athens, local cattle were poor and there was great demand for healthy animals. Sid took a train to Rushton, Louisiana, and as the train pulled through town, he spotted in the distance some fat calves standing in tall grass. He went first to a local store where he bought a loud, checkered suit, changed quickly into it, and strolled along the square, flashing bills and whistling.

"I don't know anything about stock, but Pa and Ma gave me this money and I think I'll buy me some calves," he bluffed. He was quickly surrounded by cattle dealers eager to take the innocent's money. Somehow, in the crush, the Louisianans started bidding against each other and ended up selling Sid several hundred head at far below the Louisiana market price. Sid shipped the calves to Athens and sold them for three times what he had paid for them.

Clint always attributed his and Sid's success to their boyhood training in cattle trading. "If you have to get a calf's price down to eight dollars so that you can sell it at ten dollars," Clint said, "you've got to swap a lot of spit over the fence, and you learn about people."

Just as Sid learned how to trade from his father, so did one of the most capable and ruthless oilmen of all time, John D. Rockefeller. Said the elder Rockefeller, "I cheat my boys every chance I get, I want to make 'em sharp. I trade with the boys and skin 'em and I just beat 'em every time I can."

In the Athens of 1900 a boy of eleven or twelve was considered a man and was given full responsibility for running the farm when his father was away. At other times, he was sent to town to trade the crops himself. Much of what young boys in

East Texas learned about business they absorbed while listening to their fathers. Discussion over supper was not about the transcontinental automobile races reported in the newspapers, or the technical advances of the telephone. Talk was far more locally focused—what sold that day in town and for how much.

There was one major event, however, that drew attention in East Texas, as well as around the world. It took place on January 10, 1901, several counties south of Athens, near Beaumont, in the southeasternmost region of the state.

On that day a gusher of oil blew the top off a well drilled 1,160 feet into the earth. Until then no one had known or would have cared that there was oil in Texas. But the discovery well on a marshy hillock called Spindletop changed the nation. It ushered in the age of oil as a major source of power. Liquid fuel would propel the automobiles and airplanes of the twentieth century. It would replace coal as the nation's number-one energy source, and end the oil monopoly created by John D. Rockefeller, whose Standard Oil Company pumped more than 80 percent of the nation's oil.

Before Spindletop, oil had been used mostly for lighting and lubrication, its limited supply making its use as fuel too costly. But by 1902, a year after the discovery at Spindletop, 130 wells were producing at Beaumont. Their combined production was more than that of the rest of the world.

It was still years before the Daisy Bradford No. 3 well roared in on a farm in Rusk County, spouting oil one hundred feet over the top of the derrick and raining fortunes on dozens of East Texas speculators. But Spindletop marked the beginning of the boom, and nothing else in the next eighty-eight years had such a profound effect on the lives of Texans.

As the drilling business was getting under way in Beaumont, John Murchison was beginning his career at Athens' First National Bank, which was still housed in its original two-story building on one corner of the square. Although outside it still looked much as it had when it opened, the interior had been transformed into the most dignified establishment in town, from its double glass doors to its shiny brass teller cages, its marble wainscoting and polished brass spitoons.

A farmer who came to ask for a loan from Mr. Murchison came dressed in his Sunday best and waited by a potbellied stove next to the vault at the rear of the bank. Customers straightened their suspenders and took off their hats before entering. But if the farmer felt uneasy and intimidated, it was less a result of the bank's high-toned interior than the stiff, formal ways of its owners.

John Murchison was a large man, and walked at a determined pace, looking straight ahead. His thin, hard mouth and invariably furrowed brow gave him the stern appearance as mandatory for a turn-of-the-century capitalist as the practice of addressing his wife in public as "Mrs. Murchison" and expecting the same formality from her.

He was one of the few men in town who wore a three-piece business suit to work every day, and one of even fewer to own a solid gold watch, chain, and fob. The local farmers and merchants said the time of day did not matter since they worked from "can till cain't," from sunrise when they could see until sundown when they could not. But John Murchison was more precise than that and frequently pulled his watch from his vest pocket to prove it. His coal-black hair was neatly shaped around his thick face and protruding ears. He wiped his brow with a white cotton handkerchief, which became wringing wet with perspiration during the stultifying heat from April until October. No matter how high the temperature, John Murchison rarely removed his suit jacket or loosened his tie.

John's brother, D. R. Murchison, wore a Van Dyke beard and was equally stiff and formal, which made farmers fear the trip to the bank for a loan. Although some mercantile stores continued to sell to farmers on credit, the First National had become the major lender in town, and until well into the 1930s almost all the loans went to farmers for their crops. As collateral for the loan, which usually ranged between $100 and $200, the farmer put up everything he owned: four or five cows, a mule or two, a few horses, and, of course, the farm.

A classic East Texas story is about a very young farmer who asks an older farmer's advice before seeking his first loan.

"It's no problem," explained the more experienced farmer. "You go to see Mr. Whitacker, the president of the bank. He'll lend you the money you need because it's much less than the value of the farm and he'll take the farm as security.

"The only thing that could stop him from making the loan would be if you somehow made him angry, and he gets mighty angry if anyone stares at his glass eye."

"But how will I know which one is his glass eye?" the young farmer asked.

The experienced farmer replied, "It's the one with a little kindness in it."

No other state in the union had a provision in its Constitution prohibiting branch banking, but Texas did from its inception in 1836 when there was almost too little money for one bank, let alone a branch. The reasoning for it was simple—the larger a bank (the more branches it had), the more powerful it became. Most of the early settlers had already been foreclosed, or been close to it, and they did not want to be in the hands of powerful bankers who could take away their possessions.

Most farmers did not like the changes T. F.'s sons made at the bank. Not only had the farmers felt comfortable with the more humble elder Murchison; they did not care for the new banking methods that T. F.'s sons introduced. While a man's word and his handshake were enough to get a loan from T. F., the second-generation Murchisons required that he put up the deed to his farm as collateral. Even the most optimistic farmer could not help worrying whether the Murchisons would actually take *his* farm, if the worst came.

Although Presbyterian bankers were enjoined on Sunday by the Prophet Isaiah's words not to "grind the faces of the poor," this rarely precluded their foreclosing farms or raising interest rates on Monday morning if the opportunity arose.

The only ritual observed by the men of Athens as relentlessly as Sunday at church was Saturday at the saloon. Sandwiched in narrow buildings among the mercantile stores and businesses were a number of saloons that provided one of the few hedonistic pleasures in the life of the struggling horse or cattle trader, the penny-pinching merchant, or the exhausted farmer. With a shot of whiskey came all the free lunch one could eat: barrels of pickles, pyramids of sausage and hard-boiled eggs. A customer could laugh and tell jokes, listen to the town gossip, put his dirty boots on the table, and spit manfully into the brass spitoon. The saloon was happily free from the inhibiting presence of wives. At this club a man could not only forget the trials and problems of the week past, but replace them with tall tales of his physical and sexual strength in the mandatory profane and obscene language unacceptable in front of womenfolk. On Saturday the men spilled out onto the streets, stumbling from one saloon to another. A lady seen within a few hundred yards of the square on Saturday was no longer considered a lady.

Clint's mother, known as "Miss Clara," was one of the town's leading ladies. She worked tirelessly building the Cumberland Presbyterian Church, which her father-in-law helped found. Miss Clara and her husband were devout Presbyterians and expected their children to observe strictly the Sabbath day and keep it holy. She accomplished this by not letting her children leave the yard on Sunday, except, of course, for church.

Clint and his brothers and sisters attended Bruce Academy, Athens's only private school. Shortly after Clint enrolled in grade school at the Academy, his teacher noticed that he was lagging behind the other students in mathematics. He was placed in a special class and was made to add and subtract in his head rather than on paper. Years later Murchison attributed his extraordinary mathematical mind to those early special sessions.

W. C. Bruce, a tough old educator who insisted on the title "Dr." before his name, founded and ran the Academy. In 1885 there was a hanging on Bruce's land a few miles outside of town. The body was left hanging overnight, and the next day Bruce took his students to the site, where they sat for hours sketching the remains. As late as 1941, an article in the Athens newspaper reflected on the hanging: "Despite the saying that a tree from which a man has been hanged will not flourish, this live oak is still growing more than 55 years after it was used to end the career of a killer." This kind of education, as opposed to discussion of the Constitutional guarantees of due process, helps explain why many rich Texans later became an important source of political and financial support for Senator Joseph McCarthy.

Whites in East Texas were fiercely outspoken in their hatred of blacks, and lynchings continued until well into the twentieth century. As late as the 1940s, trains and automobiles pulling into the East Texas town of Greenville passed a large electrified sign that proudly boasted, "Greenville Texas: The blackest land, the whitest people."

Bruce Academy's students were the children of Athens' well-to-do families, and the Murchison children were the richest. Clint's brothers and sisters looked the part and acted the part with their polished shoes, tailored wool clothes, and their soft-spoken, serious manner. But Clint, unkempt and on the run, looked more like a poor farmer's son late for his chores.

Although his brothers—Frank, Kenneth, and Johnny—had the distinctive facial features of their father and grandfather, Clint favored his mother's side of the family. He had large ears, a putty blob nose, and a round forehead. His face looked somewhat blurred, as though its sculptor had not finished his work. Though engagingly homely, he had certain endearing features—bright blue eyes, short-cropped blond hair, and a slow, shy smile.

Clint was the runt of the Murchison family, reaching at age fourteen his adult height of five feet six. His head was large and set low between big shoulders. His body tapered off into narrow hips and short bowlegs. Being the smallest of the Murchison boys, he wore the old clothes that both his older and younger brothers had outgrown or simply discarded. Once the clothes belonged to Clint, they quickly became even more worn and tattered. Although Clint was an aberration in his own family, his relaxed manner and dress were typical of most boys in the town. "Clint was so easygoing and easy to get along with. He would befriend anyone," recalls an Athenian who knew him when he was a boy. "Clint was the exact opposite of his sisters and brothers, who were sort of snobby. They thought they were better than the rest of the people in Athens because they were Murchisons."

Fishing clubs were being formed in the early 1900s around Athens, and the most popular was the Koon Kreek Klub, which later became a favorite fishing spot for Dallas's oil rich. It was started by a handful of Dallas bankers and merchants and a few of their friends from Athens. John Murchison was invited to join Koon Kreek, but declined, for he was neither a hunter nor a fisherman. In his view, both sports were a waste of time, as well as barbaric and especially inappropriate for the town's leading banker.

Clint was the antithesis of his father, sharing none of John Murchison's loftier pretensions about fishing. Folks on the square shook their heads as thirteen-year-old Clint and an old black man, both carrying cane fishing poles, passed them on the street. "Mr. Murchison's boy sure is nothin' like his Pa," one man would say to another. "Sure ain't," the other would reply. "There he goes again with that old nigger man."

There was an old, rangy former slave who hung around the square. He had no job and no home but plenty of time for the carefree Clint. On hot summer afternoons the barefoot Clint would meet the black man by the courthouse, and the two would head off to fish along one of the nearby creeks. The bottom lands, shaded by grotesquely twisted native oaks, offered momentary relief from the harsh Texas sun.

An incident in 1916 in McLennan County, a few counties southeast of Athens, illustrates the climate for blacks in East Texas of that time. A newspaper story explained:

Jesse Washington, a defective negro boy of about nineteen, unable to read and write, was employed as a farmhand in Robinson, a small town near Waco, Texas. One day, when the wife of his employer found fault with him, he struck her on the head with a hammer and killed her. There is some but not conclusive evidence that he raped her. He was arrested, tried and found guilty, sentenced to death by hanging within ten days of the commission of the crime. As the sentence was pronounced, a mob of 1,500 white men, who feared the law's delays, broke into the courtroom and seized the prisoner. He was dragged through the streets, stabbed, mutilated, and burned to death in the presence of a crowd of 15,000 men, women, and children, including the mayor and chief of police of Waco.

What was left of his body was dragged through the streets and parts of it sold as souvenirs. His teeth brought $5 apiece and the chain that had bound him 25 cents a link. No one was indicted for participating in the lynching.

Between 1889 and 1918, 263 blacks were lynched in Texas, surpassed only by Louisiana with 360 lynchings and Mississippi with 350. Post-Civil War Athens was a brutal place for blacks, and as a result many had left East Texas by about 1915.

Clint also left Athens in 1915 to join his older brother Frank at Trinity University, then located in Waxahachie, twenty miles south of Dallas. Trinity was a small, staunchly religious Presbyterian university that trained half of its graduates for the ministry.

John and Clara hoped that the disciplined atmosphere would provide some boundaries for the capricious Clint, as it had for Frank. But for two boys coming from the same household, their personalities could not have been more different. Unlike Frank, who had spent his boyhood around the bank listening to his father's theories on finance, Clint had been racing from one trading barn to another, swapping livestock and adding to his bank account.

Clint, who turned twenty in 1915, found Trinity to be physically and intellectually suffocating. He wanted to be outdoors rather than in the school's stale classrooms, and he was anxious to test his own skills rather than learn about heroes in history books. Three weeks after arriving, he organized a secret game of craps. After the game one of the boys reported on the others, and Clint was called into the dean's office. "The dean told me he would not expel me if I would name the other boys shooting craps," Clint recalled years later. "I thought that was a very unethical approach for men operating a Christian school."

Clint refused to name names and left Trinity on his own. Uncertain about his future, he decided the bank was as good a place as any to start. John Murchison agreed and put his son to work as a teller. For months, from early morning until early evening, Clint sat behind a cage at the front of the bank, recording deposits and withdrawals. Nearly every day he balanced the books to the penny. On those rare occasions when his books were off a few cents, he knew exactly why.

That Clint had a brilliant mathematical mind first became apparent when he was working at the bank. Complicated problems that took others as much as an hour to calculate Clint could work out in a few seconds. But he loathed the detail of running the cage, and to fight boredom he added and subtracted the deposits and withdrawals in his head.

Instead of staying in the cage, he started hanging around Stirman's Drugstore across the square. A long, narrow building with a soda fountain along one wall and chairs and tables along the other, the drugstore was the financial and political center of the town. Most men of means in Athens gathered daily at the drugstore to discuss local and national politicians, choose their city officials, and, most important of all, to make business deals. Farmers and fur traders, bankers and seed store owners started shuffling into Stirman's about nine o'clock each morning. Shortly before noon, the room was filled with Texas talk, clinking cups and saucers, the aroma of cheap coffee and pipe smoke. When all the noise reverberating from the bare wooden floor and the stamped tin ceiling made it difficult to hear, the men just shouted a little louder.

The drugstore was run by a short, fat, balding man named Winfield B. Stirman who acquired the name "Doc" during Prohibition when he provided his customers with prescription bottles containing pure whiskey. Doc and his fellow Athenians insisted that Stirman's—with its twenty-four stools and counter that spanned the length of the store—had the longest fountain in East Texas. In addition, a sign on the wall behind the counter proclaimed, "The largest dispinsir *[sic]* of Coca-Cola in all of Texas."

When Doc's better-educated customers informed him that he had misspelled "dispenser," he refused to look in a dictionary. Stirman was strongly opinionated and often wrong, but his customers were reluctant to argue with the man who operated the town's most important place of business. One day when Clint returned to the bank, he was reproached by a bank officer for spending too much time in Stirman's. Clint swung around and retorted, "I was out drumming up business for the bank while you boll weevils were just counting nickels."

Clint hated to count the small change that was not included

in the bank's legal reserves, so he bagged his nickles and dimes together. The dimes were considered legal reserves, the nickels were not. A bank examiner, on a routine inspection trip, found Clint sacking his nickels and dimes together, and demanded an explanation. Clint said he was counting the dimes as nickels and that they were not needed for the bank's reserves. The crochety old bank examiner rejected that practice and ordered him to open all the bags and count every coin. Clint spent a full day doing so, then quit the bank.

"Coins stink," Clint fumed.

Clint complained to his father that he made more money in a day trading cattle than during a month at the bank. Indeed, he had been a master at livestock swapping almost since the age of nine. So when he left the bank, he was looking for something more challenging. Only days after Clint quit, the United States entered World War I, and he obtained a contract to supply $3,500 worth of East Texas pine to the Army. Because there was a shortage of men around Athens, he went to San Antonio, chartered three railroad coaches and put them on a siding. He offered free whiskey to footloose Mexicans he found around the streets, and they came aboard. Most of the men drank so much they passed out in the coaches. In the middle of the night Murchison supervised the hitching of the cars to a locomotive, which pulled the caravan deep into Texas's piney woods. Once there, Murchison paid the Mexicans a meager fee to chop enough wood to fulfill the government contract.

On April 14, three days after his twenty-second birthday, Clint enlisted in the motor transport division of the Quartermaster Corps, hoping for an overseas assignment. Although his title was impressive, he spent his days being taught how to drive a truck, a skill he already had, around the base at Texas A & M College. He obtained a transfer to Fort Sam Houston near San Antonio, then into the infantry at Camp Pike in Arkansas, where he became a lieutenant.

His last post was at Camp Custer in Michigan, where he was given police detail and was nearly court-martialed. One incident that annoyed the brass but pleased the enlisted men was a get-rich-quick scheme he devised for the mess fund. The area around the camp was scattered with salvage lumber that the army ordered burned. Instead, Clint organized a group, collected the wood, sold it for kindling, and netted more than $15,000 for the mess fund.

From 1911 until 1917 Sid Richardson had been traveling back and forth between Fort Worth and Wichita Falls, one hundred miles northwest of Fort Worth, just south of the Oklahoma border. Although Sid earlier attended Texas's Baylor University and Simmons College, his education was cut short when his father died. Because the family was low on cash, Sid decided to try his luck in the oil fields around Wichita Falls.

The area was growing rapidly as oil companies pushed into the small town on the North Central Plains. Only a year earlier Wichita Falls had begun producing oil commercially, and large petroleum companies, as well as hundreds of lease brokers wanting a piece of the profits, moved in. The area's first major gusher came in on December 17, 1910—a year before Sid arrived—on W. T. Waggoner's ranch near Electra, in the vicinity of Wichita Falls. Waggoner was elated when the oil erupted from the ground with such force that the top of the derrick sailed hundreds of feet in the sky.

It was quite a different reaction from the one he had had when oil appeared on his ranch ten years earlier. Workers were digging shallow wells in search of water when oil surfaced in the wells. "Dammit," cursed Waggoner. "Cattle can't drink that stuff."

Wichita Falls at the beginning of this century was a typical West Texas town with no boundaries. Vast herds of cattle grazed on limitless plains, bound only by the sky that bent down to touch the land on all sides. But with the boom of 1910 came hundreds of oil's skyscrapers—derricks, each standing a hundred feet high—until the area was as closed in as the piney woods of East Texas. In this boomtown mania Sid got a job hauling pipe during the day and pushing tools on an oilwell platform at night.

Sid had even worse luck than Clint in the Army. Shortly after World War I began, Richardson tried to enlist, but he was turned down because of his bad leg. He joined the National Guard, but even there he was rejected when a colonel noticed the leg. Disappointed, he returned to the oil business, hauling pipe for the Texas Oil Company and trading leases for himself in Fort Worth.

In July 1918 a major oil discovery occurred at Burkburnett, fifteen miles north of Wichita Falls. When rancher Fowler Shields started to drill for oil on his land, it was derided as "Shields' Folly," but then a gusher came in and hundreds of lease hounds surged into the area. Because Burkburnett was not equipped to handle the overnight influx, thousands spilled over into Wichita Falls. A town of 17,000 before the boom, within six months Wichita Falls' population soared to more than 25,000. It became the headquarters for hundreds of drilling, production, and supply companies.

Between roughnecks, lease hounds, oil speculators, and camp followers, competition was tough, and not only for oil riches but for such essentials as food and beds. After six weeks of sleeping in his clothes, living on chili and eggs in the boomtown near Burkburnett field, Sid went into nearby Ranger, another slam-bang oil town, looking for a bowl of tomato soup. He found a diner, but when he asked for the soup, the waiter and cook called him a sissy and a fight erupted. Sid departed without the soup. Two days later in a drugstore the brawl continued. Another day later, Richardson spotted the cook stalking him with a gun. "I got out my pocketknife," Sid told *Look* magazine years later. "I suddenly jumped out and pushed that knife into his belly so's he could feel it. Then I made a speech about friendship and tomato soup. We shook hands while my knife was still stickin' him; then we walked back to the diner and he heated me up my soup. That was my last fistfight—I was twenty-six then—and I've loved soup ever since."

Stabbings were common in Wichita Falls as men fought for beds in the hotels or rooming houses that went up overnight and could come down with a heavy storm. Oilmen hoping for overnight riches slept in relays in rooming houses, and sidewalks were jammed with traders in oil company stocks and leases.

Those who couldn't find a bed in town hoped to find one on the Missouri-Kansas-Texas train, the "Katy," which ran three special trains daily from Fort Worth, the closest big town to Wichita Falls. An estimated three thousand persons each day headed for the Burkburnett field from Fort Worth, and Sid was on that train as often as anyone else. Despite the rugged living conditions in those early days, Richardson was on his way to becoming very rich. When the Armistice was signed on November 11, 1918, he had accumulated more than $100,000.

Only once after striking oil did Sid return to Athens on a business deal. He was twenty-four, had proved his trading expertise—and luck—in the oil fields, and he wanted to return to the cattle business. He thought he could out-trade any man in Henderson County. Indeed, he was as shrewd a trader as ever, but his cattle died of tick fever, which put him $6,000 in the red. His loss seemed all the worse because he had bought the cattle on credit with a loan from the First National Bank. John Murchison had not hesitated to give Sid the $6,000 because Sid had always repaid his loans. Deciding that the fastest way to recoup his loss was in the oil fields, Richardson headed back to Wichita Falls.

In 1917, a year to the day after leaving Athens penniless, Sid drove back into town in a brand-new white Cadillac. "I swung around that dusty square twice so's all the bench warmers would see me real good, and then I marched into the bank and paid back Mr. Murchison his money in cash. Then I drove out of town again. 'Fore the dust had settled, all those old boys got off their benches and started for the oil fields. They said, 'If that dunce can make so much money, we'll go too.'"

4

"Financin' by finaglin'."

When Clint was released from the Army, he went directly to Fort Worth where Sid was waiting for him. In his final days at Camp Custer, Clint had read magazine articles about "flowing gold" being pumped from the Burkburnett field next to Wichita Falls, and the huge oil strikes in Ranger, eighty miles west of Fort Worth. When Sid wrote and asked his boyhood pal to join him in the oil boom, Clint could not get there fast enough.

No sooner had Sid spotted Clint getting off the train in his Army uniform than he rushed his younger protégé into a local department store where he paid double to get quick service on two wool suits. When Clint protested, Sid shot back, "No, if you wear that uniform when we go around to talk to people they'll want to talk about the war. We're not talking about anything but oil."

An Army post was established at Fort Worth in 1847, but until after the Civil War it was only a frontier cow town on the cattle drive to Topeka. The first railroad came to Fort Worth, thirty miles west of Dallas, in 1876, and quickly established the town as the meat-packing and cattle-shipping hub of the Southwest. When oil was found in the small town of Ranger in 1919, Fort Worth was the closest rail center, and oil refineries quickly sprang up there.

The mania that swept Burkburnett field was at its height when Clint arrived. More than two hundred wells were flowing, and more and more acreage was presumed to have a potential for producing oil. The territory for lease trading widened with each new well that was drilled, even if the well came up dry. Rumors flowed as freely as the oil. When word spread that oil was about to come in on someone's well, immediately the land around that well would be bought up at a high price. If the well came in, the buyers won; if the rumors were simply rumors, they lost. It was the job of the lease hounds to separate the facts from the rumors, to sniff out news of developments on wells being drilled.

The potential for overnight riches, coupled with a fear of getting there too late, created panic and near hysteria as oil boomers pushed into Burkburnett at all hours of the day and night. Wichita Falls, the closest railroad town, was crowded with speculators, drillers, traders, promoters, gamblers, and criminals. The fortune seekers came by the thousands to the new black-gold rush of Texas's north central plains. Some came on horseback with only a few dollars in their pockets, while others arrived in expensive automobiles hoping to increase their fortunes. It was quickly apparent that this was no place for the weak—of either mind or body—and many packed up and left a day or two after they arrived. Others, with a dream to come away rich or richer, stayed on, and in their increasing numbers created the tremendous chaos that identified all the early oil boomtowns.

After Spindletop, thousands of wells were drilled throughout the state, and usually those that came in were in remote areas, often in the middle of a ranch that might cover half a county. The fact that no roads led to the discovery wells in Burkburnett did not stop oil boomers from cutting through farmers' fences, setting cattle free, and then destroying farmland with their automobiles and teams of mules. The farmers and ranchers, comparatively tiny in numbers, were helpless to stop the stampede.

As derricks sprang up on the horizon, so did the dozens of cheap wood shacks that became Burkburnett's hotels, saloons, pool halls, diners, and, of course, brothels and banks. During the day the streets were packed with people, automobiles, horses, mules, pipe, drills, and lumber. The town was crowded with oilmen who poured in and out of gambling halls that stayed open twenty-four hours a day. Fights for territory in the oil fields were as fierce as those in the streets. Wagons collided with automobiles, neither driver willing to give up the right of way.

The turmoil in the streets became even worse when torrential rains turned narrow, dusty, unpaved roads to mud. When automobiles bogged down in deep ruts, nothing less than a team of mules could pull them out. Men walked into banks covered to their waists in mud, if not in oil, and at times it appeared that the whole town would drown in one or the other. Sewer and water systems could not be created overnight to meet the needs of the expanding population, and the towns lacked even the most primitive health laws. Consequently, epidemics broke out regularly.

Because the towns were too tough for decent women, the wives, daughters, and sisters who came with the oilmen stayed in tents in the fields. In town were high-priced women called "oil field doves," who, like all the other entrepreneurs, benefited when the wells came in.

The risks to life at Burkburnett were many. Fires and explosions on derricks were as common as the rattlesnakes that slipped into the tents where men, women, and children slept. Men were killed when parts of hastily built derricks collapsed or storage tanks exploded. Others were maimed when drill bits flew out of control. Workers carelessly dropped matches and lighted cigarettes near gas wells that exploded into flames. Poisonous gas collected in low areas with no odor to warn of its presence.

Blood fell not only on the derrick floor but also spilled frequently in the streets, in the saloons, and in the gambling halls. Men who watched their fortunes rise with a strike, then fall with a dry well, emptied their pistols at former partners and traders and sometimes shot themselves. The crews who worked on the oil wells were called roughnecks, and the toughness necessary to survive on an oilwell rig was also necessary in every other facet of the business.

Witnesses agreed on the kind of men found in the oil boomtowns. "There would be a large assortment of outright criminals: thieves, holdup men, professional gunmen, narcotics pushers, and representatives of all other categories of crime. The Klondike had set a precedent, created a folklore of roughness, and there was at times a kind of pride in saying that a new oil town was as bad as the Klondike, or worse."

With robbers and murderers walking the streets freely, no attempt was made to arrest such mild offenders as prostitutes and pimps. The few local police who could not be bribed were too outnumbered by the influx to exert much control. Because the early towns were without jails, prisoners were chained to trees while they slept off a drunk, or, in rarer instances, until they could be transported to the county jail. But because transport was difficult, it was more common for a man who shot and killed someone to be fined $100 and released.

Men who drilled a dry well might stay on for days with no place to sleep and nothing to eat, while local saloonkeepers charged as much as the market would bear. If there had been a series of strikes, they would raise the price of a plate of ham and eggs from $2 to $5. Whiskey sold for as much as $50 a quart. A cot cost $10 a night, and even a billiard table could command a good fee for a night's rest.

The way to make big money in oil was with production. But this involved buying leases on blocks of land and drilling wells. Because Sid and Clint had no cash or credit in the early days, they started trading leases with the other fortune hunters, hoping to build enough capital someday to own their own leases and begin drilling.

After the first few weeks of observing Sid's methods, Clint had learned the basics of the oil business. He recognized that the key to buying the right leases lay in separating the genuine likelihood of oil in the ground from the mere rumors. From the start, Clint was a shrewd and savvy lease hound, carefully trading secrets with oil scouts and learning which wells were about to come in. He passed along the information to Sid. Within only a few months, they began to buy choice leases, then put the leases together into larger blocks of acreage.

Sid and Clint were a formidable team, always managing to sell their leases at a profit, and always retaining for themselves a percentage interest in future wells. As lease brokers, they made money on the wells regardless of whether wells were drilled that produced oil. But when they bought leases on land that was untested, they were betting on the "greater fool theory"—that they could find someone else to pay more money for the lease than they had. They had traded their way through cattle barns from one end of Henderson County to the other and saw no reason why they could not out-trade oilmen just as they had cattlemen. It was a skill at which they both were masters.

In the beginning Clint and Sid spent their days racing back and forth from Burkburnett to Wichita Falls to Fort Worth at night. When they were sure a well was about to come in, they bought up adjoining leases, then took the overnight train from Wichita Falls to Fort Worth. The next morning, when news broke that a gusher had come in, they sold the leases at a profit. Because the trains were almost as crowded as the oil patch, Sid and Clint always carried with them in their sleeping berths return tickets to the oil field the next day.

Within a few months Murchison and Richardson had a sizable number of leases at Burkburnett, and with a little money in their pockets, they managed to rent a room at Wichita Falls' YMCA. The building was a center of downtown activity. During the day the lobby filled with lease brokers and oil speculators, and at night men passed the hours playing bridge and poker and dominoes.

Murchison and Richardson were in the middle of a poker game when the YMCA's manager threatened to evict the players because they were shouting obscenities and profanities. Rather than sleep in the street, they wrote the forbidden words on large pieces of cardboard that they hung on walls around the card table. When arguments got heated and someone wanted to stress a point, he merely pointed to the most appropriate card.

Late one night in 1919, Richardson sat at a poker game staring at a losing hand when Murchison walked into the room. He shuffled over to Richardson, leaned over and whispered in his ear, "An oil scout just told me about a well they're testing tonight."

"Let's go," Richardson whispered back. He folded his hand and the two were gone. Outside the YMCA, they climbed into a car and raced in the darkness for the Texas-Oklahoma border. It was three o'clock in the morning when they reached the site on the Oklahoma side of the Red River. The oil crew watched as Murchison and Richardson marched confidently toward them. The crew looked at the well-dressed men and assumed they were the owners of the well.

"You ready to see if there's any oil down there?" asked one of the roughnecks.

"Yep," replied Richardson.

But after bluffing their way onto the platform, they did not need to wait for the crew to take a core sampling of the well. They could already smell the rich oil. Instead of hanging around for the well to come in, they raced back to Wichita Falls, and by nine o'clock that morning they had bought $50,000 worth of acreage surrounding the strike. Just before daylight the well came in, splattering oil all over the riverbank and into the river. News of the gusher spread quickly back to Wichita Falls, and within twenty-four hours Sid and Clint sold their acreage for $200,000.

Neither oilman underestimated the luck that was with them that night in Oklahoma, and both attributed to luck much of their riches accumulated during their lifetimes. They were proud of it. Sid boasted, "I'd rather be lucky than smart, 'cause a lot a smart folks ain't eatin' regular."

But it took more than luck to reap oil riches in the tumultuous, make-or-break early days. Only a shrewd trader could read another's mind and know when to call another man's bluff. At the height of the frenzy, promoters—on the strength of mere rumors—paid $10,000 for a lease that would produce a total of $3,500 worth of oil. That is, if the well ever got drilled.

"To some extent we lived off rumors," Clint said later. "And sometimes our own rumors."

Anyone exhibiting enough nerve and will to work could get into the oil game. A shoe salesman named Ernest Fain, in a Wichita Falls department store, impressed Clint with his selling abilities, and Clint invited him into a drilling partnership. The new company also picked up a geologist.

Prior to the 1920s, oilmen referred to geologists as scientists and generally held them in contempt. Long after Spindletop, wildcatters hunted for oil in a variety of odd ways, often relying on the occult to guide them. Clairvoyants, fortune-tellers, and spiritualists did a thriving business throughout the state. But by 1920 most of the large oil companies had geology departments. The University of Texas and Oklahoma University began churning out a large number of bright young men educated in the science of studying rock formations. It was unusual for such a small company as Murchison–Fain to hire a geologist, but Murchison did not plan to stay small very long.

Although the best place to sink a well remained a mystery in the 1920s, having a geologist on board could save time and drilling costs once the drilling had begun. Wells were drilled by the cable tool method, and as the tools were lowered into the ground, they began churning large quantities of rock and dirt, called cuttings, accumulated in the bottom of the hole. A smart geologist could examine the cuttings and determine whether oil was there or whether to abandon the well.

Murchison–Fain began sinking wells, but just as they started striking oil, a terrible blow fell. The commodities market collapsed, sending oil prices plunging. Hundreds of oilmen who were worth hundreds of thousands of dollars were suddenly bankrupted by the crash. In just nine days during the commodity collapse in 1921, oil dropped from $3.50 to $1.00 per barrel.

Sid and Clint never had a formal partnership, but their worth sank together. Suddenly all their money, as well as all of Murchison–Fain, was tied up in leases that no one wanted. "We almost lost our taw," Murchison said. They had no cash for room and board, but they still owned large numbers of leases on which they had to make rental payments, and they had loans on which the interest at least had to be paid. They were into the oil business far too deep to pack up and quit.

Instead, they reluctantly accepted the invitation of Sid's sister and brother-in-law, Anne and "Doc" Bass, to live with them until times improved. Bass, the doctor who saved Sid's leg, had given up a successful practice in Tyler to answer the call of the oil fields, and his irrepressible urge had paid off. The Basses had a comfortable home in Wichita Falls, where Sid and Clint went to live. The home quickly became a center of activity for lease hounds and scouts, speculators and drillers.

At the time, Bass was better off than the two young men from Athens. Still, Bass could tell that Murchison and Richardson were on their way to becoming very rich.

While they were staying at the Basses, Anne invited a cousin from Tyler to come for a visit and to bring her friend Anne Morris, also from Tyler. When the young women arrived, Clint was not only surprised, he was overjoyed. Clint had wanted to marry Anne for six years, and finally they were both ready.

Anne was born in Tyler on September 26, 1898, the second child and second daughter of Burk Yarbrough Morris and Edward Spring Morris. When Anne was five and her sister seven, their father died suddenly. Burk Yarbrough Morris was a great beauty, and before she had married Ed Morris, there was another man who had wanted very much to marry her. His name was Dabney White, and he was one of Texas's most distinguished business and political figures. The son of a pioneer Presbyterian minister, White came to Texas from Arkansas in 1884. He enrolled at the University of Texas and was in the school's first graduating class. He had many careers, including writing and publishing, law, banking, and insurance. He owned a number of newspapers around the state, including, for a short time, the *Houston Post*.

When a respectable length of time had passed since Ed Morris's death, Burk married Dabney. The Whites moved into a five-bedroom stucco-and-brick mansion on the fanciest block in Tyler, an elegant home that was frequently a stopping place for important political figures. When President Theodore Roosevelt visited Texas twice in the 1920s, he was entertained both times at the White home, and in the spring of 1920 ex-president William Howard Taft also called on the Whites.

Burk White was the most refined and elegant woman in Tyler. She had been educated at Hollins College in Virginia, where she was well-schooled in southern manners and hospitality. "My sister and my mother were exactly alike, both vivacious and very social," recalled Lucy Morris Runge, Anne's older sister. "Because they were so extroverted, when the Presidents came to visit it was always very relaxed and comfortable, never stiff."

Clint first met Anne in 1914, the summer before he left for
Trinity University, when he was nineteen years old. A mutual
friend asked him to escort "a beautiful young lady" to a party
in Tyler. Clint at first objected to the idea of a date with someone he did not know, but when the friend persisted, he finally
agreed. Clint was immediately attracted to Anne, who was
only sixteen. She was petite and very pretty, with large blue
eyes and honey blond hair. More even than her beauty, Clint
was taken with her charm. She had tremendous warmth and a
bubbly personality, and was the center of attention wherever
she went. She took good care of Clint at the party, introducing
him to her friends, and though he was painfully shy at first,
Anne put him at ease and he had a very good time.

During the fall after the party, Anne left for boarding
school, Ward Belmont in Nashville. For the next two years
Clint and Anne saw each other only during the summer
months and when she came home for the holidays. When she
finished school in Tennessee, her mother gave her a lavish
lawn party in Tyler. Although she had many suitors, Clint was
at the top of her list, and at the party he decided he was going
to marry her. A few weeks later he asked Anne's mother for
permission.

Clint could not have been more surprised when Burk White
said, "No." The Murchisons were one of East Texas's leading
families, and they had been established bankers for more than
twenty-five years, a very long time in a state that was only
seventy-five years old. It was also surprising to Clint because
when his parents, John and Clara Murchison, lived in Tyler in
their early married years, they were in the same social circle as
the Whites. Clara Murchison's father was also a distinguished
citizen of Tyler. Mrs. White tried to explain as kindly as possible that she felt Anne, who was then eighteen years old, was
too young to marry. Delicate though Mrs. White was in her refusal, Clint was crushed. He returned to Athens and told his
father what had happened.

John Murchison rode to Tyler a few days later to talk with
Burk White. Lucy Runge recalled the conversation: "Mr.
Murchison was a man of very few words, and he was very seri-
ous. The only thing he said was, 'Burk, please let these chil-

dren marry. Clint's not going to be a society man, but he will be a good husband and he will make a good living.' "

After only a few minutes, Mrs. White gave her consent. Dabney White, for his part, thought Clint Murchison was a good catch for the stepdaughter whom he adored. But both the Murchisons and the Whites agreed that the wedding should be delayed until Clint finished college and was established in a job. When Anne came to visit the Basses in Wichita Falls, she accepted Clint's marriage proposal and went back to Tyler to begin making wedding plans.

The wedding was Tyler's most important social event in the spring of 1920. It took place at nine o'clock in the evening, on April 17, at the First Episcopal Church of Tyler. Anne's eight bridesmaids, including her sister and one of Clint's sisters, were escorted down the aisle by Clint's boyhood chums and oil field cronies, among them Sid Richardson and Clint's older brother Frank, who served as best man.

Following the wedding, more than five hundred guests motored up the avenue lined with elm trees that led from the church to the White mansion. The home looked even more elegant than usual, decorated inside and out with white lights and pink roses. Just as the party was getting under way, the bride and groom slipped upstairs to change into their going-away outfits. When their hundreds of friends had gathered in front of the home to wave good-bye, Clint and Anne climbed into a sleek yellow Rolls-Royce and pulled away.

Carefully eyeing the car, a Houston banker whispered to another guest, "He must be a fine young man, indeed."

The Rolls, Clint's wedding gift to Anne, did more to advance his reputation than all the exaggerated talk about the hundreds of oil wells he was rumored to own. Citizens of Athens who came to the reception had for years questioned Clint's judgment in leaving the bank, but no longer. Like Sid, Clint had gone to the oil fields and come back rich.

Clint was so grateful to Burk White for allowing him to marry Anne that on the first Christmas after they married, he gave his new mother-in-law a mink coat. And after that, when he traveled to Dallas or New York, he always returned with jewelry for both Anne and Burk.

Meanwhile, fearful that Clint might decide to bring his new wife into the expanding Bass household, Anne Bass had found Clint and Anne a home of their own in Wichita Falls. Although modest, even by Wichita Falls standards, they felt lucky to have their own home.

Settled in Wichita Falls, Clint began more ambitiously than ever to buy leases. Oil prices had recovered from the crash, and he was ready to make an even bigger play in the area. As always, he put every dollar he had or could borrow into his business, so he continued to be short of cash, but he devised various ways to expand in the oil business.

"Financin' by finaglin'," Clint called it. In the beginning his practice was to trade a share of one lease for the money he needed to buy a second, a rig in exchange for a share of another rig. With such imaginative juggling, Clint was able to retain a partial interest in each lease for himself. By 1925, his income had soared to $30,000 a month.

This technique for stretching his capital astounded other oilmen, and in the coming years businessmen in Dallas and around the country marveled at the astute reasoning behind the practice. Clint's early "financin' by finaglin' "—a necessity when he had no cash—worked so well that he stuck with it for his entire life, even when he had more millions than he bothered to count. Sid built his fortune the same way.

One day Clint borrowed Anne's car, picked up Sid, and they set out to look at some oil properties. When Sid pointed to an antelope in a nearby field, Clint put the gas pedal to the floor and they took off after it. As the antelope leaped gracefully across the field, the Rolls-Royce sped behind, jumping ruts and hitting the ground with such force that parts of the car flew off—first a side-view mirror, next a hubcap. In very little time they lost sight of the antelope and got out and looked at the car. The front hood was bent, brush and sticks were jammed up under the fenders, and the shiny yellow Rolls was now a dusty brown. When Clint drove home that night, Anne looked at the car and burst into tears. "Don't worry, honey," Clint said. "The car had the best time, and I'll buy you a new one."

Anne's sister, Lucy Runge, recalls, "Anne wanted Clint to

dress up and look nice, but she did not pay much attention when he chose not to. She didn't bother him about things. She just let Clint be Clint. Anne could do no wrong in Clint's eyes, and vice versa."

Wichita Falls with its mostly unpaved roads was not the best place for a Rolls, and more than once, when Clint used it, it came home covered in mud. Late one night Sid called Clint about a rumor that an enormous well was about to blow in. Clint picked up Sid in the Rolls, and they set out for the fields to check it out. The closer they got to the well, and the farther from town, the muddier the road became, until finally they were stuck. The men climbed out of the car and tried to push it out, but it was no use. The more they pushed, the deeper it sank. The land was barren, and there was no brush or rocks to stick under the tires for traction. But if they waited much longer, the well would come in and they would miss the chance to buy surrounding leases at bargain prices.

Sid was wearing a brand-new full-length raccoon coat, and Clint began eyeing it closely. "No, I paid a lot of money for this coat," Sid said, knowing what Clint was thinking.

"I'll buy you a new one when we get the leases," Clint retorted. "Now, give me that coat."

Sid shed the raccoon, and they stuck it under a back tire. As Sid pushed, Clint stepped on the accelerator. The car came out of the mud, and they were off, leaving the coat behind.

Clint and Sid together made an amusing sight. Clint's short, slight frame supported by stocky bowed legs looked even smaller in contrast to Sid, who was over six feet tall—when he stood on his good leg. Sid was barrel-chested and heavyset, and his dark eyes were accentuated by his high forehead. Both had big protruding ears, and both dressed like the country boys that all Texans insist they are when trying to make the shrewdest deal they can.

As Clint's success grew, so did his family, and Clint and Anne moved into a larger and nicer home in Wichita Falls. As she prepared for childbirth, Anne went home to her mother's house in Tyler. Their first child was born on September 21, 1921, and was named for both his paternal grandfather, John

Murchison, and for his mother's stepfather Dabney White. He was called "John Dabney" as a child and throughout his life.

Less than two years later, on September 12, 1923, Anne gave birth to a second son. This time Anne went to Dallas for the birth, and the delivery was performed by a well-known female obstetrician. The child was named Clinton Williams Murchison Jr. Called "Clint W.," he was a tiny baby and often sick as an infant.

Only fifteen months later, on January 25, 1925, Anne gave birth a third time. Again it was a boy, and again the same female obstetrician in Dallas performed the birth. The child was named Burk Yarbrough Murchison after his maternal grandmother, and he was called Burk.

Soon after Burk was born, Clint began to grow restless in Wichita Falls. The initial excitement of the North Texas oil boom was gone, and he was anxious to sink wells farther west and to get in on the new oil play in South Texas. He dreamed of expanding his operations to encompass the entire state. Conversely, his partner, Ernest Fain, wanted to continue concentrating the company's drilling in and around Wichita Falls. They decided to split the company, Murchison taking assorted wells in West Texas, Fain receiving most of the Wichita Falls properties.

When all the assets were divided, Clint walked away with $5 million. Fields were producing around San Antonio, and there was a big play stretching west from San Antonio. In addition, south Texas was cattle country, and Clint secretly yearned to get back into the cattle business. To a few close business associates, he had even confided, "I'd like someday to own more cattle than anyone in the world."

To everyone else, he said he was moving to San Antonio to retire.

During a visit to Athens in 1925, Clint noticed an advertisement of the First National Bank in the local newspaper. In large print, it claimed, "Saving is the Secret of Success," and below that in smaller print, "The trouble with a good many people who don't succeed as well as they might is that they have more wishbone than backbone. Successful people say that thrift is one of the virtues which lies at the root of human progress."

Clint realized that one of the bank's main objectives was to get deposits, and this was an attempt to do just that. Nevertheless, the advertisement was symbolic of just how different his business principles were from the conventional attitudes of the town where he was born. The oil rush had changed everything. He knew that the Athens boys who became millionaires would do so by investing their dollars not in bank deposits but in the ground. The most ambitious men were no longer content to run their little stores and farms and gather at Stirman's Drugstore to talk about the riches being made by others on distant oil fields. Sid and Clint were among the first to leave, but they were followed by hundreds of others. More than fifty men from Athens would become oil millionaires within the next two decades. Those who remained behind deposited their dollars at the First National and continued to struggle along, just as the town did.

5

"I can't play the piano."

By 1925 Clint Murchison's wells were pulling oil from three edges of the largest state in the Union. On the flat North Central Plains near Wichita Falls, his wells continued to pump. In far West Texas, on the edge of the petroleum-rich Permian Basin, he had begun drilling, and in the cattle-rich land of South Texas his geologist already had several strikes. At age thirty, Clint was not ready to retire—in San Antonio or anywhere else. It was obvious just how restless he was when he decided not to buy but instead lease the large, white-pillared home that the family had moved into.

San Antonio was by far the most cultivated and graceful city in Texas in the 1920s. The Spanish had founded a mission there in 1718, more than a century before the first lonely log cabin was built in Dallas, and the town became famous as the site of the Mexican attack on the Alamo in 1836. By the time Clint and Anne and their three children arrived in 1925, it had also become the most important banking center in the Southwest.

In the last ten years Clint had been involved in dozens of drilling, leasing, and production partnerships with many people in many towns. After only a few days in San Antonio, the town where he had said he was going to retire, Clint had already embarked on deals with a new team of oilmen. He set up offices in one of the city's multistory bank buildings and hired a bright, young geologist, Ernest Closuit, from the Gulf Oil Corporation.

Clint planned a business trip to New York and invited Anne and her sister, Lucy Morris, to come with him. The three traveled by ship from New Orleans to New York, then checked into the Waldorf-Astoria Hotel, where they planned to stay for two weeks. During the day Clint met with bankers and oilmen, while Anne and her sister shopped and toured Manhattan. The lighted billboards on the Great White Way and the speakeasies made necessary by Prohibition may not have been quite so glamorous as they are remembered today, but they were new and exciting for this threesome whose only experience was small Texas towns and villages.

However, business forced Clint to return a few days early, and he left for San Antonio by train. He suggested the women stay on until "you have bought up everything in New York" and then return by ship to New Orleans. They happily agreed to the proposal and stayed a week longer than originally planned. Anne was the center of attention on the ship. "That cute little girl from Texas," passengers commented to one another. "She's so young and adorable. Can you believe she has three little boys?"

Shortly after returning to San Antonio, Anne noticed several very faint brown spots on her skin. But the spots were almost invisible and she put her occasional worries out of her mind. However, when she left a few days later to attend a wedding in Tyler, the spots were darker and now clearly visible. Still, she said nothing, nor was she concerned until a friend at the wedding reception exclaimed, "Anne, your eyes are so terribly yellow."

Anne asked her mother if she thought her eyes looked odd. When Burk noticed how very yellow they were, Anne told her about the spots on her body, and Burk became alarmed. They immediately suspected yellow jaundice, and Anne left that afternoon to see her doctor in San Antonio.

A few days later Clint telephoned his mother-in-law in Tyler. "I don't think it's serious, but Anne is in Santa Rosa Hospital."

The doctors did, in fact, diagnose jaundice and guessed that Anne had contracted the liver disease from dirty water or drinking glasses on the ship from New York. Unsure of the cause, the doctors were even less sure how to treat the illness. Clint did not leave his wife's side, and Dabney White brought half a dozen top doctors from around the state to examine his stepdaughter. But Anne's health grew rapidly worse, and within a few days she died.

At her death, Clint sat next to her bed, devastated. His agony and sorrow filled the hospital as he cried out loud, moaning at times, then screaming. He cried for hours.

"When Anne died, it like'd to have killed Clint," recalled ninety-seven-year-old Mrs. A. M. Barnes of Athens. "He got in his car and just drove and drove. He wouldn't come home."

Anne died on May 26, 1926, and the months that followed were the worst in Clint's life. Shattered and inconsolable, Clint withdrew into a world devoid of family and friends, business associates, even oil deals. Leaving the three children in the care of their live-in nurses, he began to roam Texas. He drove to Wichita Falls, then to various towns in West Texas, then to Tyler and Athens. He never stayed more than a day in any place, and there was no purpose to any of the trips.

"My mother said you couldn't believe how sad he looked and how lonely he was," said Mary Ann Perryman of Athens. "A few months after Anne died, my parents came downstairs, and there was Clint sleeping on their sofa. He had let himself in the house. My mother just shook her head and said, 'Poor, sweet Clint.' "

Clint did not have the comfort of religion. He came from generations of Scotch Presbyterians who believed, as John Knox had taught them, in predestination—that God had determined their destiny and they could not affect it. Clint had no such belief. He was convinced he could shape his own destiny and did so, simultaneously shaping the lives of many Texans and Americans. But if he did not believe in the Word of God, it was not because he was ignorant of it. During endless lonely nights in the various oil boomtowns, he had read the Bible from cover to cover three times and knew its contents better than many who professed piety.

As the months passed, Clint's grief grew worse. He skipped meals and began to drink heavily. Several shot glasses of straight whiskey coupled with his extreme depression were a volatile combination, and friends became alarmed. Days passed when he did not come home or call. When five-year-old

John Dabney asked where his daddy was, the nurses could not honestly answer. Finally Burk White and her daughter Lucy Morris asked if they could come to San Antonio to talk with him. Clint agreed to see them, but when he met them at the door, he looked more disheveled and distraught then ever. Burk was so shocked at his appearance that she did not wait until they were seated to blurt out, "Please let the children come live with us. You're not in any kind of shape to take care of them."

Astoundingly, Clint abruptly straightened his shoulders and pulled himself together. "No," he said. "You can spoil them all you like, but they're going to live with me. I'll take care of my boys."

Burk continued to plead with her son-in-law, but he would not relent. After they left, Clint changed from depressed to mildly happy to jubilant. Suddenly he thought how fortunate he was to have the children and how much fun he was going to have raising them. He telephoned his unmarried sister, Mary Murchison, in Athens and asked her to come to San Antonio to help in the task. Mary arrived a few days later and stayed for nearly a year.

"The new family became very close, and Clint was put off when Mary told him a year later she was getting married," recalls a friend.

But by the time Mary left, Clint had recovered and was back at the game of multiplying his millions in the oil fields. When business associates said they were glad to see he had not retired for good, Clint made light of his absence "What's a man going to do? I can't play the piano."

Thirty years later Clint confided to his secretary, "When Anne died, people said I stayed drunk for a year."

Since the discovery at Spindletop in 1901, wildcatters had been sinking holes farther and farther west. They had some success until they found themselves in the vast Permian Basin of West Texas where they punctured the dry, cracked earth again and again without finding a drop of oil. So many wells had failed to produce that wildcatters in other regions of the state promised, "I'll drink every drop of oil they find in West Texas."

But on May 28, 1923, the Santa Rita No. 1 blew in, spewing mud and oil wildly over the derrick and hundreds of feet into the sky. With the coming of the Santa Rita, more exploration began nearby on T. G. Hendrick's cattle ranch, a remote stretch of sand and scrub mesquite on the New Mexico border. When a test well came in on Hendrick's ranch, it opened up what would become the prolific Hendrick Field, one of the greatest oil strikes in the Permian Basin. New towns burst forth like desert blooms after a rain, and one of the toughest, meanest little towns was Wink, in Winkler County. With the oil came the inevitable crush of boomtowners who, in a few months, expanded Wink's population from one hundred citizens to several thousand.

There were many men and women who wandered from town to town, with no real purpose other than to experience the thrill of a newer field. They may have had well-paid jobs on rigs in the previous town, and the play may still have been big where they were, but they were lured by the newness, the adventure. They believed, or hoped, that the newer the field, the greater the potential for larger reserves. There was always more oil around the next derrick. This kind of illogical optimism was what made Texas and eventually almost destroyed it.

Although Clint was not a wanderer, he too was lured by the big potential and the big thrill, and by early 1927, he had put together drilling blocks covering more than eighty acres in the Hendrick Field. His wells began producing immediately, but he faced a new problem. Because there was no way to get the oil to market, it remained in large storage tanks on his land.

He needed a pipeline, but when he could find no one to build it, he decided to construct one himself. He first built two half-million-barrel storage tanks, and then began laying pipe in the direction of Pyote, the nearest railroad town. Some local refinery owners had, in the meantime, decided to construct their own pipeline to market, and tried to stop Clint's line. Because he had both oil and gas production on his lease, Clint decided to re-engineer his pipe to transport natural gas.

Murchison found the credit, and then a partner, Roy Moyston, to manage the gas business. The M & M Pipeline Company (for Murchison and Moyston) ran ads in the local newspaper, offering service to residents of Wink. There was no meter, just unlimited fuel at a cost of only $5 per month to residents who would lay their own line out to the M & M pipeline and tie on. Because all the pipe was laid on top of the ground, constructing a pipeline to the main line was a fairly simple task. The townspeople quickly tied in, and dusty little Wink became a sprawling web of pipe, literally full of energy.

With the success of the Wink Gas Company, Clint extended the pipeline into three other towns nearby. Soon the company had gas franchises in a dozen small towns in West Texas and New Mexico, with pipelines running from its gas storage tanks in nearby fields.

Murchison was aware that West Texas needed water at least as much as it needed energy. Now adept at constructing pipelines, he started the Cities Water Company of Texas. The firm operated out of Pyote, Texas, and tiny Lovington, New Mexico, piping drinking water to towns within a fifty-mile radius.

Natural gas was a new industry to the little towns of the Southwest, although larger cities, such as Dallas and Galveston, had used natural gas in the early 1920s. But when Murchison laid his lines along remote stretches of land in West Texas and New Mexico, where there were no large centers of population, it was a new phenomenon. Like the rail lines that had come decades earlier, the gas lines were viewed as a step forward, a measure of the town's progress.

With abundant reserves of gas in the ground, Murchison was confident that he could serve dozens, perhaps hundreds of towns throughout the Southwest. Gas was clean, convenient, and, most of all, cheap. He believed natural gas was the energy of the future.

In late 1928 Clint lived part-time in Dallas at the fashionable Maple Terrace, a Moorish structure that was one of the city's early multistory apartment buildings. He shared an apartment with a boyhood friend from Athens, Wofford Cain. Clint purchased a small gas company in Oklahoma and then looked for someone to run the company. Wofford knew noth-

ing about the gas business, but Clint came home from work
one day and offered him the job. Cain took it on the spot.

With companies scattered here and there, oil royalty checks
coming in and paychecks going out, it was difficult for Clint to
keep track of which companies were doing what. Employees
received their paychecks from as many as a dozen different
Murchison enterprises. Sometimes they came from the Murchison Oil Company, at other times Murchison Construction
Company or M & M Pipeline Company. Still other checks
were drawn on Murchison's personal bank accounts. It was a
chaotic way to run his mushrooming empire, and Clint realized it.

In an attempt to organize, he consolidated his pipeline companies and moved his headquarters to Dallas. On January 14,
1929, in Dallas's fifteen-story American Exchange Building,
Clint and his three partners founded Southern Union Gas
Company. The name was chosen to signify "the union of a
number of diverse companies, all operating in the Southwest
under one banner." Clint's elder brother, Frank, left his position as president of the First National Bank in Athens to get
into business with Clint. A younger brother, Kenneth Murchison, also anxious to share in his brother's success, came
aboard when Southern Union was founded. The fourth principal in the company was geologist Ernest Closuit, who had just
married one of Clint's sisters, Laura.

By the late 1920s Dallas boasted a population of 250,000. It
was second in the state to Houston, which had 30,000 more
people. Dallas did not yet look like a big city, although there
were signs of progress downtown. Automobiles and electric
street cars had now completely replaced the horse and buggy
and horse-drawn streetcars of only two decades earlier. But
there were only half a dozen downtown buildings with more
than ten floors, and many streets outside the central business
district were still unpaved.

It was almost a miracle that a single skyscraper, a single
street had been built in this vast, unattractive, dry, hot land.
There was no good reason for a town to grow here. There was
no confluence of rivers. Nor was there a mountain pass to
make this area of the country a good stopping point.

The town got its quiet start sixty years earlier, in 1841, when John Neely Bryan arrived at an uninhabited ford in the Trinity River. He erected a lean-to on the river's bluff, a location that would achieve fame 122 years later as the spot where President Kennedy was murdered. Bryan had come to open an Indian trading post, but the Indians had already gone. This was flat, barren country and Bryan could just as easily have settled fifty miles away in any direction.

But the hyperbole that brought Dallas into the national consciousness in the 1950s and brought it worldwide television fame in the 1980s, was there from the very start. It was a place made not by nature but by men, specifically those with a talent for self-promotion. An early victim of Dallas's exaggerated self-promotion arrived only a few years after John Neely Bryan. The settler wrote in his diary of his arrival, "We soon reached the place we had heard of so often; but the *town,* where was it? Two small log cabins—this was the town of Dallas, and two families of ten or twelve souls was its population."

For any village that was neither a seaport nor a river port, the absolute essential was a railroad. In 1872 the Houston & Texas Central Railroad completed its line from Houston to Dallas and the first wood-burning locomotive steamed into town.

But even with their north-south line in place, the town's leading citizens worried when they learned that the transcontinental Texas & Pacific Railroad planned to bypass Dallas on a path fifty miles to the south. The T. & P. railroad was pushing eastward from Shreveport, Louisiana, along the 32nd parallel, and would have provided the east-west line to make Dallas a commercial crossroads. The town's business leaders were determined to find a means, fair or foul, to bring the railroad through Dallas. A happy combination of political tricks in the Texas legislature and a $100,000 purchase of T. & P. bonds secured the connection.

This was a coup without which Dallas would have remained a hamlet or disappeared completely. Instead, within a few months, the town was bustling with more than 7,000 residents.

In the late 1890s Dallas's civic leaders began an effort to

promote development of the Trinity River as an alternate freight route to the Gulf of Mexico. Though they naively believed navigation of the Trinity could be made possible, their real purpose was to bluff the railroads into lowering freight rates. The scheme worked, and rates were quickly lowered. Dallas businessmen saved $825,000 on 3.3 million bales of cotton shipped out of the state in 1895.

The civic resolve to make Dallas bigger and better never ceased. In the first two decades of this century, Dallas businessmen continued to work hard to build a city that would be recognized nationally as an important business center. But not until the 1930s, in the teeth of the Depression, did the city really begin to achieve that goal.

The spring following the founding of the Southern Union Gas Company, Clint and Wofford Cain were vacationing in New Mexico when Clint learned that Albuquerque and Santa Fe did not have natural gas. Clint insisted they forget the vacation and get to work. Although Southern Union had enormous reserves in the giant San Juan Basin in northwestern New Mexico, there were few available markets in the area. Clint quickly obtained a franchise in Santa Fe, but Albuquerque was more difficult, as others were also seeking one.

The competitors for the franchise appeared before a city council meeting where the mayor asked which one of the men was willing to put up the most bond money.

"Who will put up twenty-five thousand dollars?" the mayor asked. Everyone held up his hand.

"Who will put up fifty thousand?" Murchison and another man raised their hands.

"Who will put up seventy-five thousand?" Murchison and the same man held up their hands.

"Who will put up one hundred thousand?" This time only Murchison's hand went up.

Before leaving the council meeting, Clint wrote a check for $100,000 on the First National Bank of Dallas. Outside the courthouse, Cain wailed, "We don't have that kind of money in the bank."

Clint kept walking, "We'll worry about that when we get

home." They caught the next train to Dallas, arriving ahead of the check. Clint went directly to the First National Bank and asked to see the chairman, Nathan Adams.

Adams was a savvy, aggressive banker who bet on men rather than balance sheets. He had first met Clint twenty years earlier when he was a dinner guest at the home of John Murchison in Athens. Clint was just a boy then, but Adams recalled a story about young Clint finding an almost dead calf by a railroad track outside of Athens. The calf had been hit, and presumably killed, by a train, and its owner was grateful when Clint offered to haul the carcass off his land.

Once home, Clint nursed the calf back to health, and a few weeks later sold it as a healthy calf. The story was embellished as Clint's business reputation grew larger in the 1930s, but Adams' nose told him Clint was a winner. Adams wanted for his bank the business of someone he already suspected might become the richest man in Texas.

He agreed to advance Clint the $100,000, convinced that the return on the Albuquerque deal would be far greater than the principal and interest. Adams was right.

During the years when Clint was away so often on business, he had a stock answer for acquaintances who ran into him in Dallas and asked, "What are you doing in town?"

"Just covering a few overdrafts," he invariably answered, and often it was true.

Friends and business associates through the years were incredulous at the enormous amounts of money Clint always owed, how the banks carried him through bad times as well as good.

"If you are honest and you are trying, your creditors will play ball," was Clint's simple explanation. And it was what he taught his sons. "If you are going to owe money, owe more than you can pay, then the lenders can't afford to foreclose."

When Southern Union won the franchise in Albuquerque, the company had undertaken a great challenge—to build the first pipeline ever to cross the Continental Divide. It would stretch for one hundred and fifty miles, from the San Juan Basin on the Pacific slope to Santa Fe and Albuquerque on the Atlantic side. Murchison personally marked the route by dropping flour sacks with flag-tipped rods from a small plane along the route. The laying of pipe across canyons, sierras, and Rocky Mountain peaks was no small task.

"Many oilmen won't drill for gas because you have to wait for the returns," said Phil Bee, who worked for Murchison for two decades. "After you find the gas, it's another two years getting a pipeline built and another two years before you start seeing income, whereas in oil the payoff is so much faster. But the gas business was perfect for Clint because he wanted the long-term payoff. He always went for the big killing years down the road."

The Southern Union pipeline company went heavily in debt. To help fund the project, Clint's brother Frank struggled without much success to sell its stock in Chicago where it was listed on the Chicago Stock Exchange. Finally, in October 1930, two years after construction began, natural gas arrived in Santa Fe. The *Santa Fe New Mexican* described the event: "A gigantic banner of yellow and blue flame leaped from the top of the tall standpipe of the Southern Union Gas Company amid the cheers of thousands and the deafening chorus of horns of hundreds of automobiles. It lit up the country for miles around."

The excitement was tempered a day later, when the newspaper's front page featured a story reporting a dozen separate injuries from gas fumes. "Santa Fe is going to have to watch its step until it learns how to handle the new fuel," the paper said. Natural gas was still an unknown fuel, and the townspeople, overwhelmed with curiosity, experimented with its use. A rash of lawsuits resulted from the injuries.

Despite the pipeline's few flaws, Clint was immensely happy with what the project had accomplished. He had reached a point in his life when he was interested in more than just challenging business deals, shrewd trading, and ingenious financing of his own projects. He wanted to play a significant role in the progress of the nation.

Although Clint neither invented the pipeline nor was the first to find natural gas, he was the first person to bring this new and superior energy source to widely scattered communities. By taking from the ground one of the earth's most valuable resources and delivering it to thousands of kitchens and living rooms, he had made life better in the growing settlements of America's new West—and he did not stop there. Murchison was becoming less and less involved in the day-to-day operations of his companies. Instead, after he acquired a business, he moved on to snatch up another. By the time the Albuquerque line was completed, Southern Union was serving gas and water to forty-three towns in Texas, Oklahoma, New Mexico, Colorado, Wyoming, and Arkansas.

With his business booming, Clint took time out to find a home in Dallas. His boys were still mostly in the care of nurses in San Antonio, and he was anxious to have them with him. He wanted a place in the country where his young sons could fish and hunt and, as he put it, "grow up close to the land."

Clint found what he was looking for fourteen miles north of downtown Dallas. The property, which belonged to the Dallas Polo Club, was a rolling expanse of abruptly changing land, of streams and brooks that ran through thick woods and open fields. Spreading across three hundred and fifty acres, it was a miniature Texas, raw, diverse and virtually untamed. The woods, like those where Clint grew up, were filled with deer, raccoons, and squirrels, and the idyllic streams and brooks, splashing over rocks and natural dams, were alive with fish. Elsewhere on the property, flat, treeless fields stretched to the horizon, resembling the vast, limitless land of West Texas. At the southwest corner, two miles from the road, was the only sign of civilization, the clubhouse.

Polo came to the United States in the 1870s, but it did not become fashionable in Texas until the early 1920s. From its inception in America, polo has been a rich man's sport, and Dallas immediately fielded eight prominent men, enough to form two teams of four. The club developed even more prestige when one of its members acquired the land for the club and developed it with polo fields, a clubhouse, and stables, where each member could board his string of ponies. The clubhouse was a small white frame house with a dining room, kitchen, and a common room where the members played cards and drank through the night.

With a few changes, Clint thought, the building would make a comfortable family home. He telephoned his sons in San Antonio. "I've bought a farm in Dallas," he told them. "You're going to like it."

Workers immediately began building two new wings for the house—one with three bedrooms for the boys, the other with bedrooms for what would become an almost endless procession of governesses. Large quarters also were built for cooks, maids, crop and cattle hands, the ranch foreman, and Clint's black majordomo and his wife, Jewel and Birdie Phifer.

When, months later, the house was still under construction, Clint grew tired of waiting and brought seven-year-old John Dabney, five-year-old Clint W., and three-year-old Burk to their new home. With the boys' bedrooms still unfinished, they slept with their father in his room, four beds side by side. If one of Clint's oil cronies spent the night, the boys would draw straws and the loser had to sleep in another room. The bunkhouse arrangement began out of necessity, but the boys loved sleeping with their father, and continued to do so for years.

Clint Murchison's farm in its early days was nothing less than primitive—and not only outside. The boys were no less fascinated with the farm's skunks and coons than their father had been as a boy tacking animal pelts to his bedroom walls. Clint permitted his sons to bring live raccoons, newborn piglets, snakes, and various wild creatures inside the house. As a result, governesses came and left almost as often as the pets.

Just as Clint had hoped, his boys played hard on the land. They hunted, fished, rode horses, climbed trees, swam in the creeks. Yet none of the children was very healthy or strong physically. John Dabney suffered from asthma and was made to wear a wool cap as protection against North Texas's chilly, damp winters. Clint W. was scrawny and sickly as a very young boy, and Burk had serious lung problems, although this was not discovered until later.

North Texas's weather was severe and destructive. Dust and sand storms blew in from West Texas in the spring, turning the sky a terrifying reddish-brown, the color of dry, burnt land. The dust ruined crops and made breathing difficult. The weather that followed, from April through October, was even more oppressive. The unyielding heat was heavy with humidity, yet the sun was so blisteringly hot that the land cracked and cratered under it. Ninety-degree and one-hundred-degree days lasted until October, and even then the relief was only fleeting. Ice and wind storms usually struck without warning in early December.

Despite the hours they spent outdoors each day, the boys did not have ruddy complexions. The fragile, wire-rimmed glasses that framed the pale faces of John Dabney and Clint W. made them look even more weak and frail. Like their father, the older boys were reserved, untalkative, and almost painfully shy. When Clint W. was only eight years old, he confided in his grandmother, Burk White, "I'm just the shyest little boy in the world."

Burk was the opposite of John Dabney and Clint W. He not only looked slightly healthier than his older brothers, he was gregarious and vivacious like his mother. He had Anne's warmth and *joie de vivre*. He had big dimples and, when he was barely four years old, he was already bouncing into the room, shaking hands with all of his father's friends. Burk's constant laughter was contagious, and he filled the house with excitement. His older brothers, conversely, could come into a room and leave again without being noticed.

Clint paid tuition for his boys to attend public school in Dallas's upper-class suburb, University Park. Majordomo Jewel Phifer served as chauffeur, driving the boys the nine miles to school and home in the afternoon. "Sometimes John Dabney and Clint would pull up in front of school in the back of a chauffeur-driven Pierce Arrow," recalled a grade-school classmate. "Other times the boys would come to school sitting on a pile of hay in the back of a cattle truck driven by one of the farmhands. How they got to school just depended on who was free on the farm to drive them to town."

The driver was frequently late picking up the boys after school, and during the winter they would wait outside in the cold. This practice was harmful to the fragile health of all three, especially Clint W., who was extremely susceptible to winter chills and flu. When he was five years old, Clint W. had a double mastoidectomy in which doctors removed part of the bone behind both of his ears. After the operation the doctors told Clint Sr. that the boy should be kept inside all day for months, under the watch of round-the-clock nurses, and that he should not exert himself in any way. Clint Sr. followed the doctors' advice, but under this regime Clint W. became willful and petulant. "He was the worst spoiled brat any parent ever had to deal with," his father recalled later.

Clint came home from work one day and found his son fussing as usual. "That's it," Clint said. He fired the nurses, then sent Clint W. outside to play with his brothers in the creek bottoms. Clint W. grew strong and healthy and was rarely sick again, but he never liked the outdoors as much as his brothers did. Instead he preferred to close himself in his room and read. He became a voracious reader of newspapers, farm manuals, and his father's magazines. He particularly liked *Popular Mechanics,* and when he was only nine, he read an article about an electronic eye, then built one himself.

John Dabney was Clint W.'s opposite. While Clint W. had a quick mind and wanted quick answers that were precise and provable, John Dabney liked to let his thoughts wander, to speculate about things that neither he nor his father could totally explain—how calves grew inside their mothers' wombs, why some crops did well one year and not the next, what caused the Civil War, why his father's friends disliked President Herbert Hoover. Endlessly curious, he was not satisfied with short, pat answers. His searching mind was revealed in *Farmalia News,* an often witty, in-house farm newspaper that he wrote and published every few weeks. Crop predictions, the births of calves, and the hiring of a new caretaker were all material for the newspaper.

John Dabney, Clint W., and Burk shared at least one common interest: They were relentless eavesdroppers on their father's frequent card games. When Clint and his cronies gathered at the card tables or roulette table, the boys would hide behind doors or under chairs, spying on the gamblers. They were alerted by the sounds of cards shuffling, the *click-clack* of chalk on a slate scoreboard for dominoes, and as the night grew late, by the noise of hands slapping the table, of cursing, shouting, and belching.

Although he tried to forbid his sons to watch his poker and gin rummy games, Clint's cronies loved to have the children around. The men spoke to the boys mostly about money, and each man offered his own bit of advice on becoming rich. They told stories of how they were born poor, but how their tough trading and gambler's instincts had made them rich. Some were even proud to admit that luck, and nothing other than luck, had made them millionaires.

"Some people get luck and brains mixed up, and that's when they get in trouble," admonished one oilman. They compared being poor with being rich, and everyone agreed rich was better. Sid Richardson described how he'd lost and won three fortunes, a story they had heard so often they could mimic him. "When I was down the last time, I said, 'I'd been poor so long it felt like rich to me.' "

Even before the boys understood the value of money, they knew that, "Count me in for ten," did not mean ten dollars, but ten thousand dollars. At card games not only were cash and chips thrown into the pot, but royalties, oil leases, automobiles, homes; even islands in the Gulf of Mexico were won and lost. A player considered it a good evening if he walked away from the table with $20,000; a great evening meant winnings of two or three times that much. These were men whose oil wells brought in or paid out more than that in a single week. If a bad poker hand cost them a twenty-acre producing lease, they were, despite rich expressions of obscenity and profanity, not really distressed. It took a certain type of person to risk thousands of dollars sinking wells. The type of men that had the stomach and stamina to keep drilling through the dry spells as well as the wet were the same type that could come to the card table at night and risk everything they owned. They were passionate gamblers.

On warm summer nights the card games were held on an outside terrace. Late one night, during a lull in the shouting and cursing, the men heard a rustle in the trees, then looked up and saw Clint W. He had been sitting in the tree for more than an hour, witnessing the continuous, rapid exchange of money and four-letter words. Clint W. was just as fascinated observing the gamblers as his father had been as a young boy watching the cattle traders at Athens' livestock barns.

If Clint W. listened carefully, he probably also heard his father using big words that neither the boy nor the other oilmen understood. "What are you saying now, Murk?" Sid would shout.

When Clint explained the meaning of a word he had just used, the oilmen looked at him skeptically, then placed bets on whether Clint was correct in his usage. They grabbed the dictionary, which Clint always had at hand, and flipped through the pages, sometimes for several minutes before they found the word. The game of betting on Clint's knowledge of the dictionary was short-lived, however, because he was almost always correct. He read the dictionary constantly, and confounded his oil cronies with his growing vocabulary. Just as rare among oilmen was Clint's refusal to use obscenity and profanity. Friends say he stopped cursing when someone told him that four-letter words demonstrated a limited vocabulary.

Clint Sr. could see that his sons had an insatiable appetite for the kind of business talk they heard around the house. When John Dabney was only ten years old, his father taught him one of the basic tenets of his business philosophy. "You can buy something and make a profit on it without using your own money," he explained, and then showed his son how it worked. He sold John Dabney a calf for $25, taking no cash but John's note for $25 plus interest. John later sold the calf at a profit, paid the note, and kept the profit.

The boys caught on quickly. If one brother was low on his allowance, another would make a loan. Clint W. was usually the creditor, and the interest rates he charged fluctuated with the desperation in his brothers' voices.

One of little Burk's playmates was Jewel and Birdie Phifer's boy, Eddie Lee, who worked as a farmhand. When Birdie, a house servant, told Mr. Murchison that a ten-dollar bill was missing from her purse, Clint lined up his sons and questioned them about the money. Eight-year-old Burk proudly pulled the bill from his pocket. "I was shooting craps with Eddie Lee and he owed me a million dollars. I just took it as payment on account."

It was not surprising that the Murchison children spoke in grown-up financial terms or that they had their own crap games, where the stakes were as high as a million dollars. Their friends were not the other little boys their age at University Park Public School who played with marbles and traded stamps. They associated with rich oilmen, such as Sid Richardson, Wofford Cain, Toddie Lee Wynne, who played with bicycle decks and traded royalties and leases. Because the farm was such a distance from University Park, the boys rarely saw other white children except in school. The few children of servants who worked on the farm were uneducated, and as the boys grew older, the farm workers' sons and daughters seemed increasingly uninteresting.

The adult world where the boys grew up was also, with the exception of the help, devoid of women. Many of Clint's oil and poker cronies were bachelors, and those oilmen who had wives brought them to the farm only rarely. A woman's touch was clearly missing. The boys were dressed in expensive clothes ordered from New York, but usually the styles were slightly stodgy.

When Clint's friends joked that he needed a new wife to help him spend his millions, his reply was always very serious: "I'm not going to choose a second mother for my sons." Clint deeply loved his children, and he loathed the notion of inflicting a stepmother on them. He steadfastly refused to remarry until they were grown.

Nor did Sid seem likely to marry. Stout and determinedly plain, he described himself as physically unattractive to women: "I look jest like a big bull lookin' through the thicket."

When Clint saw how happy his sons were at the farm, he began a master plan to develop the land—with fences, roads and bridges, and, ultimately, an enormous manor house. A new bridge was built to replace the one on the road leading from the main road to the clubhouse because it frequently washed out when the creek rose. One sweltering summer day as he stood watching workers build the bridge, he noticed how much cooler the land was near the creek, shaded by a grove of pecan and live oak trees. In this shelter from the blistering Texas sun, Clint decided to build a swimming pool and cabana.

Friends dubbed the Olympic-size pool "The Gulf of Mexico." Because it was constructed of a muddy-colored fieldstone, the water looked dark as a lake. Indeed, it was fed by a nearby spring, which also made the water very cold. Many swimming pools of the 1920s in Texas were nothing more than mud holes. Concrete or stone swimming pools with steep sides were still a rarity even in Dallas. Because many of Clint's cronies were not good swimmers, ladders were installed every twelve feet around the pool.

At one end of the pool was an enormous dressing and dining area, and next to that a barbecue. During many summer evenings a haunch of beef turned and roasted on the open spit while the men played cards at adjacent tables around the pool. Nothing could interrupt the men once the card games began—nothing other than barbecue. When one of a dozen black servants announced dinner, the men scrambled out of their chairs and lined up to fill and refill their plates.

Clint was usually the first to leave the card table, and before midnight he crept into the bedroom he shared with his sons. The boys had often been hiding, watching the party the entire evening, but when Clint climbed into bed in the dark, they always appeared to be sleeping.

6

"I was fighting for a principle."

In New York social circles, 1930 was a landmark year, marked by the debuts of two of America's most famous heiresses—Doris Duke and Barbara Hutton. The Misses Duke and Hutton would be variously known for decades as the Gold Dust Twins and the Poor Little Rich Girls. At the time of their debuts, each had inherited in excess of $50 million, and each had her own carefully appointed private railroad car.

Their lavish debutante parties were given full-page newspaper coverage, just months after the worst stock market crash in history. As thousands of the nation's suddenly jobless workers contemplated the poorhouse, the Poor Little Rich Girls traveled the world in splendor. The economic spread between the rich and the poor would become even greater as the Depression wore on. The daydreams of the roaring twenties that anyone might make a million had disappeared, but the desire to read about the rich increased. In 1933 socialist author Upton Sinclair despaired that men whose families were starving often spent their pennies not for a loaf of bread but for a newspaper, in order to read about the swells who dined on ten-course meals in the opulent mansions along Fifth Avenue.

The dream of sudden, unearned miraculous wealth was dead in most of America, but in depression-ravaged East Texas the dream was about to become a reality. In early October 1930, a year to the month after the stock market collapsed, hundreds of dirt-poor farmers joined anxious oilmen keeping vigil at a well being drilled deep in East Texas. The Daisy Bradford No. 3 was located in Rusk County, only one county

removed from the Louisiana border, a flat, arid, scrub region
of pine forests and farmed-out cotton fields.

The Daisy Bradford No. 3's beginnings were less than aus-
picious. It was the third well drilled by Columbus Marion
Joiner on the widow Daisy Bradford's 975-acre farm. After
convincing the farmers of destitute Rusk County that there
was oil under their worn-out cotton fields, he assembled huge
leases in the county. A ladies' man and smooth talker, the
sixty-seven-year-old Joiner made his theories especially be-
lievable to the fifty-four-year-old Widow Bradford. He told
her that he would drill the first well on her property if she, in
turn, agreed to relinquish a portion of her royalty interest to
him.

She agreed, and in 1927 Joiner began his first "poor boy"
well on her farm. In oil lingo, to "poor boy" a well meant to
beg and borrow not only the maximum necessary money but
also as much equipment and labor as could be had on credit.
Joiner began with a rickety, worn-out rig, rusty pipe, and local
investors who had to quit from time to time to tend their crops.
Not a drop of oil had ever been found in Rusk County, and
local farmers became increasingly dubious as months passed
and seventeen other nearby wildcat wells failed to cough up
anything but mud and water. But Columbus viewed himself as
a twentieth-century explorer and—like the man for whom he
was named—was undaunted by doubters.

His first two wells were so poorly constructed that they
broke down and had to be abandoned. But Joiner and his
weary crew were inspired in the fall of 1929 when oil was
found near the town of Van in Van Zandt County, two counties to the north. With news of the Van field to spur them on,
the crew on the Daisy Bradford No. 3 began drilling more
zealously than ever.

Finally, on July 30, 1930, more than three years after Joiner
sank his first hole in Rusk County, a drill stem test brought up
from 3,600 feet Woodbine sand saturated in oil. Word spread
rapidly, and soon hundreds, then thousands, of farmers and
oilmen flocked to the rig.

The first person to make money on the well was Daisy Bradford's nephew, who sold soda pop and hot dogs to the crowd

who came to watch. As the crowd grew, so did the variety of drink. Soon there was as much white lightning sold by boot-leggers as there was soda pop at what began to look like a camp meeting or religious revival. The ninety-foot derrick, built in a clearing in the thick woods, towered well above the tall pine trees and could be seen from miles away. It was a lighthouse, leading the way to what Joiner contended was an under-ground ocean of oil.

On the strength of the drill stem test, a boom town shot up, and by the end of summer the town, appropriately named Joinerville, had a population of 8,000. Oilmen and farmers quickly bought up leases in Rusk County at spiraling prices. Joiner became known as the "Daddy of the Rusk County oil-field," and he accepted the name "Dad" Joiner.

Each day brought more hope that the oil trapped so deep in the ground could be brought to the surface. Late in the after-noon of October 5, the hole was swabbed and it came up with oil, followed by a gurgling down in the well. The earth began to rumble and shake, and the crowds rushed to the derrick floor as oil shot up out of the hole and over the top of the der-rick. While the slick black oil rained down on them, hundreds of penniless farmers and lease owners jumped up and down, tossing their hats in the air and shouting, "Oil, oil!" Men held their faces to the sky, shouting into the oil that sprayed them. Men and women hugged and kissed each other. Amid the pan-demonium, Dad Joiner made his way over to the flow gauge. The meter indicated the well would produce 6,800 barrels per day.

The following day a story in the nearby *Henderson Times* quoted the head driller on the well: "I believe we have the big-gest thing yet found in Texas." In the following days, newspa-pers around the state were filled with stories of dozens of penniless men and women who became rich overnight, leasing portions of their farms for as much as $20,000 to $30,000 per acre.

The enthusiasm was tempered, however, when the geyser of oil that was diverted into a storage tank flowed for a few days and then ceased. When the oil stopped, there was panic among lease holders who had bought up surrounding acreage at highly inflated prices. But a few days later oil gushed in again.

The flow continued to be intermittent, "flowing by heads." It would subside and then begin again when enough gas pressure, a "head" of pressure, accumulated to bring the oil to the surface. Five days after the well came in, its flow had dropped from 6,500 barrels a day to 250. The intermittent flow was an unknown phenomenon in the 1920s, and with such confusing signals coming from the well, some oilmen happily sold their leases to men they thought greater fools, and left town. The irregular flow, they reasoned, indicated that Joiner had tapped a very limited pool of oil.

One person who did not believe that theory was Haroldson Lafayette Hunt Jr. A professional gambler, Hunt used his winnings from the card table to acquire a string of one hundred wells in Arkansas and Louisiana. With his trader's instinct and self-confident willingness to move swiftly, he had added forty of those wells to his holdings in only one year. He arrived at the Daisy Bradford No. 3 well just as the drill stem test proved positive.

Hunt was born the youngest of eight children, on February 17, 1889, on a farm in Illinois. He learned to read at the age of three and was thought to be a child genius, but he had no formal grade-school or secondary-school education. Leaving home at age sixteen, he worked his way across the country from Kansas to California, as a dishwasher, sheep herder, concrete pourer, mule skinner, lumberjack, and professional card player.

In 1921 he found the career that would make him one of the richest men in the world, when he went to the oil boomtown of El Dorado, Arkansas. He used his poker winnings to trade oil leases in Arkansas, and he was so adept at the trade that after only six months he drilled his first well. It was a success, and so were many others that followed. Hunt moved south, where he bought leases in Louisiana. In early 1930 he heard about the activity in Rusk County and of Columbus Joiner, who claimed he was about to discover a new world under the ground.

Hunt was forty-one, tall and handsome, and he looked strangely out of place when he arrived at the Daisy Bradford

No. 3, dressed in a neatly pressed white shirt, tie, and straw boater, among men in dirty farm clothes. But if he seemed like an outsider, he did not act like one. Hunt knew that Joiner, who had borrowed for years to finance poor boy wells, still had huge debts, and his creditors—even before the well came in—were threatening to force him into receivership. Hunt saw his chance to buy out the famous wildcatter.

The majors were not convinced that the Daisy Bradford was anything more than a freak, but Hunt had a hunch that the "flowing heads" indicated otherwise. If a nearby lease, being drilled by the Deep Rock Oil Company, came in, he would be convinced that Joiner had hit a very large field. Hunt scrambled to come up with $30,000 toward purchase of the Joiner lease, then went to Joiner's room at downtown Dallas's Baker Hotel to offer to buy him out. Before heading to Dallas, Hunt had carefully made arrangements to keep in close touch by telephone with one of his scouts at the Deep Rock well.

For several days Hunt and Joiner holed up in a suite of rooms at the hotel negotiating a buy-out deal. Joiner, then seventy years old, dreamed of being out of debt, but he wanted more money for his properties than Hunt had offered. On the night of November 26 Hunt got a call telling him the drill stem test on the Deep Rock Well showed the Woodbine sand was saturated with oil. With the news he had been waiting for, perhaps even delaying the negotiations for, Hunt pushed forward to clinch the deal that night.

As Hunt biographer Harry Hurt III explains:

Hunt's next move would be contested for years to come. According to Hunt's version, he immediately informed Joiner of [the Deep Rock] report. Hunt claimed that the news only confirmed what Joiner had anticipated himself.

Joiner's version was much different. According to his recollection, Hunt never told him anything about an oil-saturated core from the Deep Rock well. Rather, Joiner claimed later, Hunt told him the Deep Rock crew had drilled past the Woodbine sand without finding any oil.

But that same night, four hours after the telephone call,

Joiner sold out to Hunt for $1.3 million. The sale included
Joiner's leases on about 5,000 Rusk County acres at the center
of which was the 80-acre Daisy Bradford tract on which the
discovery well was located. Hunt paid only the $30,000 up
front in cash. The remainder was to be paid out in future oil
production from the properties.

At the same time that word spread of the Deep Rock Well,
headlines around the state began to carry the story of the deal
that would be known in the oil fraternity as the financial coup
of the decade. At the time, Hunt was a newcomer to the Texas
oil patch, but one man who now listened with interest to the
news of the Deep Rock and the Daisy Bradford wells was
Clint Murchison. He recalled that not many months earlier a
professional card player by the name of H. L. Hunt had asked
him into a drilling partnership. Clint had rejected Hunt's
offer.

By the spring of 1931, the Depression had worsened. The
economy sank ever lower; security and commodity prices collapsed; bankruptcies and bank failures multiplied; unemployment soared. Until now President Herbert Hoover had relied
on voluntary measures to combat the Depression. But by the
time Congress met in December 1931, the country's economic
state was so devastated that Hoover proposed direct governmental action.

Yet as the news grew worse around the nation, more good
news was coming out of East Texas. In Kilgore, a town of 700,
just twelve miles north of the Daisy Bradford, farmer Malcolm Crim had leased thousands of acres and had been trying
for months to get someone to sink a well on his land. A
fortune-teller ten years earlier had told him there was oil
under his land, and with the coming of the Daisy Bradford,
Crim was anxious to learn the truth. Although major oil companies usually did not act on blind faith and occultism, many
small operators did. The Daisy Bradford discovery had convinced many that a hole punctured anywhere in East Texas
would spout oil.

Crim got his wish, and on December 27, 1930, a well was
brought in on his farm. Although it was not as large as the

Daisy Bradford, the Lou Della Crim No. 1, named for his wife, flowed at a sizable 22,000 barrels a day, and Kilgore became the newest boomtown.

Geologists began to speculate that the enormous distance between producing wells implied that all the wells were tapping into one colossal field. The one-field geologists believed that beneath the East Texas earth was a vast "stratigraphic trap." The Woodbine sand, they argued, was either the shoreline or the eroded remains of an ancient sea that had once occupied the East Texas basin. The oil had been forced into it and trapped there.

The vast majority of small, independent oilmen thought it preposterous that the wells, nearly thirty miles apart, could be tapping the same pool. Meanwhile, the major oil companies had paid only minimal attention to Joiner's discovery and continued to drill in other parts of Texas and in Oklahoma. Leases between the three big discovery wells could still be bought for $10 to $15 per acre, a clear indication of how skeptically both the majors and independents viewed the one-field theory. Those who did believe the theory wondered whether the market could absorb such a huge amount of oil if it indeed existed.

Clint Murchison had carefully followed the news about the big play in East Texas, and he was convinced that the field was truly gigantic. But as others rushed into the area and sank wells, Clint was more farsighted. Knowing that the railroads could not possibly handle the hundreds of thousands of barrels that would come out of the fields each day, once the majors got into the play, Clint quickly began planning the construction of a pipeline. It would extend from the southern end of the field to the closest major railroad town, Tyler, more than thirty miles to the north. Clint planned to build a refinery in Tyler to process the oil. Any excess oil would be shipped by tank car from Tyler to the Gulf of Mexico. Early in 1931 Clint drew a circle on the map, then told his land men to lease everything they could within the circle.

"Offer whatever it takes," Clint instructed, "but make an agreement to pay as little cash as you can up front, offering in exchange to pay rentals on the lease with proceeds from the oil that's produced and sold."

Murchison's Southern Union was already heavily in debt to the Oil Well Supply Company, but he got more credit by promising that once the pipe was completed and he contracted with the major oil companies for use of the pipeline, he could pay off the debt quickly. Just as Murchison estimated, within three months the pipeline was completed, the refinery operating, and by May 1931 the combined venture showed a $100,000 profit, and he paid back Oil Well Supply Company.

Clint by now had made $20 to $30 million, some from drilling but chiefly from oil leases and pipelines. His next step was much riskier and potentially much more profitable—drilling oil wells on a massive scale.

What brought him to this decision was his mathematical genius, sharpened so many years earlier by the grade school teacher who had forced him to do his arithmetic lessons in his head.

Clint had been thinking about, and calculating again and again, the profit possibilities that derived from the combination of two extraordinary tax advantages available to oil producers.

Oil, like timber and coal, is a depletable asset. Dividends from shares of stock in a shoe factory or a store usually come from the profits, leaving the assets of the business intact, just as interest is paid on a bond but does not diminish its face value. Such dividends and interest are taxable under the federal and state income tax laws.

But income received from the sale of a barrel (thirty-one-and-a-half gallons) of oil, in contrast, is payment for selling a fraction of the asset itself, and eventually the entire asset is depleted by these sales. Because of this fact, 27½ percent of the income derived from the sale of oil was for many years exempted from income tax—an outrageously high percentage that many thought was more related to political contributions of oilmen than to fairness.

The other extraordinary tax advantage enjoyed by oil producers was the so-called oil payment, a method of borrowing enormous sums for exploration and drilling, while simultaneously avoiding any income tax at all on oil income.

Both loopholes were eventually closed, but not before Murchison and others had made tens of millions from this legal form of tax evasion. Anxious to drill his own wells in the East Texas field, Murchison tried unsuccessfully to convince his partners—his brother Frank and brother-in-law Ernest Closuit—that even more money could be made in exploration and production than in merely trading leases and building pipelines. For the first time in a long and happy partnership, Clint's ideas seemed too much of a gamble, too great a risk, and Frank and Ernest declined. Undeterred, Clint found a new partner, Dudley Golding, with whom he built an enormously profitable drilling and production company.

By the spring of 1931 the East Texas field was flowing at a half million barrels a day. One of the most bitter wars in the American oil industry was about to begin. In 1929 the average American family owned an automobile. The 26,532,000 registered automobiles in the United States in 1929 were almost three times as many as only a decade earlier. The greatest factor in the tremendous increase in automobiles on the road was the introduction of the assembly line in 1914 in Detroit's car factories. The efficiency of the assembly line allowed auto makers to cut production and retail costs dramatically. Henry Ford dropped the base price of his Model-T from $950 to $290, and thereby made the automobile available to the masses.

Although the nation's automobiles consumed seventeen billion gallons of gasoline a year, the supply that hit the market with the discovery of the East Texas field suddenly far exceeded the nation's needs. In addition, two large fields (although only a tenth the size of the East Texas field) opened that spring in Seminole, Oklahoma, and in Oklahoma City, and an enormous influx of cheap Venezuelan oil had also begun. The result was that as more wells were drilled in East Texas, oil prices began to slide—from $1.10 per barrel in October 1930, to 25 cents a barrel in early 1931, and finally to 10 cents a barrel in April 1931. Some large shipments sold for as little as 5 cents a barrel. Water, which was never in great supply in Texas, was suddenly a far more valuable commodity, selling for 10 to 25 cents a barrel.

It would be three more years before the East Texas field was pronounced the largest field in the world. Oilmen knew that it was big, but they could never have conceived that it stretched for forty miles from north to south and seven miles east to west. It was twice the size of Manhattan Island, nearly as large as the District of Columbia. The field had an estimated lifetime capacity of at least 100 million barrels and possibly as much as 500 million barrels. Eventually almost 29,000 wells were drilled in the field and only 555 of them were dry. No one had any idea that over the next few decades it would produce in excess of four billion barrels of oil or that for twenty years it would remain the largest known oil field on the planet.

Since the discovery at Spindletop, oilmen had been searching for bigger and bigger pools. They joked and dreamed about "finding a pool that's so rich I can say yes to the little wife without even listening to her demand." Someday, they hoped, they would find a field that would put them on Easy Street forever. Suddenly these dirt-poor farmers saw these dreams coming true. But just as quickly they realized that they had brought in a pool of oil that was *too* big, *too* rich. Instead of increasing their fortunes, the glut of oil pushed many oilmen into a crisis. They owed money on the wells, but could not afford to make the payments when the price of oil plummeted.

In addition, because oilmen such as Murchison ran their wells full blast to make up for the lower prices, there was growing fear that the field's underground pressure was being destroyed. Geologists warned that without enough pressure to bring it to the surface, much of the oil underneath would never be recovered. Oilmen generally responded to such warnings by blaming the problem on someone or something else, or simply ignoring it.

The ferocious competition was spurred largely by a Pennsylvania Supreme Court decision in 1889, establishing the rule of capture. Under common law the owner of the land is owner of the minerals under it. This law raised no problems for minerals that were solids. But since oil moves underground and goes to the nearest borehole or puncture mark in the earth, oil that is located under one person's lease may be pulled into another person's well. Oil migrates from areas of high pressure to areas of low pressure. When a well is drilled in an oil-bearing formation, a low pressure is created at the bottom of the well. Gas pressure brings oil from the surrounding area, often extending under a neighbor's land. In its decision, the Pennsylvania Supreme Court followed the basic rule governing the capture of wild game. Regardless of where the deer comes from, it belongs to the hunter who captures it on his own land. In the case of oil, the court ruled that it belonged to the well that brought it to the surface. The rule of capture stimulated drilling in East Texas, but it also contained the seeds of a disaster.

As early as 1929 the Texas Railroad Commission was given the authority to limit, or prorate, production in the field. The concept of proration would have been highly controversial even had enforcement not seemed so unlikely. As late as the spring of 1931, the idea that proration could be enforced in such a vast field was thought laughable. Although there were quotas on how much oil could be taken from the wells, it was rare to find an oilman who adhered to the law. On August 15, 1931, the East Texas field was producing one million barrels of oil a day. Nevertheless, there was growing alarm that production was about to be severely restricted as Texas Governor Ross Sterling studied the problem.

On August 17 Sterling did what many men would have found unthinkable. He closed down the field for an unspecified number of days and sent in National Guard troops to maintain order. The troops patrolled the wells on horseback night and day. Still, martial law was accepted with more humor than animosity, and many, in jest, called the guardsmen "Boy Scouts."

Although most small, independent operators were against proration and declared it an infringement on their right to free enterprise, the major oil companies supported it. The large companies were already so rich that they could afford to stabilize their production and accept a slower payout while the oil reservoir was studied. Above all, the majors understood that proration was essentially a method of fixing prices. In addition, if proration prevailed, the major companies would acquire more than the 20 percent of the field they now owned because they had the cash reserves to survive proration, and the smaller companies would be forced to sell out.

With the field closed for an indefinite period, Clint could not make payments on numerous outstanding loans. One of his largest was with Dallas's Republic National Bank. But before Clint could get on the phone to Republic's president, Fred Florence, the banker called to tell him to forget about his bank payments until the field reopened.

Just as Dallas's First National Bank, under Nathan Adams, had honored Clint's $100,000 hot check on the Albuquerque pipeline years earlier, Florence had also supported Clint when it was critical.

After the shrewdly generous offer from Florence, Murchison was able to use what little cash he had to finance the drilling of more wells. Oddly, the shutdown enforced by martial law did not obtain to sinking new wells, and a flurry of new drilling ensued.

Before the field was closed, 1,777 wells were producing slightly more than one million barrels of oil daily, an average of 588 barrels per well. At that time, the prices on a barrel had plunged to 10 cents and some barrels were selling for as little as 2 cents. When the field reopened nineteen days later, allowable production was cut by more than half, to 225 barrels per well per day, with a total of 400,000 daily for the field. Immediately prices shot back up—to 68 cents a barrel.

Although the price increase helped both the independents and the majors, the small oilman claimed that the 225 barrels per day he was allowed to produce was just barely enough to break even. Six days later the well allowable was cut to 185 barrels daily, and three weeks later it was again cut to 165. The Railroad Commission insisted the cuts were necessary because new wells in the field had driven total production to more than 400,000 barrels daily.

But hundreds of oilmen refused to obey the law. Some had left secure, salaried jobs and professions to try their luck in the rough-and-tumble oil field, and they had certainly not entered the game to break even. Hundreds of oilmen, therefore, exceeded the daily allowable, and illegally bootlegged the excess oil. This illegal oil became known as "hot oil."

* * *

No one ran more hot oil than Clint Murchison, and no independent operator fought proration more fiercely than he. In defiance of governmental restrictions, Clint changed the name of his company from Golding-Murchison to the American Liberty Oil Company.

During the early stages of the oil war, a field inspector, unaware of Murchison's notorious reputation, asked him if he knew of any pipelines in the area carrying hot oil. Clint answered smugly and proudly, "I believe you could look the world over without hitting a better place to find one."

Although one-third of Sterling's troops were sent home after the field reopened, the other two-thirds stayed as "peace officers" whose duty it was to pursue hot oil runners. As tumultuous as the East Texas field was in 1931, it was even worse in 1932 when the Railroad Commission issued nineteen separate orders for prorating the field and every one of them was challenged in court and invalidated.

Troubles were also brewing for Governor Sterling. In the spring of 1932 the United States Supreme Court permanently enjoined him from enforcing proration by martial law. A few months later, Sterling lost his reelection bid to Miriam A. "Ma" Ferguson. Four years earlier, she had sought office as a vindication of her husband, James A. Ferguson, an ex-governor of Texas who had been impeached as governor because of rampant corruption in his administration. Sterling won the election primarily because he had run against "Fergusonism." Now, in 1932, Ma Ferguson ran against "Sterling the Prorationist," and she won.

The proration battle, however, was far from over. Before Sterling left office, he appointed a new chairman to the Railroad Commission, Ernest O. Thompson, a former mayor of Amarillo in the Texas panhandle. Tough and ambitious, Thompson moved his headquarters into the field even before all of Sterling's troops had left.

Thompson was a staunch conservationist. Fearful that the oil pool's pressure was nearly ruined, he immediately closed the field so that a group of geologists could study the reservoir.

Although 95 percent of the oilmen opposed the principle of

proration when it was first mentioned, that percentage fell dramatically when they came to accept the unhappy fact that overproduction was ruining the field. When the field reopened on New Year's Day 1932, Thompson imposed even stricter daily production quotas. Despite his knowledge that the courts had frowned on a per-well allowable, he issued an order that each well in the field would be allowed to produce only 28 barrels daily. Inevitably, the per well allowable was invalidated in the courts, and Thompson shut down the field again. His engineers then determined that the entire field could safely produce 750,000 barrels daily. The majors complained that 330,000 barrels were the maximum the field could produce without damaging the reservoir, and that it was all the market would demand. Prices skidded from 75 cents to 10 cents.

Thompson did the only thing he could—he cut the allowable, again and again. With each cut, the price of oil rose, but with each price increase the hot oil runners increased their operations. It was a vicious circle. Reduced allowables caused higher oil prices, higher prices caused more hot oil production.

The Railroad Commission's forty inspectors assigned to supervise 600 square miles of wells could not stop the huge flow from the fields. Not only were many oilmen dishonest, but also guardsmen and even a Railroad Commission supervisor could be bribed. It was easy to understand how men who made $150 a month closed their eyes to some operations for sums far greater than their paychecks.

Oilmen smuggled oil across state borders in trucks purporting to be carrying something else. They operated unregistered refineries in the backwoods, miles from their wells, which enabled them to process the excess crude without getting caught. Chaos and defiance ruled in East Texas, and those who led the way made little secret of their refusal to be controlled.

It was said that the American Liberty pipeline was so hot you could fry an egg on it. Variations of this story, coupled with Murchison's own outspokenness against proration, made him one of the Railroad Commission's most hunted targets. But he was a hard man to catch. The Commission brought numerous injunctions against American Liberty, which Clint repeatedly dodged. When an injunction was filed against a well, Clint would switch that property into another newly created company that also contained the name Liberty. The six months it took the Commission to sort out the injunctions, one from another, allowed Clint to keep several steps ahead of the law. Few independents who adhered to the laws of proration built the size fortune that Clint did while playing by his own rules.

But the antiprorationists were shrinking in number. Not only was stealing oil a dangerous and tiring game, but the independents, like the majors, began to understand the financial advantages of conservation. Conservation effectively raised prices. It forced producers to bring the oil out of the ground at a slow enough rate that they could charge these higher prices for a longer period of time. In addition, it avoided severe damage to the pool's oil pressure.

For all the chaos created by hot oil producers, by the time Ernest Thompson came to power, the majority of oilmen abided by the rules. They took from their fields what became known as "legal" oil, an amount just at or sometimes under the daily allowable.

Jake Louis Hamon Jr., who would become one of Texas's biggest independent oilmen, played strictly according to the rules, taking only legal oil from the field. He spent tens of thousands of his own dollars trying to convict hot oil thieves whom he disdained for cheating the oilmen who played fairly. Hamon believed correctly that if the hot oilers were restrained and proration orders obeyed, the decreased output would drive prices up again, and everyone would get rich. But he opposed a growing effort by Texas oilmen to involve the federal government in bringing the field under control.

Others, unlike Hamon, were so bitter and frustrated with the Railroad Commission's ineffectiveness that they turned their attention to Washington. Despite their contempt for East Coast banks and regulation by the federal government, the oilmen of East Texas were finally so desperate they began to speak of the need for a "federal oil czar."

Washington had bigger problems. By March 1933, when President Franklin Delano Roosevelt moved into the White

House, the Depression had reached its lowest depths. At least thirteen million people were unemployed. Millions of farmers were on the brink of foreclosure, and millions had already lost their farms. Deflation was so drastic that at the end of 1932, a pound loaf of bread cost 5 cents, a head of lettuce 1 cent. Lamb chops cost a meager 12 cents per pound. At the same time, oil plunged to its lowest point, 4 cents a barrel.

"There is nothing to do but meet every day's troubles as they come," Roosevelt told the American people shortly after taking office. What interested Texans far more, however, was the man FDR chose as his Secretary of the Interior, Harold L. Ickes. A tough former Bull Mooser from Chicago, Ickes seemed likely to do whatever was necessary to stop illegal oil production in East Texas. Representatives of major and independent oil companies went to Washington to try to push through Congress what became known as the Ickes Bill, which would give the Secretary of the Interior absolute power to regulate the East Texas field.

Clint flew into Washington on his private DC-3 a few days before the vote on the Ickes Bill. But his offer to help defeat the bill was not warmly received by his allies working against it. One of them pulled him aside in a hall at the capital and whispered, "Your reputation in hot oil will ruin us. The best thing you can do for us is get back on your plane and get out of town as fast as you can."

Clint followed his friend's orders. But once back in Texas, he carefully monitored the proration struggles taking place in Washington. Even as the ranks were shrinking around him, Clint continued to urge liberty in its most unfettered form. He felt more passionately about the issue of proration than about any other political cause in his lifetime. When he listened to others describe attempts by various regulators to "close the oil frontier," he seethed with anger.

The seeds of that emotion were sown long ago. Under Mexican rule, Texans longed to be free, resented being a colony of an older civilization and the weight of its laws. Later, the powerful railroads and Eastern banks had ruled Texas towns. There were some measures to protect Texans from such malevolent powers—the Homestead Act and the provision in the

Texas Constitution against branch banking—but the greedy hand of the East Coast kept reaching out and taking Texas in its grasp, threatening to squeeze it to death.

Murchison decided that if others fighting the war against proration in Washington refused to associate with him, he would send his lawyer Toddie Lee Wynne to do battle in his place. Also from East Texas, Wynne was born in 1896, a year after Clint, in the blackland prairie town of Wills Point, a few counties north of Henderson. Toddie Lee's father, William Benjamin Wynne, had seen to it that each of his four sons graduated from the University of Texas Law School, and he instructed them, "Inch by inch and step by step, climb the ladder until you reach the top, where you can sit quietly by and look down on those who are struggling far beneath you."

When oil fever hit East Texas, each of the Wynne brothers headed for a different boomtown. Benjamin's parting advice was perhaps his most valuable. He told them to negotiate oil leases on behalf of the land owners, and in cases where the farmer could not pay the legal fee, they should take a percentage of the deal. The aggressive Wynne brothers took his advice and negotiated oil deals that yielded them spectacular returns.

Toddie Lee became the most successful of the boys. His experience in negotiating oil leases made him as shrewd an oilman as he was a lawyer. Not only was he blessed with brains and business acumen, but Toddie Lee was also extraordinarily handsome. He had deep-set blue eyes, porcelain-like skin, and perfect, movie-star features. Vain as well as good-looking, he viewed his merely average height as a flaw. For a while Toddie Lee wore his pants a few inches too short because he thought it made him look taller.

The hot oil war refused to die, and Wynne was increasingly convinced that Clint and the antiprorationists were fighting a losing battle. Nevertheless, Wynne continued to work for Clint, who seemed desperate to fight the war to its end.

Various efforts by Secretary Ickes to solve the problem proved unsuccessful, but finally in February 1935 the turbulent hot oil war was brought to an end. Victory came for the prorationists when Congress passed the law popularly known as the Connally Hot Oil Act. The new law, like earlier ones, made it illegal to ship through interstate commerce oil that was not produced in accordance with state regulations, such as the current daily allowable. But the Connally Hot Oil Act went an important step further. It stated that the government could confiscate any hot oil it found.

Murchison wanted to test the constitutionality of the measure, but Wynne begged him to let the issue die. Support in favor of the act was overwhelming, and when it was eventually tested in the United States Supreme Court, it was upheld.

From 1930 through 1934, when the hot oil war was at its hottest, more than 100 million barrels of oil were illegally taken from the field. Profits on this illegal oil were estimated at more than $25 million. But under the Connally Hot Oil Act, running hot oil had finally become too dangerous.

Many years later Clint still harbored bitterness about losing the battle against proration. In a letter to the *Dallas Morning News* in 1949, he accused the newspaper of being gullible in standing up for proration. He described the paper as merely a tool used by the big oil companies to eliminate competition.

Clint had become economically strong enough to survive any attempts by the majors to squeeze him out, and he finally saw that he would become far richer with proration than without it. But years later, defending his early antiproration stand, he insisted that his fight was not the result of selfishness, but rather that he was fighting for a principle.

Clint also came to resent the many hot oil charges against him, and said, "If I had been guilty of all the things they say I have done, I'd be under the jail, not in it."

Increasingly, Clint turned his attention away from oil and toward new projects. In 1934 he purchased an island off the coast of Texas in the Gulf of Mexico. Called Matagorda, it was a forty-mile-long, three-mile-wide buffer reef separating San Antonio Bay and the adjacent 40,000-acre Aransas National Wildlife Refuge from the Gulf of Mexico. Clint purchased the twenty miles that comprised the southern half of the island; the other half belonged to the federal government.

The island was a natural bird sanctuary, abundant in ducks, geese, turkey, and quail, as well as native nongame birds—ibis, egret, and blue heron. Title to the property belonged to the American Liberty Oil Company, whose stock was owned 45 percent each by Clint and Dudley Golding and 10 percent by Toddie Lee Wynne. The company drilled some wells, on a rumor that there was oil on the island, and even leased some acreage to the young Getty Oil Company. But no oil was found, and Clint made the island into a hunting and fishing haven for himself and his cronies.

In the early thirties the section of Matagorda that was owned by the government was barren and quiet. The government had not found a way to use the land, parts of which were regularly swept by hurricanes. The place was hilly, with some portions several hundred feet higher than others. On the Gulf side, hills made of sand dunes rolled gently down to a beach that reached for a hundred feet to the sea. On the bay side the beach was equally wide. Because there was no causeway to the island, Clint's friends and their wives arrived by boat from Rockport, the nearest mainland town. At first, visitors slept in boats docked on the calm bay side of the island. But it was not long before construction began on a clubhouse, servants' quarters, a water tower, power generator, and roads.

When Clint invited his friends to Matagorda, he described the island's spectacular hunting and fishing. The Gulf was full of redfish, speckled trout, and flounder, and the sky was thick with coveys of quail and white-wing dove. In addition, the island's tall grasses teemed with jackrabbits, deer, antelope, and raccoons. Despite the abundance of game, Clint's oil cronies and their wives preferred a far less refined sport—hunting rattlesnakes. A typical hunt began when the men and women, carrying rifles and wearing thick, high boots, piled into stripped-down convertible V-8 Fords and set out for the nearest prickly pear bush.

The bushes, a clump of cacti that could be as large as thirty feet in diameter, were crawling with snakes, raccoons, and quail. Mexicans rode on horseback ahead of the hunting vehicles and used long prongs to stir the rattlesnakes in the bushes. Out flocked a covey of quail, but the hunters ignored the birds, shooting instead at the snakes. The Mexicans bagged the snakes and brought them back to the clubhouse. Sometimes

the snakes were dissected in front of the guests to see whether
they were eating the quail. The tails were cut off and the rattlers presented to the ladies as souvenirs. Rattlesnake meat
was frequently served for dinner, but usually under the guise
of something else. The servants were admonished not to iden-
tify the meat—until the guests had cleaned their plates. On
many occasions the more gently reared visitors became sick
when they learned what they had eaten.

Clint was delighted that his friends preferred hunting
snakes to quail, ducks, or geese, hoping that all their vigor and
enthusiasm would deplete the snake population. Because of
the snakes, Clint would not allow his sons on the island. But
during hunting and fishing season in South Texas, Clint finagled—usually in a poker bet—one of his oil buddies into taking John Dabney, Clint W., and Burk fishing in nearby
Rockport. Their father boated over to the mainland to fish
with them, but he steadfastly refused to allow them on the island.

The oilmen had more success depleting the harmless jack-
rabbit population than they had getting rid of the snakes. One
long weekend they imported a pack of greyhounds, and as
they sat on the clubhouse porch drinking whiskey, they placed
bets on which dogs would kill the most rabbits.

Clint surrounded the main house and an acre around it with
a circular white wood fence lined with a wire net to keep out
the rattlers. But the fence was not always adequate protection.
Frequent heavy storms washed a new supply of snakes right
over the fence. Because snakes characteristically shed their
skins in a storm, a skin found inside the fence prompted a full-
scale search for a rattler in and around the house.

The fence also shielded the house from Hereford bulls and
cows that roamed Murchison's half of the island. Clint imported the cattle from South Texas, joking that he bought the
cattle, "so I'll feel more at home here."

The finished clubhouse was a low-hung, wood-frame bun-
galow that slept thirty-five oilmen, their wives and dogs. A
wide veranda filled with white wicker furniture swept the
length of the house, facing the Gulf. But aside from the nauti-
cal decoration of the house and the surrounding sea, Mata-

gorda did not look much like an island. It seemed like just an extension of Texas—hot, barren, dry in places, and overrun with several hundred head of cattle. It was the kind of place where a Texan could feel comfortable, and it did not take much for Clint to convince Sid Richardson to buy the barrier island to the south.

Sid was living at the comfortable old Fort Worth Club, his home for most of his life. In his two-room suite he always kept five or six suitcases packed with clothes for different climates, "so's I'll always be ready to go." Sid had visited Matagorda but had never set foot on San José Island (called St. Joe by the Texans), which nearly abutted it to the south. Still, Sid got on the phone and within a few hours made a deal to buy the island. Then he grabbed his suitcase marked "light clothes" and hopped a plane to the Gulf.

When the tide was out, guests could drive across the sand back and forth between the two islands. By the time Sid bought St. Joe, rattlesnake hunting had lost its cachet. Fish and birds were so plentiful that hunting parties of as many as fifty oilmen and bankers and their wives gathered at the two islands during weekends in the spring and fall. Between reeling in trout and shooting quail, millions of dollars changed hands on oil deals and at all-night card games. It was said that Murchison and Richardson managed to consummate more oil deals with their guests during a weekend on the Gulf Coast islands than most oilmen did in a year.

Clint and Sid's belief that the best oil deals were made in a relaxed atmosphere inspired a number of aphorisms about fishing. "The best way to judge a man's character is to fish with him or drink with him," explained Clint. "That's when he's acting the most like himself."

They applied their love of fishing to their business philosophies. When Clint said, "You ain't learnin' nothing' when you're talking'," Richardson would follow with, "Every fish ever got caught on a hook had his mouth open."

Clint and Sid also used the islands to entertain important politicians, and one of the first to visit was President Franklin D. Roosevelt. FDR had been planning a fishing trip to the Gulf when Sid learned about it and invited him to lunch at

Matagorda. When the presidential yacht arrived, FDR's aides
lifted him in his wheelchair onto the dock and then into one of
Clint's stripped-down Fords. The men toured the island in the
car, then stopped at the house for lunch. They talked briefly
about proration and other oil issues, but mostly they discussed
hunting and fishing as they relaxed on the clubhouse porch
under large fans that stirred the hot, salty air. Before the President departed, Sid gave him a gold money clip with an oil derrick and FDR's initials outlined in diamonds.

The fact that Murchison was one of the most notorious hot
oil operators of East Texas had not hurt his reputation among
the oil fraternity, in part because he was far from the only sin-
ner. Many of the state's richest oilmen had made their enormous fortunes in the 1930s in precisely the same illegal way.
Although Murchison made enemies in his struggles against
proration, he maintained a reputation as a man of high principles and strong integrity. His word was solid and his honesty
in deals unwavering. In the chaotic, rough-and-tumble oil
field, nothing counted more.

When oil was selling at 10 cents a barrel, Murchison had
contracted to sell 450,000 barrels to the Sunray Oil Company
(today Sun Oil). But that was before Governor Sterling first
placed proration quotas on the field, which decreased the output of legal oil and pushed prices up. The oil Murchison had
contracted to sell to Sunray for 10 cents was suddenly worth
68 cents a barrel. After the price jump, Sunray president J.
Edgar Pew called Murchison and Dudley Golding to his office, located two floors below American Liberty's office in Dallas's First National Bank.

"I bought oil from you at ten cents but I could not buy another drop of oil anywhere for less than sixty-eight cents, so
starting today I will pay you that price," Pew told them.

Clint interrupted. "Mr. Pew, we made a trade with you
when it was ten cents and we are going to deliver every barrel
for ten cents."

The meeting ended, but the story was widely circulated.
Years later Clint explained part of his trading success. "I

never made a deal where I couldn't go back to the same person and make another."

The deal with Sunray Oil was one of many that American Liberty negotiated when oil was selling at 10 cents a barrel. But Clint continued to meet his original contracts.

Producers Supply and Tool Company of Fort Worth now supplied most of American Liberty's equipment, and also became one of the company's chief financiers. American Liberty was so badly in debt in the early 1930s that the company's stock certificates were kept in a safe at Producers Supply as collateral. The head of the company, Sol Brachman, occasionally advanced $50,000 to $100,000 cash at a time to American Liberty so that the company could meet its payroll. The accompanying note would bear interest at 6 percent. Brachman claimed that he made far more money on the interest American Liberty owed him than on the equipment and supplies he sold the company.

As the Depression wore on and dollars became more difficult to find, Clint developed his own variation of the reversionary interest and applied it to the oil field. He sold properties at a cheap price in return for an agreement that when the property had earned enough money to pay back the buyer his investment plus interest, a half interest in further production would revert to Murchison. The deals appealed to the buyers who were mostly major oil companies needing oil for their refineries. They believed that because of proration's limits on the field, the reversionary interest would not be realized for many years in the future.

Clint had a different theory. He believed that the country was headed for another world war and that the demand for oil would increase markedly. America would need much more oil than the present limitations allowed. By the late 1930s his theory proved correct. In several cases he received his reversionary interests within six years, sold his interest for cash, and again took a reversionary interest.

Murchison did his best to use everything but hard cash to increase production. He acquired properties in exchange for oil payments, and wells were drilled the same way. Since a producing property brought in taxable income, it was far more profitable to sell the properties and pay the lesser 20 percent tax on the capital gain. The gain could be used to hunt more oil. With no stockholders clamoring for dividends, the pyramiding progressed constantly.

Murchison had such a brilliant sense of future trends that some thought he was clairvoyant. According to *Fortune* magazine:

> He sold a producing field to Atlantic Refining Co. for $1,600,000, but the price would have been much higher had he not held out of the sale 4,400,000 barrels of oil in the ground. He turned down the extra ready cash on the gamble that the price of oil would go up. When it finally did so, American Liberty sold its held-out oil at a $5 million profit.

Even the most sophisticated members of the financial community were astounded at Murchison's genius for turning Uncle Sam's tax laws to his personal profit. Marveled *Fortune*:

> Murchison, in 1938, obliged a Houstonian who wanted to sell to avoid income taxes on a field that was earning $100,000 a year. He gave the seller the tax advantages of an installment sale by having American Liberty buy the property with fifty notes of $60,000 each. These were to be paid from the proceeds of oil as produced. Murchison had purchased a property without cash. The man from Houston was able to raise $500,000 ready cash by discounting at the bank American Liberty notes of the most distant maturity. "We bought the property with pieces of paper," explained Murchison.

Just as today in Texas there is no stigma attached to being bankrupt, in the oil boom of the thirties there was no shame attached to going broke. The East Texas field, in fact, created the popular Texas attitude that an oilman who was not in debt was not very aggressive and, thus, would not become very rich. With such a flood of wealth in the massive East Texas pool, any man who waited until he had enough money to finance his own drilling would have lost out on the great fortunes being made.

Clint was involved in numerous partnerships, owned thousands of acres in East Texas with drilling and production, and controlled, either alone or jointly, several oil and gas pipeline companies. Because his empire was extraordinarily compartmentalized and increasingly complex, his staff, when asked to review his holdings, found the task almost impossible. Nevertheless, he had a sharp memory and kept in his head the complex deals he was involved in, and the money he owed to dozens of different banks, individuals, and companies.

As was common in the East Texas field, most of his deals and partnerships were made on faith—a handshake, or by telephone—with no proof in writing of the transactions, and, in most cases, with no attorney or other witness present. But even *his* memory was not perfect, and he was often surprised to receive checks of $100,000 or $500,000 in reversionary interests on wells he had completely forgotten about and on which there were no written records.

"Oil is a fairly small fraternity," explained Clint. "If you cheat someone in this business, it catches up with you, and then no one will deal with you."

Clint was a shrewder trader than most of the men he dealt with, but if there was ever a question as to the original intent or terms of a deal, Clint invariably gave way. To Clint, integrity and reputation mattered far more than one deal.

With many millions of dollars of oil reserves in the ground and huge debts at the bank, his wealth in 1934 was difficult to estimate, although it was probably more than $50 million. At the same time, hundreds of thousands of men, women, and children waited in bread lines across a country that faced the worst depression in its history. Depression prices—$57 for a used 1929 Model-A Ford, $5,000 for a Spanish stucco home in posh Beverly Hills—put in perspective just how great Clint's winnings were in the East Texas field.

Many oilmen who made millions in 1930 and 1931 slowed down as the Depression wore on, but adverse economic times had the opposite effect on Clint. He bought leases near the South Texas town of Conroe, then built a pipeline from Con-

roe forty miles south to Houston. At the same time, he built
one of the first oil recycling plants, which brought gas out of
the ground, stripped the liquid fuel, and pumped the gas back
into the formation so that it could bring another flood of oil to
the surface.

Clint learned that the vast oil storage facilities of General
American Tank Company near New Orleans were vacant
while producers in the East Texas field badly needed storage
for their unsold oil. He acquired the storage units, then won
dozens of contracts to sell East Texas crude to the giant Texas
Company.

Murchison seemed to have a magic touch. "Fields that everyone else thought couldn't possibly have a drop of oil suddenly gushed in when Clint got involved," explained one of his
geologists. "He discovered oil where everyone else had overlooked a bet."

"Clint was lucky, but he made his luck," explained a longtime bank loan officer, who funded many of Clint's wells.
"You don't get ducks unless you put out a lot of lead, and
that's what Clint was doing. He was searching for oil all over
this continent."

That the oil business had a real possibility of becoming big
industry—rather than a two-bit local business as it had been in
Pennsylvania—became evident about 1932 when major Eastern banks began to set up oil loan departments. The Texas oil
industry was about to become like the rich man's table, and the
banks lusted for its crumbs.

Sid Richardson, who never went to the East Texas field
(complaining that it was too crowded), was hitting wildcat
wells all over West Texas. Sid told Clint, "There's a man,
name of Rushton Ardrey from the Bank of Manhattan, who's
been nosing around Fort Worth, lookin' to make loans." Born
in Dallas and educated in the East, Ardrey quickly made his
name known in Fort Worth oil circles.

Brilliant and eager, it did not take long for Ardrey to see the
problems of lending money for oil wells on the customary
sixty-day notes at 1 or 2 percent interest and to devise solutions for those problems. Texans could not repay such loans
because it took longer than sixty days to get oil production.

Ardrey decided instead to offer five-year loans at 5 percent or 6 percent interest, a practice unheard of in the mid 1930s. Richardson was one of the first to get such a loan—for $1 million.

Shortly after he returned to New York to close the Richardson loan, Ardrey received a call from Murchison, asking for a meeting in New York. Clint arrived a few days later. The meeting had just begun when Clint got to the point. "I need all the money I can get."

From the start Ardrey liked dealing with Texas oilmen who were straightforward and no-nonsense. Richardson and Murchison seemed to him the opposite of the Eastern capitalist, who was often roundabout, nitpicking, and pretentious. Where Easterners required many meetings and endless contracts, Clint and Sid wanted a short meeting and a handshake. The good-old-boyism that grew out of the oil patch assured a measure of informality, of casualness, particular to Texas oilmen and a welcome relief from the staid, formal manners of Wall Streeters.

Ardrey quickly saw that borrowed money was the spur that drove the Murchison empire. Murchison found the money to buy leases, drill wells, build pipelines, and produce the oil. A wizardly oil financier, he never managed his companies or paid much attention to their profits. He was an acquisitions man, a wheeler-dealer in the truest sense.

Only after hearing from Sid of the availability of money from the Bank of Manhattan did Clint devise a plan to build a major pipeline that would require enormous funds. He explained to Ardrey that his pipeline would provide transport for the large number of independent producers in the East Texas field who did not own their own pipelines as the majors did. Until now the independents had to contract for use of other pipelines. Usually the independents had to wait in line to transport their oil, and the delays were costing them money. American Liberty Pipe Line, Clint explained, would stretch for two hundred miles, from Kilgore, in the center of the East Texas field, to the Houston Ship Channel.

Murchison sold Ardrey on the pipeline plan and received a loan that was slightly greater than the $1 million Richardson

received. Clint already had contracts to transport the oil, and
he assigned those contracts as collateral.

As American Liberty and its growing number of subsidiaries and related companies grew richer, Clint's holdings in the
Southern Union Gas Company interested him less. The Depression had hurt Southern Union's ability to raise capital,
and the company was forced to go public, selling both common and preferred stock. Clint's heart was not in anything
that had little element of risk and commensurate gain, and a
public utility was a very unrisky business.

Not only were Southern Union's "widow" stocks too tame
for him, but the company also faced major problems in meeting the requirements of the Public Utility Holding Company
Act of 1935. The act said that a company could not own and
operate natural gas systems that were not physically intercon-
nected or capable of being connected. By 1932 Southern
Union had become a complex, multitiered holding company
with seventeen subsidiaries. The consolidated company
served nearly 20,000 customers and had pipelines—most of
them unconnected—in more than forty towns and five states.

Southern Union had grown too corporate, too confining for
Clint, and the government regulation rankled his free-
enterprise spirit. Although he continued to be a major stockholder, by 1935 he had completely disassociated himself from
the firm's management.

By the mid-1930s Clint was like flypaper to hundreds of oil
deals that buzzed in and out of American Liberty's offices in
Dallas's First National Bank building. Financially strapped
farmers sold him their mineral rights at next to nothing, and
representatives from the major oil companies came calling
with irresistible farm-out deals, providing an opportunity for
Clint to explore for oil on another's acreage. He was paid a
percentage of the resulting oil—if any. The majors owned
many more leases than they had the resources or even the
manpower to drill on, and farm-outs provided the necessary
oil and gas reserves to fill their pipelines and fulfill their contracts.

During the depths of the Depression, Clint learned about
2,000 acres of land that had become available in the Trinity

River bottom just south of downtown Dallas. When agriculture prices reached their nadir in 1932, farmers unable to make mortgage payments were forced off the land, and Clint was able to acquire the property by paying no more than its delinquent taxes. He planned to convert the land into a cattle ranch called Bluebird Farms, and he ordered the ranch foreman to employ as many jobless men as he could. Clint instructed, "Anyone who comes here looking for work, give it to them." He also insisted, "Under all circumstances pay transient workers at the end of the day, for that day's work."

Pari-mutuel betting was legalized in Texas in 1933, and a racetrack was built in Arlington, ten miles west of Dallas. Clint and Toddie Lee Wynne together bought a quarter of a million dollars' worth of racehorses, which were trained and raced on a track at Bluebird Farms. But Toddie made it clear he had no faith in horse racing as an investment and that he was not in for the long haul. "I'll stay with you in this venture until we've lost the two hundred fifty thousand," he insisted.

In 1937 pari-mutuel betting and racing were again outlawed and the track west of Dallas closed. But Clint had developed a taste for horse racing and raising thoroughbreds that eventually led to his ownership of the racetrack in Del Mar, California, where he would entertain friends, including President Dwight D. Eisenhower, Vice President Richard Nixon, and Senator Joseph R. McCarthy.

7

"I figure a man is worth about twice what he owes."

One early morning in April 1936, while Clint was away on a business trip, little Burk worked his animal traps in the rain and left for school in wet shoes. A day later he had a high fever. By the time Clint arrived home, eleven-year-old Burk had pneumonia. Clint immediately put him in the hospital and, as he had years earlier, telephoned his late wife Anne's stepfather, Dabney White, in Tyler. As Burk's condition grew worse, complicated by already weak lungs, White brought in top doctors to try to save the boy's life.

Burk had been in the hospital only a few days when fourteen-year-old John Dabney telephoned his friend Carr Pritchett. John and Carr were members of the Highland Park High School band and had been planning to go out of town for a band contest. "If Burk is okay, I'll be going with the band, but if he's not, I'll be staying here."

A few hours later Carr received another call from John. "I guess I won't be going," he said, then hung up.

"That was the last time I ever heard John or any of the Murchisons refer to Burk," recalls Carr.

On the evening of April 15, 1936, during one of the season's worst dust storms, the little boy gasped his last breath and died. Burk's death was devastating to his brothers and especially to Clint Sr. While his other boys were quiet and shy like himself, Burk was just like Anne, vivacious and sociable, always bubbling and smiling. The boy loved the farm animals and befriended even the oddest creatures—snakes and cows and roosters. Clint Sr. had a snapshot of Burk in shorts and a pullover sweater, standing by a barn, holding a baby pig. For the rest of his life Clint kept the picture on the nightstand next to his bed.

Without Burk, the house was hauntingly quiet. The life that had filled it was suddenly gone, like a match that flamed brightly and briefly, then died. Clint Sr.'s friends felt the emptiness. But not a word was said. The hurt was too great.

Thirteen years later, in 1949, when Clint Jr. named his second son Burk, many of the Murchisons' closest friends were surprised to learn that Clint Jr. and John Dabney had once had another brother.

When Burk died, Clint not only lost a son, he suffered through Anne's death a second time. And as he had when Anne died a decade earlier, Clint became inconsolable. He began on the same downward spiral that led him to drink uncontrollably. He also began to roam again in his car. This time, however, his demanding oil business and masses of friends and employees drew him back to work, and he slowly adjusted to the loss.

In 1937, just a year after Burk's death, adversity struck again when the furnace in Clint's home exploded, causing a fire that destroyed several rooms. No one was hurt, but among the possessions lost to the fire was his large collection of books—including numerous well-worn dictionaries. Clint decided the time had come to build a new home.

The architect he selected, Antone Korn, had just finished building the YMCA and courthouse in San Angelo, Texas, and he was the architect of the Hilton Hotel chain, but this was his first residence. By the time construction began, Clint Sr. was traveling coast to coast wheeling and dealing, but he frequently called to check on progress of the house.

"How long are we making that center hallway?" Clint Sr. would ask. "About two hundred feet," came the reply. "Oh, let's go on and make it two hundred and fifty," the boss would instruct. Blueprints were repeatedly revised, and the house grew bigger and bigger.

Clint was impressed with the rambling kitchen at the Waldorf-Astoria Hotel in New York and was determined that his kitchen would be even larger—and it was.

In precisely the same manner that he created his business

empire, Murchison built the home entirely on credit. He was so overextended, so short of cash, that construction workers would stop for days at a time, as the owner waited for bank loans to come through. When word came from the bank, Murchison would telephone the contractor, "Go ahead."

When word got out that Clint was building the home entirely on credit, few of his friends and associates were surprised. A joke had long circulated that "Clint lost out on a ten-million-dollar deal because it required five thousand cash up front." The numbers changed periodically, but the point was always the same.

Clint's friends were astounded, however, at the 256-foot hallway that spanned the first floor. Including the guest rooms at the south end of the house and Clint's suite at the north, the house was slightly longer than a football field. "Jewel's going to need roller skates," Clint's friends laughed.

The original bid on the 34,000-square-foot house was $250,000, but when completed two years later, in 1939, it cost nearly half a million dollars.

The red fieldstone house ran north and south and faced east toward the morning sun. A wide screened porch extended the entire length of the front, looking on White Rock Creek, which ran through the property half a mile away. Despite the creek, only thick hot breezes stirred around the house. But the stultifying heat never bothered Clint. Even during Texas's summer months, he preferred to be outdoors. He enjoyed sitting in an open courtyard in the middle of the house, drinking mint juleps on hot summer evenings.

Allan Richards of Neiman-Marcus, who had decorated Clint's clubhouse on Matagorda, was also the interior decorator on the Dallas house. But Richards was shocked to find that this time each of his decorating decisions was carefully scrutinized by the boss himself. Did Clint Murchison have nothing better to do between oil deals, Richards must have wondered, than argue about chintzes and china? Shortly after accepting the job, he received a letter from Clint that reminded him he was not dealing with a new oil wife who would timidly nod her approval at his selections. Clint informed Richards that he had gotten a bid on draperies from Marshall Field & Company and warned, "Candidly, if you are too much out of line I am going to give them the business."

Richards began filling the house while Murchison was away on an extended business trip, and when Clint returned briefly and looked over the progress, he fired off another letter saying he wanted to take his time furnishing the house instead of just throwing things into the house all at once.

Later Richards was in New York when he received a letter stating the exact dimension for every piece of furniture Clint wanted in his bedroom. Among the furniture Clint wanted to put in the master suite were eight beds, not only for his sons—who were now teenagers—but also where his cronies could sleep with him, or, as he put it, "so we can stay up all night talkin' oil." A bar and kitchenette were conveniently located in an adjoining room.

Clint's favorite rooms in the house were the two he designed. One was the two-story game room with a mezzanine for his fast-growing book collection. Clint commissioned a popular local artist, Reveau Bassett, to paint murals of wildlife indigenous to Texas on the room's four walls. Bassett painted the flora and fauna most common to North Texas on the north wall of the room, South Texas on the south wall and so on around the room. As Bassett stood on his ladder, painting, Clint often sat nearby and watched. "I don't know anything about painting," he told the artist, "but if you need some advice on oil investments I'll be happy to talk with you about it."

Off the game room was the most popular room in the house, the bar. Clint covered the walls of the bar with tarpon scales from the Gulf of Mexico. "He no more had them up when they started popping off the walls," recalls a friend. "When we told him he'd used the wrong kind of glue, he didn't say a word, but by the next time he had a party those scales were plastered down for life."

The boys had their own quarters upstairs, and next to Clint W.'s room was a large photography laboratory and darkroom where he spent hours developing pictures and experimenting with the latest camera equipment that his father ordered from New York.

From late spring through early fall, servants tightly closed all the windows in the big house, and the shades were pulled to keep out the sun. Large fans circulated air, but the rooms were, nevertheless, stultifyingly hot, dark, and eerily quiet. Outside, the brown earth was cracked by the blistering Texas sun, and temperatures hovered around 100 degrees—often even through the night—with no respite for weeks and weeks during the summer.

Cattle died from the heat, and although the creek gushed like a Murchison well during the early spring, it dried up every summer. The terrible ruggedness that caused one early pioneer to remark, "Texas is all right for men and dogs but hell on women and horses," was a commonly repeated phrase as late as the 1930s.

Large brick pillars marked the entrance to the Murchison estate, but many of Clint's visitors did not arrive by car: They landed in their own planes on the old polo field, the treeless stretches of land that surrounded the field for miles in all directions making it an ideal landing strip. When the planes buzzed overhead, one of the staff drove out to the field in a Pierce Arrow and picked up the passengers. A second and third car followed, to bring in the luggage.

Clint had his own pilot and his own four-seater, twin-engine plane in the early 1930s. But when the pilot crashed the plane and was killed on a weekend outing, Clint waited before buying another. For some years he chartered planes and pilots, but he continued to crisscross the state by air, flying over Texas oil fields like a hawk looking for prey.

By the time the big house was finished, nine domestics lived at the farm, not including the dozens of workers who came during the day to tend crops and livestock, machinery and the land. When the boys became teenagers, they ceased to have governesses, and instead were put in the charge of males or, as Clint Sr. referred to them, "governors," and Clint began looking into Eastern prep schools. With the help of New York banker Rushton Ardrey, Clint got John Dabney into Hotchkiss. The same fall Clint Jr. enrolled in the ninth grade at Texas Country Day (later St. Marks School of Texas), which was and has remained Dallas's most exclusive private school for boys. Before the East Texas field came in, Texas Country

Day's students were sons of cotton kings and merchants, bankers and company executives, doctors and lawyers. But by the mid-1930s the school's ranks included dozens of sons of the newly rich oilmen. These boys fit in about as well as skunks at a barbecue.

Before oil, Texas Country Day had not been very different from the more established prep schools in the East, where privileged boys learned math and geography, but also— through association with their schoolmates—the manners and attitudes of the upper class. If Texas Country Day was striving to be as refined as Exeter or Andover, it suffered a great setback with the enrollment of the sons of the new rich oil millionaires.

"I drove a La Salle when I was fourteen, and just about all the oil kids drove Cadillacs," said John Black, one of Clint Jr.'s classmates. "Our fathers had come up in the oil fields. My father had a college education, but a lot of my friends' fathers had no education, not even high school. They'd been very poor, and now that they were rich, they wanted us to have everything."

Oil money gave many Texans a kind of wealth few had even imagined. Often they were penniless farmers who had leased their land or drilled on it themselves, sold out and moved to Dallas as rich men. Wanting no reminders of their former poverty, the oilmen showered their children with possessions— polo ponies, expensive cars and rifles, even yachts. The competition to show, or exaggerate, one's wealth was fierce at Texas Country Day. "My daddy gave my mother a ten-karat diamond," one boy would announce, prompting a new round of competition when the boys returned to school the next day.

Young Clint Murchison was the opposite of the other oil millionaires' sons. With the exception of Bunker Hunt's father, Clint's dad had made more money in oil than any of the other boys' fathers. Yet Clint Jr. never bragged. And if his father had spoiled him with material things, it was not evident at school. After a few months at Texas Country Day, Clint Jr. told a friend that he liked almost everything about the school—his classes and teachers, the school's baseball, football, and track teams. But, he said, "The boys talk too much about how rich their daddies are."

John was similarly modest. Shortly after World War II, one of John's close friends from the service was passing through Dallas. John had several times told the young man to come see "the farm" if he ever got to Dallas, so the serviceman stopped in. After getting reacquainted with his buddy, the serviceman confessed to Clint Sr.: "Mr. Murchison, this sure is a surprise. I thought I was going to see some old broken-down farm where they used kerosene lanterns. I had no idea Tex Murchison had a nickel to his name."

The sons of oilmen at Texas Country Day started drinking about the same time they started driving. The fourteen-year-olds who showed off when they were sober became twice as unruly when they were drunk. A ninth-grader who received a high-powered rifle as a birthday gift from his father pulled up to school in his Cadillac with a bottle of whiskey and the rifle on the front seat. Before classes started, he shot out the tires on the teachers' cars, theirs being the only old cars on the parking lot. One Saturday near the school, a Country Day student, unable to impress his girl with his fancy new car, climbed the nearby tower of a high tension wire and was electrocuted.

Clint Jr. did not participate in the dangerous antics that the other oil sons were crazy to try, but he was a tough competitor in the classroom and on the sports fields.

"Clint started at Texas Country Day a few months after school had already begun, and some of the kids in the class were wondering whether he'd be able to catch up," recalled classmate John Black. "In no time, he passed us *all* by. You could just assume that no matter what the subject was, Clint was going to get an A."

His ninth-grade math teacher recalls, "Clint was so smart that if the class had to make a decision they would defer to him. When he gave his opinion, that ruled. Clint was not at all like the other oil boys. In addition to being smart, he was polite and well-mannered, and he didn't cause anyone any trouble."

Clint Jr. once annoyed his English teacher, however, when he wrote at the top of an essay, "Cloudy Day," leaving it up to the teacher to guess to whom the paper belonged. The teacher, outwitted by her pupil, was unable to figure out that "Cloudy Day" translated to "Murky Sun." She asked several times whose paper it was before Clint finally stepped forward to claim it.

Getting their sons into Texas Country Day, and their daughters into Dallas's exclusive girls' school, Hockaday, was a fairly simple task for the new millionaires, but being accepted by Dallas society would prove far more difficult for the oil crowd. During the early 1930s, the city's rich began to leave the Victorian mansions they had occupied near downtown, and move north toward Highland Park and University Park. The migration five to ten miles north had actually begun some two decades earlier, when John S. Armstrong donated one hundred acres of his immense land holdings to a group of Methodists trying to start a university.

The school, named Southern Methodist University, opened in 1911 with a few buildings and a very large campus. Armstrong died in 1908, but his sons-in-law began an aggressive campaign to promote Highland Park as the "finest residential area in the Southwest, beyond the city's smoke and dust."

By the mid-thirties this was the most fashionable part of town. The Dallas Golf and Country Club was located in the center of Highland Park, and this is where the oil crowd began building their homes. Toddie Lee Wynne's mansion, resembling a giant pink birthday cake, went up just a few yards from the club's golf course. But getting into the country club was not as easy.

The oil crowd's repeated requests to join the club were steadfastly rejected. As has invariably happened through history, those with new money and new power were resented by members of the old power structure. Envy of the larger fortunes of the parvenus was frequently as important a reason for this resentment as the alleged social sins of the newcomers. But there is no doubt that many of the newly rich oil crowd had been poor East Texas dirt farmers who often lacked a high school education, let alone the table manners and fancy accoutrements of old Dallas society—and there is no doubt that it often showed.

Some oilmen referred to themselves as "just God-damned

drillers," but they did not appreciate the common remark by Dallas society that "Crude oil produces crude people."

The pre-oil people unkindly referred to the oilmen and their wives as "oilfield trash." Some of the city's most successful oilmen had risen to their fortunes from the derrick floor, but despite their millions, behind their backs, they were still referred to as "roughnecks."

Not long after Everett DeGolyer, an internationally renowned geologist, moved to Dallas, his wife was approached at a party by a member of Dallas's old guard. Making conversation, the woman said, "At Christmas our families always get together. What do you oil people do?" The comment was made in all innocence, but it indicated a consistent feeling among older Dallas society that oil people were inherently different from the rest of the human race. Ironically, DeGolyer was among the most civilized men in Texas, as *Time* magazine, wrote, "Many a Texan was puzzled over Mr. De's refusal to become merely another Cadillac-comforted caricature. He pursued learning as others pursued the black gold."

The library in DeGolyer's palatial Spanish-style Dallas home contained more than 20,000 volumes, ranging from rare editions of Copernicus and Francis Bacon to the largest single private collection of works on the Southwest. "So you're the Texan who can read," a reporter once remarked on seeing his immense collection.

Comments about the oil rich were often as caustic as they were exaggerated and indiscreet. A Dallas matron proudly announced at one of her dinner parties, "I'd sooner entertain a colored man at my table than an oilman."

Many oilmen were recognizable in a crowd by their manners or lack thereof. In the presence of oilmen, those with money predating oil often nodded knowingly to one another, their lips silently framing the single word, "Oil."

So the only club the oilmen entered easily was the one they formed in 1934, the Dallas Petroleum Club. Located in a five-story building in downtown Dallas, it was the place where men went to hammer out deals over lunch. Explained a longtime member, "It was just a place for a guy to get a good lunch and a million-dollar deal."

The club was best known for its card games that began around 11 A.M. and lasted through the afternoon. Clint Murchison ate there almost every day in the thirties, sometimes winning and sometimes losing at marathon games of poker, gin rummy, and dominoes. The club was packed with excitement as oilmen came in with the latest news from the East Texas field, and often the news prompted millions of dollars to change hands before dessert. Still, in terms of society, the Petroleum Club was a long way from the Dallas Golf and Country Club.

Oil money was unwelcome in the city's top clubs and finest homes, but it was energetically sought by the men and women who owned Dallas's retail stores, particularly Neiman-Marcus. Herbert Marcus and his four sons—especially the eldest and favorite son Stanley—were masters at stimulating and feeding the material aspirations of the newly monied.

There was a story that a barefoot woman came into the store and announced she had come in from West Texas to get "the works." Saleswomen were at first reluctant to wait on her, but she quickly changed their minds. Before leaving, she had spent more than $10,000 in cash, on clothes and jewels and a pair of shoes, explaining that her folks had oil "running out of their land." Indeed, many poor-looking folk came into the store in the 1930s, and they were often the same people who walked away with the most expensive mink coats and the fanciest gowns.

When regular customers came in, they were met by one of the Marcus brothers or by the father. "If you were a big customer, i.e., an oilman, Mr. Stanley or Mr. Herbert Sr. personally escorted you around the store," recalled a longtime Neiman's saleswoman. "Once when Mr. Stanley was taking a lady around, she was pointing to entire racks of dresses, and saying, 'I want that rack, that one too.' Mr. Stanley had the biggest grin on his face you could imagine. Naturally, he had all day to spend with customers like that."

When an oilman admired a store window and asked if its entire contents could be duplicated in his living room for his wife's Christmas, Stanley immediately said yes. There were exaggerated stories, of course, but it was not a myth that oil-men and their wives regularly bought things by the dozen, or in all available colors.

"I want to get me some of them coats that feel like buttered air," an oil millionaire shouted, racing into Neiman-Marcus one morning. He left the store a few minutes later, loaded down with ten vicuna coats that cost $750 each.

Another oilman read about a sale Neiman's was having on men's ties, then telephoned the store. "How many them ties ya got?" he asked.

The clerk said that there were quite a few, in several styles and colors. But the oilman wanted to know the exact number. The clerk counted the ties, then came back to the phone. "We've got more than a thousand, probably a thousand and fifty."

"I'll take 'em," replied the oilman.

Stories of millionaires spending $100,000 or more in an afternoon at the store made Neiman-Marcus famous around the world. If the image of the big-hatted, big-mouthed, potbellied Texan lighting his cigar with $100 bills was not born at Neiman-Marcus, it should have been.

There were also some stories that Clint Murchison would let his bill at Neiman-Marcus climb into the hundreds of thousands of dollars before he would pay it. And even then, according to popular lore, he paid his bill only every few years. In truth, Clint greatly admired the Marcuses' tremendous success, and while his bill often did climb into six figures, he paid it at least two or three times a year. As was always his practice, he paid it with borrowed money.

When Clint needed clothes, Neiman-Marcus came to him. Jack Franklin ran the men's department there, and once or twice a year he arrived at the house on Preston Road with his alterations man. Clint agreed to have custom-made whatever Franklin suggested. One afternoon Clint left his office early and went home to pick up his white tuxedo jacket before flying to San Antonio for a wedding that evening. Unable to find the jacket, he telephoned Franklin, who met him an hour later at Love Field, moments before the plane took off, with a replacement, made to Clint's measurements.

Texas's reputation was changing from Wild West to wild millionaires. *Fortune* magazine, in a 1937 article titled "Dallas in Wonderland," described the extraordinary authority Neiman-Marcus had attained in only three decades. "The store," *Fortune* said, "is like a doctor or lawyer that people swear by."

When Herbert Sr. retired, he gave most, if not all, authority to his eldest son, and Stanley handled his position brilliantly. He achieved just the right balance with the new oil customers, playing Pygmalion to thousands of Galateas from the oil fields, men and women with far more money than background. Many of them had never been out of the state, had never given a party, and some of the wives, until very recently, had made their own clothes out of flour sacks. Stanley, who was Harvard-educated and thoroughly sophisticated, showed the new oil families how to dress, entertain, and travel, and he did so without embarrassing them.

There is no other department store in the world where real jewelry is as significant to the store's profits or matters more to its customers. The reason is that when many Dallas oilmen wanted expensive jewels, they went only to Neiman-Marcus. They felt uncomfortable at Van Cleef & Arpels, Harry Winston, or Tiffany & Company in New York. The salesmen there spoke in a strange accent and looked down their noses at the oil-monied yahoos and their flagrantly unpolished ways. Conversely, at Neiman-Marcus they knew they would be treated well.

Many of Dallas's prominent pre-oil families, however, began to complain that their struggles to form a refined and respectable high society out of the dusty raw frontier town of Dallas were now for nothing. All their work, they complained, was undone by the vulgarity of the new oil barons. But Stanley Marcus publicly defended the oil crowd and once insisted, "This group has behaved, by and large, a good deal better than the Gold Rush people reportedly did."

Stanley and his father, Herbert, and Stanley's aunt and uncle, Carrie and Al Neiman, were brilliant merchants, and they would have thrived anywhere. But there is no doubt that the flood of oil money helped make their store famous around the world. So it was not surprising when a cartoon appeared in *The New Yorker* magazine in 1956, of a barefoot, threadbare woman standing by a broken-down shack in the middle of a prairie. In the distance is a huge well spouting oil a mile in the sky, and a man is rushing toward the shack to tell his wife of the gusher that she can see for herself. The caption reads, "It's wonderful, Harry! How late does Neiman-Marcus stay open?"

Of all the oilmen whose vulgar lifestyle offended old Dallas society, the most famous was H. L. Hunt, who in 1938 moved to Dallas and installed his wife, Lyda, and their six children in an oversize copy of George Washington's Mount Vernon. But H. L. was not around much during the 1930s or 1940s. In addition to his oil properties, he looked after a second set of children he fathered by another woman in Houston, and a third secret family in Louisiana. He married the mother of his Houston brood when his first wife died. Not satisfied with three sizable families, he also continued to be a notorious philanderer.

In addition to these activities, Hunt found time to support and supervise ultra right-wing and anti-Semitic enterprises. Many of the East Texas oil millionaires shared Hunt's anti-black, anti-Jewish bigotry, but not Murchison, who was absolutely free of such prejudice. Clint also was an honorable and faithful husband, and strongly disapproved of any man who had an extramarital affair. Morally and philosophically, Hunt and Murchison were planets apart.

In the 1930s the city's spirit of boosterism was as strong as it had ever been. Dallas, with a population of 260,000, was on its way to becoming a vital commercial center, the most important in the Southwest. But curiously, despite the city's growth both in population and wealth, it remained paranoid, fearful that one day it would "blow away." Dallas worried that "the customers would go elsewhere, the companies would relocate, the train wouldn't stop here anymore."

The most concerned of all were the oilmen, hundreds of whom had made their fortunes literally overnight and many of whom had lost them just as quickly. Ironically, these oilmen did not join the Dallas businessmen who were determined to ensure the continued success of the city by working for it, nor did most of the oilmen give to the city's charities.

In the mid-1930s a group of top Dallas businessmen established the Dallas Citizens Council, an oligarchy not unlike those that ruled the Italian city-states of the Renaissance. Money was a *sine qua non* for membership in the Citizens Council, but not the only one. A man had to be willing to "Do something for Dallas," to head a bond election or a fund-raising drive.

There were no women on the Citizens Council, nor any doctors or lawyers. It consisted mostly of bankers and the chief executive officers of large and important businesses, men who could commit money without consulting anyone else. These were the "yes-or-no men," as the council's founder, banker Robert L. Thornton, described them, and only one oilman joined. The Council met secretly to choose local officials and occasionally intervene if Dallas's elected officials made a decision contrary to the Citizens Council's view of "what was good for the city." With this strong feeling of boosterism underlying virtually every facet of Dallas life, the country club set thought they had a good excuse: "We won't let the oil people into our clubs because they haven't done anything for the city."

But keeping the parvenu oilmen and their wives out of Dallas's best clubs became increasingly difficult. The city's bankers could not continue to solicit big deposits for their banks and shun these same depositors socially. And, inevitably, old Dallas money began to intermarry with the new oil money. By the early forties prominent names in cotton and land, such as King and Caruth, were eclipsed by new oil names, and gradually the doors to the Dallas Golf and Country Club, the Idlewild and Terpsichorean men's clubs, opened to include the newest Dallas rich.

Edna Ferber reveals the transition in her novel *Giant,* when Bick Benedict explains to his new wife, whom he has just transported to Texas from Virginia: "Here in Texas, the cotton rich always snooted the cattle rich. And now if this oil keeps coming into Texas the old cattle crowd will look down their noses at the oil upstarts. You know, like the old New York De Peysters snooting the Vanderbilts and the Vanderbilts cutting the Astors."

Brook Hollow Golf Club was more receptive to oil wealth than the Dallas Golf Club, in part because it was newer. Ironically, by the late forties and early fifties, Brook Hollow came to be considered far tonier than the by-then renamed Dallas Country Club. Oil money built Brook Hollow into a giant, overdecorated place that aped an imaginary pre-Civil War style of life. A sprawling white clubhouse covered, inside and out, in treillage, and surrounded by weeping willows and magnolias, it is reminiscent of an era long ago—days of mint juleps and planter's punch served by soft-spoken black waiters in white coats long before the automobile had created a need for oil.

Clint became a member of the club but rarely used it. He preferred instead to entertain at home in a mansion larger and more comfortable than the clubhouse at Brook Hollow.

Matagorda Island was still a very rugged place when Virginia Long came to visit in 1937. Clint waited at the dock when Virginia, chaperoned by her mother, came across the bay from San Antonio, on a shrimp boat Clint had rented to accommodate all their luggage. Petite, blond, blue-eyed, and only twenty years old, Virginia was a radiant beauty. On that first visit to the island, she wore white shorts that showed off her tan shapely legs, and when the cowboys on the island saw how young and beautiful she was, they could not help staring. As word spread around the 40,000-acre cattle ranch that "she" had arrived, dozens of employees not-so-discreetly rode up to the house trying to get a close look at her. She looked very much like one of the great sex symbols of the late thirties and early forties, movie star Lana Turner.

Clint had first met Virginia a few months earlier when she came to a Sunday night swimming party at his Dallas home with her friend Effie Arrington, who was dating and would marry Clint's close friend and business associate Wofford Cain. Clint, who was twenty-one years older than Virginia, was immediately taken with her, and the following morning he called and asked her for a date. As popular as she was attractive, she was busy the whole week, but he persisted and she agreed to have dinner with him the following weekend. The date began a six-year courtship.

Despite the difference in their ages, Clint and Virginia were very much alike. She was carefree and energetic, and, like Clint, she was constantly on the go. Whether fishing and hunting all day at the island, or dancing all night on the roof of Dallas's stylish Baker Hotel, Virginia was always ready to have fun, and best of all, she was ready on a moment's notice. It was obvious to everyone that Clint was crazy about Virginia and she about him, but he was as resolved as ever not to inflict a stepmother on the sons he loved so much—until they were grown.

Virginia's background was similar to his. She was born in Commerce, an East Texas town slightly smaller than Athens, and, like Clint, she was the daughter of an East Texas banker. Virginia was born on January 1, 1916. "My mother said I jumped out right after midnight, and I've been jumping ever since."

When her father was not busy at the bank, he was an avid outdoorsman, and he first took Virginia hunting with him when she was barely four years old. When they returned from their first hunt, tiny Virginia stood in the doorway wringing wet and holding four bagged ducks. Mrs. Long gasped at the sight of her daughter, then accused her husband of using Virginia as a bird dog.

Tomboyish as she appeared as a girl, she blossomed into a very beautiful and feminine young lady. Before her twentieth birthday, she became a model for a clothing wholesaler in Dallas. Her father died a year before Virginia met Clint, but he had prepared her well for a life with the vigorous multimillionaire sportsman. When it came to fishing and hunting, Clint knew that most of his friends were no match for his Virginia. Not only was she a great shot, unlike other women he knew, she was not easily frightened by the unforeseen elements of nature. If a snake rattled over her boots, she stood still and waited for it to disappear. If a storm came up on Matagorda, she calmly took refuge until it passed. Most men, let alone women, did not have the sportsman's savvy that she possessed, nor her inexhaustible energy. Seeing how independent she was, from the very start Clint treated her like one of his male cronies, and he called her "chico," the Spanish word for little boy.

Once when Virginia and a female friend were at Matagorda, a storm destroyed the electrical and water towers, leaving them without lights and refrigeration. Virginia took a boat to Rockport and wired Clint, "There's been a bad storm. We need a new electrical motor."

Clint, who viewed her as invincible, wired back, "No you don't."

Virginia wired again, "You can't run this island from your office in Dallas. Send a new motor."

The next day he arrived personally with a motor.

Clint was even more fearless than Virginia. "A sunken boat formed a jetty on one side of the island where the surf was rough," recalls Virginia. "Clint and I were out in the water casting for sea trout, and I had a string of fish attached to my belt. I felt down for the string and the fish were gone, then I looked behind me and there was a large shark. I motioned to Clint about the shark and went to shore, but Clint just stood there and kept fishing. That kind of thing didn't bother him, he just called to me, 'Sissy, what's wrong with you? Come on back out here.' "

Like Clint, Virginia was an inveterate card player. She was a match for most men who challenged her to a wild-eyed, Texas version of gin rummy, and she also had the reputation of being a crack poker player. "Once, when Clint was in Mexico, I was invited to a card game and dinner at [Republic Bank chairman] Karl Hoblitzelle's house," she recalls. "I was at the table with Fred Florence and two other very smart men. I realized that I was taking Clint's place and they weren't going to be easy on me.

"Sometime during the game I asked what we were playing for and they told me ten cents a point. I figured up that I was down eight hundred dollars. Then Karl blinked the lights which meant come for dinner. When we came back to the table, I was trying much harder, really concentrating, and I ended up owing only three hundred dollars.

"When I arrived in Mexico and told Clint what had happened, he just smiled and said, 'They put you in with the big boys.' "

Clint suffered another great personal tragedy in the spring of 1938, when his partner, Dudley Golding, was killed in a plane crash. Seconds after taking off from Dallas's Love Field, Golding's plane ran out of gas and crashed into an electrical power line. Golding was more than a business associate; he had become Clint's closest friend.

After the crash Golding's wife, Georgia, urged Clint to put her on the board of American Liberty Oil Company, claiming that she had put up family money that helped get the company started eight years earlier. She wanted to appoint others to the board as well. But Clint's board had always been nominal. He had never operated any of his businesses by committee and did not propose to change now.

Clint wanted Toddie Lee Wynne, who already owned 10 percent of the company, to buy out Golding's 45 percent. Because Toddie did not have the money to do it, Clint lent him all the money he needed to buy Golding's interest. In exchange, Toddie gave Clint 5 percent of his own interest, so that the men became fifty-fifty partners. In addition to being chief counsel for American Liberty, Wynne took the title of chief executive. His first coup at the top was to get a $5 million loan from the Bank of Manhattan. American Liberty had first borrowed money there when Rushton Ardrey worked at the Bank of Manhattan, and American Liberty strengthened its ties with the New York bank when Ardrey moved to Dallas and joined the company.

The same year that Ardrey joined American Liberty, Clint hired a geologist named Albert Oldham who had been studying rock formations for more than sixteen years—considered a lifetime in the oil business of the thirties. Oldham was Murchison's kind of man. He had a master's degree in geology from the University of Chicago, but, just as important in Clint's opinion, he seemed to have a natural nose for oil. He followed his hunches as well as his seismographic charts, and exhibited none of the pretentiousness typical of the young men graduating by the hundreds from geology schools in Texas, Arkansas, Louisiana, and Oklahoma. At age ninety in 1985, nearly half a century after going to work for Murchison and many millions richer, Oldham admitted, "Some of the best things I ever did from a geological standpoint turned out wrong.

"Murchison didn't get upset when wells came up dry," Oldham recalled. "He was an oilman. He knew the hazards, the risks, and the industry percentages. Nor did he get very excited when we struck it big several times—he just took it as a matter of course. He was keenly aware that this was an up-and-down business. His philosophy was, 'You win some, you lose some.' I never had the impression he was worried about losing money. It was all a game to him, with turns that no one could predict."

American Liberty's first big strike under the direction of Oldham was in the Wasson field, one of the major finds in Texas. The Wasson field was brought in in Yoakum County, a few counties north of Winkler, where Clint had built his first pipeline in the Hendrick Field a decade earlier. The exact boundaries of the field were not yet determined, but the giant Texas Company owned some 8,000 acres of it.

In 1938 the Texas Company had produced three wells, widely separated from one another. Oldham believed the distance between the wells proved the theory that there was a sizable producing field, and he noticed that there were high structural positions that he believed would yield better wells than those the Texas Company had found.

At the same time, the Texas Company was drilling the Salem field near Chicago, which was a big market for oil. The Texas Company owned about 95 percent of the field, but the independents, who owned the other 5 percent on small tracts scattered about, had the capability of draining the field's reserves. In its haste to concentrate its efforts on the Salem field and keep the independents from taking the enormous reserves, the Texas Company agreed to farm out all 8,000 acres in the Wasson field.

"I got Mr. Murchison on the phone at Matagorda," recalls

Oldham, "and told him that it looked like the whole eight thousand acres could be producers. That same day I sent the lease broker to him, and by the next morning they had made a deal. Almost all of the two hundred wells we planned to drill had to be financed at a cost of about fifty thousand dollars per well, but Mr. Murchison made up his mind right then. Most of the major oil companies would have taken months to execute this kind of ten-million-dollar deal that took us only one day."

The Texas Company's geologist doubted Clint could make even the interest on the $10 million he sank into the Wasson field. But he recouped his investment many times over. Between 1938 and 1942 American Liberty drilled 240 wells in the Wasson field, and not one of them was dry.

Credit financing of the magnitude Clint required, coupled with the inherent and enormous risks of the oil business, gave him the dubious reputation of being one of the biggest gamblers in the oil business. But Clint was proud of his intricate deals to get huge loans. When his sons were grown, he instructed them to be similarly credit-minded, to build their fortunes using other people's money. "The only time I ever lost in a deal was when I used my own money," Clint quipped. "When you start using your own money, you start thinking you can do anything. Don't do it. Cash makes a man careless."

The Wasson field came at an appropriate time. As early as 1938 Murchison saw inflation coming, and he set out to borrow as much money as he could and sink as much as he could into the ground. He also began to think about diversifying into other industries unrelated to oil. Clint was not nearly as optimistic as most oilmen were about the future of the petroleum industry.

His first move to reduce his exposure in the oil business came in 1939 when he and Toddie Lee Wynne purchased the Reserve Loan Life Insurance Company of Indianapolis. Clint sent an employee to Indiana to study the company's books, and the employee returned with fourteen reasons why Murchison and Wynne should not make the purchase. However, the company's large mortgage loan department, and its 15 to 1 ratio of assets to capital funds, made it an attractive investment, and Murchison and Wynne borrowed $1 million to buy it. In 1940 Clint moved the company's corporate office to a small, nondescript two-story building at 1201 Main Street in downtown Dallas.

In 1939 Clint's sons were eighteen and sixteen, practically grown men. John Dabney was in his second year at Yale, and Clint was a senior at the Lawrenceville prep school in Lawrenceville, New Jersey. The fact that neither of Clint's sons seemed particularly interested in the oil business did not bother their father, but he was anxious to have them build on the fortune he had created. His plan was to acquire a wide range of companies that his sons would someday control. By the time they returned from college, they would own the controlling stock in companies so numerous and diverse that, with the help of many advisers, they could get a broad education in a variety of businesses before picking the areas where they wanted to spend most of their time, energy, and money.

While John never really expressed his opinion of his father's plan, Clint Jr. had a decidedly different plan for his life. Not long after arriving at Lawrenceville, Clint decided he was the smartest boy in the school. Indeed, after his first year, Lawrenceville's headmaster wrote a letter to Clint Sr. in Dallas, explaining that Clint Jr.'s solid A-plus average was the highest grade point ever achieved at Lawrenceville.

Clint Jr. was already beginning to consider pursuing an academic career after graduating from college. Years earlier, when he was only eleven, he had read an article in *Fortune* about the Massachusetts Institute of Technology. The article said that MIT had the toughest curriculum of any university in the country. "I'm going to MIT when I get out of high school," young Clint Jr. told his father that day.

In 1940 Clint Jr. enrolled at MIT, and again, after the first year, had an A-plus average. One of his professors, who taught physics and mathematics, was so impressed with his brilliant pupil that he invited Clint Jr. to live with him and his family for a semester. During that time, Clint Jr. made up his mind that he would pursue a career in teaching. Later the president of MIT, on meeting Clint's maternal grandmother, Burk White, said of her grandson, "Clint is brilliant. He can run a problem through the eye of a needle."

At Yale John was the opposite of his brother the egghead. Though John was very bright, and like his brother made an A average, unlike Clint Jr., John was very social. He was invited to join one of Yale's ultra-exclusive secret societies, the Book and Snake Club.

"John was always very polite and considerate, and he spoke slowly and softly with a Texas drawl," recalled one of his closest friends at Yale. "The thing I remember most about him in college was that he was very sophisticated, even more so than the boys born in the East. This seemed fairly peculiar since Texas was still a very rugged, rough country in those days, or at least we at Yale thought it was."

What his Yale friends failed to realize was that John learned about Eastern sophistication during his two years at Hotchkiss and that in many matters he was already more sophisticated than his prep school chums who were woefully naive, especially in regard to the opposite sex. As a grown man, John explained, "It's a great shock for a Texas boy to go to an Eastern school. Down in Texas you start driving a car earlier, running around with girls earlier."

One common and unhappy prep school experience that neither John Dabney nor Clint Jr. suffered was homesickness. Clint Sr. loved his sons and the boys loved their father, but because Clint Sr. spent so much time away from Dallas on business, there was never time for him to develop an affectionate closeness with his boys. When John and Clint Jr. went away to Eastern prep schools, they missed the farm and they missed their father, but the strong parental void that so many of their classmates experienced was a feeling that John and Clint Jr. had felt for most of their lives.

8

"If you trade in peanuts you can trade in watermelons too. We buy anything that adds up."

When World War II broke out in 1939, there was a strong isolationist feeling in Dallas. The isolationists believed that America had entered World War I for the most idealistic reasons and that instead of making the world safe for democracy, America had allowed itself to be outsmarted by its own allies.

But in the 1930s, as Hitler's armies marched into Austria and Czechoslovakia and the Japanese rape of China was horrifyingly pictured in newsreels and magazines, the same outrage against "barbarism" that had led to America's entry into World War I was building again. After the attack on Pearl Harbor on December 7, 1941, not a voice was heard in Dallas against America's declaration of war.

In fact, there was almost a hysteria of patriotic enthusiasm. Men who had been too young to enlist in World War I were thrilled with the chance to prove their patriotism. The eagerness to join the war was especially strong in Texas, where men had for generations envied the Texas heroes who died a century earlier at the battles of the Alamo and Goliad. Those who were declared 4F, the draft classification for men found physically unfit for service, felt stigmatized.

John Dabney did not wait to be drafted. Instead, the day after Pearl Harbor he enlisted in the Army Air Force. With typical self-deprecating modesty, John Dabney pretended that he enlisted "partly to escape the dean's descending ax."

John wrote to Clint Jr. about his experiences flying P-38s in the Mediterranean and P-40s in the China Burma India theater for which he later was awarded the Distinguished Flying Cross. Fascinated by his brother's stories, Clint Jr. wanted to enter the Marine Corps and try to get a flying commission as well. But the Marine Corps learned that Clint Jr. had a genius I.Q. and felt that his talents would be put to better use in officers' training school. He entered the V-12 program on the campus of Duke University in Durham, North Carolina.

In a letter from Duke, he confided to his father that he had believed he was the smartest boy at Lawrenceville, and, therefore, as his father had said, the smartest boy in the world. But at MIT he had met boys far smarter than he.

To allay his father's concerns that he was unsociable, Clint Jr. pointed out that his door was never locked and that in one week he had been to six dances.

While he assured his father he was not antisocial, he admitted that if he associated much longer with Marines he might delude himself into thinking he was the smartest man in the world and then he would have to go back to MIT.

By 1943, with John and Clint Jr. both in military service, their father felt they were finally grown men and he was free to remarry. On January 21, 1943, at a small and quiet ceremony at a friend's house in Mission, Texas, forty-seven-year-old Clint and twenty-seven-year-old Virginia were married.

Although Virginia's wedding picture, which appeared in newspapers throughout the state, bore some resemblance to Lana Turner, she was a much more classic beauty. What made the picture even more extraordinary was that she was not some Southern hothouse flower but a lively sportswoman who often outlasted the men with whom she fished and hunted, including her husband.

The day after the wedding Clint Jr. wrote home from Duke, congratulating his father and stepmother and confessing that for a long time he had wondered when they would marry.

A month earlier, for Christmas, Clint had given Virginia a star sapphire, which sent out many mixed signals, because she was wearing a ring but no wedding announcement was made. In fact, it was merely a Christmas present. The real thing, her engagement ring, came a few weeks later. It was a 16-karat diamond marquise for which Clint paid $125,000.

Among the lavish wedding presents they received were a

matched set of Remington rifles inlaid with mother of pearl, a gift from Sid Richardson.

Clint Jr. graduated Phi Beta Kappa with a degree in electrical engineering from Duke University, and apparently decided again that he was the smartest man in the world because he did return to MIT. He tried to go back for a master's degree in engineering, but the engineering department was already filled. Instead, Clint began work on a master's in mathematics. This time, he took with him his brand-new wife, Jane Coleman, and they bought a small home in the Belmont section of Boston.

Clint had met Jane four years earlier on a blind date in Dallas, during the summer of 1941, while he was still an undergraduate at MIT. They were both immediately attracted to each other. "Clint was very ingratiating and very, very funny," recalls Jane. "He said and did all the right things that boys were supposed to."

Jane was only sixteen at the time, and at five feet three only a few inches shorter than Clint. She had reddish-brown hair, bright blue eyes, a very high forehead, and a delicate rosebud mouth. She looked even younger than her sixteen years, and she was terrified when Clint Jr. said he wanted her to meet his father.

But Clint Sr. immediately set Jane at ease when he expressed delight that Jane's maternal grandmother was from Athens. Because her mother was a great beauty, Jane did not worry when she learned Clint Sr. had told his son, "Before you marry her, find out what her mother looks like. Then you'll know what she will look like when she gets older."

Born Jane Catherine Coleman on September 5, 1925, she had spent her early childhood in East Texas. Jane's parents, Lawrence and Quoquese Coleman, divorced when she was six, and Jane moved with her mother and grandparents, from Luling, Texas, where she was born, to Mabank near Athens. It would be impossible to overestimate how rural, both in attitude and size, these towns were. Compared to Luling and Mabank, Athens was a metropolis.

During her sophomore year in high school, Jane and her

mother lived in San Antonio, where she experienced big city life for the first time, and her first serious suitor, Clint W. Murchison, Jr. A few weeks after their first date, Big Clint asked Clint Jr. and a friend to deliver John Dabney's Ford to him in Montgomery, Alabama, where he was stationed temporarily after completing flight training. The friend drove Clint Sr.'s Cadillac while Clint Jr. and another buddy followed in John Dabney's Ford.

"We were driving along," remembered the friend who drove the Cadillac, "and I noticed the car would pick up speed without my accelerating. I was going about fifty miles an hour, then suddenly I was going seventy. Then I noticed Clint driving the Ford behind me—he'd get on the bumper and gun that Ford and it would push the Cadillac.

"After we dropped off John's car, we left Alabama and headed west back to Dallas. Myself and the other guy fell asleep in the back seat while Clint Jr. was driving. When we woke up, we realized we were west of Houston heading for San Antonio. 'We're going to see Jane Coleman,' Clint said. We arrived at a hotel there, and Clint checked into one room, then checked me and the other guy into another room. We never saw Clint the whole time we were there. He'd call us and say, 'We'll leave tomorrow,' but when tomorrow came, he'd put it off another day. Finally, about three days later, we left."

When Clint Sr. learned of the incident after the boys returned to Dallas, his only response was, "Clint W. *would* get a long-distance girl during gas rationing."

During the war Clint Jr. wrote Jane many letters promising that after the war he would marry her. Before the war ended, Clint told his father of his plans to marry, but Clint Sr. tried to persuade them to wait until they were older. Clint Jr. clearly wanted to marry at once, however, and Clint Sr. gave his blessing.

On June 12, 1945, a Tuesday evening three months short of her twentieth birthday, Jane married Marine Lieutenant Clint Murchison Jr. who was just twenty-one. At a small reception at the home of Clint Jr.'s aunt in Dallas, the young bride and groom are photographed cutting the cake together. Clint Jr., standing only five feet six but proud and erect in Marine whites, is smiling broadly at his wife, radiant in a satin wedding dress with a full-hoop skirt.

The newlyweds returned to the Marine base in Virginia where Clint was stationed for a short time, before moving to Boston. Nine months after they settled into a two-bedroom home in Boston, Jane became pregnant. A few months before the arrival date, Jane returned to her mother's home in San Antonio to prepare for the birth. Clint Sr.'s first grandchild was born on December 29, 1946. He was named Clint W. Murchison III.

In mid-1944 Clint Sr. learned some very distressing business news. An associate told him that his partner Toddie Lee Wynne had bought some oil wells in Wyoming that he was keeping secret from Clint. The two men were supposed to have a partnership in which every deal they made was to be made jointly with each man having an opportunity for an equal share. Clint had trusted Toddie Lee completely, and he had always prided himself on his ability to pick associates and partners who were honest and forthright.

The news that Toddie was operating behind his back was such a devastating blow that Clint decided he would have nothing more to do with Wynne. When Clint told Toddie he wanted to dissolve the partnership, Toddie was very reluctant to part from the man who had made him a millionaire, but he had no choice. They decided to make a list of their dozen joint holdings, which totaled more than $150 million, and then to take turns choosing whether to buy or sell. The two top assets were the production division of American Liberty and the exploration division of American Liberty (which included Matagorda Island). The first option would be decided by the toss of a coin.

Toddie won the toss and began by taking the exploration division of American Liberty with Matagorda, which Clint thought was a peculiar choice. Toddie was far more conservative than Clint and he felt sure Toddie would have preferred the production division since it was less risky and also more lucrative. He later learned that Toddie had witheld important information from him about the assets, and that in all but one case Toddie took the more valuable properties. Toddie disappointed Clint once—by dealing behind his back—and he disappointed him again, in the way the partnership was dissolved.

"Clint was very bitter in the coming years when he realized Wynne had taken most of the better assets in the buy-out," recalls a longtime business associate of both men. "Clint had dealt absolutely openly with Toddie and assumed Toddie would do the same. It really hurt Clint that Toddie didn't play fair. Toddie, after all, had accumulated a fantastic amount of wealth chiefly because of Clint."

Years later the bitterness still existed when Clint told his eldest grandson and namesake, "The biggest mistake of my life was giving up Matagorda."

When Wynne's children—Sissy and Toddie Lee Wynne Jr.—hosted a weekend house party on Matagorda, John Dabney Murchison came to the island, for the first time as a guest. Although his father no longer owned the place, John Dabney was still the most sought-after young man at the party—from the very moment he arrived. While all the other guests came by boat from Rockport, Lieutenant Murchison flew in on a military fighter plane. Clint Sr. had purchased the plane from the United States government and had it waiting for his son when he returned from the war.

At one point, Toddie Lee and Clint Sr. hoped Wynne's daughter, Sissy, and John Dabney would marry. But even if Clint and Toddie Lee had remained friends, it was not Sissy Wynne who charmed John Dabney that weekend, but a vivacious brunette named Lupe Gannon.

"I think John was thunderstruck by Lupe from the very first time he met her," recalls a friend of both John and Lupe. "She was everything he was not—outgoing, ebullient, and a real free spirit."

Born Lucille Hughes Gannon, on November 4, 1925, and nicknamed Lupe, she was the baby in a family that already included two sisters and a brother. The Gannon children grew up in a large beige brick house on Ross Avenue near downtown Dallas and near the great family mansions built about 1910 in Munger Place. The area was falling out of fashion, and when Lupe was still a little girl, the family moved into a magnificent Spanish villa on Turtle Creek.

Edward "Ward" Gannon was the leading vice president of the First National Bank and a member of the Dallas Citizens Council. Although not rich compared to Dallas's oilmen, Gannon had been part of the city's financial circles and Dallas society years before the East Texas field was discovered. Like his daughter Lupe years later, Ward was everyone's favorite host. He had a famous sense of humor and a facility for making other people feel at ease. While Ward was busy at the bank, Ethel Gannon was a warm and loving mother, devoted to her children.

"Mrs. Gannon had a beautiful face, but she was enormous in size," recalls a childhood friend of Lupe. "You wanted to climb up in her lap because it was such a big lap and she'd put her arms around you and hug you. Mrs. Gannon laughed all the time, and when she did, she shook all over, all her chins and her stomachs."

Ethel Gannon was a strong Catholic, and the family attended mass each Sunday. At the Sunday afternoon supper that followed, the family, and usually a few other families, stuffed themselves on fried chicken, pot roast, mashed potatoes, vegetables, muffins and bread, and three or four sorts of dessert.

"Lupe was always jumping about and excited about everything," recalls her friend. "She had so much energy that when she was only three years old, she was already swimming the fifty-foot length of my aunt's pool."

Lupe attended Dallas's private Hockaday School, where she was always a leader. In a picture of her fifth-grade class during gym, she is the one at the very center, holding the kickball. There are about twenty girls in the picture, but all of them are centered around Lupe Gannon. "She was always the captain of the team, always the initiator," recalls a classmate.

Ward Gannon died of leukemia when Lupe was sixteen, and she transferred to Highland Park High School. Later, to stay close to her mother, Lupe decided to attend Texas State College for Women at Denton. Then to be even closer, she transferred to Southern Methodist University in Dallas. Just a few months before her graduation, she went to the house party on Matagorda.

When the party began to break up, John invited Lupe to fly back to Dallas with him in the co-pilot's seat. She immediately agreed. "John was like no one I had ever met before," Lupe said, recalling their first meeting. "He had a very clear idea of what he wanted in life and how he was going to get it."

The guests watched the plane lift off the runway, blowing sand in all directions, and John and Lupe waving good-bye from the open window of the cockpit. As the plane's screech faded in the air, someone cattily snickered, "She has in mind marrying him."

John adored Lupe's mother Ethel Gannon. She was warm and demonstrative in her affection for him, and she gave him the kind of motherly warmth and nurturing he had never had but had sorely missed. Many times, during John and Lupe's courtship, Mrs. Gannon prepared a bed for John on the living room couch where he happily spent the night, rather than going home to the large, lonely house on Preston Road.

John and Lupe were married on March 9, 1947, at Mrs. Gannon's home. When Ward Gannon died five years earlier, he had not left a great fortune, and Ethel had to watch what she spent on Lupe's wedding. A few of the bridesmaids' gowns, bought at a medium-priced Dallas department store, came apart at the seams as the bridesmaids walked up the wedding aisle. But no one made fun of the inexpensive gowns or modest food served at the wedding reception at Brook Hollow Golf Club. Ward Gannon and now his widow and children were a part of old Dallas society, and even after the East Texas field came in, style and breeding still counted for something.

Ethel and Ward Gannon's other daughter, Jeanne, also in the phrase of the day, "married well." She married H. L. Hunt's nephew Stuart Hunt.

Following Lupe and John's wedding and a short honeymoon in Acapulco, they returned to New Haven, Connecticut, so that John could get his degree from Yale. Many of his friends had already graduated, but John could not have been happier to be back. The war was over and New England offered a serene and peaceful existence that John had missed.

The war had been very hard on him, both physically and mentally. He was sent on more than fifty difficult missions from Italy to Africa to China with no intervals of rest, and after living for months on little other than rice and pork, he became malnourished. Worse, the flying missions were tremendously stressful, and near the end of 1945 he was on the verge of a nervous collapse. When his superiors noticed his poor health and steep weight loss, he was released immediately and flown from Europe to the United States. When his plane landed in Florida, he was taken directly to a hospital and examined, then released. He recovered slowly, but not since he left New Haven in 1942 had he felt as healthy or happy as he did when he returned with Lupe five years later.

Dissolving their American Liberty partnership was a more difficult task than either Toddie Lee or Clint anticipated. A large number of accountants, auditors, and tax attorneys met almost daily for two years with Wynne and Murchison, trying to untangle one man's holdings from the other's.

Toddie had taken American Liberty's offices in Highland Park Village in the division, leaving Clint to move back downtown into a suite of three tiny rooms in the First National Bank Building. Clint desperately needed more office space and a group of advisers and administrators who could organize and manage his vast interests. His strength had always been in acquisitions, whether in acquiring oil wells or gas leases or the loans "to make the deal walk," as he put it. He was a deal maker who left the management of his businesses to others.

"If you go partners with Clint," Sid Richardson explained, "he says to you, 'Here, hold this horse while I go catch another.' Pretty soon you find you've got your hands full of Murchison's horses."

Several of Murchison's investments had been too long overlooked. He was not even quite sure what he owned and with whom, a fact due partly to the speed with which he got into and out of deals. Partnerships or agreements clinched with a handshake could be dissolved just as fast. He began to look for capable businessmen who could bring some order to his far-flung empire, and he started by hiring a longtime friend, Gerald Mann, who had been Attorney General of Texas.

An SMU football hero and All-American in the twenties, Mann came to political power with the backing of a handful of Texas good ole boys. Mann held the post of Texas Attorney General in the late thirties, then set up private practice in Dallas in the early forties. Among the men he brought into his law firm was Holman Jenkens, an aggressive and hardworking young attorney who had worked as one of Mann's assistants in the Attorney General's office. Mann and Jenkens handled many legal matters for Murchison, including several sticky lawsuits brought against him during his days of running hot oil. At the same time that Mann came aboard as Clint's administrator, Jenkens became Murchison's in-house attorney.

Clint continued to make most of his deals on a handshake, long after most oilmen used lawyers to study every detail. As a result, Jenkens was given the difficult task of drawing up contracts intended to define specifically the deal that Clint had already executed. Not only was it difficult to draw contracts on deals that had been made first and then studied, Clint usually wanted nothing more to do with a deal after it was made. He preferred to make the trade and leave the follow-through to someone else. Jenkens arrived at work at nine o'clock in the morning and rarely left before midnight.

Clint had been trying to finagle several million dollars out of a New York bank when he finally grew tired and complained to an Eastern financier: "The trouble with you guys up here, you're too slow. You spend months shuffling those papers and going to board meetings. We trade, make the deal, and let the paperwork catch up later."

He liked to complain that New York money came with too many rules and restrictions, and that he disliked nothing more than a New York banker who said he would take his request before a loan committee or the board of directors. Despite his complaints, New York was where Clint got most of his money.

Clint and Virginia spent very few evenings alone at their home on Preston Road. Part of the reason he wanted such a large home and so many servants was so that he could have groups of his cronies out to the house for dinner and gin rummy games. As the host, he had the advantage of excusing himself from the party whenever he became tired.

"I'll see you in my dreams," he said, leaving the table sometimes before dessert.

One night at a friend's home in Highland Park, Virginia got involved in a poker game. Clint was anxious to leave, but the game dragged on and on. When it finally ended and they climbed into their car, Clint cried, "I've never thought of divorcing you, but killing you, yes."

Clint was very impatient and was always amazed at the time he thought other people wasted. Virginia recalls one time when she took Clint shopping with her at Neiman-Marcus. "When word got out that Clint was in the store, Stanley Marcus came to see us. I was trying on evening gowns, about a dozen, and Stanley was bringing them to me. When we left the store, Clint said, 'Virginia, you sure did buy a lot of gowns.' I said, 'I only bought two.' He thought I had bought everything I tried on. He couldn't understand that you would waste the time to try on a gown and then not buy it."

Clint was a very generous, albeit frequently absent, host. The liquor flowed long after he had gone to bed, and he never kept tabs on the amount of whiskey his friends drank. While his parties were extravagant—fifths of the best bourbon and choice Kansas City sirloins presented by an army of servants—they were never stiff or formal.

Frank Schultz recalls being invited to a dinner party shortly after going to work as chief geologist for the American Liberty Oil Company. "My wife and I figured it would be pretty dressy, so we called Clint to ask him what to wear.

" 'Will the men be wearing tails?' we asked.

"Clint shouted back, 'Hell, if I wear tails, I've got to go out and shoot a couple squirrels.' "

Whether he was entertaining the president of Dallas's First National Bank or a hunting pal from East Texas, Clint acted the same, and he always put his guests at ease.

The wife of a friend of his recalls an elegant luncheon at Preston Road. "The waiter passed acorn squash and I took a whole one, then realized I was supposed to take just a spoonful of the squash as the other guests did. I was sort of a green country girl and didn't know much about how the rich lived. But Mr. Clint was very sensitive, and when he saw what I did, and the waiter got around to him, he took a whole squash, too."

In the early forties, Clint began planning for the enormous business expansion and double-digit inflation he thought imminent at the end of World War II. Seeing the possibilities for large growth in businesses he had yet to enter, he established a complex plan to diversify his interests by selling parts of his vast oil and gas holdings and pyramiding capital gains into new investments. In his view, the political realities were that labor unions would continue to press for higher wages, which would result in inflation. Sid Richardson agreed and spoke for both men when he explained, "We are starting on a course of inflation and I'm going to borrow all the money that I can. And I'm never going to pay it back. If I do pay it back, it will be in ten-cent dollars."

Clint wanted companies with a potential for big, long-range growth, and he planned to base his judgments on advice from his employees and on trends he saw in the marketplace. In buying these new companies, he resolutely refused to depart from his strongest principle—to use other people's money. Clint devised such a happy plan when he and Robert Young's Allegheny Corporation of New York acquired control of the American Mail Line of Seattle, a profitable, well-managed steamship company with nine ships doing business in the Orient. Allegheny and Murchison paid $2.6 million for 55 percent of American Mail's stock.

In the deal, which was vintage Clint, each party put up half the purchase price and each got half the profit. Allegheny, however, loaned Murchison all the money for his interest, taking Murchison's half of the stock as collateral. Murchison assumed the management responsibility, which in this case meant he kept the present excellent management. He indemnified Allegheny against loss and guaranteed Allegheny a 4½ percent profit. The risk Murchison took by agreeing to stand any and all losses was enormous, but his confidence in his own judgment also was great.

Very patient about returns on his investments, Clint did not care when the gains came; he just wanted to be sure that when they did come in, they were great. He never took an immediate profit if he could see a larger profit years ahead. Clint bought a half dozen well-run small and medium-size Texas banks, including 100 percent of the First National Bank of Athens. Banks were well-suited for Clint's portfolio because they did not have to be closely managed. "Anyone can run a damn bank," he said.

Among the assets sold when Murchison and Wynne dissolved their partnership was the Reserve Loan Life Insurance Company of Indiana, which Clint had moved to downtown Dallas in 1936, when it was nearly bankrupt. In 1949 he sold it to Dallas's giant Southland Life Insurance Company for $5 million.

After the company sold, Clint converted the company's two-story brick building at 1201 Main Street into his corporate office. The building had at one time been a bank, with large white pillars and a large picture window at the front. Clint removed the pillars and the front window, and painted the building beige with brown trim. The only sign on the front was a small metal plate with the address, 1201 Main. Long and narrow amid many tall buildings in the mainstream of downtown Dallas, Clint's office looked more like a general merchandise store in a small Texas town than the big-city headquarters of one of America's greatest multimillionaires.

Clint did not care what it looked like. It gave him the space he needed; it already contained a large vault in the basement, and it was conveniently located just a half block from Republic National Bank. Clint took an upstairs office, created another for his secretary next to his, and one for Gerald Mann. With space to operate, he put out the word, "I need all the smart men working for me that I can find."

One of the young lieutenants hired in the mid-forties was Phil Bee, who had received a master's degree in business from Stanford University. When he hired Bee, Clint, typically, never gave him a job description. "I learned quickly that what we were doing was advising Mr. Murchison on companies we found that had strong growth potential," says Bee.

"I was utterly amazed at the kinds of deals he was involved in and how he'd gotten into them. I knew immediately that I was not going to be applying the principles of business school here."

Another associate at 1201 Main Street recalls, "Mr. Murchison put me in charge of keeping the books on all his cattle operations in Mexico. What he handed me to start with was a small shoe box, which contained all business records of the previous twenty years."

Clint did not read the earnings reports and other business material that flooded the offices at 1201 Main. If he had an idea to buy a company, he skimmed through a synopsis of its assets and liabilities, then called someone into his office to study the report in more detail and explain it briefly to him. Afire with energy and ideas, Clint explained, "If you trade in peanuts you can trade in watermelons too. We buy anything that adds up."

One of the deals he learned about that grabbed his interest was an opportunity to buy a controlling interest in the New York publishing house Henry Holt & Company. The deal had numerous attractive features, not the least of which involved his sons' futures. "There's no finer heritage I could leave my boys than a publishing business," he said. His original plan was to put together a little chain of Texas newspapers to give John Dabney as a graduation present, and he scouted around the state looking for a good buy.

Unable to find one, Clint asked his associate Don Carter to put out the word in New York that he was interested in a publishing house. When an investment trust put a 13 percent block of Henry Holt & Company common stock on the market, Carter snapped it up for Murchison.

John Dabney was soon to graduate from Yale, and a publishing career seemed even more appropriate for his son when Clint learned that the man who gave the firm his name in 1866 had done so just after graduating from Yale. But Clint never bought companies for personal or sentimental reasons unless he believed they also would be profitable. The more he studied the book publishing business, the more he believed Henry Holt & Company had strong, long-range potential as a moneymaker. Holt was a large publisher of high school and college textbooks, with potential to be even larger. He anticipated correctly that men returning from the war to finish college on the GI program would buy record numbers of new textbooks. In addition, while many economists in the mid-1940s predicted the postwar boom in baby foods, baby clothing, and suburban housing, Murchison looked even further ahead and predicted the increase in high-school textbook sales a decade in the future.

Henry Holt was the first major publicly owned company in which Clint purchased stock. Despite its aristocratic name in textbook and trade publishing, the company was not doing as well as it could. Clint thought Holt lacked a business-minded leader, and he went outside publishing circles to Wall Street in search of a new person to take over. He chose Edgar T. Rigg, then a vice president of Standard & Poor's, and in 1949 Clint persuaded Rigg to become Holt's president. After listening to Clint's predictions about increased demand for textbooks, Rigg gave the company a new direction. He began by creating a formidable organization of editors and salesmen for the textbook division, which had been badly understaffed. In addition to more manpower, Rigg gave the textbook division much more scope and money.

At the same time Rigg took over the presidency, Murchison bought more Holt common stock in the open market. Then he advanced the firm $200,000 by buying its preferred stock, becoming Holt's dominant shareholder.

The company also had a well-known and reputable trade division, which accounted for a much smaller percentage of Holt's sales. Its authors ranged from poet Robert Frost—a pillar of the firm's literary prestige since 1915—to Hollywood gossip columnist Sheilah Graham to best-selling authors United States General Albert C. Wedemeyer and Wall Street financier Bernard Baruch.

When Murchison first purchased Henry Holt in 1945, there was some fear at the company that the Texas millionaire was seeking an outlet for the kinds of right-wing political views often associated with rich Texas oilmen. Some even snickered about the irony of a man who had never finished college publishing college textbooks. But Clint did not intrude in Holt's editorial affairs—with one exception. In the late forties he became a disciple of a seventy-eight-year-old Vermont country doctor, DeForest Clinton Jarvis, and his health-restoring recipe of honey and apple-cider vinegar. Clint suggested to Rigg that Holt publish a book on the doctor's earthy remedies.

Rigg told Holt's editorial staff of the idea, but it was not enthusiastically received. However, Holt's editors reluctantly agreed to produce *Folk Medicine* in a modest edition of 5,000 copies. When the book came out, the demand was overwhelming. Holt could not print enough additional copies of *Folk Medicine* fast enough. The book sold more than a quarter of a million copies and became one of the biggest best-sellers in the company's history.

Clint received in the mail every trade book the company published, and his book collection grew rapidly, but he never once visited Holt's offices in New York. Once when Rigg needed to discuss business with Clint, he flew to Dallas and the two departed on one of Murchison's planes for a hunting trip south of the border. In Mexico, Rigg explained sales figures and decisions by Holt's board of directors, while Murchison, between shots at white wing dove and wild turkeys, merely nodded or replied, "Fine, sounds like you boys know what you're doing."

During one dove-shooting trip in 1950, Clint told Rigg that he heard *Field & Stream* magazine was for sale. Clint had been an avid reader of the magazine since his childhood and had high regard for the opinions of *Field & Stream*'s staff writers. The magazine was an industry leader with 800,000 circulation and more advertising than any other outdoor publication. Best of all, it had even greater potential for long-term growth as magazine publishing was a growing industry with hot competition for circulation. Clint asked Rigg to buy it for him. Rigg and the magazine's owner managed to agree on a price slightly above its over-the-counter $12 a share, giving Murchison control for about $950,000.

Those in New York publishing circles again were skeptical about the intent of a Texan involved in publishing. But Clint's suggestions were never more potentially dangerous—or ill-conceived—than the time he suggested *Field & Stream* make it policy to put an attractive fisherwoman on the cover. The magazine's editors politely ignored the suggestion.

As Murchison's organization grew, the number of employees at 1201 Main Street soon outgrew the office space, and many employees found themselves working out of various closet-size rooms scattered about the city. Attempting to bring more centralization to his diverse empire, for the moment, had in many ways further compartmentalized it.

Clint never paid any attention to such details as where his associates worked, how they got there, or what they wore. He cared what they had to say about a deal, whether they could find new ways to finance projects, how close they came on their cost and revenue estimates.

He never carried any money, not even pocket change. The men at 1201 Main Street, when they left home in the morning, made sure to have enough money to pay for Clint's lunch or parking meter, as well as their own, in the event they left the building with him during the day. Far more important to the millionaire wheeler-dealer was a worn rabbit's foot, which he carried with him in his pocket at all times.

Clint wanted his mind free to spin deals, leaving others to look after life's small but time-consuming details, things that nonmillionaires must tend to daily—having cash on hand, gasoline in the car. His mind did not slow down when he left the office. He continued to be preoccupied until he arrived home and often long after that. At home he had a black Cadillac limousine and chauffeur, but he always drove an old blue Chevrolet to work. One day one of his associates at work played a trick on him and put a white Oldsmobile in the parking spot where Clint kept his blue Chevrolet. The keys were in the ignition, and Clint drove the car all the way home and back to work the following day, never noticing it was not his car. Instead of buying a new car when his Chevrolet caught fire, he merely gutted the inside and put a wooden chair in the spot where the driver's seat had been.

He was a fast driver and drove at a steady speed, never slowing for potholes on the road to his farm or for other cars. His friends called him Barney Oldfield because he was always pushing ahead, holding the pedal to the floor. Clint was pulled over several times and ticketed for speeding. A friend recalls his words to the officer when he was stopped on the road to Athens from Dallas. "Better go on and give me another ticket now," he volunteered, "I'll be coming back through here in a few hours."

Clint almost never wore a suit or even a sports coat to work. He usually dressed in an open-neck, short-sleeve shirt and khakis. He rarely put on the tie he kept in a closet in his office, but he did use a necktie in place of a belt to hold up his pants, a fashion his son John Dabney later copied. If he bothered to wear socks they often did not match. Sometimes he came and left his office in shorts, sandals, and an old worn straw Panama hat. In his left hand he held a Camel nonfilter cigarette at the end of a skinny wooden holder. When people on the street pointed him out as one of the richest men in America, the response was usually an astounded, "Who? *Him?*

Those who knew of Clint's reputation before they met him in person were often shocked at his small frame and five feet six inches height. Again and again, after being introduced to the financial giant, acquaintances would later say, "I always imagined he would be so much taller."

Despite his short, stocky legs and the paunch that hung over his belt, he was an extremely graceful man. His step was so light and so smooth that at times it seemed he barely touched the ground when he walked. When he needed his secretary, he never called her into his office. Instead, he glided to his door, leaned casually against the doorjamb, weight on one leg, hand on hip, then spoke to her. Many times he startled her when he appeared in the doorway, for she had not heard him approach, even across the bare wood floor.

He always addressed her as "Mrs. Van Buren," even after she had been his secretary for twenty years, and no matter how urgent a matter, he never raised his voice to her. But he kept her so busy with dictation and answering the phone during the day that she had to come to the office at night to open and file a mountain of daily correspondence. The letters he dictated were usually no longer than a sentence, and sometimes they were only a few words long. But he sent hundreds of letters on hundreds of different subjects to hundreds of friends and business associates each week.

For the first several months that Murchison occupied 1201 Main, it was in relative anonymity. But it would not be long before businessmen and promoters began coming in off the street, hoping to make a deal, and reporters arrived seeking an interview. One of the earliest Dallasites to learn that important deals could be consummated in this nondescript building was a street bum who wandered in seeking a handout. Clint gave him a ten-dollar bill, with the result that he came back every week. The man desperately needed a bath and Clint preferred to keep his odorous new client out of his building. Typically, therefore, he struck a bargain satisfactory to both sides. When the bum needed funds, he stood outside on the sidewalk and whistled up to Clint. Moments later from the second-story window came a ten-dollar bill at the end of a long string.

9

"We'd have paid thirty thousand dollars to have had them *not* visit us."

Many days at 1201 Main Street were hectic, even frantic. Murchison and his advisers struggled sometimes for hours trying to hammer out complicated deals. On several occasions when the negotiations lasted too long and Clint grew tired, he would simply stand up in the middle of a meeting and walk to the door, with the parting words, "You boys fight it out, I'm going fishing."

Clint had a new island in the Gulf, which he thought far more spectacular than Matagorda. Much farther south and much more remote, it was located in Central Mexico's Tamiahua Bay. Shielded by a peninsula, Isla Del Toro—so named because it was in the shape of a bull's head—was nine hundred acres of treeless ranchland. Clint cleared the land of squatters and imported three hundred head of Brahma cattle, one of only a few breeds capable of withstanding the tropical heat and insects. But even though Brahma thrived on the island, efforts to haul them by barge to Tampico were often foiled by strong Gulf winds. Isla Del Toro proved to be a better fishing and duck hunting haven than a cattle operation, and Clint built a sprawling, rustic home on El Toro where he and his guests spent long, lazy weekends.

Isla Del Toro was only a very small parcel in the extensive Mexican land holdings Clint had acquired by the end of the forties. He owned some 500,000 acres spread over five separate ranches throughout central and eastern Mexico, including a 300,000-acre ranch that he owned but had never visited.

Clint first became interested in Mexico in the early forties, when American Liberty acquired a small hunting lease just a

141

few hundred miles south of the Texas border. To Clint, Mexico seemed an extension of Texas, only more pronounced in character. If Texas was vast and rugged and remote, in Clint's eye Mexico's chief attraction was that it was even more so.

On one trip south of the border Clint learned about a place called Hacienda Acuña, a group of six ranches spread over approximately 75,000 acres in Mexico's Sierra Madre Range. The ranches, named for the Acuña family who had once owned the land, were located in the eastern region of Mexico in the state of Tamaulipas, ninety miles from modern civilization. Clint was warned that Acuña was isolated and nearly impossible to get to, but he was determined to see it.

Leaving Virginia behind in Tampico, he took a train to the little town of Gonzales, where he borrowed a car. He drove as far as he could, until the road stopped some twelve miles from the center of Acuña. Clint convinced a local farmer to take him the rest of the way through the mountains by ox cart. Along the way the cart broke down, and Clint and the farmer made the last six miles of the trip on burros.

When he arrived at the Corazón de Acuña—named for the heart-shaped rock formation in the bed of a nearby waterfall—he was astounded at the beauty of the area. Spanish moss hung from the trees, orchids were in full bloom, and seas of wildflowers growing out of huge rocks waved in the gentle wind. The land was virgin and budding with new life, while, at the same time, ancient, an untouched relic of another century, another world. This was headquarters for all of the Acuña ranches, and a few small huts that housed the Mexican cowboys and their families were scattered about. The old homestead, with its roof torn off and walls crumbling, was now a century-old Spanish ruin.

The primitive beauty of this subtropical area far exceeded Clint's expectations. When he returned to Tampico, he told Virginia, "I have found the paradise of the world."

In the forties in Mexico land titles were acquired with great ease. There was a common saying that, "If you owned a map to the land and said the land was yours, you owned it." Clint got a map to Hacienda Acuña's 75,000 acres, then with $10,000 acquired a two-year option on the land. The option was contingent on his ability to have a road built from Gonzales to the center of the ranch within two years.

With the help of a local rancher who led the way, Clint and Virginia traveled into the mountains to pick the site where they would build a magnificent home. "We made the trip on horseback, and it took eight hours," recalled Virginia, "and we only stopped once on the way to shoot a wild turkey for our dinner. We cooked it on coals buried three feet in the ground. We slept that night in sleeping bags on the hard stone floor of the old homestead. There was no roof, and the moon was so bright it lit up the mountains, and we could see the Acuña ranches in all directions. This was where we built our home."

The climate at 3,000 feet was ideal, warm during the day but cool at night. But not everything was idyllic about that first trip. "When we got back to the hotel room in Tampico," said Virginia, "I took off my shirt and noticed my back was covered with ticks." She also noticed that a suitcase full of her jewelry was missing from the closet of their hotel room. Among other jewels, the suitcase had contained her engagement ring and, in the descriptive words of a fellow Texan, "a necklace of cabochon emeralds the size of hen eggs." Despite the help of a former FBI agent and various Mexican policemen, the jewels were never recovered.

What attracted Clint most to Mexico was what attracted him to the oil business and to so many of the companies he acquired: its potential. In Mexico he saw tremendous opportunity to develop the land, the agriculture, the abundant minerals, and he could do it with a large supply of cheap labor. The people wanted to work, and the resources were there. The paradise he talked about was more than simply a beautiful location. It was a world that offered endless opportunity.

Clint wanted to house and educate the Mexicans who were living on the land, and he immediately put them to work. He built houses with running water, and he built a school and brought a teacher from Gonzales, to teach both the adults and children basic English and math.

Clint put the Mexicans to work tending a few thousand head of cattle he imported from other parts of Mexico, and clearing the land for the big ranch house and a nearby landing strip. He had earlier bought a DC-3, the *dernier cri* of thirties aircraft, and named it the *Flying Ginny.* Clint never called his wife Ginny, but it had a better ring to it than the *Flying Virginia.*

"The plane was supposed to hold thirty, but by the time Clint got finished fixin' it up with bars and card tables, it held only sixteen passengers," a friend recalls. "So he went out and bought two more planes to follow the DC-3 when he took big parties to the ranch."

Even with access by air from Tampico, Mexico, and Brownsville, Texas, Clint was determined to build the house importing as few materials as possible. He began by bringing carpenters, tilemakers, brickmasons, and stonecutters to the ranch.

The foundation and walls of the new home were laid with rock chiseled by hand out of Acuña's mountains. Walnut, cedar, and pine trees were felled, and sawmills were constructed to dress the wood for beams and flooring, doors and shutters. Carpenters' shops were built, and the Mexicans were put to work constructing furniture and cabinets to fill the house. Virginia went to New York and searched for a place to buy yards of leather with which to cover the chairs, but was politely informed that genuine cowhide was not sold by the yard. Returning to Acuña, she had the Mexicans gather skins from the ranch, and she personally bolted pieces of leather onto Acuña-made chairs.

While the main house was being built, Clint and Virginia took friends to Acuña, where they slept in an old, crumbling adobe house with a thatched roof. Guests were politely shown the one-stall outhouse some twenty yards away, an amenity unappreciated by some. Clint's close friend Wofford Cain hated roughing it, and on his first night at Acuña he woke everyone else as he cursed his way to the outhouse. Wofford had become a millionaire with Clint's help, and one of his favorite self-indulgences was shopping at Sulka, the international haberdashery. That night at the ranch, Wofford was wearing monogrammed Sulka green silk pajamas with a matching robe and matching green suede slippers. As he gingerly made his way to the outhouse, he used one hand to keep his long robe from dragging in the dirt, and in the other he held a cigar. When he reached the outhouse, he took a long drag on the cigar, opened the door, and blew in a cloud of smoke before entering.

"Goddamit, Clint," Wofford shouted at breakfast a few hours later, "this is the first and last time I'm coming down here until you get indoor plumbing!"

No indoor plumbing also meant that these Texas millionaires and their wives who were draped in jewels from Neiman-Marcus, and who by now were quite accustomed to the luxuries of the very rich, each day rode horses to the foot of a natural waterfall a few miles from the house where they bathed in ice-cold water.

The architect of the main house was the same man who had built many of the Spanish-style mansions in Dallas and had gained local fame as the architect of Highland Park Village, one of the first shopping centers in America. The sprawling twenty-room home was built in the shape of a horseshoe whose galleried central courtyard was built around a large barbecue. The porch, which circled the courtyard under a low-hung red-tile roof, was furnished with handmade rocking chairs and benches. Climbing roses and bougainvillea covered the pillars that supported the roof.

Clint and Virginia went to Spain to buy furnishings that could not be built on the ranch—lamps made from old cathedral candlesticks, porcelain, pottery, and fourteenth-century Spanish desks and consoles. Skins of ocelots and mountain lions shot on the ranch were thrown over the cool red-tile floors of the house. Heavy velvet curtains with tassles and fringe draped the home's large windows, and bleached white skulls of Texas longhorn cattle decorated the walls. The home was both rustic and elegant.

A few small houses were built around the main building to accommodate the large staff of cooks, maids, gardeners, hunting and fishing guides, the butler and chauffeur, and full-time pilots. Another dozen small buildings some three hundred yards away housed the permanent Mexican residents who worked the cattle operation.

"It sounds presumptious, but what I've created here gives

me a feeling of achievement," Clint confided to a friend. "I feel I've really got me a place."

Not content just to raise steers and cows to fatten and sell, Clint also brought in dairy cows from Wisconsin and started a cheese factory on the ranch. Also eager to diversify his holdings in Central America, he bought a silver flatware factory in Mexico and built a meat-packing plant in Costa Rica.

Clint quickly increased his Acuña land holdings from 75,000 acres to 125,000 when he bought adjoining ranches. By the late forties he had 10,000 head of cattle on his Acuña ranch and his various other ranches in Texas and Mexico. Typical Texas hyperbole put his herd at ten times, sometimes fifty times that number, but when he was regularly asked by curious New York bankers how many cattle were in his herd, he invariably answered either "not enough" or "hard to tell." His Eastern friends did not realize that asking a man the size of his herd was as vulgar as asking how much money he had.

Clint built Acuña to get away from his everyday business at 1201 Main Street, but he also used it as an important business tool. Whether it was the chairman of a company he wanted to buy or the president of a New York bank where he wanted credit, he invited the very biggest fish he was angling for to enjoy the luxury of Acuña and to get to know him, and vice versa, in the way he had always thought was the most important—while hunting, fishing, drinking.

New York Central Railroad chairman Robert Young was a frequent guest at the ranch, and in the fall of 1949 he called Clint from New York. "I told the Duke and Duchess of Windsor about Acuña and that it would be a most unusual place for them to visit when they're here this spring."

"Great, I'll have the *Flying Ginny* pick them up in New York," Clint shot back excitedly.

"Uh, that might be a problem," answered Young. "Wally doesn't fly."

While alternate travel plans were studied, a more pressing concern was the completion date on the house. With several rooms still unfinished, the timetable for construction was moved up by several months to prepare for the royal visit. Immediately after the Christmas holidays, word leaked to the press that plans were in the works for the Windsors to visit Acuña and El Toro. Suddenly society columns from New York to Mexico were filled with speculation about the event. When the news of the visit was confirmed in late January, newspapers described in detail preparations for the ten-day visit. The *Dallas Morning News* ran photographs and even a half-page reproduction of the blueprints to Acuña's magnificent ranch house. The papers explained that the Windsors would make the journey from Palm Beach to the ranch aboard Robert Young's private railroad car. Young was a powerful figure in New York and throughout the country, and the notion that the royal couple planned to travel to the wilderness of central Mexico aboard Young's private car made the trip seem all the more exotic and glamorous.

Invited to accompany the Windsors and Robert and Anita Young were Charles Cushing of the Boston Cushings and Edith Baker, a member of New York's old guard and widow of George Baker, a major stockholder in New York's First National Bank, and one other Dallas couple. Naturally, all of Dallas society hoped for an invitation, but the guest list was limited to twelve.

Carrie Neiman, of Neiman-Marcus, had read the news with interest, and had just the right suggestions for Virginia in readying Acuña for the visit. In her late sixties, Mrs. Neiman was a tall, regal-looking woman, and she was unquestionably Dallas's leading arbiter of style. "It would be nice if you had some linen hand towels with the duke and duchess's monogram and their crest," Carrie said. Service being what it was at Neiman-Marcus in the 1950s, the personalized hand-embroidered towels were ready within three days.

In late January Virginia left for Mexico, where she spent several afternoons with the staff rehearsing how to serve tea. She tried to teach her Mexican help every detail of the English custom—from making delicate watercress sandwiches to pouring the tea—most of which they quickly mastered. More difficult was teaching them even the simplest English words. Despite Virginia's efforts, José the butler and most of the other servants insisted on calling the duke *El Rey* (the king) and the duchess *La Reina* (the queen).

Although it probably amused the former Edward VIII, it doubtless delighted Wally, who fought and pleaded all her life to get a grander title than merely "duchess." What she yearned for but her brother-in-law and niece refused her was "Her Royal Highness."

During the early afternoon of February 4, word came to the ranch that the royal entourage had reached Gonzales, the closest town, which was thirty miles away. With no telephone or even a short-wave radio at the hacienda, Clint established his own means of communication with the outside world. A Murchison plane from Gonzales buzzed over the house at Acuña, and the staff watched for a stream of toilet tissue to fall from the plane. They followed the streamer until it landed, then picked up the cardboard roll and found the note inside. It read, "They've arrived in Gonzales." Although the distance to the ranch was only thirty miles, the terrain was so rugged that the trip took nearly four hours.

The group of six had traveled for three days by train from Palm Beach to Tampico, Mexico, to Gonzales. They looked exhausted when they were met at the train station by the Murchison staff, most of whom were Mexican and spoke no English. But Edward spoke fluent Spanish and did so at a rapid pace almost the entire way to the homestead. The drive up the mountains in a caravan of station wagons was more difficult than the entire rest of the trip had been. The path carved out of rugged terrain could hardly be called a road; it was just barely passable at points. When they arrived at the house, they were physically sore from being jolted and jostled each foot of the way.

Guests had always arrived at Acuña by private plane. But if Bob Young and the others were discomforted by the train trip, they were too polite to show it in front of the duchess who was terrified of flying. When Edward was governor of the Bahamas during World War II, and he and Wallis took the regular shuttle to Miami, passengers dreaded seeing her board the plane. Each flight, she insisted on being blindfolded and forbade the other passengers to smoke, fearing that the plane would catch fire.

It was a good thing Clint sent a cattle truck to bring the luggage from the train to the ranch house. The party arrived with some 150 pieces of luggage, 104 of which belonged to the duchess. Twenty of the duchess's pieces were enormous steamer trunks, and the contents of all her luggage were carefully indexed.

After greeting her host and hostess, Wallis went directly to freshen up. Moments later she opened the window of her guest bathroom, which looked onto a courtyard where the rest of the party was gathered. "They're marvelous," she shouted, waving one of the crested towels out the window. Virginia was surprised when Wallis took all twelve towels home with her.

The Duke of Windsor once remarked about his ability to get along with his wife. "It helps in a pinch to be able to remind your bride that you gave up the throne for her." Despite his sacrifice, the duchess always had the upper hand.

She was excessively overprotective of her husband and seemed to watch his every move, snapping at him for this, or scolding him for that. Toward his wife, he was like an obedient child. Virginia recalls taking a box of chocolate-covered creams to the ranch for the royal visit.

"After dinner we were all still at the table when the duchess spotted the duke reaching for a chocolate. Just as he was lifting one from the dish, she screeched, 'Daaaviiiiiid!' He dropped it instantly and no more was said.

"After a few days at the ranch, the duchess wanted her hair done. We tried to explain there was no one in Mexico to do it, but she was determined to have it done, so we sent our plane over to Tampico to pick up a hairdresser. The woman did a terrible job with her hair. I tried to warn her, but she didn't listen. Another time she wanted hairpins. I gave her some of my bobby pins, but she insisted they were wrong and wouldn't do what her hairpins could do.

"The duchess's maid was with her all the time, but she was not very helpful, so Wallis would ask our help for things. One morning Jewel came rushing to me and said, 'Mrs. Murchison, the duchess is hollering for some ink.' "

While Wally was often demanding to the point of difficult, she was also, on at least one occasion, very helpful. Late one night the furnace blew out and the house became quite cold.

As the rest of the house party stood in the living room, the duchess climbed into the furnace room, found the pilot light, and relit it.

The guests hunted mountain lions and jaguars and shot various game birds, including wild turkey, blue rock pigeons, quail, chachalaca (Mexican pheasant) and paloma blanca (white wing dove), a Mexican favorite. Known among Texans as the "Cadillac of hunting," white wing dove hunting was also one of Big Clint's favorites.

The Murchisons' white wing dove parties launched from Acuña on the *Flying Ginny* and flew to one of several of Clint's ranches in Mexico. When the plane came to a stop, the hunters climbed out and Clint stationed them at various points on or near the dirt runway, which was usually the only place on the ranch clear of brush and trees. Each guest was assigned one Mexican boy to collect the fallen birds, while Clint took three or four helpers for himself. If their host seemed greedy, first-time guests quickly learned the reason why.

Clint was a snap shooter and an excellent shot. When the boys around him shouted, "Paloma!" he looked to see where they were pointing, then, holding a .410 shotgun in his left hand, he fired, cocked, and fired again. Most of the time two birds fell with his two shots. The Mexican boys never stopped running, retrieving the birds as fast as he shot them. To the astonishment of newcomers, he always returned to the plane with four or five sacks of birds, four or five times as many as anyone else.

The Windsors loved watching Clint hunt, and for many years afterward talked about the fun they had shooting white wing dove. But nothing thrilled the duke more than the two turkeys he shot. "He wanted his picture taken with those turkeys from every angle imaginable," recalls Virginia.

Moving the party from Acuña to El Toro island was a tremendous ordeal. Wally had her maid, Edward had his valet, and the Murchison staff numbered more than twenty. Nevertheless, the move took a full day, and again the guests were worn out when they arrived at El Toro. During the trip Clint never let out of his reach a small black alligator suitcase. When they docked at the island, Virginia and Edith Baker watched

Clint climb out of the boat still clutching the case. They finally whispered, "What's in that suitcase?"

"Wally's jewels," he replied.

"My God!" both gasped. "Why didn't you tell us sooner? We could have picked the lock."

Each day the group split up and set out from the island in various fishing boats. Once, at the end of a long day of fishing, the battery went dead on the boat carrying Young, Edith Baker, and the duke. Back at the house, Virginia held dinner and Clint sent out a larger boat to look for the missing guests. The duchess, Clint, and the rest of the group nervously paced the floor until five o'clock in the morning, when the missing threesome finally came through the door.

Edith was a great sportswoman and said she was never frightened during the time they were stranded in the bay. She was, however, quite embarrassed when she needed to use the toilet on the boat. The duke drank very heavily away from Wallis's critical eye, and before midnight he passed out on the floor blocking the door to the toilet. Edith explained to Virginia later, "What do you say to the man who was once the king of England when you have to use the rest room and he's lying in front of the door passed out on the floor? I finally just stepped over him into the bathroom."

"I really rather enjoyed myself, you know," the duke reportedly said upon his return. "Very relaxing, a dead motor."

Sid Richardson found the idea of his boyhood pal playing host to the Windsors a fairly amusing one, and for a long time afterward he kidded Clint for having several suits made for the occasion. The story was later embellished by Texans who claimed Clint bought a completely new wardrobe for the visit.

There was endless gossip about the Windsor visit, some of it true but much of it false. There was no truth to the rumor that the Murchisons paid the duke and duchess $30,000 to visit them in Mexico. When Virginia told Clint that this was being said behind their backs, he retorted, "We'd have paid thirty thousand to have had them *not* visit us."

But the duke seemed truly to enjoy the visit. Several months later at a party at Mary Sanford's home in Palm Beach, Virginia was seated on Edward's right when he leaned over and whispered in her ear, "I had the best time I've had in my life at your ranch. I'd come again if only I could get the duchess to fly."

Ironically, at the same time that Murchison was diversifying his investments, he embarked on what would become his biggest oil and gas venture. Although he retained a large stock position in the Southern Union Gas Company, he was increasingly disgruntled with the government regulation imposed on the company by the Public Utility Holding Company Act. The fixed profit ceiling, as well as reduced speculative possibilities, cramped Murchison's wheeling and dealing style. Because Southern Union was chiefly involved in the distribution of oil and gas, rather than exploration, it operated in the conservative manner of a utility.

But Clint was attracted by one of Southern Union's subsidiary companies, Delhi Oil, whose chief objective was exploration. In 1948 he convinced Southern Union to spin off to its stockholders shares of Delhi, and Murchison became Delhi's largest stockholder.

Delhi played a significant role in Murchison's business career, not only because it was hugely successful but also because with Delhi he departed from many of his previous business practices. When he organized the company, he offered each of its five executives the chance to buy stock at 10 cents a share. They saw a great opportunity, and when the company later went public, their stock sold for $10 a share, one hundred times what they had invested. Clint, in only a few years, had made millionaires of the five executives—an accountant, a manager, a geologist, a pipeline specialist, and a petroleum engineer. This method of making his associates rich became a Murchison trademark.

"If you've got a good man working for you, make certain he dies rich," was the way Clint explained his impetus for sharing the pie. He felt that his employees would do a better job if they had a financial interest in their operations, and he encouraged his associates to borrow money to buy stocks in his companies.

"If you tried hard and produced for the company, Clint wanted to make you a millionaire," recalled Frank Schultz, chief geologist and 5 percent stockholder of Delhi. "There were more than fifty people in Dallas for whom Clint made fortunes of between one million and thirty million."

Clint became chairman of Delhi. It was the only public company in which he took a title and played an active role in devising long-range plans and strategy.

Delhi's offices were located in a run-down two-story building a few streets from 1201 Main Street. The first floor belonged to the Gossard Corset Company, whose motto was, "We live off the fat of the land," and the second story had previously been a coffin warehouse. Ignoring what it lacked architecturally, Clint got a good deal on the lease and snapped it up. In 1950 Delhi was a tiny company, as were most independent oil companies, with only eight employees, including the secretary. Murchison came by very infrequently, and when he did, he usually slipped in through the back door to avoid seeing anyone. Even in such a small operation, four or five of Delhi's employees had never met the company's founder and chief stockholder.

Not long after Delhi was getting started, Clint was on his way to work when he approached a young man on the road whose car had broken down. Clint offered a lift to the man, who explained that he worked for Delhi Oil. "I'm a personal adviser to Clint Murchison who owns it," he said. Clint said nothing, and the two politely parted ways when Clint dropped him off at Delhi's office downtown. A few months later, at a large meeting of Delhi's shareholders, Clint, seated center stage on the dais, waved to the young man in the audience.

Under Murchison, Delhi began aggressively searching for oil and natural gas and building pipelines throughout the Southwest and Rocky Mountains. "If a good drilling or pipeline deal comes in, grab it," Clint told his men at Delhi. Clint's geologists knew East Texas and West Texas, and could have multiplied Delhi's riches without ever straying from those fields. But because he loved the gamble and the risk of the oil business even more than its profits, he sent his geologists and drilling crews farther and farther from the Eden of Texas oil— into Mississippi, Louisiana, Arkansas, New Mexico, Oklahoma, Wyoming, and Colorado.

Between 1950 and 1953 he put some $25 million into exploration, an astoundingly high figure for a company as new and small as Delhi. But Murchison could move from field to field—spending $5 million on exploration in each place—and not feel overextended. "So long as you add value," he explained, "debt is sound."

Delhi's huge gas reserves in the ground were worth little if there was no market. But it was never very long before a market developed for the gas, which was then worth millions. Murchison's sale of his reserves in the Barker Dome field marked a financial breakthrough in the petroleum industry, as well as a personal triumph.

Southern Union had paid $40,000 in 1930 for a lease on what was to become the Barker Dome field. Twelve years later the first producing well came in. Sixteen others quickly followed, and estimates were that the field had a trillion feet of natural gas. Delhi, as an offshoot of Southern Union, had a large stake in the field, which straddles the New Mexico and Colorado border, east of the Arizona and Utah line. Murchison approached the El Paso Natural Gas company with an offer to sell them his gas. El Paso had a contract to build a gas pipeline to supply southern California, and another to service northern California. El Paso found itself in need of much more gas.

El Paso offered to buy Delhi gas for 5 cents per thousand cubic feet (mcf). Murchison's original thought was to sell El Paso 12-cent gas and to join it in ownership of the new pipeline. But under Federal Power Commission rules, if Delhi took a piece of the pipeline it would become a regulated public utility restricted to a 6 percent return. Further, since Delhi's gas sales to the pipeline would not be considered arm's-length transactions, the FPC would regulate the wellhead price. Wanting no part of government regulation, Murchison dropped the idea to join in ownership of the pipeline.

After two years of negotiations, in 1950 Delhi and El Paso reached an agreement. Instead of selling Barker Dome gas to El Paso, Delhi sold its leases to El Paso for $3 million. In addition, Delhi retained an overriding royalty graduating from 5 cents to 7 cents or more on all gas produced from the field. El Paso assumed all drilling and operating costs.

Clint brilliantly maneuvered the deal to his satisfaction. As a royalty holder rather than a seller of gas, Delhi was removed from regulation as a public utility in interstate commerce. The sales price plus the royalties brought the revenue from Barker Dome gas to his original asking price of 12 cents per mcf. In short, he got his price with no interference from the Federal Power Commission.

Two years later Murchison made a second arrangement with El Paso that made him even richer. He sold Delhi's 100,000 acres of leases in the Blanco–La Plata area of the San Juan Basin—a result of Delhi exploration in the forties—and again kept an overriding royalty. The two deals together were estimated to bring Delhi $100 million.

Clint pyramided his gains, paying no stockholder dividends, but, instead, plowing profits back into Delhi. At the same time he negotiated the Barker Dome deal, he spent $5 million finding a trillion feet of natural gas in the western Canadian province of Alberta. Again, he had huge reserves but no market.

The energy boom in Canada began in force in 1947 when a large pool of oil was discovered south of Edmonton. With the oil there was a tremendous supply of natural gas. Most of the companies operating in the area viewed gas as a nuisance. They ignored it, capped the wells, and moved on looking for oil.

Clint did the opposite. He formed Canadian Delhi, which became the first company in Canada to explore for natural gas rather than oil. Other oil companies who were operating around his wells saw little use for what Clint was doing. There was no local market for the gas, nor any potential market within two thousand miles. But Clint was already devising a plan to pipe the gas from Alberta.

There were a few other groups of oilmen, both Canadian and American, who also were talking of exporting Alberta gas. Most of the promoters thought the most obvious market was the West Coast, which was the last major industrial area of the United States without an adequate supply of gas for its growing markets. In 1948 Alberta had appointed a commission to establish ground rules under which oil and gas could be exported from the province. The next year Alberta's government-appointed Conservation Board began to hear export applications from promoters, whereupon the export issue took its first step toward becoming one of the most hotly debated in Canadian history. The crux of the problem at this early stage was the question of whether there were enough reserves to take care of the future needs of Albertans.

From the beginning most Albertans who lived in towns and villages were able to count on an abundant supply of very cheap fuel. "Though they lived in one of the coldest winter climates in the world, a farm family could expect to heat their homes and their water, do their cooking and keep their barn warm for about sixty dollars a year. In districts where a major gas line was close, farmers were in the habit of simply going over to the gas line and hooking it in to their barn. The vast cavern of natural gas beneath the farm or the thousands of cubic feet running by in a pipe was part of the everyday life and folklore of Alberta."

Alberta was slow to allow its gas to be exported, and the issue quickly became a national one. Murchison had a clear understanding of the Canadian political climate and became the first person to propose building an all-Canadian pipeline across the country. It would be the longest in the world—stretching some 2,000 miles from energy-rich Alberta across the massive Canadian Shield in northern Ontario to the commercial cities of Toronto and Montreal.

When Murchison delivered his plan to the Canadian government, there were already five major promoters who had applied for a permit to export Alberta gas to different regions of the United States. But while the other promoters' schemes seemed to exploit Alberta's resources exclusively for their own financial gain, Murchison's plan had touched a patriotic nerve. Immediately, the idea of an all-Canadian natural gas pipeline became associated with the precedent of the Canadian Pacific Railway.

Still, although they liked the idea, most Canadians did not believe it would work. The major obstacle seemed to be the gigantic Laurentian Shield, the world's most ancient rock, the breadth of which had through history defied Canadians to make a single country of east and west. For the modern-age pipeline, the Shield's wilderness was the most threatening territory in the world. Composed of myriad lakes, swamps, bogs, and solid rock, it seemed an impossible barrier to cross. Many observers openly scoffed at Murchison's plan to build a pipeline across the forbidding Shield, calling it, "a pipe dream, not a pipeline."

But there was one man willing from the start to consider seriously Murchison's plan. His name was Clarence Decatur Howe, Canada's Minister of Trade and Finance, and he had become one of the country's most important and influential political figures. Although dubious about the pipeline's feasibility, Howe was interested in Murchison's idea. On their first meeting to discuss the pipeline plan, Howe got to the point. "Mr. Murchison, have you ever traveled over the Canadian Shield? I come from there. It is a little more rugged and a lot colder than Texas."

Murchison, undaunted, explained to Howe that the severe climate would be no problem, and because dry gas is not affected by cold, the pipeline could be laid above ground. He described his experience laying a 150-mile pipeline across the Continental Divide, from New Mexico's San Juan Basin on the Pacific slope to Santa Fe and Albuquerque on the Atlantic side.

From the start it was obvious to Howe that Clint had more than just a monetary interest in the project. He talked with a passion about the thrill he experienced each time he delivered energy to an area where there had been none before. From his days in West Texas, where he first built a pipeline from Wink to the tiny nearby commercial centers, he viewed pipelines as a measure of progress, a step into the future. For Murchison, the sense of personal accomplishment was enormous.

Howe found Clint's enthusiasm contagious, and the two men took an immediate liking to one another. They had met briefly once before, at the formal opening of New York's La Guardia Field in 1939, when Murchison was a director of

American Airlines, and Howe was Canada's Minister of Transport. Howe had been a guest at Acuña in the forties.

But Howe was also much closer to the group of Canadians who formed Western Pipe Lines Ltd. and were Murchison's chief rival for a pipeline permit. Western's scheme was to export Alberta gas to the United States.

Murchison knew that his best chance for getting a license to build the line was to show that the line should not leave Canada. "You Canadians don't know the value of gas," he told the government Conservation Board. "When you do, you won't want to be on the far end of a line from Texas."

In 1951 Murchison formed Trans-Canada Pipe Lines, a subsidiary of Canadian Delhi, and became a fierce competitor of Western Pipe Lines. Although Western had as its sponsors three of the largest investment firms of Toronto, Montreal, and Winnipeg, by 1953 Trans-Canada had spent more than twice as much as Western in feasibility studies on potential markets, on the costs of construction and buying right-of-way. Hundreds of miles of the route through northern Ontario were sparsely populated. The Trans-Canada Highway, which the pipeline would follow, was just a dirt or gravel road in places, and access roads to the pipeline from the highway would have to be cut out of rugged terrain.

The project took a major step forward in 1954, when Howe proposed that Western and Trans-Canada merge, and the two groups agreed. The resulting company, Trans-Canada Pipe Lines, received a permit to build a privately financed pipeline proposed by Murchison across the Laurentian Shield.

The shotgun marriage solved only one of many problems, for the new company faced enormous hurdles in financing the project which had a projected cost of between $150 million and $200 million. Further, there were problems finding a steel mill with a capacity to manufacture some 2,000 miles of pipe, and willing to commit itself to make that much pipe for an unproven and highly risky project.

By 1955 Clint had spent $10 million shoring up reserves for the pipeline which was not even in its construction stage. At the same time, a strong anti-pipeline sentiment began to emerge. Stories about Murchison filled the Canadian newspapers, in which he was almost invariably described as "the richest Texas oilman and one of the richest of American capitalists." He came to be viewed by Canadians as a money-grubbing American out to exploit the natural resources of Canada.

Cartoons in Canadian newspapers depicted Murchison in the typical Texas oilman caricature—with a loud tie, a ten-gallon hat, and always smoking a large cigar lighted with crisp green banknotes.

The criticism bothered Clint enormously, and in the spring of 1955 he wrote a long and impassioned letter to Howe explaining that making money was not his chief purpose in this enterprise and pointing out in detail how very little he stood to make financially. He viewed this giant undertaking as the capstone of his career, a final monument to his business acumen and courage, before he retired.

But Clint became so disgruntled with bureaucratic delays that by the late fifties he turned all responsibility over to Frank Schultz, Delhi's chief geologist. "We went through seven years of hearings to get a permit, then a terrible expense proving we had enough gas reserves to keep [the pipeline] operating," recalls Schultz. "Clint hated the red tape. All of this began to wear so thin on him that he wouldn't go to Canada."

Despite efforts to do otherwise, Trans-Canada finally had to turn to the government for financial assistance, and construction began in the late fifties. The actual building of the pipeline, however, was anticlimactic for Clint, who had turned his attention elsewhere. The company—of which Canadian Delhi owned about 10 percent—turned a profit in 1961, and four years later Clint sold his stock to a Canadian firm.

Clint later looked back on the pipeline with enormous pride completely disproportionate to his economic gain. While Murchison's financial reward was small, relative to the effort involved, he had never before felt such a profound sense of personal accomplishment. When completed at a cost of $200 million, Trans-Canada Pipe Lines became the longest natural gas pipeline in the world. The company that Clint started with a few gas reserves scattered around Alberta is today a $4-billion-a-year firm with pipelines throughout Canada and the United

States. It is the second largest carrier of natural gas in the world.

After John Dabney graduated from Yale, he and Lupe moved back to Dallas, but only briefly. Clint Sr. was worried about his elder son's health. John Dabney's asthma was worse than ever, and he was still exhausted and nervous. One weekend when John and some friends were hunting at El Toro, Clint brought a doctor from the Mayo Clinic to the island to observe John in a normal, relaxed setting without John's knowing the real purpose of the doctor's visit. The doctor, whom Clint introduced as a hunting buddy, managed to stay near John most of the weekend, after which he told Clint, "John seems to be over the nervousness, but it's his asthma I'm worried about." The doctor said it was important for John to be in a dry climate until his health improved.

Clint Sr. immediately put John and Lupe on a plane to Santa Fe, New Mexico. "You can come back when you feel better," Clint Sr. said. "Besides, it's good for a young couple to start out on their own, not too close to their parents."

Soon after John and Lupe settled into their adobe house in New Mexico, John took a job with the First National Bank of Santa Fe. The bank was small and stuffy, and John, soft-spoken and casually dressed, did not look like the Yale-educated son of one of Texas's biggest millionaires. But in this role John began a financial career in exactly the same position his father once had—as a teller.

John and Lupe loved the relaxed, slow pace of Santa Fe and would remember it as the happiest time in their lives. During their eighteen-month stay they returned to Dallas only once—for the birth of their first child. The boy, born in the spring of 1948, was named John Dabney Murchison Jr. He was called Dabney.

"Not long after the baby was born, Pop and Virginia came out to visit us in Santa Fe," says Lupe. "We lived in a little house, and up on the hill behind our house was a pig farmer. There were pigs all over the hillside. When we greeted John's dad, I was wearing a Mexican dress and carrying the baby in a straw basket. John was wearing a Mexican shirt and sandals.

We were very happy, but Pop and Virginia took one look at us and the house and said, 'You're packing right now and coming back to Dallas immediately.' "

Boston was as suited for Clint Jr.'s temperament as Santa Fe was for John's. In and around Boston, Clint Jr. frequented a milieu of intellectuals from Harvard, MIT, and Wellesley. Even in this environment Clint Jr. was viewed as a scientific genius and an eccentric. He loved to spend an evening at the home of a professor, or a fellow graduate student, where the conversation about mathematical or scientific theory lasted well into the morning hours. On such evenings Clint would not say a social word, but on the subject of math and science he talked at great length. He was a voracious reader of dozens of technical journals, and, given the chance, he could explain the latest theories he had read, explanations so complex in their detail that the hosts and other guests were astounded and often baffled.

Jane went along with what Clint wanted, but she was not at all comfortable in this setting. She had attended the University of Texas for two years, and SMU her junior year, but when she and Clint married, she dropped out of school a year short of graduating. "When Clint was getting his master's degree and trying to decide on a career," Jane remembers, "I said to him, 'If teaching is what you want, then please let me know, and I'll go back and get a degree. I can't be walking around here with no brains.' "

Clint Jr. was trying to decide whether to become a math teacher or an engineer. But he was never forced to make up his mind. His father made it up for him near the end of 1949, when he sent a letter to Boston that said little more than, "Dear Clint W., Come on home. Love, Dad."

Shortly after Clint returned to Dallas to work, Clint Sr. received a letter in the mail from the MIT professor with whom Clint Jr. lived as an undergraduate. The professor told Murchison that it was a great loss to science that his son Clint had gone into business.

Since 1942 Clint Sr. had been telling his sons about the companies he was acquiring in their names. But not until Clint Jr. and John Dabney returned to Dallas did they realize the extent of their worth and their responsibilities. They found themselves in control of a complex private partnership, Murchison Brothers, containing stock (usually a majority interest) in some twenty companies throughout the country.

Clint Sr. instructed his sons to use the partnership as a base to build on. "Have at it," he told them, and his sons listened. When they entered the business world, both still in their twenties, they had the confidence to surge forward, making mistakes along the way, but quickly commanding respect locally and soon nationally as well.

PART
TWO

10

"We've got vice and versa."

When the boys arrived at 1201 Main in 1949, they shared some similarities. Both had both been educated in Eastern prep schools and Ivy League colleges. Both married Texas girls, and each had two young children. Together, they had come home to work.

But the two brothers had grown apart during their years away at school and the war. John, who was twenty-eight in 1949, enrolled at Hotchkiss when he was sixteen and had been away from Dallas for twelve years. The camaraderie or closeness the brothers felt in the odd, isolated, all-male household in which they grew up had almost disappeared. Their personalities, which were never very similar, became markedly more different when they started in business. Clint Jr. was even more shy and more introverted than he had been before. He was abrupt to the point of being impolite.

John Dabney, on the other hand, while still far from gregarious, was warm, kind, and pleasant. Clint Jr. hated social events and spent most of his time in the office making deals, and when he was away from the office, in an endless series of adulterous affairs. John, with Lupe's help, became involved in Dallas society and charities, and in travel.

Despite their personality differences, from the very start in business, the brothers were a team. Everything they owned, they owned equally, right down to the last million. Their father had seen to that, and Clint Jr. and John planned to continue the practice. In the beginning and throughout most of their lives, their investments were made through Murchison

Brothers. In typical Murchison fashion, the partnership had no written agreement.

To help his sons manage their investments and find new ones, Clint Sr. hired James H. Clark, who was from an old-line investment analysis firm in Chicago and who had earlier handled the refinancing and reorganization of Clint's Southern Union Gas Company. Clint Sr. was impressed with Clark's analytical mind and his disciplined, businesslike approach. Prior to World War II, Clark had worked on Wall Street, and after the war he joined the Chicago firm of Duff & Phelps, where he quickly climbed to the position of senior partner. His future in Chicago looked bright, but he wanted to be more than just successful. He wanted to be very rich. When Clark was at Washington and Lee, his father had died and there was not enough money for him to finish college. From that point forward, he was deathly afraid of being poor. When he read about Murchison's voracious appetite for making money, he saw a chance to make millions and to be safe from ever again being in need.

Ironically, when Clark was thinking about coming to Dallas, his associates warned him, "You're not going to Texas and get in with that wheeler-dealer, are you? You could end up broke."

Clark arrived in 1950 and immediately began to demonstrate his analytical skills. He was given the role of chief of staff, in charge of advising the brothers on their investments. In effect he was also reviewing Clint Sr.'s investments, most of which now were in the name of Murchison Brothers. But Clark's orderly supervision of the sons' investments was often disrupted by Clint Sr. The boss repeatedly undercut Clark, buying and selling companies for the boys or himself without consulting Clark beforehand or informing him later. When Clark objected, Clint Sr. tried to exercise more restraint, but it was difficult. Murchison was a pragmatist, but he also had an uncanny imagination and a supple, far-reaching mind, and he never could make himself look too hard or too long at a balance sheet.

Clark often set aside money for a deal, then found that Clint Sr. had stepped in and, without telling him, used the cash to fund another. Clint Sr. wanted his money working for him at all times, and he could not stand to have cash sitting in a bank. "All you need is eatin' money," he explained about his relatively minuscule cash position.

Clint Sr. thought his sons should begin in business each choosing a field of interest and concentrating in that area. "Clint Jr. loved everything that had to do with construction," recalls an associate who arrived at 1201 Main in 1951, "and John liked everything that did not have to do with construction."

Before World War II ended, Clint Sr. saw there was going to be a need for inexpensive housing for the large numbers of servicemen who would be returning from the war. Looking ahead, he purchased several dozen acres of cleared land eight miles north of downtown Dallas and invested in a new type of construction, called INS-CEM (insulated cement) houses. Although the houses were soundly built and ranged in price from only $7,000 to $9,000, they looked just like cement blocks. In addition to being unattractive physically, the development was considered too far from downtown.

Clint Jr. and his family moved into one of the INS-CEM houses, and Clint Sr. put his younger son to work selling them. Clint Sr. thought the job of salesman would help bring his young son out of his shell, especially with the help of Robert Thompson, whom he assigned to supervise selling the houses. Thompson was one of the most outgoing, fun-loving, gregarious men Clint Sr. had ever known. Born in New Mexico, Thompson met Clint Sr. in the forties in Washington where Thompson was a lobbyist. During World War II Thompson served as a captain in the marines. He was some twenty years younger than Clint Sr., but when he returned to Dallas he married one of Virginia Murchison's best friends, and the wedding was at the Murchisons' Preston Road farm.

Everyone was Bob's friend, whether he knew the person or not. He was known to walk into a party and jump up on a table and tap dance. His friends said he could excite a crowd, amuse his friends, and seduce a woman simultaneously. A reporter once described him as "having enough charm to coax partridges out of mesquite." Thompson was the opposite of Clint

Jr., about whom someone said, "He has the personality of a used tea bag."

When Clint Jr. was working closely with Thompson, he became only slightly more outgoing, but the two grew to be fast friends, and Thompson became the instigator of the wild parties, crazy pranks, and womanizing for which Clint Jr. became famous. "Because Clint Jr. had married when he was so young and right after getting out of the service, he had missed out on a lot of fun," says his stepmother, Virginia Murchison Linthicum. "He had never really dated anyone other than Jane, and most of his life had been spent concentrating on his academics. Soon after Bob and he began working together, those two started getting into a lot of trouble."

Virginia recalls receiving a telephone call one day from her stepson in New York. "He called to ask me how to order a limousine. That was the first sign I had that he was playing around."

Clint Jr. and Thompson were so busy raising hell and running around that they had almost no success selling the fifty-two INS-CEM homes. But Clint Sr. was determined that someone would be able to sell them. Virginia and Clint Sr. had become friends with a smart young millinery buyer at a Dallas department store. The woman, Ebby Halliday, had tremendous success in selling dozens of hats to Virginia and her friends, a fact that did not escape Clint Sr. He was a great salesman and admired anyone who shared this talent. One day when Virginia came home from a day of shopping, Clint said to her, "If Ebby can sell you all those hats, she can sell those INS-CEM houses."

He offered Ebby the job, and she took it. Within nine months she sold all fifty-two houses, and she never returned to the millinery business. Instead, she started her own real estate firm, and within a decade built a Dallas-based fortune and a reputation to match. She became, and is today, one of the top residential real estate brokers in America.

When Clint Jr. was relieved of his responsibilities with the INS-CEM houses, he bought the City Construction Company, a Dallas street-paving concern. Using credit as his father had taught him, Clint Jr. put up only $32,000 in cash to buy the firm, and paid for the remainder with an $80,000 promissory note.

He hired Robert Thompson as his partner and operating head of the firm. The young company had more than its share of problems during its first few years. With its first successful bid, Thompson and Clint Jr. landed a contract to pave two suburban streets. They had their bulldozers ripping up one of these streets when irate city inspectors arrived on the scene and pointed out that the other street was to be paved first. Thompson had his workmen patch up the ravaged road as best they could and then move to the proper street. After it was paved, city inspectors took a core drilling, decided the concrete did not meet specifications and that the street would have to be torn up and repaved. Upon hearing the news, Thompson vomited. Clint Jr., typically, showed no emotion, but asked with a grin, "How do you go about ripping up a new street?"

Soon Clint Jr. expanded City Construction into a conglomerate of companies involved in the building of roads and highways, bridges, dams, and houses. Each time he bought a new firm or expanded into a new area of heavy construction, he borrowed heavily, using as collateral his growing company. His original $32,000 investment pyramided into Tecon Corporation, a general construction company whose assets within two years totaled more than $10 million.

Although Tecon was an acronym for Texas Construction Company, when Clint Jr. was still in his twenties, he regularly bid on such large projects that business associates joked, "His company's called Tecon, pronounced tay-con, because he'll 'take on' anything."

One of Tecon's biggest projects was a contract to remove some two million cubic yards of a rocky hill that threatened to fall into the Panama Canal. On June 7, 1954, *Time* magazine reported,

> Seven contracting firms, among them Morrison–Knudsen, the world's greatest earth mover, rushed engineers to the canal to study the great fissure splitting the hill. But it was the young and aggressive Tecon Corp. of Dallas that put in the winning offer. . . . Tecon is headed by Clint Murchison

Jr., 30-year-old son of the multimillionaire Texas wheeler-dealer. Eager for the worldwide attention that the job will create, up-and-coming Tecon agreed to move shale from the hill . . . and to finish the job in 15 months. . . . Tecon will probably collect around $3,391,000 for the job.

The story explained that Tecon would have to perform "some tricky engineering feats, for the massive rock of Contractor's Hill lies atop soft shale. Breaking it up will take at least 1,000,000 pounds of dynamite. If a careless or badly planned blast drops any of the rubble into the canal, the contractors will have to dredge it out at their own expense."

Business associates at 1201 Main and friends asked Clint Sr. to step in and stop young Clint from risking what could be his entire fortune on the Panama Canal deal. "This is so risky," one associate warned, "and he has so little experience."

But Clint Sr. refused to interfere, saying only, "If he makes a mistake, he'll learn from it."

Tecon accomplished the feat with no major disasters. Although the Panama Canal contract did not net even close to the $3.3 million estimated, it did bring Tecon the national and international recognition Clint Jr. wanted. Further, it made clear to everyone around him that Clint Jr. had his father's penchant for big deals, big risk, and Clint Sr.'s unwavering self-confidence that he could pull off virtually any deal he set his mind to. But while Clint Sr. was not arrogant, his son was. Clint Jr. operated on the cocky assumption that the bigger a business opponent, the harder the opponent would fall.

Big Clint sometimes worried that his young son was playing the game of business too loosely. Once when Clint Jr. plunged into a residential deal, one in which his father thought a smart operator could make a million dollars, Clint Jr. lost half a million.

"You can afford to go broke once," Clint Sr. warned, "but that's all."

When John began working at 1201 Main, his father put him under Don Carter's wing. Carter, a savvy and aggressive investor, had worked in Wall Street brokerage firms before joining Indiana's Reserve Loan Life Insurance Company as an

investments analyst. Clint wanted John to have a Wall
Streeter's knowlege of the stock market. John had had some
experience in finance during his brief banking career in Santa
Fe, but not the kind necessary to handle, much less expand, his
voluminous portfolio.

In 1951 Clint Sr. read a book about the life insurance industry titled *The Safest Investment in the World.* Clint knew that
insurance was more than just safe—it was profitable—and he
asked Carter to find some insurance companies for Murchison
Brothers to buy.

Clint Sr. had had success with his Reserve Loan Life Insurance Company of Indiana, and with Atlantic Life Insurance
Company of Virginia, which proved to be even more profitable. Clint purchased Atlantic Life on Pearl Harbor Day,
1941, for $1.8 million plus a capital contribution of $300,000.
When he bought the company, an old and staid firm, Murchison made some big changes. He instructed that the company
keep its cash to a minimum and concentrate on buying and
selling in common stocks and other equity fields. Atlantic
made loans in which it required the borrower to give or sell
some of its shares. In one case, Atlantic's lagniappe—or gratu-
ity—of 1,500 shares, worth nothing when the loan was made,
was bought back by the company that issued it with a five-year
5 percent note for $500,000. In the eleven years from 1941
until 1952, the company's assets jumped from $34 million to
$71 million.

John kept a careful eye on Atlantic Life, watching its progress but without interfering in management. He and Carter
had been studying the industry for more than a year when they
learned that a large block of Lamar Life Insurance Company
of Jackson, Mississippi, was for sale. Murchison Brothers
bought 40 percent of the stock, at $100 per share. Clint Sr.
then made an offer to buy all outstanding stock at the same
price. Swiftly and shrewdly, the family acquired more than 98
percent of the company.

These early deals were soon dwarfed by much larger purchases. John and Don Carter looked at nearly all the big insurance companies in the United States before deciding to buy a
large block of the Life and Casualty Insurance Co. of Tennes-

see. Clint Sr. figured the deal in fifteen minutes on the back of a used envelope, then made an offer to pay $40 million for control of the $254 million Tennessee insurance company. Clint Sr. then turned the transaction over to Murchison Brothers. John later became chairman of the board of the giant and very profitable company.

The family continued to expand its life insurance portfolio, and eventually John began to make the decisions on what to buy and sell. In July 1959, in the name of Murchison Brothers, he purchased $15 million worth (17 percent) of stock in the Gulf Life Insurance Company of Jacksonville, Florida. John also had under his supervision the half dozen banks scattered throughout Texas that Clint Sr. bought in the 1940s.

John also took charge of the family's investment in Henry Holt & Company and became a member of its board of directors. Not only did Clint Sr. never once visit Holt's offices, he did not need to ask his son much about Holt's profits: He saw the earnings reports. By 1952, just a few years after the war ended, Henry Holt's textbook sales were the highest they had been in their history. Holt had become the leading publisher of high school textbooks, and among the top three of college textbooks.

To Murchison's delight, president Ed Rigg explained, "All that was needed was someone to run the company as a modern business instead of a literary tea party."

The volume of textbook sales in general doubled in the fifties. Holt's turnover hit $23 million in 1959; net profits after taxes came to $2 million, or 8.7 percent of sales, well above the industry average and eleven times earnings of a decade earlier. Taking into consideration a three-for-one split of the common stock in 1957, the stock appreciated 1,400 percent in a decade.

During the fifties, under the Murchisons' ownership, Holt also bought magazines, including *Popular Gardening.* And Clint tried several times to buy *Popular Mechanics,* a magazine he and Clint Jr. had read and loved for twenty-five years, but he was never able to reach an agreement with the magazine's owners.

* * *

When John began in business, he was slow and methodical, very careful and conventional. He was bright and had received an excellent education, but the enormous responsibilities thrust on him when he was still in his twenties were overwhelming at times. Before getting into a deal, he did not merely listen to a promoter. He did his own research, considered and then reconsidered the opinions of many experts in the field. Several times he delayed making a necessary decision for so long that the advisers at 1201 Main had to make one for him. But John was applauded by his associates for his diligence after making his deals. He reviewed the investment at regular intervals and met regularly with the company's CEO, as well as its chief financial officer.

Clint Jr., on the other hand, was very quick to make up his mind, and he did so without the help of others. He treated Jim Clark and the other advisers at 1201 Main as though they were his father's lackeys, men he viewed as inferior intellectually, unnecessary baggage. Not only did Clint Jr. move quickly from one deal to another; he then left his investments untended. When he did receive a financial report, he rarely gave it more than just a passing glance. Before he had sealed one deal, he was preparing to make another.

"We've got vice and versa," Clint said of his sons, "One of my boys makes up his mind too fast, the other won't make it up at all."

Not only were the brothers different in their approach, but Clint Sr. also showed two conflicting approaches to business. With the help of Jim Clark, he operated less out of his hip pocket than ever before. He might rework a potential deal or abandon the idea altogether if it did not fit into the scheme of his investments. At times he could be even cautious, heeding the advice of those around him. But he still maintained his lifelong passion for plunging, and this was the side that more often dominated.

The Murchison organization came to have two conflicting personalities, one that loved risk, the other that operated more conservatively. Conservative was always a relative term at 1201 Main. What was viewed as conservative buying and selling there would have been seen as one continuous roll of the dice at most organizations.

A flip of the coin was an index to Clint Sr.'s personality. Many of his associates preferred the side of him that intuitively leaped and plunged into deals more than the side that carefully thought out deals beforehand. But Jim Clark struggled to control the carefree plunger in Murchison, recognizing that the boss himself often regretted some of the deals he had made and soon after sold.

Clint Sr. instructed, "Cut your losses and ride your winners," but Clark felt that he carried the practice too far. When Clint decided to get out of a bad deal or sell his stock in a company (usually a controlling interest), he often did so without warning the company's directors, owners, partners or other large shareholders. When this happened, the directors repeatedly and often frantically tried to reach him by phone or mail to ask why he had sold out. Clint rarely took the call or answered the letter. That was in the past, and Clint had no interest in or time for the past.

Clark felt this was a dishonorable way to do business, and he saw a relatively simple way to avoid the problem. "If you'd be more careful before getting into a deal," he said, "you wouldn't have to cut it off."

When Clark lectured Murchison about his plunging, Clint just looked up at him sheepishly and said nothing. Even with Clark's help, the organization continued to lack structure and direction. Many hours were wasted by employees who joined the company but were unsure of their responsibilities. There were no clear divisions indicating where one person's duties left off and another's began. Many men who were hired in the late forties and early fifties were given no title or even the vaguest job description.

Steve Rooth, a Princeton undergraduate, had just finished Harvard Business School when he was hired by Murchison. After a few workless weeks had passed, he asked one of the more senior men at the firm, "What am I supposed to do?"

"Look through the files and learn about the companies we own," came the reply. That proved to be a very lengthy and time-consuming task. One of the companies Rooth was given to supervise was Cabell's grocery, a small group of curbside convenience stores. At about the same time in Dallas, Clint Sr.'s good friend Jody Thompson was starting a similar group of stores called 7-Eleven. When Ben Cabell became mayor of Dallas, the family sold 75 percent of its stock to Clint Sr.

Clint believed in the concept of a national chain of curbside convenience stores when 7-Eleven was nothing more than a small Dallas company with big dreams. Clint wanted Earl Cabell, who took over as head of the company, to open a chain of such stores across the country. But Earl and his family were not interested. Meanwhile, Jody Thompson was hounding Clint to sell him his Cabell's stock. Unable to convince the Cabells to expand, Clint sold out to the Thompsons.

Before the war ended, Clint saw transportation as a fast-growing industry. During the war it was difficult to buy a car, and Clint assumed it would remain so for some years afterward. Looking to the future, he bought $7 million in bonds of the Missouri Pacific Railroad. The bonds, with their accrued interest, were purchased at a large discount and proved to be a highly profitable investment.

As the result of a series of mergers, he became a 26 percent owner of the Trailways Bus System, beginning in 1944 when he and some associates bought three Dallas-based intercity bus lines on borrowed capital. He had the opportunity to buy two other much larger bus companies based in other cities, the Santa Fe Trail Transportation Co., a subsidiary of the Santa Fe Railroad, and nationwide Continental Trailways. Both had become very rich during the war and had not been paying dividends to their stockholders. Clint had acquired the companies through American Liberty Oil Company, which had a loss carry-forward that would make the bus companies tax free. When one of Clint's associates in the deal marveled, "You bought those bus lines without a red cent," Clint just grinned.

A few years later Murchison paid $1.6 million for Dallas's only taxicab concern, City Transportation Company, and retained its former owners to run the monopoly. Clint wisely sold it at a hefty profit before the city of Dallas took away its exclusive franchise.

In addition to trains, buses, taxicabs, and ships (American

Mail Line), Murchison also owned a Texas airline for a short time. Although cars became readily available after the war, the transportation companies made a handsome profit during the years he owned them.

During the forties his investments had been focused primarily in Texas and in the South and Southwest. But Murchison was eager to give his organization more national and eventually international scope. He was able to accomplish this with the help of Jim Clark, who had strong connections from Chicago to Seattle, and Don Carter, who had remained well connected in New York. Carter was a burly and sometimes brusque man who acted as a sort of lease hound, sniffing out attractive, growth-oriented deals in New York and around the country.

Clark and Carter both became very rich very fast, but not through a weekly paycheck. Clark, who was making $50,000 with his firm in Chicago in 1949, took almost a 50 percent cut in pay when he joined the Murchison organization at an annual salary of only $30,000. Carter was never paid a salary at all, but he kept an office at 1201 Main.

Both men became millionaires in the same way that dozens of others did who worked for or with Murchison. Clark and Carter found lucrative companies for the family to buy or invest in, then Clint offered them an interest in it. The boss encouraged his employees and associates to borrow money to buy stock in companies he owned, and in most cases Clint cosigned the notes.

Steve Rooth was amazed when he learned that Murchison wanted his employees to have a share of his deals. When Rooth was managing Murchison's investment in Cabell's, Don Carter asked him what his financial interest was in the store. Rooth told him he had none, and Carter, surprised, retorted, "Well then, you'd better go talk to Mr. Murchison about it."

Clint did not hesitate a moment. "You can have five percent of our stock." Grateful for the offer, Rooth did not have the money to buy 5 percent of the stock.

"That's no problem," said Clint. "You go tell Ernestine to write a letter to [Horace] Blackwell [at Dallas's First National

Bank] and sign my name. Tell her the letter should say I want you to borrow seventy-five thousand dollars, and any time they don't like the loan, I'll pick it up."

Of course, Rooth did not get the prime rate. Only the boss at 1201 had the privilege of borrowing money from Dallas banks at this lowest of interest rates, which was 3.5 percent in the early fifties. It was highly unusual for any oilman or venture capitalist to be given the prime, but Clint was not the average oilman or venture capitalist. He was a very unusual credit risk.

Murchison borrowed an enormous amount of money, and while he was often late in repaying his loans, he always repaid them. Many times when the note came due and the bank did not have its money, Clint was unreachable in Mexico, and the bankers had to wait for his return. But if he was at his office, he always picked up the phone and spoke with the bank officer.

"Give me thirty days," he would say.

Or if he was in a "tight," as it was known in the oil business, he would say, "I'll have it to you within ninety days." And he always did.

His word was his bond, and bankers respected him immensely, not only for his honesty in repaying his loans but for his brilliance in being able to. Clint's ability to crystallize a complicated financial situation into simple horse sense endeared him to his immense collection of banking and business cronies.

Clint Sr. guaranteed many loans for friends and associates, and he was stung from time to time. But what disappointed him most in his business life was not losing money. The times he was most hurt were when he trusted an associate and the associate let him down. When he learned someone had used him, he took it as a personal affront to his judgment. Clint Sr. never cosigned a note unless he believed in the person wanting the loan, and he tried to deal only with people he thought had integrity. He believed that mankind was generally good, that if you trusted a man, he would be trustworthy. This trust in associates was a hallmark of Clint Sr.'s business empire, and it was a principle his sons believed in just as strongly.

Clint Sr. carried the practice so far that he refused to take precautions against the possible dishonesty of others. A partner in Mexican ranching said he could not forget the signed blank check Murchison gave him to conclude a cattle deal. "I wouldn't have had the nerve to take a chance like that with my own brother," the cattleman said. About 1950 Clint set up a bank account in which his partners in Mexican ranching merely had to fill out checks—already signed by Clint—that were then drawn on the First National Bank of Dallas. This unrestricted check-writing practice continued well into the 1970s.

But Clint Sr.'s losses from sharpers were trivial compared with the huge expense and time he would have had to devote to prevent them. After finding good men to run his companies, he left them alone to do the job. Despite this practice, he never had a company go bankrupt while he controlled it.

Clint Sr., his advisers, and his sons spent an enormous amount of time with lawyers working out ways to pay the least amount of taxes on companies they bought and sold. It was time well spent, for they almost always found methods to get around paying the maximum. The Internal Revenue Service came calling regularly, many times after discovering a loophole. But usually by the time the government caught on to Clint's schemes, he had gotten far more out of the deal than the back taxes cost him.

Clint Sr. regularly avoided paying taxes by incorporating a highly profitable company into one with a huge loss carryover. This was a technique he had learned earlier in the oil business, and one he mastered with Consumers Company of Chicago. Jim Clark told the Murchisons about Consumers, a sand, gravel, rock, and ready-mix concrete firm. Murchison bought a controlling interest in the company in 1951 after a breathlessly short period of deliberation. From that point he moved even faster, liquidating the company's unprofitable fuel division and using the proceeds to buy outstanding company stock. This gave him 70 percent of a stock that quadrupled in price in twelve months—from $25 a share in 1951 to more than $100 a share in 1952.

To avoid paying tremendous capital gains taxes if he sold Consumers, he planned to merge it with his Frontier Chemical Company in Wichita, Kansas, which desperately needed cash.

Just as the merger was about to take place, one of Murchison's contacts at the Chase Bank in New York called him with news that the giant Folansbee Steel Company of Pittsburgh was for sale and that Chase would supply the financing if he wanted to buy it. The three companies were merged. Folansbee had a huge loss carryover, which offset Consumers' profits, and Frontier Chemical got the cash it needed.

Clint was interested in science and technology, and bought a controlling interest in Ohio's Diebold, Inc., maker of office-systems equipment. Diebold had developed a $2 million microfilm machine and had a research laboratory bursting with new ideas. The company was sound, its management was good, and it gave Clint the opportunity to compete with such giants as Eastman Kodak and Remington Rand. The competition was not unlike that he faced as an independent oilman against the major oil companies.

Clint also became active in the purchase of city-regulated water companies, the largest being Indianapolis Water Company and the Philadelphia Surburban Water Co. These might have been viewed as widow stocks, except for one important difference. Unlike the widow who bought the utility company stock and lived off the dividend, he bought it for the bigger gains, for the growth he predicted. The widow took the dividend to buy groceries. Clint took the dividend to pay interest on the loan he needed to buy the stock.

By 1952 the nondescript building at 1201 Main had become an internationally famous address. Opportunities for Clint to invest in New York Stock Exchange companies, in oil, banks, and real estate around the world, flooded the offices each day. He jumped at many of the big opportunities, as well as much smaller and more unusual deals. He was asked to invest not only in established companies but in ideas that had not even been patented, from frozen foods to household detergents.

When someone came to Murchison's office and asked him to buy the Tidy-Didy diaper service, he was immediately interested. Two minutes into the meeting, it seemed that Clint was growing restless, so the seller asked, "Well, would you like to buy it?

"Sure," Clint snapped. "There's a baby boom."

One promoter told Clint about an opportunity to acquire some Western desert land that was dotted with small extinct volcanoes. The old volcanoes, the promoter said, could be tapped for irrigation to make the desert bloom. Clint agreed to give the idea a try and invested a few thousand dollars. Although it failed, it was exactly the kind of deal he liked. Often the more far-fetched and untested an idea, the more it grabbed his attention.

Sometimes 1201 Main was called "the patent office," and there was a saying among Dallas businessmen: "If the dog won't hunt at the bank, try Clint." In other words, if the city's bankers would not agree to lend money to a business or new idea, there was someone else in town who might. Even officers at Republic National Bank, if they refused to make a loan, suggested, "Why don't you try your luck at 1201 Main? It's just a few doors from here."

Clint actually turned down a far greater percentage of deals than he agreed to, but the Murchison name had become magic. By the mid-fifties people were lining up in the lobby at 1201 Main to see the boss. Many were turned away at the door by a discriminating receptionist. Others, who made it as far as Clint's outer office, sometimes had to come back several times before they finally got a minute with him.

Eventually Clint met in person with most of the people who came to see him, but the meeting usually lasted no more than a minute or two—even when he liked the deal. If he felt someone had wasted his time, he described it as "nickels holding up dollars." No matter where his office was, he always made sure to have a back door, an escape route when visitors waited out front to see him.

Many requests for money were made in person, but many more came by mail. Even when he wanted a part of the deal, Clint dictated responses that were usually no more than a sentence or two and sometimes just a few words. When a growing staff of secretaries found it impossible to keep up with the enormous amount of correspondence, he put together a form letter that served as a rejection letter.

At times he invested in a deal merely to help a friend. An old black man Clint had known from Athens wrote to him one day, saying, "I'd like to raise some hogs."

Clint wrote back, "What are you going to feed them?"

The black man responded, "Oats."

"Go on over to the bank," Clint wrote back, then telephoned the First National in Athens and told an officer to let the man have a loan.

Clint thought that luck had played a role in his success, and he never lost sight of the fact that fate could have dealt him a different card. Acutely aware of his own former vulnerability, he was always generous to people around him who were in need. When a one-time acquaintance from his days in Wichita Falls came to his office selling neckties, Clint chatted briefly with him, then bought all eight dozen of the ties. He had heard that the man lost all of his money in the oil business.

At the same time throngs of people hounded Murchison to invest in their projects, he received countless letters from friends and strangers trying to sell him things, usually the types of things he had been known to buy in the past—airplanes, yachts, Rolls-Royces, racing stables, homes, islands, expensive jewelry. He had a pat response for most of the offers, and he used it on Stanley Marcus when he wrote Clint about an extraordinary diamond for Virginia.

"Dear Stanley, Virginia's got a diamond. Clint."

Clint was always rushing here and there, just as he had as a boy when he had raced from one cattle barn to another. He loved to talk on the telephone, but he never said "hello" or "good-bye." He simply began talking, and when he was finished he just hung up the receiver. Friends and business partners never seemed to be offended. "Clint can't be figured like an ordinary man," someone said. "Clint is just Clint." Clint Jr. imitated his father in exactly the same way, always dispensing with the niceties one expects to hear on the phone.

Clint rarely reflected on the accomplishments or the mistakes he had made in his life. That was history, not to be brought up again. If friends asked him to discuss any aspect of his past, he invariably replied, "That's yesterday's bird's nest." He was always moving ahead, always pushing forward. He and his sons were as unpretentious as the building in which they worked. But this unpretentiousness did not always carry down through the organization. Once, when a telephone call came in asking for Mr. Murchison Sr., the receptionist admonished, "It's pronounced MURK-kiss-on, not MURTCH-iss-on." A few seconds later the caller responded, "Thank you very muck."

In the early fifties much of Murchison's financing was being done through private placements. Instead of selling securities to the public, he was borrowing from banks and insurance companies. Jim Clark had arranged for financing through Bankers Life Insurance of Lincoln, Nebraska, and Modern Woodmen of America in Illinois, among others. When Murchison began borrowing large sums from these insurance companies, their directors approached Clark with a concern.

Before a loan is made, the borrower's lawyer is supposed to give his opinion of the loan, but the insurance companies were nervous taking the opinion of Holman Jenkens because he was in-house counsel to Murchison. They feared that the public might view the Murchison-Jenkens relationship, in regard to borrowing, as a conflict of interest. The insurance men asked Clark to speak with Murchison about hiring an independent law firm, rather than Jenkens, whom they referred to as a "kept" lawyer.

One of the lawyers representing one of the insurance companies was Bill Bowen. Clark recommended to Murchison and Bowen that Bowen leave his firm in Chicago and start an independent firm with Jenkens in Dallas. Murchison agreed, moved his office to the first floor of 1201 Main and rented the new law firm the entire second floor. The insurance companies felt comfortable with the new arrangement, and Clint took advantage of their warm feelings, arranging for even bigger and better loans.

Jenkens and Bowen did not get along well, however, and split after only one year. But the law firm grew quickly to include Jenkens and two new senior partners, as well as a half-dozen junior lawyers. Although the firm was technically independent, its chief client continued to be the Murchisons. Walter Spradley, who became a senior partner of the firm in the fifties, recalls an undying loyalty Jenkens and others felt toward Murchison.

"Holman worshiped the ground Clint walked on. Whatever Clint wanted, Holman was ready and willing and eager to do it. Because Clint was so honest and so smart and he wanted to see you succeed, he had a fantastic ability to instill loyalty. No one was more loyal to Clint than Holman, no one idolized Clint more."

As Clint's empire grew, he relied on Holman more and more and was grateful to have him just a floor away. With his lawyers, his advisers, and his sons in the same building, Clint rarely saw the need to leave 1201 at lunch or any time during the day. Nor did he have the time he once had to gamble away the hours at cards after lunch at the Dallas Petroleum Club.

Instead of going out for lunch, he decided to convert part of the building into a dining room. Everyone who worked at 1201, as well as many other employees still scattered in various office buildings around the city, were served, gratis, a hearty noonday dinner ranging from steak and potatoes to fried chicken with cream gravy, served on white tablecloths by black waiters in crisp white jackets.

The new dining room was dubbed "the little petroleum club," and oil was usually discussed at some point during lunch. But the resemblance between Clint's dining room and the other Petroleum Club stopped there. Clint forbade drinking, gambling, or dirty jokes in his dining room, fundamentals that were mainstays through booms and busts at the Petroleum Club across town.

Clint's establishment was never noisy or boisterous. On the contrary, it was remarkably quiet, especially when the boss was there. Clint's very soft, low voice set the tone. He rarely laughed out loud, and his low chuckle was usually lost under the noise of clinking plates and silverware. Obscenity and profanity were forbidden; Clint had dismissed employees and cut off friends who cursed excessively.

Big Clint did not like it at all when Clint Jr. entered his office one day cursing and shouting about a bad deal. Clint Sr. listened for ten or fifteen minutes, without saying a word, but he appeared disgusted when his son left his office. A business associate who overheard the incident recalled Clint Sr.'s comment a few weeks later. "When he heard that Clint Jr. wasn't elected a director of Brook Hollow Golf Club, Clint Sr. said, 'They probably didn't want such an objectionable person on their board.'"

The brothers' vice-and-versa personalities were obvious in nearly every way they approached business. Clint Jr. could take a simple deal and commit it to failure by making it complicated and convoluted. John, conversely, gained confidence in his own judgment, and as the years passed he began to show a special knack for looking at a complicated deal, then working out its problems and making it succeed.

Again, big Clint showed both of these opposing tendencies. Like Clint Jr., he loved the thrill of watching a deal evolve by taking into account tax considerations, borrowed money for financing, and long-term planning, which often resulted in an unnecessarily roundabout, difficult plan for what was originally a very simple deal. At the same time, like John, Clint Sr. was a master at looking at a complicated balance sheet and bringing forth a quick decision.

Clint Sr. almost never second-guessed his sons or reprimanded them for their mistakes. But once when Clint Jr. lost a large amount of money in a deal, Big Clint lectured him: "There's nothing wrong with losing money. You expect that to happen at times when you're investing, but we've got experts on all these subjects all over the country." Then raising his voice, "The trouble with you is that you don't check with any of them."

In fact, Clint Sr. had for years done the very same thing, preferring much of the time to make deals based exclusively on his own judgment even when a large group of advisers and attorneys was at hand. When Clint Jr. plunged into deals, he was emulating his father's impetuous side.

Jim Clark continued as chief adviser and chief of staff, but under a new organization called Investments Management Corporation decisions would be made by a committee of its directors. Investments Management was responsible for overseeing all of Murchison Brothers' holdings as well as all of Clint Sr.'s holdings—except for his cattle operations and

Delhi Oil and its subsidiaries, which Clint Sr. continued to run independently. IMC was comprised of an eight-member executive staff, with five voting officers—John, Clint Jr., Jim Clark, Gerald Mann, and Mrs. Vaughn Hill, who served as unofficial treasurer. Clint Sr. recognized that Mrs. Hill was overqualified as his secretary and would be more valuable as a manager. One day he came into the office and instructed her, "Get yourself an office and me a new secretary."

Each Murchison-owned company took on its board one or more IMC representatives as a director or officer. IMC had the Murchison trademark of giving advice on financing and policy to the companies it owned, but rarely interfering in day-to-day operations unless local management turned out to be bad, which, to the Murchisons, meant their investment was unwise.

Clint Sr. continued to borrow heavily from Murchison Brothers, a technique his sons watched and learned. By borrowing and investing in the partnership, their father kept his net worth at or below zero. He hoped to die with a negative net worth (he had already provided for Virginia) and thereby ensure that his sons paid no inheritance tax. He believed he could accomplish this merely by making all of his deals in the name of Murchison Brothers. It was an amazingly lucrative scheme in his sons' view. They had the benefit of their father's shrewd business judgment, without having to pay inheritance taxes on its rewards.

With the forming of IMC, Big Clint began to take more of a peripheral role in his sons' investments. He did not want to appear to be looking over their shoulders, and on rare occasions when he attended IMC meetings, he sat in a corner of the room, at a distance from the large directors' table. Clint Sr. was ready for his sons—now in their early thirties—to take control of their financial destiny. In addition, he was spending more and more time vacationing in a new and fashionable playground for the rich in Southern California.

11

"Joe McCarthy's done the greatest possible service to this country."

The Texas oilman was a different breed from the Texas cattle rancher of an earlier era who, when asked by a Yankee why he did not get away during the hot summer months, paused a moment and said, "Why, because it's hot *everywhere* in Texas."

How times had changed was evident in the early fifties when one social historian wrote, "Ah, the Texans. They flock into the Beverly Hills and Bel Air hotels with increasing gusto and alarming bankrolls."

Clint and Virginia were not among the flashy crowd poolside at the Beverly Hills Hotel in whose bungalows former Texan Howard Hughes conducted his business and bedding operations. But they had begun to migrate west during the summer with their friends. They took the *Flying Ginny* to a small, quaint, and relatively unknown seaside town south of Los Angeles, called La Jolla.

The serene setting of La Jolla and its relaxed Casa Mañana hotel belied the exciting fast pace established by Texans for whom La Jolla's chief attraction was the nearby Del Mar Race Track. No one from Texas, young or old, pretended they had come to La Jolla to rest and recuperate. They went to indulge in a sport famous for its element of risk—betting on horses—and no one enjoyed a day at the track more than Clint.

"Clint loved to pick horses and was always the best at it," says Virginia. "His mind worked so fast that it was easy for him to look at the odds and the numbers and decide in two or three minutes which horses he wanted. He won many more times than he lost, and most of the time when he won, he won very big."

Del Mar was heaven to Clint during his and Virginia's first summer in La Jolla. They arrived at the Del Mar Turf Club midmorning and stayed the entire day, drinking mint juleps, eating ham or corned-beef sandwiches, socializing with friends, and betting on almost every race. Clint liked Del Mar so much that he wanted to own a hotel in La Jolla. He tried to buy the famous Casa Mañana, but its owners refused to sell. Unable to find another hotel to buy, he decided to build one. The property he chose had been a girls' riding school on the edge of town. There he built the hotel and converted some of the existing riding stables into cottages. Aware of the Spanish–Mexican tradition, in California as in Texas, Clint named it Hotel Del Charro, a *charro* being a handsomely costumed gentleman horseman.

When Del Charro opened in 1951, it was immediately a fashionable spot, not only with Texans who came as the invited—as well as uninvited—guests of the Murchisons, but also with the Hollywood movie crowd. William Powell, Jimmy Durante, Betty Grable, Joan Crawford were regulars at Del Mar during the day and at Del Charro at night.

Clint and Virginia hosted dozens of parties, where movie actors and actresses mingled with Texas's richest oilmen. Many evenings began poolside at the hotel, where a large staff of waiters provided the guests with an endless supply of mint juleps, straight bourbon whiskey, as well as other spirits, which never "flowed in heads," but continuously. Joan Crawford always carried her own flask of vodka, and while she was usually reserved at the start of the evening, as the contents of the flask began to disappear, she became increasingly extroverted. The flask must have been very light the night she was introduced to Sid Richardson because she practically threw herself into Sid's arms.

"Everyone around the country knew that Sid was a billionaire, and there had been a lot of press about him right at that time when we introduced Joan to him," recalls Virginia. "She followed him around so much that he finally came and sat on the couch between me and Effie Cain, so that Joan couldn't get near him. He was very shy around women, and he didn't like it at all when they flirted with him."

Sid never married and almost never had a date, unless the woman was a close friend. It was always a mystery why Sid remained a lifelong bachelor, but he never told anyone the reason, not even Clint. However, Clint remembered that as a young man in Athens, Sid fell in love with a girl he hoped to marry, but she married someone else. He was badly hurt by the incident and Clint sometimes wondered if Sid had avoided another romantic relationship to avoid being hurt again.

In his sixties during Del Mar's heyday, Sid was the eldest among his circle of cronies, and their wives and girlfriends started calling him "Uncle Sid." The name fit his warm, avuncular, and often bashful personality. He addressed most women, including Joan Crawford, as "ma'am," and when he spoke to them, he half glanced away, avoiding their eyes.

Sid's facial furrows were arranged around quiet hazel eyes, and his thinning hair accentuated his large ears. In the words of one writer, his face was "as pleasantly seamy as an old dog's."

Despite his large, barrel-shaped body, he moved about easily with a rolling gait. "That swingin' walk of mine is my own invention," he said. "My left laig's a inch and a quarter shorter than the other. So I practiced me a walk that wouldn't make me limp. Took me a year—now I take long steps with the long laig, short steps with the other."

His easygoing manner belied his cynical view of women. In a 1954 article in *Look* magazine titled "The Case of the Billionaire Bachelor," he said, "I noticed that when the women found out I had me some money, they began wantin' me."

Letters from females flooded his office, he said, but he never responded to any of them. Instead, he created a corny credo, "Do right and fear no man; don't write and fear no woman."

Clint's guests at Del Charro—many there for the summer—took turns picking up the tab at large dinners and cocktail parties. They took turns, that is, with the exception of Sid, who was extravagant in big ways but frugal in little ones. One night, after a large party ran up a hefty tab, Virginia signed Sid's name to the bill and tacked on a generous tip. Sid never said anything about it to her, but he was outspoken another time when he mistakenly left $7,000 in cash in his cottage.

Sid had already left Del Charro and was aboard his DC-3 heading for Dallas when a maid found the cash, seventy one-hundred dollar bills, strewn across his unmade bed. She brought the money to Clint, who reached Sid on a short-wave radio. Sid had not missed the money, but when Clint said he tipped the maid fifty dollars for returning the money, Sid shouted over the radio, "Why the hell were you so damn liberal with my money?"

Once, on a return trip from Europe aboard the *Queen Mary,* Sid received a mid-Atlantic telephone call from his crony Amon Carter, the flamboyant publisher of the *Fort Worth Star Telegram.* Carter wanted Sid's commitment to give $37,500 to a Fort Worth charity. When Sid hesitated, Amon threatened to reverse the charges and make the call collect. Sid quickly agreed to ante up the $37,500.

Richardson and Carter were close friends, and both men, in one evening of gin rummy, had many times lost to the other a good deal more than $37,500. Like Sid, Carter kept a room at the Fort Worth Club where the two spent many nights playing cards. The gin rummy and poker games endured the ups and downs of the oil business, even when all of Sid's other bills went unpaid. During a three-year dry spell, he ran a tab at the Fort Worth Club that reportedly climbed to $100,000 before he paid a cent of it. Because Sid and Clint were eternally optimistic and always manifested an air of luckiness, their debtors were willing to carry them through bad times, until their luck returned. However, at one point Sid was so deeply in debt to the Fort Worth National Bank that the Federal Reserve Board stepped in and ordered the bank to limit the amount it loaned him.

For years Carter depended on his newspaper and other holdings to carry him through down times in the oil business—he had to. He was one of the all-time "dry hole" champions. But when he finally struck, he struck it big. In his office, under the glass top of his desk, Carter kept the proof of his first gusher—a $16 million canceled check.

Not long after Del Charro opened, the manager told Clint about a brilliant eighteen-year-old piano player whom he had engaged to perform in the hotel's nightclub. Clint thought it was a fine idea, but said he would not attend the performance. "I spent enough of my life listening to my sister Mary play the piano."

Coaxed into it, he stopped squirming in his seat after the first few seconds of the performance, and at a pause in the playing, he told Virginia in a very loud whisper, "He plays a lot better than Mary."

The audience roared, and many recalled the incident later, when they read that the eighteen-year-old had become one of the world's most famous pianists. His name was Liberace.

Not only movie stars and Texas oilmen but also state and national politicians poured into La Jolla during the summer. Aware of the power of oil money, the politicians were not shy about befriending the oil folks. One of Sid and Clint's earliest friends at La Jolla was J. Edgar Hoover, director of the Federal Bureau of Investigation. Hoover was a great fan of the Del Mar track and a longtime guest of Casa Mañana. But when Del Charro opened, J. Edgar quickly switched his allegiance to Clint, and he always took the same cottage.

J. Edgar told Clint how much he liked Del Charro, but, candidly, he had one criticism. "I'd have to rate it second to my favorite hotel in Florida only because there, when you walk out of your room in the morning, you can pluck an orange right off a fruit tree."

Clint listened without responding, then instructed the manager to find and have delivered to the hotel fruit-bearing plum, peach, and orange trees. That night, after J. Edgar went to bed, gardeners planted the trees outside his cottage. When he stepped out of his door the next morning, he found the garden full of trees thick with luscious fruit. Clint prided himself on being a good host.

At the track Clint was usually first to place his bet, not only because he was quick to make a decision, but because others waited to bet exactly as he did. They did not always follow him, however, when he placed $3,000 or $5,000 on a long shot. Yet, when his long shots came in—as they often did—the others in the group cursed, "Damn, I should have stuck with Clint."

Like Clint, Sid placed big money on the horses—$1,000 or

$2,000 on even money, as much as $10,000 on a long shot. Neither man acted much different whether he was winning or losing. If Clint lost as much as $5,000 on a race, he might say, "Well, I'll pick it up the next time," but his expression did not change.

Each man bet on the horses the same way he gambled in business. Clint studied the numbers, Sid went with his hunches. Both downplayed the constant thrill they felt betting on horses. "We just like to watch the ponies run," Clint told reporters who asked him about his and Sid's apparent addiction to betting.

Virginia enjoyed more than just watching and betting on horses; she and Effie Cain, the wife of Clint's partner Wofford Cain, owned a stable of thoroughbreds. Although Clint was no longer interested in horses as an investment, Virginia had some considerable success at the game. On September 11, 1954, her horse "Blue Ruler," with jockey Willie Shoemaker, won the $25,000 Del Mar Futurity.

By 1952, newspaper reporters and photographers had begun lurking around the bushes at Del Charro, looking for a story. While photographers would have clicked their cameras furiously at the sight of Joan Crawford chasing Sid Richardson around the pool, the reporters were after even bigger stories. They came looking for Senator Joseph McCarthy of Wisconsin, who had become the most controversial and one of the most powerful politicians in America. During the summer of 1952, at the height of his power, McCarthy was a regular at the Del Mar Turf Club and at Del Charro.

Reporters who hid in the bushes did not have difficulty picking the senator out of the crowd that gathered for cocktails every afternoon by the pool. He was always the loudest and the drunkest of the guests, and he usually had an anxious group of oilmen gathered around as he told horror stories about Communists waiting and ready to destroy America. No one at Del Charro seemed more profoundly interested in the stories or more fearful of communism than Clint.

He had not met McCarthy until 1951, but he had been electrified by his spectacular speech a year earlier in Wheeling, West Virginia, in which the senator claimed that President

Truman's administration was infiltrated with Communists. Murchison thought McCarthy's charges were exaggerated, but he did believe in the senator's basic allegations.

With the growth of hostility between the United States and the Soviet Union following World War II, there was throughout the country an increasing apprehension about domestic Communists. A *Fortune* magazine poll revealed that by February 1948, 10 percent of the American public feared Communists could rise to dominate the nation, and another 35 percent believed "Commie pinkos" were already in control of important sectors of the economy.

For nearly a decade the House Un-American Activities Committee had conducted blatantly publicized investigations of Communists in government, unions, and business. HUAC had existed for years and had been damaging to the basic civil liberties on which the country was founded. Innocent individuals suffered blacklisting and loss of jobs as a result of the Committee's persecution. But not until McCarthy's speech in Wheeling did anticommunism become the central political issue in America. Only a week before the Wheeling speech, McCarthy had been one of the least-known senators in Washington. All too soon the hottest, most controversial issue in America would be described by its opponents in a word, "McCarthyism." Backed by racists and extreme right-wingers, as well as more moderate Americans, McCarthy's voice was being heard around the nation. What he lacked was money, and he went to Texas to find it.

He could not have picked a better place. The welcome McCarthy received in Texas was even more extraordinary than the Wisconsin senator dreamed it could be. As *Fortune* explained in 1954,

> McCarthy, the rough-and-ready Marine, challenging Truman, smiting left-wing college professors hip and thigh, appealed to the Texans' combativeness as well as their conservatism. The American system was being attacked by subversives; nowhere had that system reached a fuller flowering than in Texas; nobody had more to lose should the at-

tack succeed; McCarthy was determined that it should not succeed. It was that simple.

Not only did Texas oilmen have the deepest pockets of any group of businessmen in America, but they were more fearful than anyone else in America that what McCarthy was telling them was true. Quite apart from any Communist threat, Texas oilmen, many of whom had made their fortunes literally overnight, feared that their wealth could disappear precisely as fast.

Many of the richest oilmen were among the most insecure businessmen in America. True, they had made great fortunes, but how much of their wealth was a result of ability and how much of it was due to luck? If luck was a major factor, as it almost always was initially, then how could a successful oilman feel any assurance that, if it was taken away, he could make it again?

Steadily improving geology was replacing some of the luck with science, but Everett DeGolyer, one of America's best-known geologists, said, "Given the choice between the best geology in the world and a little bit of luck, I'll take luck."

Richardson swore, "Luck has helped me every day of my life," and his most famous slogan, "I'd rather be lucky than smart cause a lot of smart folks ain't eatin' regular," expressed the secret fear of many in the oil crowd who knew—as all gamblers do—that luck comes and goes.

McCarthy was a virtuoso at playing on this insecurity. He told them that Communist subversives were taking over America. Texans did not have far to look to understand McCarthy's contention that the "Commies" would nationalize all industries, including oil. Right across the border in Mexico, in 1938, President Cardenas had nationalized all oil properties and given the former owners, both American and Mexican, a pittance as compensation. The losses were tremendous.

Texas's own Martin Dies Jr. was the man who pioneered the techniques later used by McCarthy. Dies, a congressman from East Texas, had been the first chairman of the House Committee on Un-American Activities in 1938. It was under his chairmanship that HUAC began compiling lists of citizens suspected of subversive affiliations.

Part of the reason most Texans did not take note of Dies's investigations was that there had as yet been no Hiss trial and no Communist conquest of Eastern Europe and China. Even more importantly, in the forties, the East Texas field was still being discovered, and most oilmen were preoccupied with making their first twenty or thirty million. Not until the 1950s did they start worrying about losing their wealth. By that time many oilmen in retrospect viewed Dies as a hero. "We should have listened to that guy years ago," they said. What they had lacked in enthusiasm for Dies they made up for in their passion for McCarthy.

Texans loved Joe McCarthy not only because he was a foe of communism, but also because he was a strong and devoted friend of oil. McCarthy linked communism with liberals who, he pointed out endlessly, were trying to cut back on oil's many special privileges. His association with Texas's richest oilmen began in 1948, when he met Houston's Hugh Roy Cullen, who had invested some $1 million in right-wing radio propagandizing. In the 1952 national campaign Cullen and his sons made thirty-one contributions ranging from $500 to $5,000 backing candidates for the House and Senate who were not only right-wing but specifically favored the interests of oil.

In 1950 Senator McCarthy voted for passage of the Kerr-Thomas Natural Gas Bill, which would have deregulated the industry. The measure was vetoed by President Truman. A year later McCarthy fought an amendment to a new tax act that would have cut the oil depletion allowance from 27½ percent to 15 percent. Seven months later he voted for the tidelands oil resolution, which gave to the states' use (and, in essence, to private oil companies) additional rich, offshore oil lands.

To such a good friend in the Senate, the oil rich of the Lone Star State opened their wallets. If he needed money to defeat a foe, he merely picked up the telephone and a check arrived from Texas. The national press dubbed him "The third senator from Texas," a title the oilmen loved.

Four of the richest men in Texas—Cullen, H. L. Hunt, Sid

Richardson, and Clint Murchison—were also four of McCarthy's strongest supporters. During the McCarthy era they became known around the country as "The Big Four."

H. L. Hunt—who by the early fifties was considered the richest man in America—contributed nothing to Dallas's civic and charitable causes. But like Cullen, Hunt regularly gave money to defeat "leftist" candidates for the House and Senate. In 1951 he founded an ultraconservative organization called Facts Forum, a key source of misinformation for Red Scare activists. Facts Forum produced a radio program that, at its peak, was broadcast on 222 stations across the United States, as well as a news column carried in 1,800 newspapers. Hunt used Facts Forum to promote Joe McCarthy's causes and the possibility of McCarthy as a presidential candidate.

"It isn't just that Hunt is to the right of McKinley," explained a Dallas oilman. "He thinks that communism began in this country when the government took over the distribution of the mail."

Hunt was believed to have spent more than a million tax-deductible dollars annually on Facts Forum. In addition, he wrote a novel, *Alpaca,* in which he described his vision of an ideal government—one that would give more votes to citizens who paid more taxes and would limit the income tax to a maximum of 25 percent.

Hugh Roy Cullen, for his part, advocated the abolishment of all income taxes and substitution of state and federal sales taxes, predicting that such a tax system favoring the rich at the expense of the poor would result in "the greatest kind of prosperity." Although Richardson and Murchison did not make such outlandish suggestions publicly, they, of course, also favored any system under which they paid less taxes.

Richardson's relationship with McCarthy was far more tenuous than that of the other big three. In 1950 he supported the senator and that he thought McCarthy had "done some good work." But he was never nearly as vocal about McCarthy as his fellow Texans. He had far more political aplomb. "I don't see how I could be friendly with Sam Rayburn and Lyndon Johnson," Richardson complained, "and be friendly with Joe McCarthy, too."

Sid had become close friends with Senator Lyndon Johnson, who, among other favors, introduced Sid to John Connally. Richardson had said he needed someone to help look after his varied interests, especially in relation to Washington, and Johnson thought Connally could be useful. An aggressive lawyer who had served for some years as Johnson's administrative aide, Connally had an insatiable affinity for the rich. Richardson, who lacked most social graces and wore old, rumpled suits, was impressed with Connally's poise and his dress, and after a short meeting at Sid's suite at the Fort Worth Club, Connally was hired.

Richardson tried to move away from the issue of McCarthyism, but his friends and associates gave it enormous attention. It had the full support of the state's oldest and most influential newspaper, the *Dallas Morning News,* both in news stories and staunchly conservative editorials, as well as the support of Texas Governor Allan Shivers.

Shivers in 1954, with the backing of his fellow millionaires, tried to enact a law that would make membership in the Communist Party a crime punishable by death, an idea that some said, "out-McCarthy'd McCarthy." Shivers adoringly signed and presented McCarthy with a scroll proclaiming the senator "a real American, and now officially a Texan." McCarthy's brash, gambling, and intuitive political instincts and his limited social graces appealed to Texans who felt uneasy around polished Eastern "thinkers."

Murchison became much closer to McCarthy than any other Texan. He threw multi-thousand-dollar contributions the senator's way, and gave him the use of his fleet of airplanes. He also provided McCarthy with numerous stock market tips and financial advice—a service that Murchison gave other politicians as well.

He tried to teach McCarthy how to make money investing in stocks using other people's money. The senator, like Clint, was a consummate gambler. But unlike Clint, who put his big money in businesses, McCarthy threw away huge sums, including the political contributions of his backers, at the crap tables in Las Vegas, and at racetracks from Washington to La Jolla.

Being blind drunk is usually a handicap for a gambler, but in McCarthy's case it was on occasion a guarantee of making money. A bodyguard of H. L. Hunt recalls that one way Hunt found of subsidizing the senator was to lose at gin rummy to McCarthy whatever sum he planned to give the senator. This required considerable discipline on Hunt's part because he was a wizard at cards and was accustomed to winning. The task was frequently made easier, however, when McCarthy passed out drunk at the card table and Hunt simply gave the bodyguard the cash he wanted the senator to have. The bodyguard stuffed the money in McCarthy's pocket, then carried him home.

Although McCarthy came from one of the northernmost states in the country, and Murchison one of the southernmost, there were stunning similarities in their backgrounds. McCarthy's grandfather settled in Center Township, Wisconsin, in 1855, and after purchasing acreage sight unseen, cleared his land and built a log cabin with his own hands. The very same year in Texas, Clint's grandfather, T. F. Murchison, settled in Henderson County. He too built a log cabin with his own hands. Although McCarthy's chief interest in fighting communism was to advance his own political career, he fooled Clint for many months. Like Clint, he talked of his hardworking ancestors, his small-town roots and patriotic ideals. He described "McCarthyism" as synonymous with "Americanism."

Murchison had unusual foreign policy views for a far-right conservative; he was an internationalist and believed in aid to underdeveloped nations. But his political philosophy on domestic issues was far to the right and fit exactly into the mold of his fellow Texas millionaires. During the Eisenhower–Stevenson campaign of 1952, Murchison printed and distributed some 600,000 copies of an arch-conservative pamphlet he called "The Native Texan," whose headlines included, "With Adlai You Can't Even Pick Your Own Doctor," "McCarthy Charges Treason," and "Truman Stays Faithful to Stalin in Oregon."

Murchison, an ardent supporter of states' rights—especially those of Texas—was nevertheless eager to meddle in the affairs of other states if it meant helping defeat a political foe of McCarthy. Murchison gave McCarthy some $40,000 to defeat his outspoken critics, including $10,000 to defeat Senator Millard Tydings of Maryland and $10,000 to unseat Senator William Benton of Connecticut.

Because so many rich Texans were making similar contributions, the myth was born that any politician who challenged McCarthy was marked for political extinction, with oil money paying the costs of burial. But Murchison claimed his support for McCarthy was strictly to "hunt Reds" and not for help on oil problems in Washington. "Hell, I've got ten men in Washington who are better thought of than McCarthy," he said. "I don't need him for influence."

Clint not only supported McCarthy financially; he also established a personal relationship with the senator. McCarthy was thirteen years younger than Clint, but Clint treated him like a brother, whisking him off to hunt at Acuña, fish at El Toro, gamble at Del Mar, or meet his friends at Del Charro. "I tell you," Clint told reporters in 1951, "I think he's done the greatest possible service to the country. He fears nobody, and he's certainly got those Communists feared to death of him. I'm for him all the way."

Clint ended his letters with the promise, "I'm with you, Joe, to the bitter end." But this proved to be untrue.

Competing with McCarthy for the attention of both Sid and Clint was the election of the next President. Both men were strong conservative Texas Democrats. For decades there had been no effective Republican Party in the former states of the Confederacy, only the Democratic Party whose nomination in the primary, therefore, constituted election. As a result, the Democrats were divided into liberals and Dixiecrats, the latter often at least as conservative as the Republican Party. But the moment for a revived Republican Party in the Old South arrived during the Truman Presidency.

Murchison and Richardson were outraged with Truman on three scores. He had vetoed the Congressional tidelands bill, which would have guaranteed Texas's title to the mineral deposits for ten miles off the Gulf coast, and he vetoed a bill that would have deregulated the oil and gas industry. His greatest sin was his strong opposition to the depletion allowance. Most oilmen cut their ties with Truman after his 1950 budget message, when he said, "I know of no loophole in the tax laws so inequitable as the excessive depletion exemptions now enjoyed by oil and mining interests." Murchison thought so little of Truman that he customarily spelled the President's last name with a small *t*. In addition, Murchison and Richardson were frightened by Adlai Stevenson, front-runner for the Democratic nomination, whom they viewed as an extreme liberal.

In the spring of 1952 General Eisenhower was stationed at NATO headquarters in Paris. Members of both political parties were hoping to draft Eisenhower, but at that point he was uncommitted, both on whether he would run and, if so, on which ticket. Rather than wait for him to make up his mind, Richardson traveled to Paris for a meeting with the general. During the visit Richardson pledged Eisenhower several million dollars if he would decide to run—on either ticket.

Sid also carried with him a letter from Murchison, echoing the appeal. Murchison was more specific, saying that he doubted Eisenhower would be able to get the Republican nomination, and, therefore, urged him to run as a Democrat. Murchison told the general that even looking at things as optimistically as possible, as a Republican he could only hope for a bare majority which would haunt his administration.

As a Democrat, Murchison explained, the President would have a strong majority in Congress. Eisenhower was, of course, aware that Sid's and Clint's contributions had helped maintain a Democratic Congress in 1942. In fact, the Democrats received sizable oil funds as late as 1944.

In 1941, Sid became a petroleum adviser to President Roosevelt and traveled to Washington regularly. A few days after Pearl Harbor Sid had a stateroom on a crowded train en route from Dallas to Washington. Just before the train left the station, an Army brigadier general came aboard. Sid unselfishly invited the stranger to share his stateroom until a berth could be found. He did not hear his companion's name again until two years later, when he learned that the man, Dwight D. Eisenhower, had been named commanding general of the Allied forces in Europe.

In the 1930s Richardson had bitterly resented government power, but in the 1940s, as a member of Roosevelt's advisory council, he had begun to understand that power. Still, although he liked FDR as a friend, he wanted a conservative President, and he found that leader in Eisenhower.

By August 1952 Murchison, too, was convinced that Eisenhower was the best man for President, and he wrote from La Jolla to a business associate in Dallas that he had spent ten days with Eisenhower and J. Edgar Hoover, and that they believed that the Democratic presidential candidate, Adlai Stevenson, would be used by radicals to destroy America's proud traditions.

Clint was worried that Eisenhower would not win the New Hampshire primary against the favored Robert Taft. But he was wrong, and wrong again when he predicted Ike could not win the Republican nomination in July 1952. During the campaign, when Eisenhower came out in favor of Texas ownership of the tidelands, Governor Allan Shivers and many of Texas's richest and most powerful citizens who were conservative Democrats, switched their party affiliation. Ike carried Texas with 1,100,000 votes to Stevenson's 970,000. Never since it joined the Union had Texas shown such support for a Republican.

Texas exemplified an important change in what had been called the Solid South, as well as a change in the country. Since the Civil War the states that had formed the Confederacy regularly voted for the Democratic candidate against the party of Lincoln and the carpetbaggers.

Texans and other Southerners prided themselves on being "Yellow Dog Democrats," meaning they would vote for any Democratic candidate even if it were a yellow dog. But Eisenhower proved that a Republican, if he were a popular enough figure, could carry Southern states, not only Texas but Tennessee and Virginia, among others. He won the election with 33,936,000 votes to Stevenson's 27,315,000.

Eisenhower was helped to the presidency with many Texas-size donations. Because Sid did not make his financial contributions directly to Ike, but rather through a third party—so there would be no record—it is difficult to estimate just how many millions he gave the general. Whatever amount Sid contributed to Eisenhower, it did not make a dent in his bankroll. After years of ups and downs in the oil patch, he finally, in 1939, made a billion-dollar fortune that he would keep for the rest of his life.

Sid's big break came when he discovered the Keystone Field in West Texas. Richardson drilled 385 wells in the Keystone Field and only 17 were dry holes. By 1943 his underground fortune in the Keystone Field alone approached $800 million.

Sid became a frequent guest at the White House, sometimes eating dinner with the President and Mrs. Eisenhower three or four days in a row. When friends asked what kinds of political issues they discussed, Sid retorted, "Hell, we talk religion, not politics."

One of the stickiest problems facing Eisenhower when he took office was the McCarthy scandal. Americans, including many conservatives, were becoming disillusioned with the senator and his increasingly unscrupulous and brutal tactics, and many wanted Eisenhower to condemn McCarthy publicly. Eisenhower's willingness to shake McCarthy's hand, just after the senator had denounced General George Marshall, outraged many people. Eisenhower confided to close associates that he loathed McCarthy but feared that a direct presidential attack on him would enhance the senator's credibility among his right-wing followers.

Richardson's feelings about Eisenhower were almost idolatrous, and, seeing the problems McCarthy was causing the President, Richardson refused to have anything more to do with the Wisconsin senator. "Sid," Clint explained in 1954, "thinks I'm crazy to get mixed up in this business."

Clint also felt strong admiration for Eisenhower, whom he sent personal gifts as well as sizable political contributions. Thanking Clint for some of the sausage the Texan made at home by the bathtubfull, Eisenhower said that by his and Mamie's reckoning it amounted to a full year's supply.

And Clint's support of McCarthy was beginning to lessen as well. He was disappointed that McCarthy's exaggerations of Communists in the federal government weakened what would otherwise have been a strong case. Clint was also growing tired of McCarthy's egotism and inflexibility, and his unwillingness to listen to views contrary to his own.

"After Joe came out with that figure of two hundred and five Communists in the government, and then wasn't able to produce the names of more than thirty-five or so, I thought he ought to admit publicly that he had been wrong. He could then have hammered hard on the right figures. I tried to get him to do this, but he wouldn't—I guess he figured it would be bad tactics."

Murchison began to suspect what many of his friends had been telling him for more than a year, and some for more than two years—that McCarthy was driven by his own political ambitions and that he lacked even the slightest degree of prudence or judgment. Murchison suggested to McCarthy that he should stop random "name calling" and instead quietly and carefully document his charges.

Not only Sid, but many of Clint's closest friends and associates told him to cut his ties with McCarthy. Jim Clark's wife, Lillian, refused to attend parties at Del Charro or anywhere else where McCarthy would likely be. Clint agreed with much of the criticism, explaining, "He *is* beginning to bungle." But he would not cut his ties completely—at least for a few more months.

The beginning of the end for McCarthy came in the fall of 1953, when he pressed hard for access to the Defense Department's confidential files on loyalty and security. McCarthy charged the Army with harboring and protecting Communists and traitors. Shortly before the now-famous Army–McCarthy hearings, Murchison flew to Washington for a private meeting with the Wisconsin senator. Once again he urged McCarthy to exercise some restraint, to show a "proper spirit of humility."

Murchison not only disliked the senator's random, undocumented charges against the Army; he disdained McCarthy's lack of personal self-control. The senator drank constantly, beginning at breakfast when he sometimes downed a glass of whiskey with a tablespoon of orange juice. At Del Charro, McCarthy sat drinking by the pool until three or four o'clock in the morning, then stumbled to his cottage, slept for two or three hours, and woke up ready to go again.

He was a terrible bore, telling lengthy off-color jokes, often in the presence of ladies. Clint disapproved strongly, and more than once left the party, disgusted. One evening at Del Charro McCarthy challenged another guest to lean his head back and balance a marble on his forehead, then see if he could drop the marble through a funnel McCarthy stuck in the man's trousers. When the man bent his head back, McCarthy poured a bottle of bourbon down the man's trousers. Fortunately for McCarthy, Clint was not present.

But Clint did witness another incident at Del Charro that was the final blow to his relationship with the senator. It happened just a few weeks before the Army–McCarthy hearings were scheduled to begin. McCarthy, his wife, and a dozen or so other guests of the Murchisons were seated by the pool at Del Charro. Clint usually retired early, often by nine o'clock, but on this evening he was still there listening to McCarthy, on a roll, loudly spraying charges in all directions about Communists in the defense department. After many drinks too many, McCarthy began insulting his wife, Jean, and then stood up and madly flung her, fully dressed, into the swimming pool. Clint shot up from his chair and made his way to his cottage. Early the next morning Clint sent an associate to McCarthy's room. The messenger had only a few short words for McCarthy: "Pack your bags and get out."

Clint later confided to a close associate, "I finally had it when he pushed Jean into the pool. That did it for me."

Clint followed the Army–McCarthy hearings on television during the spring of 1954, and finally came to view McCarthy as many of his closest associates had for months. On television the senator came across as a bully whose accusations were clearly not based on facts. Angry, surly, and obviously drunk much of the time, his slovenly appearance and slurred speech contrasted poorly with the soft-spoken, clearly reasoned, meticulous words of Joseph Welch, the Army's attorney.

When the United States Senate at last displayed enough courage to pass a bill censuring the senator, "McCarthyism" was finally discredited. Like most bullies, he retreated, increasingly hid in his whiskey bottle, and died only a few years later.

Clint's brief, passionate, and finally disappointing honeymoon with Joseph McCarthy had a definitive influence on how he was thereafter perceived locally, nationally, and internationally, except by his few intimates. He was now lumped together with all the antiblack, anti-Semitic, antiliberal, cliché right-wing Texas oil millionaires.

Only a handful of people knew or cared that Clint was the same person who as a boy had fished regularly with a black man, unmindful of or unconcerned about the critical whispers this conduct caused. Nor did they know that when some Athens blacks wanted a swimming pool, Clint gave them the money to build it. While several of Clint's closest friends were outspokenly anti-Semitic, Clint simply had no racial prejudice. He judged people by other criteria.

McCarthy was Clint's learning and disillusioning experience, just as Vietnam would be America's. It is difficult as the twentieth century ends to believe and understand the simple patriotism of those born at the end of the nineteenth. Clint cared genuinely about his country's well-being. He was not a student of America's history or of the nuances of its Constitution. But he loved his country and he believed, as fewer and fewer Americans have recently, that the person who ran the country could mean the difference between whether America thrived or merely survived.

In the late fifties Clint invested nearly $1 million in making *The Alamo,* a historical account of the great Texas massacre, starring John Wayne. The movie was a failure at the box office, but that did not bother Clint. He had never intended to make money on the film. His purpose was patriotic.

Just a few months after McCarthy was censured, national magazines had already begun asking "What ever happened to Joe McCarthy?" Amazingly, nearly a year after McCarthy was brought down, his spirit, if not his name, was at work in Dallas. A handful of the city's archconservatives began attacking the Dallas cultural institutions, beginning with the Dallas Public Library when they insisted that a work of Pablo

Picasso, "a self-professed Communist, be removed from the wall." The library's director immediately obeyed the command, prompting a *Dallas News* writer to suggest a credo for Dallas in buying books and displaying art: "If anybody objects, yank it down or ban it from the walls or burn it up."

After months of remaining silent, some of the city's leaders finally spoke out, charging that the right wing must be brought under control. One wag complained, "Next thing we know, we'll be looking at Venus de Milo wearing a bra."

But with the library coup, the archconservatives gained even more momentum. The biggest controversy began in 1956 when the Public Affairs Lunch Club, the Inwood Lions Club, a post of the American Legion, and others insisted the Dallas Museum of Fine Arts favored "liberal" modern art. These groups charged that the museum, a tax-supported municipal institution, favored "red" artists over more traditional artists. The so-called patriotic groups attacking the museum saw modern art and communism as one and the same, and insisted the museum remove from its walls all works by "Communists."

The Dallas Museum, like the library, buckled under the pressure of its attackers, took down works the attackers insisted were made by "Communist" artists, then issued a statement by its board of trustees, saying, "It is not our policy knowingly to acquire or to exhibit the work of a person known by us to be now a Communist or of Communist-front affiliation."

The New York Times and a host of other national publications immediately castigated the Dallas Museum for this policy, and a group of civic leaders criticized the museum "for allowing art to become political." Under fire, the trustees changed their stand and wrote a new policy, stating, "The Dallas Museum of Art is to exhibit works of art only on the basis of their merit as works of art."

The *Dallas News* summed up the new policy in a headline, "Museum Says Reds Can Stay." Ironically, the trustee who introduced this new "art for art's sake" policy was Clint Murchison Sr.'s chief adviser, Gerald Mann. Even more ironic, John Murchison so strongly disapproved of the museum bowing to political pressure—especially its anti-modern-art stand—that he began to plan a new museum, the Dallas Museum for Contemporary Art, which would open only a few years later.

12

"What the hell did you say was the name of that railroad?"

Soon after Murchison opened Hotel Del Charro, he and J. Edgar Hoover were chatting by the pool when the FBI director casually volunteered, "If I had the money that's spent at racetracks, I could do a wonderful job building character among the nation's young people."

It was then that Murchison conceived the idea of acquiring the Del Mar Race Track—at that time controlled by a private commercial syndicate—and using the revenues to help boys. He established Boys, Inc., a philanthropic organization that would distribute money to various youth organizations around the country. With their plan in mind, Sid and Clint one day wandered into a California facility run by Boys' Club, an organization that helps boys from low-income families. Sid and Clint were introduced to the director of the organization, who took them on a tour of the facility. Impressed with what they saw, Sid asked, "Is there anything you need?"

The director replied, "Well, we could use some new uniforms."

Sid retorted, "No, we meant something like a building."

The Boys' Clubs in California and other parts of the country would become Boys, Inc.'s principal charity. By law, a charity cannot earn business income, but Clint and Sid finagled a way to do so. With the help of more than a dozen lawyers and accountants, they conceived a complex corporate arrangement for acquiring the racetrack and paying for it with its own earnings. Under the plan, Boys, Inc. would own the track but would sublet it to a separate corporation. Boys, Inc. would receive most of the profits from the track as "rent" rather than "income," thereby eliminating the federal government's tax bite.

The lease entitled the holder to use the 265-acre, state-owned Del Mar facility for horse racing for about two months every year, contingent on the annual granting of a racing permit by the California Horse Racing Board, also a state agency. From the time the track opened in 1937, the lease holder had been a corporation called the Del Mar Turf Club. Bing Crosby and some Hollywood friends were the original holders of the club stock before it shifted to others in later years.

In 1954 Clint and Sid acquired 7,000 shares of Turf Club stock at about $400 a share on behalf of Boys, Inc., a $2.8 million transaction, with the understanding that the debt would be paid off from future earnings of the track. This plan was essentially the same as the oil payment plan, in which the cost of drilling a well was paid for out of future oil production.

But the racetrack plan was even more complex than the oil payment. The Turf Club, with Murchison-appointed directors, subleased the racing franchise to a new corporate entity called Operating Company. The Turf Club then gave the ownership of this sublease to Boys, Inc.

The genius of Murchison's plan was in the tax dollars saved. Other comparable California tracks, such as Santa Anita and Hollywood Park, ended each racing season in the 1950s with profits of more than one million, divided among stockholders. Del Mar, under Murchison's leadership, ended a forty-two-day racing season with stated profits of only about $50,000. The track's net revenues were approximately ten times that amount, but they were paid out as an expense in the form of "rent" to Boys, Inc.

The Internal Revenue Service had not ruled in favor of or against the plan when it went into operation in 1954. But although the track operated for ten years without an IRS ruling, it became a major tax dispute. The crux of the dispute was whether the money, more than $350,000 a year, which went to Boys, Inc., was truly rent and thus untaxable as a business expense of Operating Company or essentially a business operation. State and federal tax officials argued that Boys, Inc. was not organized and operated exclusively for charitable reasons, but primarily for the purpose of liquidating its own indebtedness. The plan, tax officials charged, was a device by which the foundation bought the track on the installment plan out of the track's own profits.

Indeed, for the first four years under Murchison's control, revenues were channeled into paying off the purchase price. But beginning in 1958, Boys, Inc. reported distributing more than $1 million annually to numerous organizations that helped needy youngsters and fought juvenile delinquency. Although grants were made to some Boys' Clubs on the East Coast, most were made to those Clubs in California and Texas.

The track's status as "leased state property" was unparalleled in the country, which, in and of itself, caused problems for the IRS. Murchison's arrangement in acquiring and operating the track was so complex that he not only found dozens of loopholes, he completely baffled tax officials. The federal government simply could not find a way to prohibit the arrangement. Murchison's extraordinary scheme continued until 1969, when the lease expired, and the track's managers, facing strong political opposition, decided not to renew its lease.

Not long after Clint and Sid acquired Del Mar, Clint began planning a much larger venture, to purchase and operate similarly a half dozen big racetracks around the country. Naturally, Sid and Clint planned to borrow the capital to make a minimal down payment on the tracks—they had acquired Del Mar with a cash outlay of $10,000 to $15,000. But when their idea hit the front pages of newspapers from Los Angeles to New York, it caused a flurry, and not only among horse racing enthusiasts and the IRS.

Fundamentalist Christians and other religious sects came out strongly against the Texans' plan, charging that gambling money, or, in their words, "dirty money," should not be in any way connected with America's youth. Government officials and big business complained that the plan was nothing more than a tax dodge. Racetrack owners, who had not been approached to sell their tracks to the Texans' chain, saw the potentially enormous competition and spoke out in stern opposition.

Clint tried to combat the charges coming from all directions. "This is no tax dodge," he insisted. "We have the Rockefeller Foundation and the Ford Foundation and others. Why not Boys, Inc.? It appears to be just as hard to give away money intelligently as it is to make it."

Many Americans believed Texans, and especially these two men, already had too many tax advantages. The depletion allowance was viewed by businessmen in other industries as unfair and overly generous to an industry that was already among the richest in the country. Making the issue even more prickly was J. Edgar Hoover's connection. Not only was J. Edgar wrongly credited with devising and executing the plan by which Sid and Clint acquired Del Mar, news stories indicated that he was considering accepting Clint's suggestion that he retire from the the FBI and become director of the string of tracks. Although Hoover told Clint he did not want the job, he was neither firm nor final in his rejection of it. Clint continued to press him to take the role if the plan went through.

The public's negative feelings about Hoover's involvement in the scheme were expressed concisely in a letter to the editor published July 16, 1954, in *The New York Times:* "I hope Mr. Hoover will not lend himself to this undertaking. It would tend to popularize gambling and it would set a very bad example. If these Texas millionaires want to help underprivileged boys, let them do it with their own money, not with the money the American people would lose on race-track betting."

Although the plan met with far more criticism than praise, there were also outspoken individuals who favored the general idea, as stated in another letter to the editor in *The New York Times:*

"Theoretically, a good end should not be brought about in a bad way. However, here we face a factual situation, not a theory. It is a fact that the race tracks are operating and making millions annually in profit. It is a fact that human nature is such that race tracks will, alas, continue to exist and make profits for many years in the foreseeable future. More power to these Texas wheeler-dealers."

Quite contrary to the fundamentalist Christian belief about

gambling, Clint thought the owning and operating of a race-track, if part of the proceeds went to charity, was a worthy and virtuous undertaking.

By 1956 Clint and Sid were in the process of acquiring two major racetracks outside of Chicago, two in New Jersey, and one in Detroit. But because the IRS had not decided whether to give the umbrella racetrack plan a favorable or unfavorable ruling, the sales contracts could not be made final. The IRS hedged on the ruling for months, then years, and the negotiations eventually collapsed.

Although the plan for a chain of tracks failed, Clint accomplished the essence of his goal with Del Mar, which paid no federal taxes from 1954 until 1964, and which contributed nearly $4 million to help needy and underprivileged boys throughout America.

If few things in life are as certain as taxes, few things bothered Clint as much. The most hotly debated tax issue among oilmen was the 27½ percent depletion allowance that gave oil operators an enormous tax break. As Cleveland Amory said in a *Holiday* magazine article in February 1957, taxes are such a large part of the oil business that the state might well be called "Taxes, U.S.A."

Oilmen argued that without the depletion allowance they would stop taking the risks necessary to find new oil reserves. In 1954 Sid Richardson claimed that he had spent the previous three years and $15 million looking for oil without bringing in a single well. And Clint claimed that Delhi Oil ran up a $690,000 deficit in 1953 because almost half of the fifty-six wells the company drilled were dry. Only the depletion allowance, they claimed, kept them hunting for oil and oil prices from soaring.

During the start of the fifties, some United States senators were trying to pass a bill that would cut the depletion allowance to 15 percent, with the result that consumers might have to pay a little more for their oil and gas but the government would receive an additional $300 million in annual revenue. Delaware's Republican senator John Williams insisted, "As long as there is oil, people will be looking for it, depletion allowance or no."

Although most non-Texans probably agreed with Williams' assumption, Texas oilmen became furious when the subject was even mentioned. They hated the term "allowance," for in their view it connoted "government subsidy," when in fact many oilmen viewed the "depletion percentage" as a God-given right.

During the late forties press baron Henry Luce hammered hard on the issue in *Time* and *Life*. An eight-page spread in the April 1948 issue of *Life,* titled "Southwest Has a New Crop of Super Rich," described the favorable tax situation.

Said the article:

> The tank cars of oil and fields of cattle are the basic ingredients of the Southwest's wealth. But almost as important are peculiarly favorable provisions of the U.S. income tax laws. The oilmen and ranchers can take far larger deductions than most businessmen elsewhere, which helps account for the Southwest's impressive number of expensive cars, furs, and mansions. It also helps explain why Neiman-Marcus has nearly 300 charge accounts that run over $50,000 a year.

Time once jabbed Murchison directly in an article that said, "One big reason Murchison is able to swing such varied deals is the tax bonanza enjoyed by all oilmen. This is the depletion allowance which permits them to pocket 27½ percent of their gross income (up to 50 percent of their net) before paying a cent of taxes."

Indeed, many times when a company of Clint's had substantial—or even small—taxable profits, he would instruct his associates, "Let's drill that up." But Clint found some grist of his own for Luce, when he learned that the press barons of Washington had convinced the United States government to give them a special postage rate—because of the alleged importance of the magazines to the citizens' welfare. Clint charged that Luce, with his special postage rate, had an unfair advantage over other businesses. Naturally, Clint's opinion did not receive nearly the amount of press that Luce's did.

By the early fifties Clint began to think that Henry Luce had it in for the oil industry. At every turn, it seemed, one of Luce's magazines took an unfavorable slant in its articles about the oil industry. Clint voiced his complaints to Luce in a series of letters, but was unable to get Luce to back down.

Clint explained to Luce one of his most unusual, most innovative ideas for the oil industry. He had devised a plan to inject cheap foreign oil into East Texas's depleted field.

Clint remembered World War II when U-boats were sinking America's tankers and America was depending on foreign sources for oil. He was concerned that if World War III broke out, the United States would be on its knees. Clint believed that the United States could assure itself enough oil reserves by using the 60-percent-depleted East Texas field for storage. The U.S. government could condemn the field, buy cheap oil from Middle East and South American countries, and pump it into the ground by reversing the pipelines.

Many people throughout America viewed Clint's idea as extraordinarily innovative. Others thought it ludicrous. Luce simply ignored the idea, preferring to hammer away on the issue of depletion.

Clint tried another approach. He was a brilliant economist with a far-reaching mind and extensive vocabulary. He was fascinated by the power of the pen, and he believed that if he could write articles for *Time,* he could help interpret world events. At the very least, he could give the articles a slant *he* preferred. He wrote a number of articles on the subject of international affairs and sent them to Luce anonymously, thinking they would have a better chance to be published if Luce did not know Clint had written them. He was disappointed when the articles never appeared.

But finally Clint was given the ultimate exposure in Henry Luce's most powerful magazine when his picture appeared on the cover of *Time.* The well-known illustrations of Artzybasheff for *Time*'s covers combined a realistic portrait of the subject with symbols of what had brought the man (or very occasionally woman) to this peak of recognition.

On the cover of the May 24, 1954, issue, bannered THOSE TEXAS MILLIONAIRES, the subject was identified as "Clint Murchison: A big wheeler-dealer." The cover showed

Clint—wrinkles, double chins, putty blob nose, elephant ears—in a symbolic straw cowboy hat, surrounded by a wagon wheel rimmed with dollar signs.

Then as now, the rich Texan was viewed by the rest of the world as a combination of boor and clown, and Artzybasheff's portrait contained not a hint of flattery, but the artist's sensitivity revealed this anything-but-handsome Texan's power, passion, and essential decency.

The story, titled "Tycoons: The New Athenians," also mentioned a half dozen of Texas's "big rich," but the focus was on Murchison. "Murchison is the first of a brand-new breed of Texas oilmen," the story explained. "Having made his millions in oil, he is now using them to further the popular Texas ambition of buying up the rest of the U.S.

"Murchison has built up an empire of 48 companies, with 50,000 employees and an estimated $350 million in assets—not to mention scores of lesser investments. No sooner has he bought a ship line than he wants a railroad, no sooner a candy company than he gets a grocery."

A map of the United States titled "Murchison's Millions" accompanied the story, and seventeen of its states were dotted with drawings of Murchison holdings, ranging from a hotel in California to a water tank in Indiana to an outdoor movie theater in Louisiana.

Murchison was a natural for a *Time* cover story. He was one of Texas's biggest oilmen, yet had strayed far from the oil patch, buying businesses from New York to California, from Canada to Mexico. He was also a good subject because he was politically controversial, while at the same time the most likable and colorful of all Texas oilmen.

The story that catapulted him onto the cover of *Time* had for months been receiving coverage on the business pages of America's newspapers and in its business magazines. Most business stories are quickly forgotten, but this one was remembered and embellished for years to come because of an anecdote.

Texas-born tycoon Robert R. Young had been, in the words of *Time*, "trying to catch an iron horse—the $2.7 billion New York Central Railroad." When he ran into difficulty in his campaign to win control of the Central, then the nation's second-largest railroad, he knew just where to turn. From Palm Beach, Young telephoned Murchison, "I need your help."

He wanted a friendly buyer for 800,000 Central shares, owned by the Chesapeake & Ohio Railroad. Murchison immediately agreed to put up $10 million to buy 400,000 shares of Central stock at $25 a share, then called Richardson and asked him to do the same. Richardson took the call just as he was headed out the door for a round of golf. In his haste he agreed to the deal, but when he returned he called Murchison again.

Richardson, startled to learn that he had committed not to half of a $10 million deal but a $20 million deal, cried, "What the hell did you say was the name of that railroad?"

When chided about this later, Sid said defensively, "Well, Clint mumbles so." Even if Murchison did mumble—and he did—the fact is that he and Richardson were powerful operators who dealt in millions but also retained their easygoing small-town trader outlook. They were hard drivers, but they were not driven. They were tireless deal makers, but it was a game they enjoyed.

Friendship was one reason for the purchase by the oilmen who planned to vote their 800,000 shares in favor of Young in his bitter proxy fight for Central's chairmanship but, as *Business Week* observed, "Those two don't lay out $20 million just to help a friend."

"Murchison and Richardson jumped at the deal," wrote *Time,* "because they know that Bob Young is an expert at parlaying shoestrings into golden chains." Not many months earlier Young had sold Murchison a 24 percent interest in his huge Investors Diversified Services, whose three subsidiaries sold savings certificates and other securities. Murchison's $5 million investment had grown to more than $7 million in three months.

The New York Central operation was performed quickly and painlessly, and abiding by the first article of faith in Clint's religion, "Thou shalt not use thine own money."

Time explained, "[Murchison] and Richardson did not

have to put up a cent of their own money, but borrowed the entire $20 million.

"They got more than half the money from Young's own Allegheny Corporation and his business associate Allan Kirby. With it, they got an option to sell 50 percent of the stock back to Allegheny at the $25 price they paid."

Five months later, when Young had won his control, Murchison and Richardson sold their shares with no loss and no profit except that they had won a powerful ally for future deals in Bob Young. But in business wars, as in national wars, alliances are not forever. Wall Street financier Allan Kirby had been a powerful and effective ally of Clint's in this fight, but only a few years later he would become the archfoe of Clint's sons in their biggest and most dangerous takeover attempt.

Alliances and betrayals on Wall Street have been one of the few constants in America's business history from before the time Cornelius Vanderbilt gained control of the New York Central in 1867 right up to today's most brutal takeover attempts. But neither Murchison nor Richardson was afraid of the Wall Street warriors. In fact, they found tangling with them at least as exciting as hunting rattlesnakes on Matagorda or wild boars at Acuña.

In the course of the Central fight, Richardson and Murchison were forced to testify in a New York Supreme Court. When Murchison told the court-appointed referee Robert Fitzsimmons that the New York Central deal was a "strictly run-of-the-mill investment," Fitzsimmons asked Clint, "Well, how much are you worth?"

"About five, six or seven million."

"A twenty-million-dollar deal is a pretty big bite for a man worth only one-third that amount."

Murchison later amended his original estimate. He was really worth, he guessed, "about thirty million" and added, "I consider money to be the same as manure. If you pick it up and put it out in the fields and till it, you get good returns."

"Twenty million dollars," snapped Fitzsimmons, "is a lot of fertilizer."

By the time the New York Central story hit the newspapers, legends about Sid and Clint were already legion. Dun & Bradstreet, according to local lore, once characterized Richardson this way: "Estimated worth $500,000,000. Pays bills promptly."

Eastern bankers unfamiliar with Murchison's and Richardson's love of credit were fascinated at the relaxed, almost nonchalant way in which the two described borrowing millions of dollars. One time, Clint and his cronies were gathered at the Dallas Petroleum Club when geologist Everett DeGolyer initiated a conversation about man's greatest inventions. Clint sat quietly listening, as the oilmen offered their opinions—the light bulb, the automobile, the wheel. When someone finally asked for Clint's opinion, he did not hesitate a moment. "The promissory note."

Clint and Bob Young became close friends during the New York Central deal, and Clint and Virginia were often guests at the Youngs' many homes. Bob, who came from a tiny town in West Texas, had long since traded Texas ruggedness for New York, Newport, and Palm Beach suavity. When Young was a nineteen-year-old student at the University of Virginia, he met and married Anita O'Keeffe, younger sister of the artist Georgia O'Keeffe. Anita was, in the phrase of the day, "a tearing beauty," six years older than Bob, very sophisticated and very assertive. They complemented each other in much the same way that Clint and Virginia did. He was brilliant and quiet, she was beautiful and outgoing.

Young's rise was swift. Out of college, he joined a top Wall Street firm, where he was made a partner in only a few years. He quickly acquired the trappings of East Coast wealth: a luxurious Park Avenue apartment, a summer home in Newport, a winter home in Palm Beach, and a home for all seasons in White Sulphur Springs, West Virginia.

Clint was very fond of Bob, but always felt uncomfortable as his houseguest. Virginia recalled a visit to the Youngs' estate in White Sulphur Springs, "Their servants were so formal, and the valet who was assigned to Clint never left his side. Clint finally drew the line when the butler preceded him into the bathroom, drew the bath, and stood waiting for Clint to climb in. Clint said, 'That's okay, you can wait outside the door. I've been bathing myself since I was three.' "

Another time, the Murchisons were guests at Montsorrel, the Youngs' opulent Palm Beach mansion. Young always took tea in the afternoon. Joining him were a handful of guests, mostly neighbors who also wintered at the luxurious Florida resort. When they assembled in the drawing room, perfectly groomed waiters primly passed delicate teacups and finger sandwiches.

Unlike his terribly refined host and the other Palm Beach gentlemen, Clint had great difficulty balancing a teacup and saucer on his knee. One minute he had the cup and saucer in his hand, then on the coffee table, then he held them in front of him, one hand on the saucer, the other on the cup's handle. The whole time he squirmed uncomfortably in a formal French chair.

Seeing how ill at ease Clint was, Young finally asked, "Would you rather have a drink?"

"Yes," Clint replied impatiently, "I'll have a double martini."

Anita had superb taste, and her homes were the envy of her guests. She had an extraordinary eye for color and style. Georgia O'Keeffe said late in her life that Anita would have painted circles around her had she not been afraid to free her imagination on paper. But Anita often duplicated Georgia's painting on the wall by putting a similar still life on a table in front of the painting.

The O'Keeffes that Bob and Anita owned were mostly colorful pastels of flowers, never the rugged Southwestern landscapes for which O'Keeffe is no less famous. Anita was not reticent in describing her distaste for New Mexico, saying she was amazed that her sister could live "in that barren, dry, ugly country."

Virginia many times told Anita how much she liked Georgia's works and that she would like to own one. But Anita repeatedly told Virginia, "Don't buy one. I'll give you one."

Anita never kept her promise, and Virginia never knew why. A possible explanation is that Anita feared Georgia would refuse to sell one of her works to the Murchisons. By the

1940s Georgia had become so successful that she could afford to indulge her wish to sell only to people she thought demonstrated a sensitivity to her work. Her paintings could not be purchased like a share of stock, Georgia insisted. Although Anita admired Clint enormously, she may have wondered whether Texas oilmen "qualified" in her sister Georgia's view.

The Youngs kept an apartment at New York's fashionable Waldorf Towers. Clint had many times stayed at the adjacent Waldorf-Astoria Hotel, beginning with one of his first trips there with his first wife, Anne, in 1926. As a regular and a Texas oilman, he was treated well, especially by the hotel's manager, Oscar, whom Clint instructed on everything from "charging a higher price for his rooms" to "the correct way for his staff to cook vegetables." When Young suggested Clint lease an apartment at the Waldorf Towers, Clint agreed it would be convenient, and in the mid-fifties, the Waldorf was added to the list of Murchison homes.

Clint was, in fact, eager to switch his allegiance to the Waldorf from the Plaza Hotel after an unfortunate incident in the mid-fifties. Clint left his Dallas office late one afternoon, met his pilot and plane, and departed for New York in a cotton suit. When he arrived at La Guardia, it was very chilly so he grabbed an old hunting jacket that was on the plane. He stepped off the plane and climbed directly into one of his limousines which took him to the hotel. When he entered the Plaza, he was wearing the three-quarter-length hunting jacket covered with blood and feathers.

The reservations clerk took one look at him and said, "*You* don't have a reservation here."

In his quiet way, Clint said, "Well, I . . . I think I do. Would you mind please checking again?"

"No, we have no room for you."

Finally Clint pulled out a 14-karat gold card that his friend and owner of the hotel, Conrad Hilton, had given him. The engraving read, "The bearer of this card, CW Murchison, will be accorded the hospitality of any Hilton."

Clint was quickly shown a suite, but it would never have occurred to him not to walk into the Plaza in an old, smelly, dirty hunting jacket.

Clint liked the Stork Club in New York, and the club's manager, Sherman Billingsly, liked him. He rarely sent a check to Murchison's table, a kindness that made Clint uneasy. One evening when the manager sent a complimentary bottle of champagne to the table, Clint told the waiter to bring him a bill for the bottle. When the waiter returned several minutes later, he told Clint that Billingsly refused to charge him for it. "In that case," Clint retorted, "tell him to send a case of it to the Waldorf."

Bob and Anita Young were wonderful to Clint and Virginia, introducing them to their New York friends, whisking them from Broadway shows to clubs to museums. But usually Clint retired right after dinner. The apartment was quite large, and easily accommodated several Dallas friends who were frequent houseguests when the Murchisons were in New York. On more than once occasion Clint was already at work at 5 A.M. in the living room when he heard his houseguests stumble in the door. He teased them, "You're sure up early."

Clint's relationship with Young was all too brief. In January 1958 he had been at Acuña and had not heard any news for several days. When his plane touched down at his Athens ranch, one of his servants rushed to his side and told him that Bob Young had shot himself to death in the billiard room of his Palm Beach mansion. Clint knew that Bob had faced financial problems during the months leading up to his death, and in the coming days his suspicions were confirmed by business associates who said they believed Young committed suicide because he thought he was broke. In fact, Young's fortune had fallen dramatically, but many of his associates viewed it as a temporary setback. Anita Young was the sole beneficiary of Bob's estate, reportedly estimated at $20 million. By 1958 standards, Young had left her a very rich woman.

Virginia kept in touch with her until Anita's death in 1985. Virginia's last hope that Anita would give her an O'Keeffe disappeared when she learned Anita left all ten of her O'Keeffe oils and five pastels to the Robert R. Young Foundation.

Following the publicity on Clint's association with the New York Central and the *Time* cover story, even more mail than

usual flooded the offices at 1201 Main. A hundred letters a day
was typical. Most were from people Clint had never met or
had met only briefly years earlier. Much of the mail that came
from around the world was addressed simply, "Clint Murchison, Dallas, Texas." One letter was addressed "Clint Murchison, Texas Millionaire," and another, "Clint Murchison, in
care of Stanley Marcus, Dallas, Texas."

There was some unfriendly mail, but most letters were from
fans, and much of it included solicitations for money. The
Time story inspired a rash of new publicity, from national
magazines and newspapers across the country, as well as the
interest of Edward R. Murrow and his popular CBS television
show *Person to Person.*

Clint limited the publicity about himself and his family by
refusing to be interviewed for many of the stories. But to Murrow, he was uncharacteristically cooperative, and in March
1955 he allowed Murrow's camera crew to film the inside of
the twenty-nine-room mansion. Murrow conversed casually
on film with Virginia and other members of the family and
closed the show with a person-to-person interview with the
legendary oilman. During the interview Murrow asked if
there were any businesses he would advise viewers to avoid.

"If they would take a page out of my book," Clint reflected,
"they would quit the chicken business. I've gone busted in it
about five times."

Although the *Time* cover story further enlarged his national reputation, he continued to rank far down the list of the
most powerful men in Dallas. Other oilmen and bankers were
far more prominent locally. Because his financial and personal
interests were so vast, Clint never became caught up in the
local spirit of boosterism. The men who ruled Dallas, via the
Citizens Council, were intimately acquainted with the city,
how it breathed and prospered. Clint, conversely, was busy
flying all over America, overseeing his far-flung interests,
meeting politicians in Washington or California, bankers in
New York. Dallas, for Clint, was no more than a base of operations, an address at which to receive correspondence.

Clint never became part of the Dallas establishment partly
because he did not feel strong ties to the city. He was not born

in Dallas, nor did he make his money there. Most of his family still lived in Athens, as did many of his friends. Several of his closest friends—Wofford Cain, Sid Richardson, and, at an earlier time, Toddie Lee Wynne—were not a part of the old Dallas establishment either. Like him, they had moved to the big city, but their hearts were still in East Texas.

With a few exceptions Clint did not give to local causes and charities. Oilmen were not accustomed to giving, in part because they did not need the tax write-off that has always spurred charitable giving. More importantly, oilmen hit a psychological stumbling block when they contemplated parting with dollars. Most of the richest also had great debts, and even when they owed nothing, as very few did, they never felt that they had a solid fortune to depend on. Many of their fellow oilmen had seen their fortunes disappear literally overnight, and while some won them back, many others did not. Even men in the $50 million range and up felt that their fortunes were only as good as their luck.

Like Hunt, Murchison was criticized by the Dallas establishment for his lack of philanthropy. When the *Time* magazine story appeared and listed his wealth at $350 million, a figure many Dallas businessmen thought was deflated (*The New York Times* said he was worth $400 million), the criticism grew worse.

An outsider would have been amazed that most of the criticism came from the rich, the power structure, and not from the poor or middle class. For generations, middle-class America has idolized the rich, but Texans take the phenomenon a step further. They seem to want the rich to succeed even at the expense of the poor and middle class. Part of the reason the middle and lower classes in Texas supported the enormous tax breaks afforded oilmen (i.e., depletion allowance) was the inherently optimistic feeling that they, too, might someday strike oil or great riches. When they "arrived," they would want those same advantages. The masses viewed Murchison not as a greedy oilman, uncaring or unmindful of society's needs, but rather as a sort of folk hero. He was a Texan's Texan, a symbol of the great wealth that thousands were trying to achieve.

In 1957 *The New York Times* named Murchison among the seventy richest men in America, a category that included New York's Vincent Astor and John Hay Whitney, Detroit's Mrs. Edsel Ford, international socialite Doris Duke, a few Wilmington du Ponts, and all of the third-generation male Rockefellers (David, John D. III, Laurence, Nelson, and Winthrop).

By the early sixties, when Clint Jr. and John Dabney were making multimillion-dollar deals weekly, their net worth was a constant source of speculation and gossip. Local newspaper articles estimated the father and sons' worth anywhere from $300 million to $1 billion. "They aren't as rich as the Hunts," friends and business associates said, "but they are a close second."

Whatever else the *Time* story did, it tore down the shroud of secrecy behind which the Murchisons had been able to operate for years. No longer could they buy and sell companies in their own name, but would henceforth do so under various aliases. Although Clint Sr. had at various times in the past been forced to operate this way, the practice was now a necessity. The mere fact that the Murchisons were involved in a deal made it newsworthy. Nor was the family ready to rest on its accomplishments. As *Time* explained, "Murchison has no doubts about which of his many big deals gives him the most pleasure. Says he: 'The next one.' "

13

"Murchison does everything by the ten thousands."

When executives of Clint Sr.'s far-flung companies had important business to discuss, they often found themselves boarding a plane for Dallas's Love Field, then heading for the Koon Kreek Klub, a millionaires' hunting and fishing lodge seventy-five miles southeast of Dallas. In a sturdy wooden rowboat on one of the club's five stocked lakes, Clint and his out-of-town associates made some of their most important business decisions.

Many of these men were used to making deals in the nation's most expensive dining rooms and clubs, and those who knew or cared about fishing were used to a rather more exotic form of the sport—fly fishing on some Scottish laird's racing brook, but not sitting in a rowboat on a still lake in the hot Texas sun, swatting mosquitoes, and waiting for the fish to bite.

The club's original mix of Dallas businessmen and local farmers changed during the thirties and forties so that by 1950 its members were almost all from Dallas and were mostly oilmen. But other than the wealth of its members, not much had changed about the club from the years when Clint was a boy growing up in Athens. The members still gathered for supper in a weatherbeaten wood clubhouse where they served themselves, boardinghouse style, fried fish and fried chicken, turnip greens, black-eyed peas, creamed corn, and peach cobbler. The evenings were filled with drinking and marathon gin rummy games, and a hefty dose of Texas good ole boy back slapping and camaraderie.

The club's main attraction was the fish. Five man-made

lakes, spread over 8,000 acres of swampy woodland, were stocked with varieties of native black bass, white perch, and Clint's favorite, bream. A tasty type of local sunfish, bream (pronounced "brim" in East Texas) is usually no larger than a man's hand, but unmatched in fight per ounce. Bream fishing requires no trolling, casting, or reeling, but simply pulling up to a brush pile at the lake's edge, hanging a cane pole over the side of the boat, watching the wiggly worm fall to the bottom, and waiting for a bite.

"Once you get over a bed of them, you can't work fast enough," Clint told an astonished female reporter from New York who came to the lake on assigment for *Sports Illustrated.* Despite the multibillion-dollar combined net worth of its members, she explained, "The club remains cultivatedly unpretentious. A stranger coming upon [it] in the east Texas wilderness might mistake it for the summer headquarters of the Salvation Army."

She was one of the first and last working journalists ever to make it through the club's front gate. It was precisely the simplicity of the fishing at Koon Kreek that Clint loved. "Brings a man back to his roots," he said. As for the luxury of a guide in every boat, who baited the members' hooks and removed the fish therefrom, Clint explained, "Gives a man time to do a little figuring."

Fishing for bream became such a popular sport that club members named this preoccupation the "Athenian Disease." Just as there were dry spells in the oil business, however, the anglers found that some years were better than others. Once when the bream stopped biting at Koon Kreek, member Sam Gladney built his own lake down the road.

Clint was a regular at the new bream lake, and to repay Gladney, an executive of the Sun Oil Company and a friend since the early days of the East Texas oil boom, he took out an oil lease on the property at a dollar an acre, the proceeds to go toward stocking the lake. Several years went by before Clint drilled on the lease, but when he did, he brought in a well. "Ruined the fishing," Gladney mused, "and we had to go back to Koon Kreek."

In addition to fishing, duck hunting was a popular sport.

According to a story in the local paper, "The club has 13 blinds on the lake. In the fall and winter ducks abound at one blind, and it is claimed more ducks are killed there than at any other in Texas. At that blind 3,000 ducks were killed last year."

The blind was number 11, the one that Clint and his friend Ike LaRue year after year managed to pick in the members' annual drawing to see which blinds would be theirs for the season. One year before the drawing, some of the members looked into the hat for number 11, and as they suspected, it was missing. It was never proven that Clint and Ike had pocketed the ticket, but from then on the tickets were closely guarded.

A longtime Athenian recalled the annual drawing. "You could see some of your buddies become more upset if they drew a not-so-good blind than if they'd come up with a dry hole."

The members were no less distrusting of one another in card games. "They put the spitoon in the middle of the card table," says a Henderson County historian, "because they were afraid to turn their heads to spit."

In the 1940s Clint read a magazine article that said the fifty-hour work week would soon be reduced to forty. He calculated that with shorter weeks, the average working person would have 20 percent more free time than before. As a result, Clint believed, people would travel more. He quickly snapped up an offer to buy—sight unseen—the Royal Gorge Bridge and Amusement Park in Canon City, Colorado, whose assets were slightly less than $1 million. The park's chief attractions were a 1,053-foot-high toll bridge spanning the Colorado River and a scenic railway that climbed from the river to the top of a cliff. Royal Gorge was one of Clint's most profitable investments, yet twenty years later he admitted, "I've never even seen the durned thing."

Clint also recognized that workingmen would have more leisure time for sports, which to him translated to hunting and fishing, and he purchased James Heddon's Sons, the best-known manufacturer of fishing tackle in America. The Michigan-based company, with assets of $2.8 million in the early 1950s, already had excellent management, and Clint assumed correctly that it could become even more profitable.

Despite his love of fishing in its simplest form, Clint was always interested in the newest fishing equipment Heddon turned out, and he wanted his buddies to see what money could buy in the way of tackles, hooks, and lures. Shortly after he bought Heddon, a salesman came to Koon Kreek to demonstrate the company's latest products, hundreds of different tackles in virtually every shape and every color of the rainbow. At the end of the weekend a few of the members asked the salesman what he wanted for everything he had brought with him.

"Three thousand dollars," the salesman replied.

Overhearing the conversation, Clint instructed the salesman, "Just go on and give this stuff to the guys here and charge it off to advertising."

Over the years Koon Kreek had as its guests many powerful politicians and captains of industry from around the country. Teddy Roosevelt was entertained there often, although, according to local lore, Teddy's cousin Franklin could never get through the front gate.

One of Koon Kreek's more amusing visitors was Pete Kriendler, who owned and operated New York's famous "21" club. Clint first started going to "21" in the 1930s when it was still a speakeasy. He had remained a regular customer over the years, and when it became the watering hole of America's rich and powerful, Clint Murchison was not the least important of its customers. Even in "21," where Fortune 500 executives, United States senators, and Hollywood movie stars were commonplace, heads turned when Murchison walked in, especially after his face appeared on the cover of *Time*.

"At one point when Clint was coming to '21,' he was considered the second or third richest man in America," recalls Kriendler, "but he never gave that impression. He didn't care where he sat, and he loved bourbon whiskey, but he never ordered it by brand name."

Clint enjoyed the casual atmosphere of "21" and the personal service that Pete Kriendler and his brothers gave their regular customers. What amazed and amused him the most was not the service or the famous customers who lined the bar at lunchtime, but that "21" charged eight dollars for a hamburger. "I can't get that for a steer," he cried.

In 1953 "Mr. Pete," as his friends knew him, had just returned from a month in Africa with theologian–doctor Albert Schweitzer when he received a phone call from Clint.

"Mr. Pete," Clint said excitedly, "you're coming down here to go fishing. I want to take you to the KKK."

"To the *Klan?*" Pete asked, disbelieving.

"No. To the Koon Kreek Klub."

Pete was relieved with his friend's reply but said he had to decline. "I've got a business to run. I can't just take off and go fishing the way you Texas millionaires can."

When C. R. Smith, the founder and president of American Airlines, got word of what happened to his buddy Clint, he had his vice president, O. M. "Red" Mosier, call Kriendler in New York. "You can't do this to the big boss," Mosier told Kriendler. "When Clint asks someone to come fishing, it's not a request, it's a command."

A few days later a complimentary round-trip ticket from American Airlines arrived in the mail and Pete was on his way to Texas and the "KKK." In Africa with Dr. Schweitzer, Kriendler had grown a six-inch moustache, three inches long on either side of his face. On his last day at Koon Kreek, a group of dirty, unshaven oilmen grabbed him and held him down as New Orleans surgeon Alton Ochsner shaved off the right half of the moustache. When Kriendler got back to New York, he filed a $100,000 lawsuit against Ochsner and the others who conspired against him—$1 for each hair. The newspapers picked up this sensational story, causing panic among some of the pranksters before they realized it was a joke.

Kriendler spent many more weekends at Koon Kreek and quickly learned about the fine art of Texas brag. "Those guys at Koon Kreek always bragged about how well they cooked their quail," says Kriendler. "They burnt them up in my opinion, so one time I went down there with a planeload of quail and showed them how to cook it. Later Clint would bring wild quail with him from Texas and Mexico for us at '21' to prepare for him. Those Texans never said anything about steaks because they knew our steaks were better than theirs."

Not every multimillionaire oilman was invited to join Koon Kreek. In the 1950s membership was limited to 145, with a regular waiting list of several hundred. Sid Richardson did not become a member until 1957, just two years before he died. "It was sort of a joke at first, to keep Sid out," said one of the members. "It got to the point where everyone was making fun of him because he had more reserves in the ground than anyone else in the United States. He was the richest man in America and he couldn't get into Koon Kreek."

One weekend in the early 1950s Clint was fishing with Ike LaRue, who had lived in Athens all his life. Ike tried to talk Clint into retiring to Athens. "Murk, why do you want to keep working? You've got more money than you and your children and grandchildren could ever spend."

Clint did not reply, he just smiled. A few weeks later, Ike called Clint in Dallas. "Murk, do you want to go fishing?"

Clint shot back, "No. You've got two large freezers full of fish. Why do you want to keep fishing? You've got more fish than you and your children and grandchildren could ever eat."

No story better illustrates Clint's love of business and making deals than this. It was the game of business that mattered, the sport of making a deal that lured him. The fact that by 1950 he and his children and grandchildren seemed financially set for life had no more to do with Clint's desire to keep making deals than the number of fish in Ike's freezer had to do with Ike's desire to keep fishing.

Although Clint was not ready to retire in the early 1950s, he did want a weekend place in Athens. But he needed a place that was either near an airport or had its own landing strip where he could come and go when business demanded. The Athens Airport was too small to handle the *Flying Ginny* and others of Murchison's fleet of airplanes. He tried to convince Koon Kreek to build a landing strip, but the members strongly objected, arguing that they paid a $2,500 initiation fee and $250 annual club dues to keep the place as simple and rustic as possible.

Unable to change their minds, Clint bought 4,000 acres up the road and began to develop a place of his own. He called it Gladoaks, the compound name of his fishing buddies Sam Gladney and Doak Roberts. Even before he found the land, he had decided to develop the property into a fabulous spread replete with orchards, pine trees, stocked lakes, duck blinds, cattle, a sprawling home, and, most essential of all, a long, broad runway.

Clint rented giant earth movers to cut a swath 3,300 feet long and 100 feet wide through brush oak and scrub oak for the landing strip. On a road from the main gate to the house that crosses the runway, he posted a warning sign, "Watch for Airplanes."

John Rogers, who worked for Clint from 1951 until 1969, recalls that the grass runway, which was frequently overrun with cattle, was so busy with corporate planes trying to land that some days the sky was thick with planes circling overhead.

"The landing strip could take a jet, with the result that there were always millionaires flying in and out of Gladoaks," says Rogers. "They came and went constantly."

As a boy, Clint picked peaches for pay in Athens, and he had long dreamed of owning a commercial peach orchard. At Gladoaks he planted a 300-acre peach orchard with 20,000 trees representing 30 different varieties of peaches. He also planted 10,000 pine seedlings, 30,000 dogwood trees, and 10,000 strawberry plants. "Murchison does everything by the ten thousands," a friend laughed.

He built two large lakes, which he stocked with 100,000 bream, bass, and crappie. He hired a crew of fishing guides and regularly invited his pals from Koon Kreek to fish at his place. "The fish are biting," translated into a fishing invitation, and the Koon Kreekers raced over to Gladoaks as fast as their Cadillacs and Rolls-Royces would take them.

His new venture in East Texas fell under the name of Anderson County Land & Cattle Company, ANLACO, and included several hundred head of Brangus cattle, the most popular breed of East Texas. The Brangus is one of the oldest American breeds and combines the best of the Brahma, which is capable of withstanding heat and insects, and the Angus, which fattens well to produce U.S. Choice steaks. Typically, it was not long before Clint's herd had increased into the thousands.

Clint loved the country-style food that was served in East Texas, and he loved Mexican food, the spicier the better, and there was nothing he enjoyed more than Early Caldwell's tamales. Early was a black man who had peddled tamales in Athens since 1919. He and Clint were about the same age and had hunted and fished together as boys. When Clint was in Athens, he was Early's biggest customer. The only car Early ever owned was a Model-A Ford, which he drove when he searched the fields for corn shucks for his tamales. Several times Clint tried to buy him a new car, but Early refused.

"I'll take it out in tamales," Clint pleaded, but the tamale man shook his head and said, "Mr. Clint, my Model-A can go in the sand hills where those newfangled cars can't. And that old Model-A of mine'll shake all the meanness out of you."

When Clint found something good, he wanted to share it with his friends, and he began sending Early's hauntingly hot tamales by air to friends around the world. It was not long before Dallas millionaires caught on and began flying to Athens just to pick up tamales.

Another of Clint's discoveries was a pair of calf-high, slip-on leather boots that he bought in Chicago. He wore the boots during the summer as well as winter, with shorts as well as long pants. One of Clint's friends went to the store in Chicago to exchange his pair for the right size, and mentioned to the store clerk that they were a gift from Mr. Murchison.

"Am I ever glad to know you," the clerk said. "Please tell me, who *is* this Mr. Clint Murchison?"

He then took the man to a back room and showed him a file of more than three hundred names of people to whom Clint had sent the boots as gifts.

By 1957 John Dabney and Clint Jr. had taken complete control of Murchison Brothers, operating independently of their father. They continued to ask his advice from time to time, but in no way did they depend on him for help in making an investment. Not only was Clint Jr. very confident of his capabilities, as he had been from the start, but also John Dabney had slowly but determinedly gained confidence in himself. Even when the boys were first starting in business, Clint Sr. kept them on a loose rein. He wanted them to consult their advisers but in the end to make their own decisions. Clint tried not to second-guess them, and he rarely offered unsolicited advice. After seven years of operating in the same building as his sons, he thought they could be even more independent of him if he moved out of the office at 1201 Main Street.

Clint got a good deal on a piece of property north of downtown, on Mockingbird Lane, just off the newly built North Central Expressway, the first major freeway linking the burgeoning suburbs of the north to downtown Dallas.

Jim Clark continued at 1201 Main, as adviser to the brothers. But Clark was increasingly frustrated with Clint Sr. "The unhappiest time I can remember for my dad at work was around 1957," recalls Jim Clark Jr. "He had gotten together eight million dollars and had put it in the bank ready to pay off some loans. On Friday afternoon Clint Sr. had his secretary call the bank to find out his balance. The bank said eight million, so Clint took the money out and used it to finance a deal over the weekend. He hated having that much money sitting in the bank. When Dad came in Monday morning, it was gone, and he had to call several bankers and tell them he couldn't make the payments on the loans as he had promised.

"Dad was really upset over this, and told Clint, 'You can't do that. It was set aside to make these loan payments.'

"Clint apologized and said, 'Let's get to work and see if we can find the money someplace else.' "

Late in 1957 Jim Clark started experiencing periods of sleeplessness, and in January 1958 he checked into Boston's Massachusetts General Hospital suffering from a nervous breakdown. Jim Clark Jr. attributes his father's breakdown in large part to his inability to impose order at 1201 Main.

"Dad was an extremely disciplined and organized person, and while he could cope with Clint Sr. who sometimes plunged into deals, he could not cope with Clint Jr. who always plunged. When Clint Sr. moved out of the building and Dad was dealing more with Clint Jr., it was a nightmare."

Not only did Clint Jr.'s free-wheeling business practices upset order at 1201 Main, but also Clint Jr. was having extra-marital affairs that were anything but discreet. This would not have caused problems for Jim Clark if the Murchisons had not been so famous and if journalists had not been interested in the intimate details of the personal lives of the very rich. But because the Murchisons were big news and Clint Jr. was a flagrant adulterer, Jim Clark frequently found himself trying to cover up potential scandals.

Once, at the precise moment when the Murchisons were trying to buy a major American company, Clark spent all night on the phone trying to talk a well-known Washington columnist out of printing an item about one of Clint Jr.'s affairs. Clark succeeded in keeping it out of the papers, but whether it was cleaning up Clint Jr.'s fast and furious plunging in business or the residue of his adulteries, this was not the kind of work Clark could tolerate.

Jim Clark finally ended his regular association with the Murchisons in 1958. He spent the last twenty years of his life building the greatest private collection of Piet Mondrian paintings outside of Holland. At his death in 1979, Clark had donated more than fifty works of various artists to the Dallas Museum of Art, constituting the basis of the museum's modern art collection.

At his new office on Mockingbird, Clint continued to snap up companies. By now he had large holdings in many major industries, from oil, insurance, and finance to publishing and heavy manufacturing. But by the end of the fifties it was obvious that Clint was staying in the swing of business primarily for the thrill of it.

When one of his friends complained that rich men work just for charity, Murchison retorted, "*I* don't. I work for fun."

One of the companies he had the most fun owning was the Daisy Manufacturing Company, world's largest maker of BB guns. The firm's most famous product was the Daisy Air Rifle, a gun Clint had owned and loved as a young boy. He wanted his four young grandsons to experience the excitement of knowing that their grandfather, "Pop," owned Daisy Air Rifles. In 1957, when he learned that the Arkansas-based company was for sale, and that its projected sales that year were $11 million (up a few million from the year before), he purchased an 83 percent controlling interest. Typically, Clint did not interfere with the company's management, which was superbly headed by a grandson of Daisy's founder.

While he was as fervent as ever in his desire to keep working, it was obvious that he could not keep up his former breakneck pace. He was sixty-two years old in 1957, when he moved into his office on Mockingbird, and talking more and more of "retiring to the sunny valleys of Mexico."

On a trip to Acuña in 1958, Clint suffered a stroke. As a result, his speech was slurred and his walk was wobbly, but both afflictions were so slight they were almost unnoticeable. Nevertheless, Clint and Virginia flew directly from Acuña to the Ochsner Clinic in New Orleans. Clint checked in for a few days of tests, then flew to Baylor University Hospital in Dallas. At Baylor doctors opened a clogged vein in his neck that had caused the stroke.

After his stroke he began spending more time at Gladoaks, and doctors from Dallas, as well as other specialists from around the country, flew in regularly to check his health, and, of course, to fish. "I've got the fishing poles, I'll count on you to bring the stethoscopes."

Clint told his doctors, "I feel insecure in my walking, very wobbly, especially when I drink," but he never complained.

By 1959 his memory had begun to fail, and he asked his secretary to begin listening in on his phone calls and making notes in case he missed something, but, ever the gentleman, Clint warned her, "If it's George Greer, I think you won't want to stay on the line." George's prose became a little purple at times.

Clint went to his office on Mockingbird less and less frequently, but he kept in touch from Gladoaks with his business dealings and associates. Clint and Sid continued to call one another, always collect, at least two or three times a week. The call was usually placed between 4 A.M. and 5 A.M.

Sitting at an oak card table in pajama bottoms and an old pullover sweater, cigarette in one hand, coffee cup in the other, Clint waited for Sid to pick up the phone and accept the call. Then he mumbled, "What's the dope?"

They discussed possible deals in which they could act as partners. "Count me in for five," meant $5 million.

Early one Sunday morning he wanted to call John in Dallas. "Dial up John Dabney and Lupe," he told one of his Athens cronies who was summoned to Gladoaks for breakfast, usually around 6 A.M.

"Now, boss, let's not call John and Lupe," the friend replied. "You know they went to one of them big society deals in Dallas last night. They're going to be real tired and probably still asleep."

Clint insisted on placing the call and told the help to wake John. Clint talked to John for five minutes about a matter of such immediate importance as peach crop predictions for the next decade.

Clint had so many interests and his friends were of such different socioeconomic backgrounds that in a single morning on the phone he discussed such varied topics as: a new law governing insurance companies, a good bowl of chili, how a recent political event in China might bring about World War III, how legislation in Washington was going to affect real estate values in America, his favorite whiskey, a new book on the poetry of Robert Frost, how well the fish were biting at Gladoaks, a genetic experiment for crossbreeding cattle, horse racing in California, oil discoveries in the Middle East, his grandchildren.

The next morning he addressed two dozen entirely different topics.

On the first day of October 1959, Clint overheard a workman at Gladoaks say something about Sid Richardson. Listening more closely, he heard the man say that Richardson had died the day before. Clint immediately returned to the house, called his secretary in Dallas, and asked her to call Sid's nephew Perry Bass in Fort Worth. The phone rang at Gladoaks a few minutes later. "Uncle Sid died in his sleep last night at St. Joe," Perry said. "We wanted to make some arrangements before we called you, Clint."

On September 29, 1959, Sid and some fishing buddies had gone to St. Joe's island and retired early. The next morning when Sid was not up at his usual hour, friends looked in on him, and he appeared to be sleeping. A little later one of the guests grew concerned and checked him again. He found Richardson dead.

Sid died in the night of an apparent heart attack. He was sixty-eight years old. Newspapers around the world described him as the fourth or fifth richest man in America. His only Texas rival for "richest man in America" was H. L. Hunt. But while Hunt had a larger daily income from producing oil, Richardson owned more proven oil reserves—more than any other individual and more than several of the major oil companies.

The same day that Clint Sr. learned the news about Sid, John Dabney and Clint Jr. flew from Dallas to Gladoaks to be with their father. They knew how sad he must be, and they stayed for more than a week.

Virginia was on a trip around the world and called immediately when she heard the news. She said she would come home, but Clint quietly told her not to. "There's nothing you can do."

Hundreds of calls of condolence jammed the telephone lines at Gladoaks. President Eisenhower was among the first to call, followed by Senator Lyndon Johnson, Speaker of the House Sam Rayburn, and evangelist Billy Graham, a close friend of both Richardson and Murchison.

Graham gave part of the eulogy at Sid's funeral a few days later in the packed 1,780-seat Broadway Baptist Church in Fort Worth. Graham spoke dramatically, leaning from the pulpit, which was adorned by a large white floral cross sent by President and Mrs. Eisenhower. Among the hundreds gathered were a large group of East Texas Baptists who before and after the services reminded several of Richardson's heirs that the billionaire had pledged $100,000 toward construction of an auditorium for Athens' First Baptist Church but that the money had not yet come in.

The Baptists need not have worried. The Richardson Foundation saw to it that the money was given, the auditorium built, and dedicated, as Sid wanted, to his mother, Mary Richardson. Sid had been baptized at the church when he was twelve years old, and he was buried only a few blocks away at the Athens City Cemetery.

Billy Graham tried with no success to comfort Clint, reminding him that, "Sid slipped away in his sleep without pain." But, as always, Clint had great difficulty accepting the death of someone he loved. This time he had lost his oldest and closest friend.

As a multimillionaire who trusted people implicitly, Clint had been cheated and betrayed, tricked or disappointed by a number of men in his long career. But Sid's friendship had been ideal. In a letter to a friend, a week after Sid died, Clint revealed that he had never had a disagreement with Sid in all their many years as business partners and friends.

Neither man was as colorful without the other. Their aphorisms and folksy expressions were best when they were a combined effort, one man acting as the other's straight man. Even the sound of their names went together, Sid Williams Richardson and Clint Williams Murchison. When they were photographed in front of the New York Central Building at Grand Central Station, each in a rumpled suit and tie, each politely holding his hat in his hand, they still had an air of casualness, a confidence of country boys who had made good.

In his will Sid left five trusts, one to his sister, Anne Richardson Bass, and one to each of his great nephews, Sid, Edward, Robert, and Lee Bass. The trusts were the foundation of the present multibillion-dollar Bass fortune.

More than $100 million went to establish the Sid W. Richardson Foundation. Among its many philanthropic functions, the foundation established a museum on the ground floor of a building in downtown Fort Worth that is a replica of an 1895 period building. The museum today houses fifty-two of Richardson's works of Remington and Russell.

For years before Clint married Virginia—and later when Virginia was away traveling—Clint and Sid spent many nights together, sleeping in the same room. After turning out the lights, they lay awake talking of politics and fishing, oil and cattle, but mostly, in the dark of the room, they spun new deals, a pastime they had shared since they were young boys. Neither man ever lost his love of spinning ideas into dollars, of adding millions to his millions.

"Every kid ought to be raised in a small town because it gives him a chance to study human nature," Sid explained about his and Clint's enormous wealth.

As he grew older, he added, accurately, "Me and Clint'll be tradin' till they bury us."

PART
THREE

14

"I asked my friends what people around the country think of when they think of Texas. Most of them said, 'Cowboys.'"

In 1958 one of the owners of the Los Angeles Rams football team invited Clint and Virginia to be his guests in the owner's box at Los Angeles Coliseum. On the way to the game, the Rams' owner was describing the thrill of owning a professional football team. Clint listened carefully, then asked candidly, "Did the Rams make any money last year?"

"Oh, no," came the swift reply. "It's just a fun thing."

Clint would never forget those words. What concerned Clint Sr. was Clint Jr.'s relentless efforts to acquire a National Football League franchise. It was rare for Clint to worry about his sons. Mistakes were okay in Big Clint's view. He went along with Clint Jr.'s contract to widen the Panama Canal, even when close associates told him to step in and stop his son from risking the family fortune. But from the very start, and for the rest of his life, the father worried that his younger son's idea for turning a professional football team into a sound investment was too risky, too daring, too unlikely.

Clint Sr. believed that while Clint Jr. was a genius, he was also unbalanced. He frequently failed to see the practical side of ideas, the bottom line. When Clint returned to Dallas, he repeated the Rams' owner's comment to his younger son. Typically, Clint Jr. was absolutely unmoved by the remark or its implications. It would not alter his plan in the least. "Clint Jr. was very strong-headed," notes an intimate. "The more you told him something couldn't work, the more he was going to prove to you that it could."

Never before or again would Clint Jr. feel more passionate about anything than he did about owning a professional football team. Clint Jr. had loved football from the time he was a young boy. At prep school he weighed only 125 pounds, stood only five feet six, and had tiny hands, but he had superb hand and eye coordination and he made a scrappy halfback on the Lawrenceville team.

Professional football made its debut in Texas in September 1952, when a twenty-one-man syndicate of industrialists and oilmen bought the losing New York Yankees NFL football team, moved it to Dallas, and renamed it the Dallas Texans. The Texans' first game in Dallas was against the New York Giants, former crosstown rival of the Yankees turned Texans. The Texans scored first when a gifted young Giants halfback named Tom Landry fumbled a punt at his own 22-yard line.

In the stands watching Landry fumble was twenty-nine-year-old Clint Murchison Jr. who wanted so much to support the struggling Dallas Texans that he bought twenty season tickets. His enthusiasm waned after a half dozen disappointing losses by the Texans, but he still liked the team so much that at mid-season he offered to buy it. The owners seemed interested in selling, but when Clint asked to look at their books, they declined and the sale fell through. After just one season the Dallas Texans folded. Clint was determined to bring professional football back to Dallas, and he began aggressively searching for an NFL team to buy. Two years after the Texans left town, Clint came close to buying the San Francisco 49ers, but again he was unsuccessful.

The price of an NFL franchise had increased an incredible 6,000 percent in just over two and a half decades, from $10,000 in 1933 to $600,000 in 1959, causing some shortsighted critics to insist that Clint had arrived too late on the scene. But Clint believed professional football was still an infant industry, bound to become vastly more profitable because of television. Clint never believed he could make a large year-to-year profit on a professional football team, but he was lured by the buy-low, sell-high potential. Most of all, he simply loved football and wanted Dallas to have a franchise.

In 1958 he came very close to buying the Washington Redskins for the going price of $600,000, and bringing the team to Dallas. Redskins owner and manager, George Preston Marshall, appeared eager to sell because his team was doing poorly and he allegedly needed the money. Under the terms of the deal, Marshall would stay on as the Redskins manager for five years. Because Clint was busy with other businesses in Dallas, Tom Webb, who handled the Murchisons' financial and political interests in Washington, negotiated the deal with Marshall.

After a long and arduous negotiation, terms were agreed on and Clint drew a cashier's check for $600,000. But just as Webb was preparing to announce the sale to the press, Marshall called and said he wanted to stay on as manager for ten years rather than five. Marshall had changed the terms several times already, and when Webb called Clint to tell him the news, Clint shouted into the phone, "Tell him to go to hell. The deal's off."

Clint decided his best chance at owning a team was to start one himself, and in February 1959 he met with Chicago Bears owner and coach George Halas, chairman of the NFL expansion committee. The NFL had decided to expand its twelve teams to fourteen in 1961, and Clint was excited at the prospect of Dallas being included in the expansion.

On August 29, 1959, six months after their first meeting, Clint met again privately with Halas, this time in Houston. Clint pressed Halas to make a statement about whether Dallas would get a franchise. He told Halas he needed to know not only if it would happen but when, so that he could negotiate for a Cotton Bowl lease and dissuade Lamar Hunt from starting a Dallas team under a new league. Clint believed that Hunt, the quiet, personable youngest son of H. L. Hunt, was under the assumption that Dallas would not have an NFL franchise—or at least not for several years. Halas was impressed with Clint's eagerness to field a team. Even more importantly, he was anxious for the NFL to establish a Dallas team to "get off on equal footing" with Hunt's ball club. Halas agreed to give Clint a franchise, contingent on a vote by the NFL owners in January.

When Lamar heard the news, he was furious. He was indeed under the impression that Dallas would not have an NFL franchise, and he had already spent a great deal of time and money planning a team—the Dallas Texans—as well as a new league. In August 1959, just two weeks before Halas announced that the NFL would expand into Dallas, Lamar had met in Chicago with owners from Houston, Los Angeles, Denver, Minneapolis, and New York, to establish the American Football League. Hunt and the other five owners each put up $25,000 for their AFL charter franchise.

When Clint learned how angry Lamar was, he decided to make a peace offering, and on September 1, 1959, he went to see Lamar at his office. "Lamar, if you want to own a team this badly," Clint reportedly said, "why don't you take the NFL franchise?"

When Lamar declined, Clint said, "Well, then at least come in fifty-fifty with me."

Lamar again declined, explaining that he had commitments to five other team owners whom he had just brought together to charter a new league. In the coming months Hunt was publicly outspoken against the NFL, calling the move into Dallas "sabotage." The NFL's purpose in fielding a Dallas team became even more obvious when it announced the Dallas expansion would occur in 1960, a year earlier than the original date, to coincide with the starting season of Hunt's Dallas Texans.

Murchison hired the organization's key administrators during the fall of 1959, months before the vote was taken. The first man Clint spoke with was Texas E. "Tex" Schramm, who had spent ten years with the Los Angeles Rams, first as publicity director and later as general manager. Schramm later joined CBS as assistant sports director, where he remained until George Halas introduced him to Murchison in 1959. During their first meeting Schramm explained to Clint the importance of having a direct line of authority in operating a ball club. Schramm told him "the only person the players should be responsible to is the coach and the only person the coach is responsible to is the general manager and so on up and down the line."

Clint knew immediately that Schramm was capable and knowledgeable enough to turn his dream into a reality. Schramm was well-schooled in running a ball club, and during his time with CBS he had studied teams throughout the country—their trends and innovations, failures and successes. Clint's philosophy fit Schramm's exactly, and he made it clear that his mode of operating was the same as his father's and his brother's: "Get the best men for the job and let them run the show." Ten days after their first meeting, Schramm was hired as general manager.

Clint and Schramm wanted as head coach a smart thirty-seven-year-old former defensive coach for the New York Giants by the name of Tom Landry. After playing halfback for the New York Yankees, Landry had moved to the Giants, where he was a tough defensive back for six years. For two years after that, he was both a player and a coach before becoming a full-time defensive coach in 1956. Under Landry's leadership, the Giants had become the best defensive team in the league. Clint remembered Landry's fumble in Dallas in 1952, but since then he had heard the coach described as "the thinking man of football."

Clint liked the fact that Landry had been known as one of football's leading intellectuals. He was cool and calculating about the game. As was the case with Clint, emotion had no place in Landry's makeup. Even when he was playing football, Landry had characteristics unmatched in the NFL; while others played the game, he studied it.

Landry had gotten a college degree in industrial engineering, and coaching football was not in his long-term plans, but he decided to try it for a year or two. The general who had brought military precision to the Giants' defensive unit, however, soon found himself in charge of a group of inexperienced, out-of-step foot soldiers.

The NFL still had to approve unanimously the Dallas franchise, and it appeared Clint's old nemesis, George Preston Marshall of the Redskins, was going to vote against it. The Redskins had fans throughout the South and Southwest, and Marshall feared some of those loyalties would be lost to Dallas. The NFL owners were a fraternal, clubbish group of rich men, and Marshall put out the word that he would not vote for Dallas because he found Clint to be "personally obnoxious."

A few years earlier, when Clint was trying to buy the Redskins, Marshall had fired Barnee Breeskin, who had written the words to the Redskins' fight song and led the band that played in the stadium. Breeskin, knowing that the Murchisons had bad feelings toward Marshall, asked Tom Webb if he would like to buy the rights to the fight song, "Hail to the Redskins."

Webb felt that these rights might someday be useful as a bargaining chip in buying the Redskins, and he paid $2,500 for the rights. In anticipation of getting his franchise, Clint went to the league meeting in Miami Beach in January 1960, where the board would vote on expansion. A few days before the vote, Clint and Marshall, who had not met, each dined one night with a group of friends in the same restaurant. Knowing the antagonism that existed between the two men, no friend of either was daring enough to introduce them.

Later Clint telephoned Marshall in his hotel room. "George, since no one will introduce us, I'd like to introduce myself."

Marshall invited Clint to his room, but when Clint arrived he was not given the warmest reception. "You took my fight song," Marshall charged.

Clint did not know that his associate Webb had the rights, but he quickly learned that Marshall cared passionately about the song. In fact, for more than a week, the Washington press had been lambasting Murchison for his "dirty trick." One columnist claimed, "Taking 'Hail to the Redskins' away from George Marshall would be like denying 'Dixie' to the South, 'Anchors Aweigh' to the Navy, or 'Blue Suede Shoes' to Elvis."

But the two men, sitting in Marshall's hotel room, reached an agreement. Marshall agreed to vote in favor of the Dallas franchise on January 28, 1960, in exchange for the rights to his song. Clint paid $550,000—$50,000 for the franchise, $500,000 for the players to be drawn from existing teams. The purchase caused one wit to comment, "He bought it for a song."

Not everything in Miami Beach seemed so cheap. For the fun of it, Clint had taken with him to Miami a dozen friends and associates, on two Murchison airplanes. While the NFL met in several sessions, Clint and his friends lounged by the pool at the luxurious Kenilworth Hotel. Clint was footing the entire bill for his party of friends for what was supposed to be a two-day meeting.

But the league meeting lasted eleven days, during which time his group's bar bill alone could have stretched from Miami to Dallas. After the vote was announced in Clint's favor, a reporter rushed up to him outside the meeting room. "Sir, are you prepared to come up with five hundred fifty thousand dollars cash?"

"I better be," Clint said dryly, "or I won't be able to get out of the hotel."

Back in Dallas, Schramm scrambled to put together a football team whose first game was scheduled in seven months. Although John Murchison's financial stake in the team was the same as Clint's—Murchison Brothers originally owned 95 percent of the company—it was incorrectly assumed in Dallas that John was not involved. And most people thought Clint Jr. was only a 50 percent owner, and that his friend Bedford Wynne owned the other 50 percent. This misconception was inspired in large part because Bedford, a nephew of Clint Sr.'s former partner Toddie Lee Wynne Sr., acted as the front man for the organization, while Clint kept a low profile. In fact, Wynne owned only 5 percent of the team.

One of Schramm's first decisions—to name the team the Dallas Rangers—turned out to be a bad one. Dallas already had a baseball team by the same name, but Schramm believed the team was about to leave town. When the Rangers baseball team stayed, he and Murchison were forced to come up with a new name. "We thought and thought and thought," says Schramm. "I asked my friends what people around the country think of when they think of Texas. Most of them said, 'Cowboys.' "

The Cowboys had not been permitted to participate in the draft in December 1959, because Murchison did not have a franchise at the time. As a result, the team was badly crippled, but Schramm paid the Rams $5,000 for their scouting files on players who had not been drafted, and used his connections from coast to coast to sign free agents for the still-unofficial NFL team. The player situation was not vastly improved

Virginia Long in 1943 when she became engaged to Clint Sr.
(Courtesy Virginia Murchison Linthicum)

Lt. John Dabney Murchison during flight training in the Army Air Corps, November 1942. *(Courtesy Carr Pritchett)*

(Left to right:) Clint Jr., Jane Coleman Murchison, and best man John Dabney at Clint and Jane's wedding, June 12, 1945. *(Courtesy Virginia Murchison Linthicum)*

Building the house at Acuña in the late 1940s. At center are Clint Sr. and Virginia. *(Courtesy Virginia Murchison Linthicum)*

The Duchess of Windsor's visit to Acuña in 1950. With her are Clint Sr. and Robert Young. *(Courtesy Virginia Murchison Linthicum)*

Clint Sr., Wofford Cain, and Sid Richardson In East Texas. *(Courtesy Virginia Murchison Linthicum)*

Clint and Virginia in 1954. *(Courtesy Clint Murchison Memorial Library)*

Sid Richardson advising Clint who is leaving for Canada on the "Flying Ginny." *(Courtesy Clint Murchison Memorial Library)*

Clint Jr. proposing a project to his brother and father. *(Courtesy Clint Murchison Memorial Library)*

Time, May 24, 1954.
(Courtesy Time *magazine)*

Clint Sr. at his
Gladoaks work
table in his
everyday dress.
(Courtesy Life
magazine)

Dallas Cowboys founders at the beginning. (Left to right:) Tex Schramm, Bedford Wynne, Clint Jr., Tom Landry.
(Courtesy Tex Schramm)

Clint Jr., Jane, and their four children in front of their three-bedroom house. (Top left:) Clint III, (bottom, left to right:), Robert, Coke Ann, Burk.
(Courtesy Life *magazine)*

Lupe Murchison at home, 1960.

John, thirty-nine, and Clint Jr., thirty-seven, on *Time*'s cover, June 16, 1961. *(Courtesy* Time *magazine)*

Clint Jr. with an electronic scrambler on his telephone to discourage wIretapping. *(Courtesy* Life *magazine)*

John and Lupe
Murchison in front of
their home in Vail,
Colorado.
(Credit:Toni Frissell)

John and Lupe at
daughter Mary
Noel's wedding,
1974. *(Photo by
Dian Malouf,
Courtesy Lupe
Murchison)*

when the franchise was granted. The Cowboys were given only twenty-four hours to select three players from each of the twelve NFL teams. But each of these existing NFL teams was allowed to protect twenty-five names on its roster, leaving the new expansion team to pick from many of the least capable, the oldest, or injured players in the league. "It reminded me of the words on the Statue of Liberty," says Schramm, " 'Send me your tired, your poor . . .' "

The 1960 Cowboys had to pick from the worst pool in the history of the NFL draft, and with only twenty-four hours to make their selections, Schramm and Landry did not have the luxury of picking the best of the available players. They had the much more elemental problem of making sure they had players for each position on the team.

If the Cowboys' ineptness showed on the field—and it did—it showed to very few people. Professional football was still a novelty, one that received almost no attention in a city whose football loyalties had long been directed to the collegiate Southwest Conference. It seemed highly unlikely that Dallas could or would support a professional football team, and in 1960 it had not one but two teams vying for fans.

Before the 1960 season began, Lamar Hunt's AFL brought a $10 million antitrust suit against the NFL. The suit charged that the older league attempted to move in and monopolize cities where the AFL was trying to operate. The NFL counter-charged that the AFL had moved into cities where NFL teams already existed and therefore was guilty of the same attempts. Hunt argued that the size of the market made the difference between free competition and attempted monopoly, and insisted that Dallas, a town of less than 700,000 in 1960, could support only one team—and his Texans got there first.

With the AFL's antitrust suit in the courts, both Clint's Cowboys and Lamar's Texans opened their first season in 1960 and both played at the Cotton Bowl, located on the State Fair of Texas fairgrounds. Size-conscious Texans were quick to brag to out-of-towners that the Cotton Bowl with its 75,504 seats was one of the largest stadiums in the NFL, second only to Cleveland Municipal Stadium. But the professional game, played on Saturday nights and Sunday afternoons, was an anticlimax to the wildly popular Saturday afternoon collegiate games, and as a result had a meager following in Dallas. There were no turnstiles in the Cotton Bowl in 1960, and it was just as well. The first Cowboys game brought a crowd estimated at slightly more than 20,000, and that was by far the highest attendance it would have all season.

Because Hunt's Texans reserved most Sunday afternoons at the Cotton Bowl for its games, the Cowboys had to settle for Friday nights and Saturday afternoons, with the result that they were competing for fans with high school and college games being played at the same time. Each Cowboys game for the remainder of the year saw spectators straggle in at the rate of 10,000 to 15,000, with rainy day lows of as few as 4,000 or 5,000. To those in the stands, and especially to the owners, the numbers seemed even smaller.

What little interest in professional football existed locally was divided between the Cowboys and the Texans. From the very beginning it was clear that although both Murchison and Hunt were concerned with the bottom line, neither was going to give up without a hard fight. Hunt's league was featherweight compared to the long-established heavyweight NFL. Because of this, the press made the Texans the "underdogs," a notion that amused Murchison. "Well, I'll be damned," he said. "That's the first time I've ever heard anyone call a Hunt an underdog."

Both teams campaigned hard for public favor, and both used a lot of promotional razzle-dazzle. The Texans distributed thousands of complimentary tickets in the most imaginative ways. Some were released in helium-filled balloons, others came in packages of corn chips. In a gimmick called the School Teacher Caper, Lamar hired twenty-five high school teachers to drive around town trying to sell tickets. Though this attempt failed, there was a bright side for Lamar. He fell in love with and married one of the teachers, Norma Knobel.

For their part, the Cowboys commissioned a star middle linebacker to ride around Dallas in a sleek and shiny convertible, attempting to peddle season tickets, but he too had little success. After several games came and went with no outpouring of fans, the press began to make fun of both teams, suggesting, "Why not save time at the start of the game, and instead of introducing the players, introduce the fans?"

A song, written about the 1952 Dallas Texans, was resurrected in 1960 about both Dallas teams:

> Oh give me a home
> Where the millionaires roam
> And three hundred grand is just hay.
> Where seldom is allowed
> A discouraging crowd,
> And the Cotton Bowl is jammed every day

At one Cowboys game, 8,000 spectators rattled around the stadium, and when it started to rain, they all scurried for cover under the press box—where Clint was sitting—and under the top section overhang. From Clint's view, it looked as if the Cotton Bowl were empty. He later confessed that the sight was so discouraging he did not go back to the press box for another two years.

In fact, the comment was probably made in jest, for Clint felt confident that crowds eventually would come. In the meantime he decided to have fun with the low attendance figures. When New York restaurant owner Toots Shor sent him two tickets to a Dallas game at Yankee Stadium, Clint sent Shor in return 10,000 tickets—four full sections—to an upcoming Giants game at the Cotton Bowl. "It was the least I could do after he got me those two tough tickets," Murchison said. Shor always contended his Texas friend got the best of the deal.

Clint met a radio broadcaster from a Paris network who was in Dallas on assignment. Displaying his puckish sense of humor, he invited the Parisian to broadcast five minutes of one of the Cowboys' Sunday afternoon games on a Dallas radio station. The man did so, in scarcely intelligible English, but it inspired not a single comment from the listening audience, convincing Clint that a radio audience did not exist.

Still, Clint never gave the impression of being worried.

Once, with a game just six days away, he asked Schramm how many tickets had been sold. "Seven," Schramm said.

"Well, why would anyone want to buy tickets now, anyway?" Clint said. "It's too early."

He even made fun of the personal rivalry between himself and Hunt. "In between lawsuits," Murchison laughed, "Lamar and I get along well."

A relentless prankster, Clint donned a red Texans' blazer and arrived at a Texans booster club gathering. He stuck his head in the door, smiled, waved to the group, then left. A few weeks later, at a gathering at Clint's home, some friends wheeled into the party a large gift-wrapped box. Clint pulled the ribbon and out popped Lamar.

While such tomfoolery seemed anything but acrimonious, friends and business associates of both men began to wonder, and many worried, how long the competition could continue.

A story circulated that a friend of H. L. Hunt telephoned the old wildcatter and warned him that Lamar risked losing a great deal of money if he continued to bankroll the Texans.

Hunt, so the story goes, asked, "How much?"

"About a million dollars a year," the friend replied.

"In that case," H. L. responded, "it will take him a hundred and fifty years to go broke."

Attendance figures of 30,000 were needed to break even, and many games drew less than one-third that number. Both teams made far less on gate receipts and television revenue than their operating costs. After watching Pittsburgh battle Philadelphia at the start of 1961, Clint told Pittsburgh Steelers owner Art Rooney how much he enjoyed the game. "It's the first game I've watched since joining the NFL that didn't cost me fifty thousand dollars."

Although Clint loved to plunge into deals, just as his father did, he also had his father's extraordinary patience to wait for the return on his investments. By the end of 1960, his Cowboys investment was $1.3 million—$700,000 in losses, plus the $600,000 price tag for the franchise. He expected to lose far less than that during each of the next four years, but he did not expect to break even or see a return on his money until 1965 at the earliest.

The financial yardstick that had always mattered more to Clint—his buy-low, sell-high measurement—was increasingly reassuring as his predictions that the cost of a franchise would continue to soar in the 1960s proved correct. In 1966 the Atlanta Falcons entered the National Football League at a cost of $8.5 million, nearly fifteen times what Clint had paid for the Cowboys franchise just six years earlier.

Clint believed his team would prevail in Dallas, partly because the Cowboys had the attraction of bringing to town established NFL teams and their star players. Hunt was not only saddled with building a team, but he was also committed to the enormous task of building an entire league. As early as 1961, *Sports Illustrated* said the Cowboys had a better chance than the Texans for financial success. Still, on the surface it seemed the Texans could win the battle for fans. The Cowboys finished the 1960 season last in the Western Conference, with a disconcerting record of eleven losses, one tie, and no wins, while the Texans finished with eight wins and six losses. But the records were not comparable because all the AFL teams the Texans played were new, inexperienced expansion teams in 1960, while the Cowboys played only established and tougher NFL teams.

The Cowboys' crowds were smaller than the Texans', but they had a much higher percentage of paying fans, and their tickets were more expensive. Because none of the AFL teams was drawing large crowds, gate receipts were always small for the Texans—at away games as well as at home. But the Cowboys profited nicely from large crowds in other NFL cities.

Television both helped and hurt the teams. It brought revenue of $150,000 to the Cowboys in 1961, but often when the Cowboys were on the road, the Texans were playing in the Cotton Bowl and vice versa. The televised game of the Cowboys cut into the live gate of the Texans in Dallas, and the televised Texans games did the same to local Cowboys games.

The Cowboys started their regular season in 1961 much better than they had a year earlier, largely because they were able to participate in the NFL draft. During their first regular season game against the Pittsburgh Steelers, they gave the fans a reason to shout. Down 24–17 in the final 56 seconds of the game, the team scored two touchdowns and won the game 27–24, their first victory.

Although the Cowboys had managed to draft former Southern Methodist University quarterback Don Meredith, a hometown boy and pride of the Mustangs, Meredith played second string to the team's number-one quarterback, Eddie LeBaron. There were shrill cries of protest when Meredith walked the sidelines, and when LeBaron made mistakes, Dallasites booed him loudly. Meredith, the club's first high-priced rookie, became more prominent in 1962, when Landry introduced his quarterback shuttle system, alternating LeBaron and Meredith on each play as he called the game from the sidelines. Meredith quickly learned that Dallas fans were not merely against LeBaron, they booed any and all Cowboys who performed poorly.

Meredith was to get his most shocking taste of crowd disapproval at the very first pre-season game in 1963. When he was introduced, the crowd booed him so loudly he thought they intended to run him out of the Cotton Bowl. But because Meredith was an exciting player—he liked to scramble and throw on the run—he could turn a loud or angry crowd into a wildly cheering mob. Murchison, sitting in the stands or in the owner's box, showed no emotion during games. With his keen eyes peering through thick horn-rimmed glasses he looked as if he would be more at home on Wall Street than in the Cotton Bowl. But Clint loved the dynamics of the game, and although he did not react outwardly to what happened on the field, he was excited by Meredith's flashy style.

Saddled with a bad team because they missed the 1960 draft, Tex Schramm and his assistant Gil Brandt combed the country scouting for players. Both men believed that building a winning football team depended on success in recruiting quality players from the top college ranks. This philosophy was the basis on which the Cowboys became one of the leading recruiters in professional football. In fact, Schramm and Brandt were so accomplished in their fact gathering that they actually found themselves with more data on each potential draftee than they knew how to process. After much discussion on what to do with the mass of information they accumulated,

Schramm decided the only way to handle it was with a computer.

The kind of home or business computer available today did not exist in the early sixties, but Schramm contacted IBM, and one of its subsidiaries agreed to develop a program for the team. The program took almost two years to plan and develop. After much anticipation, the computerized scouting system was completed in time for the 1964 college-player draft. Among the half dozen top players selected that year through the use of the innovative computer system was a quarterback by the name of Roger Staubach.

The Cowboys' use of the computer revolutionized scouting in professional football, and by 1967 it was copied in one form or another by every team in the league. Not long after IBM began developing the computer program and it appeared the Cowboys were in Dallas to stay, Clint told reporters he did not intend to take a loss on the team forever. Some immediately suspected he was giving up the battle, until he added, "Nor do I think I will have to."

A reporter asked Clint if he thought it would be smarter to move an unprofitable team to another city or to stay for prestige reasons. "Oh, it would be smarter to leave," he replied soberly. "If you stayed and threw away money you would be a fool in everyone's eyes." Then he added, "That's why Lamar should start looking for another city."

Both Clint and Lamar believed that if the other would leave town the one who remained could survive and eventually thrive. Fans agreed, and began clamoring for a Texas-style shootout on the football field. The winner would stay while the loser would have to fold his team or leave town. Because of the tepid reception given both teams, a much repeated joke was that the winner would *get* to leave town.

As citizens called for a Cowboys-Texans duel, *Dallas Times-Herald* sports editor Blackie Sherrod chided his readers, "Dear hearts, the way the public turned out for both Texan and Cowboy games this year, it could ill afford to demand anything, even mustard for the hot dogs."

The *Times-Herald* ran a surprisingly candid story, claiming that if there were such a game, the Texans would probably win

it. That evening, when sports editor Blackie Sherrod returned
home from work, he found tied to the railing of his second-
story apartment a small goat. A note was attached to a string
around its neck: "Dear Blackie, Throughout the controversy
over football coverage, I haven't been too concerned, but you
finally got my goat, which is herewith enclosed. Clint."

Asked why he sent the goat to Sherrod the editor and not
the person who actually wrote the story, Clint replied, "There
are two things in a man's life in which logic plays no part, and
one of them is sports."

Newspaper coverage, both ball clubs believed, was crucial
to their success. Schramm each day used a ruler to measure exactly how many column inches the Dallas papers devoted to
the Texans and how many to the Cowboys. By 1962 the battle
of the ball clubs was being labeled a millionaires' standoff, and
a hint of class consciousness began to creep into the rivalry.
The less affluent citizens of Dallas sided with Hunt's team,
while the more socially prominent, white-collar Dallasites
backed Murchison. Clint, still in his thirties, and Lamar, not
yet thirty, were seen by many outsiders as merely rich men's
sons playing with Daddy's money, and much of the choosing
of sides related more to their fathers than to them.

Contrary to stories that bankers and other influential men
who did business with the Hunts sided with the Hunts, while
the Murchisons' bankers and business associates sided with
the Murchisons, the people who publicly chose sides were
small in number. Most men in the Dallas business community
refused to give their loyalties to either team for fear of damaging some potential future business relationship. The Cowboys
ended the 1961 season with a much improved record of four
wins, nine losses, and one tie. And, financially, the following
season looked much brighter for the Cowboys even before it
began. Their television contract with CBS would be double
that of the previous two years, or approximately $300,000. But
the biggest good news came in February 1962, when the AFL
lost its antitrust suit. A Dallas judge ruled that the NFL had
not monopolized professional football competition because it
had not prevented the formation or successful operation of a
new league.

The good news, however, did not immediately translate to the football field. The Cowboys lost all five of their pre-season games. The regular season, however, was more encouraging, with five wins, eight losses, and one tie. In three years the team had moved from last place in the Western Conference, to sixth place in the Eastern Conference in 1961, to fifth place in 1962.

The Texans finished the 1962 season as the AFL champions, and they beat the Cowboys at the turnstiles. But they came in seventh out of eight teams in their league in attendance, and it seemed only a matter of time before the more established NFL team in Dallas would take charge.

Hunt was discouraged over losing the antitrust suit, and for the first time, in December 1962, he began to talk of moving his team to another city if that was what it took to survive. It was obvious the Cowboys had no plans to leave town. "As long as the Texans are here," Clint explained, "there will be two teams."

The Cowboys' financial loss for the 1962 season was $600,000, down $100,000 from the previous year. Since its founding, Clint had poured some $2 million into the team, not including the cost of the franchise, and was still not expecting to break even or see a meager profit for at least two more years. But the highest hopes of the Cowboys in their three-year history were about to become reality.

On February 8, 1963, Hunt announced that he would move his franchise to Kansas City. The Dallas Texans, who would be renamed the Kansas City Chiefs, had been offered numerous perquisites, such as free use of a stadium for two years and a guaranteed sale of 25,000 season tickets. It was senseless, Hunt explained, for him to continue losing money on the football venture, and his poor attendance figures in Dallas were hurting not only his team but, more importantly, the entire AFL. Lamar saw the eventual merger of the two leagues, and if his team were in another city it could possibly survive, but not if it stayed in Dallas.

The Texans had reportedly lost $3 million, but as the AFL champions, his team could leave town with its head high, not bowed in defeat. The more salient point of Hunt's departure escaped the notice of very few football fans and very few among Dallas's financial community. Murchison was a tough man to beat.

Through sheer tenaciousness, Clint had won the AFL–NFL battle in Dallas. But crowds did not suddenly jam into the Cotton Bowl to cheer the Cowboys. Attendance in 1963 climbed 23.9 percent from the 1962 levels, but it brought the average to only 26,961 per game in a town of three-quarters of a million people. Nevertheless, the Cowboys were attracting a large television audience and were beginning to look like the glamour team of the NFL. Their uniforms—dark blue jerseys with big white stars on the shoulders and shiny, white helmets with big navy-colored stars—probably had more to do with their image than their performance on the field. Like all professional football players, the Cowboys were heroic in size, and their star-blazened uniforms with subliminal connotations of theater and movie stars, as well as army generals' stars, created a shiny symbol of glamour and glitz.

The most important contributor to the Cowboys "star" image in the early 1960s, however, was the international reputation of the city itself. Dallas was a mythical and magical land of oil wells and millionaires and Neiman-Marcus, a land of sapphires and sables where people traveled by private plane and Cadillac limousine. The Cowboys on television gave Americans a powerful and exciting glimpse of the biggest, most boastful state in the Union.

In 1964 attendance figures jumped to 38,237 per game, an increase of 41.8 percent from the previous year. Gate revenue also climbed dramatically, from $750,000 in 1963 to surpass the $1 million mark in 1964. The Cotton Bowl was only half full at most games, but the Cowboys were beginning to round up the fans. They now faced having to perform on the field. Not long after Hunt announced the plans of his departure, Cowboys coach Tom Landry proudly remarked, "I don't know when it's coming, but the Cowboys are going to be a great football team."

Even as vague as the prediction was, most people in Dallas who followed football at all thought it was highly optimistic, considering the Cowboys' dismal four-year record of thirteen wins, thirty-eight losses, and three ties.

Landry could say all he wanted about the Cowboys becoming a great football team, but the fans were not buying it. They began calling for Landry's resignation, charging that the coach was responsible for the Cowboys' disappointing performance. Rumors circulated that Landry would soon be drawing unemployment checks. When a reporter asked Murchison whether it was true that people within the organization were calling for Landry's resignation, Clint responded curtly: "No one has said anything to me about it, and they better not."

The rumors ceased in February 1964, when Murchison announced that not only would Landry not be fired, he would get a new ten-year contract. Because he had one year remaining on his original contract, the new one assured his job with the Cowboys for eleven more years.

Fans and other NFL owners and coaches, even Schramm, were stunned. The contract was the longest in the history of the NFL, and it was being given to the NFL coach with one of the worst records ever. Clint responded to the astonishment with typical smugness. "Tom has been with us four years, and this will round it out to an even 15," he told reporters. "This is in line with my philosophy that once you get a good man, hold on to him."

Indeed, the contract assured Landry's stay in professional football. "I had become a born-again Christian a few years earlier," Landry recalls, "and I felt the contract was God's way of saying that football was the place for me. I decided then and there that I would make a career of it."

Family associates of the Murchisons were not as surprised by the ten-year contract as outsiders were, largely because they had witnessed for years the Murchisons' dogged loyalty to the people running their companies and because when the Murchisons got into a business they did so for the long term. If success did not come to the Cowboys until the late sixties, that was acceptable to Clint. Most professional coaching contracts were from one to three years, during which time the coach had to have a good record if he wanted to stay. Clint believed that the decade-long contract would give Landry time to concentrate exclusively on building the foundation for a great team, rather than trying to please the team's owners with one winning season after another. Secure in his job, Landry could plan and develop long-term strategy for future greatness. It was an innovative idea and one that proved tremendously successful.

Some football enthusiasts bitterly joked that the eleven years of his contract gave Landry a full year to work on each defensive position of the team, and, after that, he would get another eleven-year contract to work on each offensive position.

Still, insiders knew that Clint was a man of his convictions, a man so arrogant and self-assured about his judgment that he repeatedly defied conventional wisdom. Much of the time he was right in disregarding the opinions of others, as he proved to be in the case of Tom Landry. But skeptics saw something even more telling in the contract decision. It was a move completely in keeping with Clint's predilection for seeing what the majority wants and then doing the opposite. The more his associates—or in this case, the people of Dallas—told him Landry would not do, the more determined Clint was to prove he would.

Two years later, when the Cowboys lost several games in a row, a friend of Murchison's took him to lunch to try to cheer him. "There's a silver lining in all of this," the friend said. "At least Tom's only got nine years left."

If Clint did not seem to mind the ups and downs of football—and there had been many more downs than ups—it was because, even in the early days, he was having more fun as owner of the Cowboys than he had ever had in his life. Not only did he love the sport; he loved the life that went with it. He and his buddies showed up at training camp with swizzle sticks and party hats, had their pictures taken in Cowboys uniforms, played hard at night when they traveled as "bachelors" to away games, and attended cheerleaders' tryouts in Dallas.

The cheerleaders in the early sixties were teenagers from Dallas high schools. Although innocently named the "Cow Belles" and dressed in typically chaste high school cheerleading outfits of that era, some of the girls were anything but innocent. Clint and his buddies attended the tryouts, then introduced themselves to the girls afterward. Great prestige came with being an NFL cheerleader, a fact of which Clint took full advantage. Clint, then in his late thirties, met a few of the teenage girls secretly and individually away from the Cotton Bowl.

Sitting in the stands with a friend, Clint once joked about one of the cheerleaders, "Notice the one on the far left. She's completely out of synchronization." Then, with a grin on his face, he added, "That's okay. She has other talents."

The Murchisons shared the steamy, unair-conditioned press box at the Cotton Bowl with hoards of print and television reporters. Much of the time in the early fall, the temperature in the glass-enclosed booth climbed into the 100s, but the heat, as well as the outcome of most games, was made more bearable for the owners by an endless supply of mint juleps.

The noise level in the press box bothered Clint Sr. more than the heat, and at one game he became very annoyed with a few newspaper reporters who were cursing loudly at each play on the field. Because he was wobbly on his feet, he instructed Virginia, "Go over and tell them to stop using those four-letter words."

Virginia rose from her seat and walked over to the reporters who were cursing the loudest. Up close, they looked like former football players, and after seeing the size of their necks and shoulders, she timidly backed away. Returning to her husband's side and sinking into her chair, she whispered, "You do it."

Clint Sr. loved football, and he was proud that his son had been victorious in the fight with Hunt, but he still worried that the team would not make money. Even more worrisome, in Clint Sr.'s view, was that Clint Jr. was devoting a disproportionately large amount of time and effort to the team.

By 1961 the Murchisons had become embroiled in a major battle in New York for control of the giant Allegheny Corporation. And, at least for the next several months, in terms of dollars and financial power, the fight for Allegheny would dwarf the importance of a few million dollars invested locally in a struggling football franchise.

15

"Get happy or get out."

There were devoted Big Clint-watchers not only in Texas but all across America. They studied what he bought or sold with the hope of profiting from his moves. But when he and Sid in 1954 had invested $20 million dollars in New York Central stock, no one believed that he was suddenly interested in railroads as an investment.

A century earlier railroads might have been Clint's chief interest—they were the seminal business of the nation in the industrialization of America that followed the Civil War. No group surpassed in greed or guile the great railroad robber barons: Dan Drew, Jay Gould, E. H. Harriman, Cornelius Vanderbilt, and Collis P. Huntington. Because their railroads could make or break a town by stopping there or passing it by, they were able to extort millions in America's West.

Clint knew that his grandfather, T. F. Murchison, had bent the knee to Jay Gould to avoid the railroad bypassing Athens. Clint had spent much time and effort influencing state and national legislation to benefit the oil industry, and he knew that in his grandfather's time the railroads had been able to demand and receive from the state of Texas alone, thirty-two million acres, more than one-sixth of the state's area.

But now, half a century later, why was Clint buying railroad stock when airplanes and automobiles were carrying more and more travelers and trucks were hauling more and more freight? Railroad stocks had become "widows' stocks," the kind of investment Clint had always avoided because it had no great growth possibilities.

The Clint-watchers were certain that his professed motive,

his friendship for Robert Young, was not his primary one. Experience had taught them early that friendship is rarely the primary motive in the jungle of business.

Only a few weeks after Murchison and Richardson voted their 12 percent share of the Central's stock in Young's behalf, the prize Clint's eyes were on became clear to everyone. It was another major asset of Allegheny Corporation that Young then permitted Clint to buy—130,000 shares, or 24½ percent, of the voting stock of Investors Diversified Limited, the large Minneapolis-based financial services conglomerate that controlled $3.4 billion in assets and generated more than $52 million in cash every day.

For a man who devoutly believed and had taught his sons to believe that cash was something to spend, to spread like manure, to parlay and play with, here was a stupendous playpool of power and opportunity. In a series of eleven joint venture stock deals, the Murchisons and Allegheny split the profits and Murchison indemnified Allegheny against loss and agreed to give Allegheny about a 5 percent return annually on its investment.

When Robert Young won control of the New York Central with the help of Murchison and Richardson, it attracted the attention of the Banking and Currency Subcommittee of the United States Senate and dismayed the committee chairman, Senator Herbert H. Lehman, whose family investment bank was one of Wall Street's oldest, most powerful, and most conservative. His subcommittee was investigating the proliferation of such proxy battles.

On June 9, 1955, Senator Lehman called Young to testify before the subcommittee and demanded, "How much of their own funds did Mr. Murchison and Mr. Richardson put up?" Young explained that neither Texan had put up a dollar of his own money and called the arrangement "the cleverest deal in my financial history."

The senator's contempt was withering. "It was a clever deal all right, too clever for my old-fashioned standards."

Senator Lehman's objections were on moral grounds, but there were Allegheny stockholders and their attorneys who believed that the mutual backscratching of Young, his longtime associate Allan P. Kirby, Murchison, and Richardson was not only immoral but also illegal and that money was to be made by bringing a lawsuit charging that "the corporation's affairs were conducted in the interests of a small group of insiders."

There were a number of such lawsuits over the next five years, and in various out-of-court settlements, Young and Kirby paid Allegheny several million dollars. Murchison was required in one settlement to indemnify Allegheny against certain losses, but his most painful penalty came on Christmas Eve of 1959, when Kirby urged him to give back to Allegheny his voting shares of IDS, in exchange for nonvoting shares. Although Clint did not realize it at the time, this exchange would come to haunt the Murchisons.

Clint's health had been deteriorating, and such prolonged and public fights had never been to his taste, even when he was at his peak. Now, when he testified before a special referee of New York's State Supreme Court, Clint could still put on a good show. He referred jocularly to Sid as a "rich, fat old man" and laughingly admitted it when he was accused of vastly underestimating his own worth. But for a man who all his life had pursued privacy, these were not happy experiences. These seemingly endless legal fights were making the only game Clint had ever cared about far less fun. Then something happened that dramatically changed the field. In January 1958 Robert Young committed suicide.

Young's death marked a turning point in the Murchisons' position with Allegheny. A native Texan and a speculator on a scale with Murchison, Young appreciated and admired Clint's way of doing business. But when Young disappeared from the scene, little respect was paid by Kirby to the close business relationship that had thrived for decades between Young and the Murchisons.

Kirby, who had been Young's silent partner and financial backer, clearly disdained the freewheeling Murchison style and now moved quickly and forcefully to increase his power. When Kirby and Young bought IDS in 1949, they had paid less than $2 million for it, and IDS had grown until it now controlled assets of $3.4 billion. That Young could have sold a large share of such a valuable asset to Clint Murchison Sr. in early 1954 still rankled Kirby. He was further angered that, in his view, the Murchisons had used their control of IDS for their own personal benefit.

The terrible disadvantage they now faced was a direct result of their earlier agreement to give up their 15 percent of IDS voting shares for nonvoting shares. In effect, they had handed Kirby control of IDS because Kirby controlled Allegheny, and Allegheny, as a result of the switch, now held 48 percent of the IDS voting shares. But the Murchisons had had little choice. Had they not agreed to this settlement, Kirby threatened to settle his liability without them and leave them to fight the stockholders' suit alone.

There was the possibility, however, that if they went along with Kirby, in the future he would enable them to make up for this loss by means of more joint ventures with IDS, like the eleven that the Murchisons had made when Young was in command.

Once they gave back their voting shares they soon realized they were being squeezed out. IDS officers and directors whom they had installed were replaced by Kirby's men, and in 1960 Kirby kicked the brothers themselves off the board.

John brought in John Connally to try to settle the dispute, for it seemed Connally, an Allegheny board member, was the only Texan whom Kirby and his men liked and trusted. Connally absolutely mesmerized the Wall Streeters. But for all his charm and political savvy, Connally's attempts to reinstate the brothers on the board were in vain. John Murchison then exhausted every means he knew to resolve the conflict with Kirby. But he failed at each turn. As a last resort, the Murchisons determined the only means of regaining control of Allegheny was to institute a proxy fight. It would become the biggest, most bitter proxy fight America had ever seen.

In retrospect it seemed obvious that only Bob Young's mythic charm had kept such unalike allies as Kirby and the Murchisons together even briefly in their pursuit of power and profits. Without Young, the rupture in Kirby's and the Murchisons' relationship was inevitable. Clint Sr. did not become involved in his sons' fight with Kirby, but he regretted that he had not done more to befriend Kirby when Young was living. Clint Sr. always believed, and his experience proved, that when powerful businessmen got together in the relaxed atmosphere of fishing at Koon Kreek or hunting at Acuña, they could reasonably resolve their differences and strike a deal that was profitable to both sides. "Kirby was an odd man," says Clint's widow, Virginia Murchison Linthicum, "but Clint always felt that the fight with Kirby could have been avoided if only he could have treated Kirby to a weekend at Acuña."

The hatred of "Eastern bankers" felt by citizens in the West for more than a century was one of the few constants of America's history, and Allan Kirby was an almost stereotypical example of the rich, conservative Eastern establishment financier. He came from "old money." The son of a founder of the Woolworth chain, he increased his inherited wealth fivefold, to $300 million and made himself the biggest individual stockholder in Woolworth, New York's Manufacturers Trust Company, the New York Central, and Allegheny.

The "withdrawn, willful, inscrutable grand seigneur" of a twenty-seven-room Morristown, New Jersey, mansion, Kirby fit into the old-rich pattern of lavish extravagance combined with petty parsimony. He decorated his mansion with paintings by Rembrandt, Gainsborough, Reynolds, and Gilbert Stuart, but shined his own shoes. He had quintupled his personal fortune as a silent partner and was now convinced that by assuming an active rather than a passive role in Allegheny he could again increase his wealth dramatically—at the expense of the Murchisons.

John and Clint Jr.'s decision to institute a proxy fight was viewed as madness by most of America's business community. But the Murchisons believed that IDS, the prize at the core of the fight, was too great to lose.

One of the problems in America for small investors in this country has been how to invest in the country's growth without sinking all their capital in a single stock. To fill this need mutual funds grew in popularity in the 1920s and 1930s. These combined the few hundred or few thousand dollars of individual investors into a sum large enough to diversify its investments and also provided the opportunity for quick redemption of the small individual investments into cash.

After World War II the variety and size of such funds grew enormously, and by the late fifties the very largest was Investors Diversified Services. IDS tried to appeal to the individual, and it managed this in part by being the only mutual fund in the country with its own sales force that dealt directly with individuals. The company emphasized that it was not an impersonal financial institution on Wall Street, but a more personal company based in Minneapolis, the heartland of America. IDS was first with the slogan that it "Brought Wall Street to Main Street."

Kirby was much richer personally than the Murchison brothers. Already the largest stockholder in Allegheny, he could, with or without the help of friends, simply have bought enough shares of Allegheny to get control. Like that of most older Wall Street tycoons, Kirby's view of the Murchison brothers was the prevailing Texas stereotype—callow, ignorant, loud wheeler-dealers with the manners of farm boys and the morals of con men.

The brothers, and especially John, would show Wall Street they were far different from this caricature. Because Clint Jr. handled Murchison Brothers' interests in real estate and construction and John had specialized more in finance and insurance, John would call the proxy shots.

The war had to be fought on Kirby's turf. Murchison Brothers leased offices in midtown Manhattan and brought almost all of their Dallas staff to New York. Clint Jr. spent a few days each week there, but for John and Lupe, New York became home. They flew to Dallas as often as possible during the weekends, but their weekdays were spent in Manhattan. They leased a $17,000-a-year suite of rooms at the fashionable Hotel Carlyle on Madison Avenue, and hired well-known decorator Ed Bennesch to make it even more comfortable. The Carlyle was thirty blocks from Murchison Brothers' offices at 48th Street and Madison, and John walked to and from work every day.

Insiders believed from the start that the brothers had a fighting chance because they were more aggressive and better organized. They hired two of the country's top proxy solicitation firms, and thereby insured that neither would work for Kirby. The Murchisons were extraordinarily cautious, burning all waste paper connected with the fight and speaking about it only on a scrambler or pay telephone.

They divided the country into eighty regions, and every one of Allegheny's more than 20,000 shareholders in every region was personally contacted. In a handful of important instances the call was made by John or Clint Jr. Their purpose was to convince the stockholder that their modern, up-to-date management as opposed to Kirby's old-fashioned, atrophied management would eventually result in a rise in price of the stockholders' shares.

Many Allegheny shares were held by stockbrokers in street names and bank trust departments. For these professional money men to hear personally from the Murchisons was not only flattering but also made obvious the difference between the aggressive efforts that could be expected from the young Murchisons and the tired management to be expected from Kirby who was older than the boys' father. It had long been said on Wall Street that Allan Kirby ran Allegheny as if it were his personal investment company and private fiefdom. Clint Jr. and John Dabney and their co-workers in their conversations with shareholders did not contradict that view.

The brothers, when interviewed by *The New York Times,* news magazines, and business magazines, carefully and constantly characterized themselves as underdogs. It was good publicity, of course, because it contrasted so obviously with the wild-and-woolly Texan picture of them painted by Kirby. But more important—in fact, probably the single shrewdest move the Murchisons made—was their relentless "poor-boying," which fooled the Kirby camp and stopped them from winning by the simple expedient of buying enough shares for control.

As in many conflicts, image was often as important as substance. As part of their naive-boys-from-the-country act, they expressed surprise at finding "rustlers and brand changers" in the big city. And despite rumors to the contrary, the boys projected a unified front. Asked if they had differences between themselves, they insisted they were "closer together than the hands of a clock at twenty minutes of eight."

But for all the playacting and posturing by both Kirby and the Murchisons, as the months wore on and the battle became tougher, there was one fact the Murchison camp felt was absolutely essential to keep secret or else the rest of the public relations would be for nothing. The terrible pressures of the fight were taking a devastating toll on John. His eyes were puffy and his cheeks drawn. He smiled less and appeared preoccupied and worried. He started smoking again, after having quit for nearly a year.

To relax, John and Lupe began visiting art galleries in the evenings. Soon they were purchasing contemporary works of art, reading books on avant-garde artists, attending lectures. But even when John was buying art, Allegheny was clearly on his mind. "John never discussed business with me, but I could always tell how the Allegheny fight was going by the art he bought," recalls Lupe. "When he bought bright or fun pop art, it meant the negotiations were going well. But dark, gloomy pieces, and he bought a lot of those, meant the fight had taken a turn for the worse."

Murchison Brothers was not only trying to win a proxy battle; the partnership faced a barrage of related lawsuits and injunctions and complicated negotiations with federal agencies. At one point the struggle became so intense that John was dangerously close to a nervous breakdown. Although he was the key element to victory, he had no choice but to return to Dallas to rest. When he flew back to New York three weeks later, he threw himself back into the whirlwind.

While John fought the business war, Lupe faced additional worries. Her greatest concern other than her husband's problems with Allegheny were her four young children. They were in the constant care of a governess at home in Dallas. But seeing her children only on weekends, and sometimes not even then, made her feel guilty and depressed. Increasingly, she was torn between her obligation to be with her husband and her obligation to be with her children who desperately needed their parents' love and attention. Lupe might have divided her time between New York and Dallas, but John would not allow such a compromise. He had to have Lupe with him all the time, and despite the guilt she suffered, her husband came first. "If I don't go with him, some other woman will," an intimate recalls hearing Lupe say. Lupe was well aware of how attractive John was. "Women adored John," she says, "and I used to get my feathers up over it."

But Lupe's decision to devote virtually all her time to her husband would later cause deep resentment from her son and major problems in her relationship with him in the years to come.

With no family or longtime friends in New York to turn to, Lupe relied on her Catholic faith to help her through this difficult period. She regularly walked the several blocks to St. Patrick's Cathedral, where she prayed and asked for guidance. "Our time in New York was the most difficult in our marriage," Lupe says. "One lesson we learned, though, was that life isn't just a hand-me-out. You have to work for what you want to achieve."

That John Murchison and Clint Jr. were viewed as achievers was obvious. *The New York Times* observed: "The Murchison sons are pecuniarily in the class of such café society notables as James (Woolworth) Donohue, and Huntington Hartford 3rd. But instead of spending their time as men-about-town, they work in the world of finance, real estate, and insurance, as earnestly as a bank teller bucking for a $300-a-year raise."

In one national story the brothers were described as eager bird dogs ranging across the nation, sniffing out deals and supplying capital, entrepreneurial vigor and acumen in vast areas of the economy. A cartoon that appeared in *The New Yorker* pictured a shopkeeper and his wife standing in front of their store in New York, with the caption, "I wonder if those Murchison brothers could use a nice little novelty store in the East Sixties."

The press was far kinder to the Murchisons than to Kirby in the hundreds of stories in *The New York Times, The Wall Street Journal,* and dozens of papers across America fed by the wire services. Many of these, like *Life* magazine's, contrasted the "two great American economic baronies—the rough-hewn Texas beef, oil, and money combine and the elegant eastern financial syndicate." The contrast was illustrated by *Life* photographs—Kirby's Rolls-Royce with its "APK 1" license plates, and the rear end of a large Brangus steer bearing the Murchisons' 7L brand.

In these stories the Murchison brothers' flair for public relations was obvious. *Life* pictured John, Lupe, and their four little children, smilingly surrounding one of their giant bronze sculptures in the foyer of their Dallas home, as opposed to Kirby, "a moody and withdrawn figure," pictured sitting alone and scowling on the ferry to New York.

Kirby's only public relations effort, intended to demonstrate the present management's interest in the stockholders' welfare, backfired. For more than thirty-two years, since Allegheny's founding in 1929, the company had never paid a dividend. Suddenly, just eleven days before the crucial stockholders' meeting scheduled for May 1, 1961, in Baltimore, Kirby had the company declare a dividend of five cents a share.

John immediately ran full-page newspaper advertisements with a cartoon of Kirby throwing "5-cent chicken feed" to the stockholders. The ads successfully made Kirby appear both cheap and desperate and indicated how out of touch he was with Allegheny's stockholders. Kirby was a conservative who cared about dividends, while most Allegheny stockholders were hoping that the stock would rise in price and cared nothing for a token dividend.

In the ten days prior to the Baltimore meeting, more than $60 million was invested in Allegheny shares. Kirby was reported to have bought in the open market $3 million of stock in one day, and a total of $13 million. The Allegheny stock-buying splurge was the biggest of any single stock since the crash of 1929.

The most credible estimates indicated that Kirby and his associates controlled about 3,200,000 shares and the Murchisons with their supporters some 2,800,000, but 4,922,486 shares were needed for victory, the total potential vote of common shares being 9,844,970.

Clearly the decision lay in the hands of the company's small stockholders, some 500 of whom were expected to come to Baltimore. The morning of the meeting, Kirby insisted to the press that he owned or had proxies for a majority of Allegheny's shares, and the Murchison brothers made the same claim. The meeting was adjourned to allow the tellers to count.

As the days and weeks went by, the suspense mounted. People who had no financial interest wanted to know who had won the fight that had been going on for more than a year. Days before the official tally was announced, the news leaked out that the two boys from Texas had won, and the superbly organized team of young businessmen they had put together was widely likened to the perfectionist political troops young Senator John F. Kennedy had organized to sweep him to victory at the Democratic National Convention a year earlier.

And there were those who pointed out that the Kennedy clan also stayed at the Hotel Carlyle, including former Ambassador Joseph Kennedy who had taught his sons, "Don't get mad. Get even!"

The official tally was impressive. Of some 9,200,000 shares voted, the Murchisons had obtained 5,026,000 and Kirby's forces only 4,172,000, a very safe margin of almost 855,000 votes.

One of the most remarkable facts about the fight was the extent to which Wall Street had been seduced by the Murchisons. Wall Street and the professional financial community were Kirby's world. There he had been known as a sophisticated and successful investor for twice as long as the Murchison brothers had been in business. It was amazing that Allegheny shares held in Street names by stockbrokers and other professional trustees were voted four-to-one in favor of the brothers from Texas.

In the glow of victory it was fun to remember that one of Kirby's lieutenants had scoffed at the Murchisons' yokel outfit as a "vehicle put together of glue, string, turpentine, and wind."

For the Texans victory was sweet, especially since it clearly established the brothers as successful in their own right. After years of being known only as "Clint's boys," they were now called "Clint's whiz kids." But John's interviews with the press continued to be soft-spoken and witty with no mention of some top Wall Street figures who had been betting against him until the tally was completed.

"We lost our shirts in uranium," John volunteered to a *New York Times* reporter who congratulated him on confounding Wall Street, "and in electronics—we haven't done anything at all. We missed the boat completely on that one."

To a reporter in Baltimore he joked, "We're going to pay a six-cent dividend next year. That's a 20 percent increase." Asked by *Time* what advice he had for Allan Kirby, John answered, "He should do what he used to tell us to do: either get happy or get out."

The highly publicized proxy victory catapulted the brothers onto the cover of *Time* magazine, just seven years after their father had the similar distinction. Clint Jr. and John Dabney, pictured in Brooks Brothers suits, looked somewhat more sophisticated and Eastern than their father, who had been pictured in a straw cowboy hat. Yet sketched behind the boys' portraits was the noose of a lasso circling the skyscrapers of Wall Street, a hint that they still maintained at least a tie to their Texas roots.

The *Time* story, titled "Texans on Wall Street," began with the Texas tale that "the reason Dallas has one of the nation's busiest airports is that outbound jets are loaded with Texas businessmen heading for Wall Street to borrow money. . . . John Dabney Murchison, 39, and Clinton Williams Murchison Jr., 37, flew to Manhattan [last week] not as supplicants but as conquerors."

The article explained in detail how the two Texas youngsters had defeated the far richer Kirby who "still owns 34 percent of Allegheny and could buy outright control if he had a mind to."

Like the rest of America's financial community, *Time* wondered whether John, temporarily acting as Allegheny's president, would conduct the company's affairs in his father's wheeler-dealer fashion or in a more conservative Wall Street style. The story said, "Last week John Murchison, who ordinarily wears no hat, even went out and bought the current Wall Street fashion in summer headgear—a straw boater."

Although the assumption was partially incorrect—in non-business situations John always wore a hat of one type or another—the point was well made.

Close friends wondered whether the straw boater was not only a symbol of a new style of doing business, but whether it indicated that Texas had lost John and Lupe to New York permanently. John loved everything about New York. He not only kept himself at the forefront of contemporary painting, but was also anxious to know what was happening in the popular arts. No sooner had he heard about the "Twist" than he rushed to the Peppermint Lounge to learn the dance from its creator, Chubby Checker.

The two and one half years that John and Lupe spent in Manhattan during the Allegheny fight had been, and would always remain, the most exciting, most difficult time in their marriage. Lupe recalls, "John remembered his boarding school days and his college days in New Haven as very happy times, probably the happiest in his life. In New York, he was thrilled with being on the cutting edge, and it was so much more his style than Dallas.

"Even though the fight for Allegheny had been very difficult for him, when we got control, he wanted to move to New York, to buy a home on Sutton Place and make that our permanent residence."

Lupe was against the idea. She loved Texas as much as John loved New York, and she feared that the stress her husband went through during the Allegheny fight was due in part to the strains of living in a big city. She had become accustomed to the breezy openness of her twenty-nine room Dallas mansion, whose windows she kept wide open from early fall through late spring, and she loved to walk barefoot in the morning through acres of cutting gardens at their sprawling estate.

There was another even more important difference between the kind of life John wanted and what Lupe wanted. She clearly missed the recognition that came with being a Murchison in Texas, and she yearned to return to the familiarity of her hometown. But what Lupe missed about Dallas, the spotlight, was what John so disliked. He wanted to hide in New York: in effect to live an anonymous life. Still, when Lupe insisted on returning to Texas, John agreed reluctantly. In the meantime, however, they continued to live part-time in New York while John searched for a new chief executive for Allegheny. All too soon, he realized his corporate struggles were far from over.

The dozens of battles in the Murchison brothers' long war against Kirby were fought not only in a variety of state and federal courts in a variety of jurisdictions but also before the Interstate Commerce Commission and the Securities and Exchange Commission.

The multiplicity of these suits was not merely a course of action designed by lawyers to multiply their fees. As in any war and even in any great battle, a number of fights usually take place on many different fronts: a feint here; a surprise attack there; a variety of efforts to find the enemy's weakest point or an unforeseen advantage.

The Murchisons were so convinced that the settlement Kirby had forced on them, to exchange their voting shares in IDS for nonvoting shares, was a conspiracy and a fraud that they sued him for $100 million. They took the case all the way to the United States Supreme Court, but they lost.

The *Time* magazine cover story of June 16, 1961, that reported John and Clint Jr.'s brilliantly orchestrated victory over Kirby had suggested that perhaps the last had not been heard from him. In fact, the very next day after the vote count in Baltimore, Kirby had secretly begun his campaign to make their victory Pyrrhic and to regain control from the Murchisons. Kirby plans did not long remain a secret.

Every move that John made to fulfill his promises to improve Allegheny and IDS, Kirby fought, in every possible venue: the boardroom, the courtroom, the public press. Aware that the Murchison brothers had, in the proxy fight, shrewdly used the press, while he had disdained to, Kirby quickly demonstrated that at sixty-nine, he was not too old to learn.

The New York Times regularly reported, almost gleefully, his "war-like moves" and his sharp words: "[The Murchisons] won election last year on a platform of promises which they have not fulfilled and criticism of an investment policy which they have not changed. . . . The contrast between their propaganda while they were seeking control and their lack of performance since they gained control should be a matter of grave concern to all shareholders of Allegheny."

Indeed, John's lack of performance on his promises was a matter of grave concern to him, but he found that every major move he proposed was immediately blocked by Kirby. During the proxy fight he had promised to recapitalize Allegheny's most profitable holding, IDS. He proposed to split the stock ten-for-one, to combine both the voting and nonvoting class into a single voting class, and to "reward" Allegheny's stockholders by giving each of them a pro-rata right to buy the new shares owned by Allegheny. This would also, John pointed out, provide new investment funds for Allegheny. But no sooner had John sought permission from the Securities and Exchange Commission for these changes than Kirby fought it and won.

John was also considering lightening Allegheny's almost 1,000,000 share holding of New York Central stock by giving each Allegheny stockholder rights to subscribe to the Central shares—the kind of move his father had mastered when he spun shares of Delhi Oil exploration company out of the Southern Union utility company. What John was proposing would give the Allegheny stockholder the choice of whether to keep or sell the New York Central stock.

John was also considering having Allegheny buy in some of its own shares because he felt it had become overcapitalized when, during the proxy fight, hundreds of thousands of shares of preferred had been converted to common. This would increase the value of Allegheny shares for those who wanted to stay in and increase the demand for shares for those who wanted out.

John's victory was increasingly hollow as not only active opposition by Kirby frustrated him but even the mere threat of Kirby's opposition. John had made himself president of Allegheny "temporarily" while he searched for a top-rank executive to take over for him. Among those rumored to have been offered the job were former Treasury Secretary Robert B. Anderson and former Chase Manhattan Bank Chairman John J. McCloy. But no first-rate executive would even consider stepping into the middle of what was constantly characterized as the bitterest business fight in American history.

As the vendetta continued, both investors and observers could justifiably wonder what the Texas whiz kids had actually accomplished after more than a year, other than moving Allegheny's offices a few blocks up Park Avenue from the New York Central Railroad executive offices at the Grand Central terminal building to new, fancier, walnut-paneled, orange-carpeted offices on the twenty-fifth floor of the Manufacturers Hanover Trust Company building at 230 Park Avenue.

In Baltimore, at John's proxy victory, a Dallas reporter had asked him what it had cost the Muchisons to win the fight, and John admitted that it had cost between $500,000 and $1 million. But he added, smiling, "It was worth it."

Yet now the Murchisons were wondering whether the few million dollars they made in the proxy fight were worth the time and effort involved. The clear answer came all too soon. Less than a year and a half after their proxy victory, John and Clint Jr. were reported to be discussing a sale of their controlling interest in Allegheny and, in one of the ironic coincidences frequently found in big business where the top players are so few in number, the Murchisons were said to be offering their Allegheny interest to the same Minneapolis investor, Bertin C. Gamble, who in 1949 had sold his 90 percent control of IDS to Allegheny for less than $2 million. The total value of IDS in the early sixties was about $300 million.

When the rumors that the brothers were selling to Gamble proved to be true, many Allegheny stockholders were incensed. Among the angriest were those who had allied themselves to the Murchison cause in the proxy fight but were given no notice that the Murchisons were fleeing the field. That they were not the only allies ever so deserted did not lessen their fury.

"I feel I may have been sold down the river by the Murchisons," declared one owner of 40,000 Allegheny shares. "When I went in with the Murchisons last year, it was with the definite idea that they would accomplish things. I gave stockholders my word and backed my word with additional stock purchases.... Frankly, I'm a little disappointed."

The brothers' flight set up a spate of rumors that they were in deep financial trouble and that all their investment holdings were up for sale. Rumors that the Murchisons were especially desperate to dump their holdings in Daisy Manufacturing and Delhi-Taylor Oil could not have been more untrue.

In Dallas Clint Jr. declared the rumors of financial troubles false but shrewdly explained that any investment he and his brother had was for sale at any time for a price. He emphasized, however, that with 25 percent capital gains tax to be paid when such investments are sold, and the need then to find other places to invest the money, the price would have to be pretty good.

The shares Bertin C. Gamble bought from the Murchisons were later bought by Allan P. Kirby and two associates, giving him control of 59 percent of Allegheny's voting shares. Asked why he had agreed to buy 1,000,000 shares of Allegheny stock at $10.50 per share on top of his already huge investment in the company, Kirby answered, "Pride. Family pride. As nearly as I can remember until the proxy fight with the Murchisons in 1961, I never got licked."

16

"Clint was trying to be like his father."

In 1959 John and Lupe rode a tractor up a snow-covered Colorado mountain with an old friend from Yale. When they reached the top, over 11,000 feet, it was late in the afternoon, and the sun was glinting off endless rows of purple mountain peaks.

From this spot on the mountain John's Yale friend described his plans for what he hoped would become a world-renowned ski resort. The mountain had four bowls for skiing, including one schuss slope with a drop of more than 3,000 feet. John saw immediately that this could be one of the most magnificent ski slopes anywhere. And the mountain was only one hundred miles from Denver. Its greatest attribute was its beauty. Crystal streams splashed through the pristine aspen forests that draped the mountainside.

It took John's kind of imagination to envision a ski resort here. A few houses and a small grocery store were the only specks on the floor of the valley below. The land had for decades belonged to local sheep ranchers whose life-style could scarcely have been more primitive. There were no roads, only narrow paths that the sheep had trodden out of the mountainside. That this tiny village could somehow become a famous international ski resort called Vail would have seemed farfetched to most people. Postwar skiers wanted fast lifts, groomed snow, and ski patrols. But these essentials were expensive, and the ski season was not only short but—in those days before snow-making machines—unreliable. Only one or two ski resorts in the United States had ever made money.

But John liked challenges, and after seeing the mountain, he agreed to be one of fifteen initial investors in Vail. John viewed his original $10,000 investment as a risk, but precisely the kind of risk he liked to take. The odds were similar to wildcatting in the oil business. If he lost the money, he could write it off against his huge profits. If he made money, that was obviously better. In either case, while $10,000 was not an inconsiderable sum in the late 1950s, it was an insignificant fraction of John Murchison's worth.

But the financial profit he might make from his investment in Vail was far less important than the fun he was going to get out of it. John loved to ski and had even owned a ski area in Santa Fe. He and Lupe had skied in Aspen in the late 1950s, and it was there that John's friend from Yale, George Caulkins, invited him into the Vail partnership.

It was not long before word spread that the elder son of Clint Murchison Sr. was a Vail investor, and the publicity payoff came immediately. In the June 1961 *Time* magazine cover story about John and Clint Jr., Vail was listed among John's assets. Although John now owned about 10 percent of Vail, the story gave the impression that he was the controlling partner. In his typically modest way John called Caulkins and apologized that the story incorrectly portrayed him as the chief stockholder. But Caulkins was delighted with the publicity, and especially with the timing of it. Vail planned to open the coming fall, less than six months away. The ski resort needed national publicity, and the fact that John Murchison was connected with it gave it enormous and immediate credibility.

The Murchisons, while often viewed as big risk takers, also had the reputation of being very shrewd. Skiers from around the nation were suddenly excited by the prospect of a new mountain in Colorado, and ski buffs from Texas assumed that if the rich Murchisons were connected with it, it would be bigger and better than anything seen before.

That their assumption was correct became obvious the moment they got to Vail and saw a large contemporary house being built high on a cliff above the town. Long before Vail was fully financed, let alone operating, John hired a top Dallas architect to build his dream home. The result was a five-story house, glass on three sides. The fourth side, the home's most extraordinary feature, was the mountain's hard, exposed stone face that formed one of the interior walls. A *Town & Country* story, including architectural plans, described the house and decoration, and Lupe explained poetically, "Our house is always full . . . without people it's a crying window." The story went on to explain that, "Although Vail's trails were designed for all classes of skiers, the town was designed strictly with the 'upper' classes (social and economic) in mind. Those who set rather than follow trends now go to Vail."

Because John and Lupe had built the first house and picked the choice site right in the heart of the slopes, they could buckle on their skis at their own front door, and guests who arrived by car boarded a gondola lift that carried them from the carport right to the house.

John had grown up in the hot, dusty, dull, flat scrub oak country of Texas, and to him the Rocky Mountains were an ineffable glory. Because his Vail house was so far removed from his Wall Street wars and the pressures of Murchison Brothers in Dallas, this became the favorite of all his homes—the isolated, luxurious hideaway that everyone dreams of but few attain.

John often piloted one of his own planes, usually a Beechcraft Twin Bonanza, to and from Denver, and a friend recalls one trip back to Dallas. "John had an almost ecstatic enthusiasm about the sense of freedom that flying high above the earth gave him. He had important business waiting for him in Dallas, but the clouds were so beautiful and fluffy that he circled the plane around and played in them."

The house became a point of pilgrimage for the most chic ski buffs in America, where the caviar and dry martinis never ran out. John and Lupe always brought with them to Vail one of their planes full of friends from Dallas. In addition, après-ski parties on the top deck of the Murchison home always included a number of new friends from around the country who had built homes at Vail, or who dropped by in their own private planes from Sun Valley and other Western ski resorts.

Following John's lead, scions of the nation's richest families, as well as dozens of corporate executives and even one soon-to-be President of the United States, Gerald Ford, built homes at Vail. Because of John's connection, Vail also became very popular among rich Texans.

John was proud of the trend he had set and was happy that his friends built magnificent homes that made Vail even more sought-after and valuable. Just how important this was to him was obvious when fellow oil-rich Texan Herbert Hunt, third son of H. L. Hunt, built a house next to John's. When John saw it, he complained of Hunt's frugality. "Gosh, Hunt, why'd you go and build such a little house?"

Within two years of its opening, Vail had arrived. As *Sports Illustrated* wrote in 1964, "Never has a mountain leaped in such a short time into the four-star category of ski resorts," and *Holiday* magazine compared it favorably to Kitzbühel, Cortina, or St. Moritz, "but at Vail the ski chalet has been shouldered aside by the ski château; [it is] the sort of place good skiers hope to go when they die."

John took great pride in Vail and contributed not only his money but his ideas. "He built a chapel and a hospital at Vail, and he brought merchants to the town," recalls another pioneer of the area. "When these things succeeded, he felt immense satisfaction."

In the mid-seventies Harry and Richard Bass of Dallas (not related to Sid Richardsons' nephews of Fort Worth) wanted to take a controlling interest in Vail. They approached John with an offer to buy his stock, but John was not sure he wanted to sell.

"Maybe we should try to take control ourselves," John told George Caulkins, who had brought him into the partnership at the start. But John decided against it when he remembered his frustrating battle for control of Allegheny. "Besides," John said, "I have to see the Basses at the [Dallas] Petroleum Club, and I don't want to be in the awkward position of being in a business fight with them."

There was another reason John wasn't interested in fighting for control. He enjoyed having a part in the financing and in the creative design of Vail, and he enjoyed watching it grow from a tiny, remote village into an internationally famous ski resort. He knew the land would become more valuable with time, but he never thought the Vail Corporation would become a hugely profitable venture. In some ways John viewed Vail the way Clint viewed the Cowboys. John loved skiing, Clint loved football. Both men had built something where nothing existed before. But the brothers were also different in the gratification they needed. Clint, who never ceased struggling to be the success his father was, needed the Dallas Cowboys for his ego. John, conversely, did not have to prove things to himself or others. He ultimately decided, *if the Basses want my stock so much, I'll sell it to them*—and he did.

Just as John found a way to turn his love of skiing into a profitable investment, he was even able to make money out of his favorite hobby, flying. By the early sixties, the number of Murchison aircraft totaled thirteen. Eleven of these were housed at Dallas's Love Field where the Murchisons shared a hangar with Delta Airlines. Love Field, Dallas's main airport, was nine miles from John's home.

For even easier access to his planes, John built a private airport two miles from his Preston Road estate, and, finding enough other plane-owning friends, he was able to convert the airport from a rich man's luxury into a profit-making enterprise.

John's hideaway in snowy, mountainous Vail had no appeal to Clint Jr., who had hated cold weather since his boyhood. He often recalled the many times when he and John Dabney and Burk shivered in the cold waiting for Jewel to pick them up from school. Nor did Clint Jr. care much for his father's Acuña ranch or Isla Del Toro in Mexico, for the Athens ranch or Matagorda. These weekend retreats were fabulous for hunters and fishermen. Clint Sr. and John Dabney both loved the rugged outdoors and enjoyed spending weeks hunting and fishing in rough country. But Clint Jr. had never, even as a boy, liked to hunt or fish.

Clint Jr. wanted an island because his father had an island, but he wanted a sunny place in the Carribean that, unlike Matagorda, was warm year-round and where the sand was pure white and the water crystal clear. He searched for nearly two years before he found Spanish Cay (pronounced Spanish

Key), a two-and-a-half-mile-long and quarter-mile-wide coral reef in the archipelago of the Grand Bahama Islands. The uninhabited island's glistening white sand stretched from the shoreline to myriad tall palm trees that swayed softly in the ocean breeze. Taking a lesson from his father, before he purchased Spanish Cay he made sure that it could accommodate a 5,000-foot landing strip.

As his father had at Matagorda, he built power generators and water tanks, a radio tower for the airplanes, roads to and from the runway. He landscaped Spanish Cay with flowering trees and bushes and designed and built the sprawling main house as well as six separate guest cabanas linked with walkways overhung with flowering vines. Clint hired a Dallas architect and engineer, but rarely asked their advice, preferring instead to build the island exactly to his own taste. "Clint Jr. wanted our input from time to time, but he never really gave us any creative rein," says a Dallas architect who worked with Clint. "He was the most unbelievable perfectionist I've ever known."

Just how particular Clint Jr. was became obvious in the early fifties when Big Clint bought one hundred acres of land across from his own Preston Road farm. He offered the property to Clint Jr. and Jane, and suggested they make it their home. Big Clint thought his grandchildren should grow up "close to the land," just as he and his sons had, and he recognized that as Dallas was rapidly growing north, the land was becoming more valuable.

But Clint Jr. turned down the offer, saying the land was not right. There were not enough trees in places, or it was too hilly here or too flat there. His father was hurt when Clint Jr. rejected the gift, but Clint Jr. was not about to accept anything that was, in his view, less than perfect. He and Jane spent the next two years searching for just the right piece of property. "We looked and looked, and when he couldn't find exactly what he wanted," recalls Jane, "I finally said, 'Clint, are you sorry we didn't take the property across from Pop?' He said, 'Well, yes. Maybe we should have taken that.' "

Jane would have preferred to refurbish an old house in Highland Park, but her husband wanted to be in the country.

"Clint was trying to be like his father," says Jane. "He wanted to build a big fabulous house, and he was personally interested in designing it and developing the land just as his daddy did."

Clint Jr. finally found what he was looking for about three miles south of his father's house and eleven miles north of downtown Dallas. He got title to the twenty-five acres in 1954 and began to design his dream estate. The new house that Clint had in mind would come none too soon. Jane had just given birth to their fourth child.

After having two sons, Clint III and Burk, who was named for Clint's brother who died as a child, Clint had been disappointed when his third child turned out to be a girl. He wanted three sons, just as his father had had. But Clint came to adore the little girl, Coke Ann, who was named for Jane's mother and his mother. Clint and Jane then had another boy, whom Clint named Robert after his best friend Robert Thompson. The six-member family was still living in a very modest and now very cramped three-bedroom, two-bathroom house, an arrangement Jane hoped would be short-lived.

But Jane soon realized the new house was a long way, possibly years, from being built. After nearly a year Clint was still working on the blueprints, needlessly scrapping plans if they contained a minor flaw. Finally he decided that the house would be 43,500 square feet, in the shape of a horseshoe and would cover an entire acre of property. At last construction began.

The house was built of limestone rock, hewn at Acuña in Mexico. Mexicans chiseled large pieces of the rock from a quarry on the ranch, then loaded them onto railroad cars that carried them to Dallas. More than a year after construction began on the house, after several railroad cars full of rock had already been shipped, Clint Jr. ran into a friend in Dallas who was headed for Acuña. "Could you take a message and have them send up another seventeen thousand rocks?" he asked matter-of-factly.

The time it took to put up the stone structure was as nothing compared to the years Clint would spend completing the interior. He cared desperately about details, and this soon became painfully obvious to Jane. "Clint would debate for hours about whether the moldings should be two-and-three-eighths inches or two-and-four-eighths inches wide," recalls Jane. "I couldn't see what made the difference in an eighth of an inch, but he could."

Clint was fascinated with the chance to use what he had learned at Duke and MIT to create a state-of-the-art computerized home. The electronic system he designed and built was so intricate that even *he* was intrigued by its complexity. Hundreds of switches and buttons triggered hundreds of different functions, and he reworked the system again and again until it was flawless. Curtains closed and opened with the push of a button; an electronic bar made drinks to order; appliances came out of the walls in the kitchen.

"Before he bought a stereo, he kept touching the buttons on different components, maybe for an hour or more," recalls a friend. "He was trying to decide which felt smoother and easier to the touch."

He worked for years perfecting a large screen television, when big-screen TV was still little more than a concept. The flick of a switch opened the living room ceiling and down came a large television projector. A screen appeared on a far wall and the camera projected large-screen, brown-and-white TV. He wired the front gate so that it opened and closed with the push of a button, and he built an electronic eye that formed a wall around the house and sounded an alarm if penetrated.

While Clint became completely absorbed in the electrical problems he encountered, Jane was becoming increasingly impatient for him to finish the house. Despite his promises that the place was close to being completed, by 1960 she began to wonder whether her children would all be grown by the time they moved. Robert, the youngest, was six years old and still sharing a room with his eight-year-old sister.

Impatient as Jane was, however, she tried not to complain too much. "I fussed about the house taking so long, but I didn't really push too hard. How could I? It was Clint's hobby. He loved what he was doing."

To develop the remaining twenty-four acres, he hired the well-known Dallas landscaping firm Lambert's. Typically, he allowed them very little creative leeway.

"We came up with an overall plan for the property," recalls Henry Lambert, "and Clint Jr. had something to say about virtually every foot of it. There were hundreds of large trees to be planted, and he cared about every one of them. He would stare at a tree for hours, trying to decide if it was turned just the right way on the property. It took months for him to decide just how a row of shrubbery should curve along the drive."

Jane had been content to let Clint have full say on the building of the house, but she was surprised when he insisted on handling the interior decoration without her as well. He had decided it would be in the style of Mies van der Rohe contemporary, and he proceeded to select every lamp and every sofa and every ashtray without consulting Jane.

"Other women were totally in charge of their houses, and their husbands tended to business downtown," says Jane. "That's what I expected when I married Clint, but that was never the case."

Frustrated at being shut out of decisions about her home, Jane turned her attention to another outlet—charity work. Soon she was involved in a number of fund-raising projects for Dallas arts groups. Clint agreed to attend some of the benefit balls and society cocktail parties, but he hated every minute of it. This became a turning point in their marriage. A major problem was Clint's severe inferiority complex in social settings.

It was difficult enough for him to say "Hello," to someone on the street; for him to carry on cocktail conversation was next to impossible. The more Jane tried to become a part of the social scene, the more Clint backed away from it. Big Clint and John were also shy and uncomfortable in large social gatherings, but they were always cordial and often charming. Clint Jr. did not have this ability. He thought of himself as the most brilliant businessman in Dallas and one of the smartest men in the country, but his confidence in himself disappeared at five o'clock. When the cocktail hour began, he reverted to a frightened, neurotically introverted little boy, incapable of even the briefest and most superficial small talk.

He often tried to mask this pathological shyness by acting

rude and aloof. A friend recalls being at a party with Clint when another man walked by. The passerby warmly greeted Clint, but Clint merely stared at him blankly. The man with Clint was so embarrassed he turned to him and demanded, "Why didn't you speak to him?

"I saw him yesterday," Clint said plaintively. "How often do you have to speak to someone?"

John Murchison was able to make friends with people who were of his own class. He established friendships with the cream of Dallas society—corporate executives, bankers, doctors, architects—sophisticated men who were well educated, belonged to Brook Hollow Golf Club, who read books, drank fine wine, and took their families to Europe in the summer.

Jane wanted the same type of friends for herself and for Clint. But Clint befriended another type of person entirely. He began hanging around a number of crude, uneducated, skirt-chasing, hard-drinking sycophants, who quickly recognized and played on Clint's deep insecurity. Backslapping and garrulous, these men were eager to carry the conversation, allowing Clint comfortably to say nothing. In very little time, some of them served an even more important function. They introduced him to the women who would become his sexual partners, a job that was relatively easy, for Clint was not picky about the women he wanted to sleep with. Likewise, most of the women, when they learned his name, were only too willing to go to bed with Clint Murchison Jr.

Dallas-based Braniff Airlines became the official carrier of the Cowboys, and Clint flew with the team to all its away games. If Jane was with him, he sat at the front of the plane with his head buried in a book. But if she was not along, he liked one of his right-hand men to sit with him and carry on a conversation with the stewardesses.

Clint formed close friendships with these skirt-chasing buddies, and seemed exceedingly grateful that they played the adultery game with him. Clint kept informed of parties the stewardesses had in Dallas, as well as in other cities. At these parties, when Clint's buddies paired off with the young women, friends always looked after Clint. "If we were at a party and Clint wanted to meet a woman, me or one of the guys would have to go up and get the woman and bring her around for Clint to meet," says one friend "He could never approach anyone. He was too shy."

In the early sixties, being young, attractive, and single were requirements for becoming a stewardess. "There was not a stewardess that Clint didn't want to take to bed," recalls one of his buddies. "He was so in love with these girls that he stopped flying on his private planes and flew commercially."

Just as he enjoyed attending Dallas Cowboys cheerleaders tryouts, Clint found there was much to be gained in attending graduation ceremonies of Braniff stewardesses. These young women, just out of flight school, were an entirely new flock of potential bed partners, and he was always looking for fresh, young talent.

"Clint always sat in the back row during the Braniff graduation ceremonies, and he carefully eyed the stewardesses as they paraded by," recalls one of his procurers. "After the ceremonies he'd point out a few girls and say, 'Go get their phone numbers.'

"When I'd tell the girl, 'There's Clint Murchison Jr., the owner of the Dallas Cowboys, sitting out there in the audience, and he wants a date with you,' she would jump at the chance."

When Cleveland was in Dallas for the 1969 playoffs, Browns owner Art Modell stopped by Clint's house to watch the college all-star game on television. Bedford Wynne was there with Clint, and the two were going over pages of lists while keeping an eye on the game on television. Modell was impressed that Clint and his right-hand man were so carefully taking notes on college players they might draft. But when he looked more closely, he noticed the names were not John or Bobby or Randy, but Pam, Cathy, and Susie. What had Murchison and Wynne so engrossed were lists of Braniff stewardesses. Before each Cowboys season Clint got to choose which stewardesses would be used for Cowboys charter flights that year, and he spent hours carefully studying the problem.

When he was in Dallas, Clint routinely arrived home in time for an early dinner with Jane and the children, and he usually retired early. If this gave the impression everything was blissful at home, he gave the opposite impression at 1201 Main where he spent hours each day scheduling his extramarital affairs.

Clint was looking for new hobbies, especially since his house was now almost completed. During the spring of 1963—one year short of a decade after purchasing the Forest Lane property—he finally agreed with Jane that the time had come to move into their new home. They wanted to open the house with a large celebration of his fortieth birthday, and Clint decided the theme of the party would be "Christmas in September." He began months of planning for the extraordinary affair. On the day of the party, September 12, workmen arrived with truckloads of artificial snow, which they scattered generously over acres of the estate. They draped the glistening snow over bushes and tree branches and built banks of it along the drive. The estate looked like a winter wonderland display in a department store window.

Even more magnificent than the snow were the beautifully lighted trees, which appeared to be bathed in a glowing moonlight. Clint had achieved this natural effect by permanently fixing thousands of spotlights in the tops of the trees. The hundreds of beautifully tended live oaks that had been so artistically and carefully planted, one by one over the years, now shone brilliantly and would for years to come. One of Clint's secretaries was astounded at the $1 million cost and the years spent on the lighting job, but the result now seemed worth it. Clint could leave all the lights burning at once, as he usually did, or he could operate the lights individually by merely flicking different switches on a massive control panel. As the guests stood on the terrace by one of the swimming pools, they watched as large clusters of trees lighted on the estate, then fell dark, as other parts of the property were displayed, in the most fabulous light show they had ever seen.

The inside of the house was even more extraordinary, but many of the guests were unaware of this on their first visit, for Clint had spent a fortune to avoid showiness. The newfangled gadgets and their intricate switchboards that he had masterminded at a cost of millions of dollars were all carefully hidden from view. The television sets and stereo components were built behind hand-finished walnut paneling which opened only for viewing and listening. The only signs of the electronic drink machine were the spigots that portruded behind the bar when a button was pushed. Even the underwater viewing room into his mammoth swimming pool was carefully hidden by a small door and narrow flight of stairs. Another swimming pool, just for Jane and Clint, sparkled in the artificial moonlight right off the master bedroom. Clint, who never failed to amaze his friends, managed to show off one of the most magnificent homes in the world while somehow remaining incredibly unpretentious.

After Clint Sr.'s stroke in 1958, his twenty-nine room house became an increasing burden to him. Even with the help of a dozen servants, the mansion was suddenly too large with too many steps to maneuver. But when he talked about selling it, Virginia objected. She wanted it to stay in the family. Because Clint Jr. and Jane already had their Forest Lane property, Clint Sr. offered the house to John and Lupe. Someone came up with the idea that Clint and Virginia and John and Lupe should merely switch houses. John's children could grow up in the same wonderful Texas-size mansion their father had, while Clint Sr. would be more comfortable in John and Lupe's three-bedroom ranch-style home in North Dallas. Best of all, the house switch could be accomplished without any money changing hands.

The only person not keen on the house trade was Lupe. She felt a woman's elemental desire to create her own home, her own way, to her own taste, but the Big House, as it was called, had her father-in-law's indelible imprimatur, from the tarpon scales in the bar, to the wildlife murals on the four walls of the game room, to the rustic cabana and spring-fed swimming pool. Despite Lupe's ambiguous feelings, she, John, and their four children, ages three to twelve, moved to the mammoth Georgian home, which, in 1960, was still far out in the country. Because the bridge on the Preston Road entrance had finally washed out once too often, the back driveway from Keller Springs Road was now the main entrance.

Lupe immediately busied herself with transforming the richly appointed but masculine mansion into a far more regal and elegant home and one that was absolutely hers. She removed the rusty screened porch from the front of the house so that only an elegant slate terrace remained, and much to her father-in-law's unhappiness, she removed the tarpon scales in the bar. But Lupe still had a long way to go to put *her* mark on *her* new home. "We had very little furniture and the walls were almost completely bare," she recalls. "After we had lived in the house about a year, I finally asked John, 'How are we ever going to fill this place?'"

They found a solution in New York. John and Lupe had been in their new house only a few months when Murchison Brothers became involved in the fight for Allegheny. Not long after moving to New York, they began visiting art galleries, particularly those exhibiting the latest American artists. They bought a few works, and a few more.

The empty walls at home in Dallas were the main catalyst in John and Lupe's interest in collecting. But their interest did not long remain so superficial or cosmetic. They became fascinated with the New York art world, with the young contemporary artists of the late fifties and early sixties, and they began to pursue their interest with fervor. They bought some of the very early works of Helen Frankenthaler, Robert Rauschenberg, Morris Louis, and Sam Francis. Although these artists would become four of the most important contemporary artists of the twentieth century, they were not when John and Lupe became interested in them.

In addition to collecting art, Lupe wanted to help young artists, and she and four friends founded the Park Place Gallery in New York. In the tradition of the Florentine arts patrons of the Renaissance, Lupe and the other founders invited eight young artists to use the gallery to show their works. In the years since, five of the eight have become recognized internationally. Among the best known is Mark Di Suvero.

While Lupe was involved with the gallery, John was buying one work after another. He cared nothing about Impressionists or Old Masters, preferring instead brand-new works. Because these artists were so new they had no history, and because most of the works were comparatively inexpensive, John bought quickly and on impulse. "John had a very good eye," recalls Andre Emmerich, one of New York's most successful contemporary art dealers. "He was a good judge of what would be important twenty years later."

It was an exaggeration to say John was known as the Texan who could read, but it was no exaggeration that in the early sixties he was *the* Texas deal maker who had a sophisticated interest in abstract art. "He was the opposite of many Texans who came to me over the years with the feeling that we New York Jew dealers were out to screw them," recalls Emmerich. "John never acted that way. He loved buying art and he loved learning about it. He was very unusual because he never had the inferiority complex so many Texans had."

Not only did New York dealers quickly learn about the Murchisons, artists as well came to know and like them. In addition to buying several paintings of Helen Frankenthaler before her stature as an artist was widely recognized, John and Lupe had her as a guest at Gladoaks in Athens. John felt, as his father had, that the best way to get to know someone was to entertain him or her at one of the Murchison homes. When Ms. Frankenthaler accepted the invitation to come bass fishing in East Texas, she could scarcely have imagined that she would be accompanied in her rowboat by the Murchison butler in full uniform and that he would bait her hook and string the fish she caught.

Kenneth Noland, who was painting concentric circles on square canvases, knew there were not many Texans buying his works in the early sixties and even fewer who could appreciate his nonrepresentational art. "The thing that impressed me about the Murchisons was that they had a genuine interest in my works," recalls Noland. "So many wealthy people buy art for investment reasons or because they are seeking status, but that wasn't the case with John and Lupe. They seemed to truly care emotionally and passionately about the art."

John and Lupe liked Noland's work so much that they not only purchased his paintings for their home; they bought Nolands for their airplanes and for John's office. They were so enamored with one of his works they bought, a cat's-eye painting (an oval shape with a disc in the middle), that they made it their personal logo: They put an emblem-size reproduction on the side of their cars; they used it as a banner that flew with the American flag on their front lawn, and they reproduced it for party invitations. Lupe even had it reproduced on the tips of her skies. Noland was so flattered that he said nothing about potential copyright violations.

While John distinguished himself in New York as the art world's favorite Texan, his passion for modern art was not contagious back home in Dallas. A few years earlier John had been one of the founders of the Dallas Museum for Contemporary Arts. He and the other founders, including Betty Marcus, of the Neiman-Marcus merchant family, were two decades ahead of their time when they conceived the idea of a Contemporary Museum for Dallas. Their idea was to have a museum that would exhibit the works of current artists, those whose reputations were so new they could not at that time have won their way into the staid Dallas Museum of Fine Arts.

In fact, the Contemporary Museum was in large part a reaction to the Dallas Museum of Fine Arts' unenthusiastic acceptance of modern art. The ages and backgrounds of the trustees of the older art museum made them predisposed toward old, accepted art as opposed to difficult-to-understand contemporary works. This natural predisposition had been exacerbated by the McCarthy scare, when the Museum of Fine Arts had allowed art to become political.

Most people in Dallas did not like contemporary art, but the small band of people who supported the Contemporary Museum got behind it in a big way. John and two other leaders of the new museum paid the several thousand dollars a month in operating costs for a large building on a beautiful section of rolling land along Turtle Creek Boulevard.

The Contemporary hired a top-notch director from New York's Museum of Modern Art, Douglas McAgy, and quickly established itself as the avant-garde museum of the Southwest. It took many courageous steps, none more daring in the ultra-conservative climate of Dallas than the Oldenburg Happening. Up to this point in America, art was conceived to be objects hung on walls or set on stands to be decorously worshiped or at least studied. However, a few of Dallas's young rich, led by John Murchison, were part of the new movement that said art should be the opposite of decorous and stationary. It should move and change and make loud noises, and frighten as well as exalt, and maybe even disappear.

McAgy and Murchison decided to bring Swedish-born artist Claes Oldenburg to Dallas to direct a "happening." Only the bravest 10 percent of the museum's 1,500 members dared to show up for the event, which was held outside after dark. The guests, holding a long rope, walked single file through two small buildings behind the museum where a number of artists were doing different things. One was making a salad, another was playing a violin, some were dancing, others were sawing wood. After winding through the buildings and outside again, they looked up and saw Oldenburg's wife dancing around a papier mâché tree supported by a rope on the museum's roof. She cut the rope, the tree fell to the ground, and the happening was over.

The police showed up and Murchison and McAgy had to explain that what had occurred was simply a happening. Some of the participants, frankly shaken and doubtful at the moment of truth, would look back on it twenty years later as a high point when they were leaders of the pack rather than merely part of it. Oldenburg had become a mythic figure in Dallas almost overnight.

Despite the support of wealthy individuals, and its ambitious effort to educate Dallas to new art forms, as well as new artists, the Contemporary did not have enough financial support to survive, and in 1963 it was forced to merge with the Dallas Museum of Fine Arts. The DMFA, even if it did not like modern art, recognized the worth of the Contemporary's permanent collection, which had grown to include works by Renoir, Matisse, Buffet, Courbet, Dufy, Grosz, and Tamayo, among others.

Although the Contemporary Museum itself no longer existed, modern and contemporary art would never again be shunned or ignored at the Fine Arts museum. Murchison and the Contemporary's other founders insured this by making it a provision of the merger that the two museum's boards of directors would be combined as well. The energy that resulted when these two boards got together was tremendous, and the next decade was one of the Dallas Museum's most productive.

But the early sixties were still a very conservative time in Dallas. The vast majority of rich businessmen and their wives still viewed collecting even traditional art as odd. An interest in contemporary art was viewed as a pastime particular to homosexuals or Communists.

"The idea of an establishment Petroleum Club deal maker who was into buying abstract art was very different," says Harry Parker, former director of the Dallas Museum of Art. "John and Lupe were vanguards of taste, and they were living in the forefront of society and change. But to many of their friends the art was crazy. When John brought his hunting buddies and oil cronies home for dinner and they saw his art collection, they must have thought he had flipped."

There were plenty of skeptical looks, snide whispers, and raised eyebrows on September 21, 1961, when hundreds of friends and family came to the Keller Springs Road estate to celebrate John's fortieth birthday. Although their friends had facetiously dubbed it "Le Petit Chateau," inside the house was still relatively bare and what furniture there was was dwarfed by the cavernous size of the rooms. No one, however, failed to notice the few dozen shockingly abstract paintings on the walls.

The birthday party began with a black-tie, five-course seated dinner on the front terrace. Lupe imported a 120-piece orchestra from Houston to perform during dinner, as well as a Dixieland band from New Orleans and an all-black gospel church choir from Dallas's inner city. Midnight was ushered in with fireworks, but the real fun began when the Dixieland band started to play and the church choir began to sing. Formally dressed couples, carrying their champagne glasses, danced to the church choir, marching and swaying and gliding across the lawn, singing "When the Saints Come Marching In."

The party was the first of many that would establish Lupe as one of Texas's greatest hostesses. It was also the first glimpse many of John and Lupe's friends had of their extraordinary taste in art, a taste that was for the most part neither admired nor understood.

Clint Sr., Clint Jr., everyone in the family but John and Lupe had difficulty accepting the art. "My mother did not speak to me for months," recalls Lupe. "Then one day she said to me, 'The rumors are true. People in Dallas think you and John are crazy.' " And it was not a generational problem. John and Lupe's oldest children, who were just becoming teenagers, were so embarassed by the paintings that they refused to invite their friends home.

That the children did not understand why their parents filled the home with such unusual objects is not surprising. John and Lupe were away so often that they rarely had time to discuss with their children something as esoteric as the avantgarde art with which they were so enthralled.

In fact, although the children were no longer babies, they continued to live separate lives from their parents. Their chauffeur drove them to and from school, cooks and butlers prepared their meals, their governess bought their clothes, attended school functions, took care of them when they were sick, and helped them make their most important early decisions. Barbara Jeanne, John and Lupe's youngest child, recalls that her upbringing by her governess, Mrs. Golden Hale, began almost at birth: "When I was born, Mrs. Hale literally carried me out of the hospital." Mrs. Hale was in complete charge of where and how the children spent their vacations. "Mrs. Murchison would say to me, 'You go over to John's office and tell his secretary how much money you need for the trip,' " recalls Mrs. Hale. "I did and then I'd arrange for our stay in several Holiday Inns. We'd pile into the car and the chauffeur would drive us around the country. Mary Noel still says to me, 'Why did you always have us stay in a Holiday Inn, of all places?' "

While the Murchison children toured the country by car and stayed in Holiday Inns, their parents traveled to the most exotic parts of the world. At almost the same time that they built the Vail house, John and Lupe fell in love with Australia. Murchison Brothers started exploring for oil all over Australia in the mid-sixties when there were only two other exploration companies on the continent.

"We bought a charming house in Sydney that was right on the harbor," recalls Lupe, "and while John was working, I started buying art. Sometimes we would camp out in sleeping bags on the Australian outback for three weeks at a time. It was a pioneering experience that we loved."

Despite the international reputation for sophistication and luxury that Dallas's Neiman-Marcus had earned for the city, the overwhelming majority of citizens at every economic level were fundamentalist and ultraconservative. At the First Baptist Church, the largest of its denomination in the world, the hellfire-and-damnation fulminations of its pastor, the powerful Reverend W. A. Criswell, were indistinguishable from those preached half a century earlier by Billy Sunday, who had discovered that such pyrotechnical preaching was more profitable than baseball. Dallas was a place where you were saved or not saved, born again or damned, with us or "agin" us, and this black or white attitude was no less absolute in matters of politics than in those of religion.

The Dallas Museum of Art was attacked, but modern art was not, after all, a life or death matter. A far more serious problem expressed itself when hundreds of citizens insulted and mobbed Lyndon Johnson and his wife in a downtown hotel, and later spat on and hit Adlai Stevenson. The city's businessmen began to worry about the political climate, saying, "They're going to have to add a line to the city limits sign: CITY LIMITS OF DALLAS—UNSAFE!"

The event that most dramatically confirmed the world's view of Dallas as a dangerous place occurred at 12:20 P.M. on November 22, 1963, when President John F. Kennedy was murdered on its streets. That the murder was committed by a Marxist madman instead of a right-wing madman was a bitter and inconsequential irony. Around the world Dallas was labeled "The City of Hate." Dallas's ordinary citizens became angry that the city had acquired this image and worried that its bad reputation would slow or even end the city's growth. Neiman-Marcus president Stanley Marcus, one of America's greatest image experts, in his store's 1964 New Year's Day advertisement suggested:

> Finally, we think that Dallas should forget about its "civic image" as such. The best public relations comes from doing good things and by not doing bad things. Let's have more "fair play" for legitimate differences of opinion, less cover-up for our obvious deficiencies, less boasting about our attainments, more moral indignation by all of us when we see human rights imposed upon. Then we won't have to worry about the "Dallas image"—it will take care of itself.

But would it? What "good things" would ever redeem the city in the world's eyes? What individual or corporate good deed could ever erase the obscene example of murder?

17

"Wanta buy two seats for the Dallas Cowboys? Struck oil lately?"

Following the assasination and Stanley Marcus's injunction, the citizens of Dallas were searching for things that were right with their city. They needed to lessen their insecurities about Dallas, a city that outsiders viewed as a small, brash, nouveau riche cliché that flaunted its wealth, promoted extremist politics, and had murdered the President. Only those who lived in Dallas understood its strengths—the hardworking, church-going businessmen, the dramatic skyline, the strong unity among civic leaders. But these strengths had existed for decades. The people needed something more powerful to erase the negative image.

They found it in the Cowboys. Almost everyone agreed that the symbol, more than any other, that cast Dallas in the best light around the world after the assassination was its young and exciting football franchise. Despite the team's mediocre record, when Cowboys games were televised nationally, the hometown crowd saw their Cowboys as a bright symbol of what was good about Dallas.

Men and women, from bankers to schoolteachers to bus drivers, found in the Cowboys a reason to be proud of their city, and the reasons were as varied as their life-styles and the size of their wallets. The powerful Citizens Council was worried that the adverse publicity Dallas was receiving in the national press would hurt the city's ability to attract new industries and conventions. But the council also quickly recognized that a professional sports team was a strong drawing card, and one that few other cities in the Southwest had. The Citizens Council began to play the card at every opportunity, boasting of the Cowboys in the same breath as the "can-do" business atmosphere, its pool of nonunion labor, the city's commitment to cultural arts, and its warm, sunny climate.

Thousands of Dallasites who went to bed at night and woke up each morning feeling guilty about the assasination and wondering if, in fact, something *was* wrong with their city, as the rest of the nation claimed, could scream as loudly as they wanted for Dallas on Sunday afternoons at the Cotton Bowl. For many people, the team became an outlet for this wrenching guilt and frustration. Whether the Cowboys won or lost, they provided the people with a cause, one that they began to back with increasing numbers and energy.

While the team projected a sparkling image on national television, if its popularity was to continue, it needed to start winning. Although it finished the 1964 season with a disappointing five wins and eight losses, in 1965 the Cowboys became a rising power in the NFL. They got off to a good start with two impressive pre-season victories, but in the third game injury-plagued quarterback Don Meredith hurt his arm and was sidelined. The Cowboys lost the game and then suffered four more consecutive losses. On November 21 an overflow crowd of 76,251 jammed into the Cotton Bowl for a game against Cleveland, the Cowboys' first home sellout. But despite their numbers, the fans could do nothing about the team's disappointing performance on the field. Landry used his famous shuttle system with two rookie quarterbacks, and the team lost to Cleveland 24–17.

After two wins followed by six consecutive losses, Landry put the injured Meredith back in for the game against the Pittsburgh Steelers. But it turned out to be the Cowboys' worst game of the season. They lost 22–13 against Pittsburgh, then the weakest team in the NFL. Following the game, Landry was so distraught that he walked to the locker room, closed the door, broke down and wept. This uncharacteristic action by the stone-faced and seemingly unemotional coach marked a turning point for the ball club. Landry knew his team lacked consistency, and switching back and forth, using first the rookie shuttle system and then the injured Meredith was only contributing to the problem. He announced that Meredith would have the quarterback job, win or lose, for the remaining seven games of the season.

With Meredith, the Cowboys won all their remaining games and finished the season with seven wins and seven losses, placing them second in the Eastern Conference. Although the Cowboys were trounced 35–3 in the Playoff Bowl in Miami, few in American sports failed to notice that Dallas was a comer.

Locally, the Cowboys became an overnight sensation and were quickly dubbed the "Darlings of Big D." Three or four thousand fans crowded into the small airline terminal at Love Field to cheer the players when they returned from away games. The days when far fewer fans than that shuffled around the Cotton Bowl on Sunday afternoons were quickly forgotten.

The 1965 season showed a spectacular 45.3 percent increase in attendance over 1964. The first two home games in 1965 attracted 120,943 fans, only 7,557 less than the total annual attendance at Cowboys home games in 1960. A lack of fans would never again be a problem for the Cowboys. Ironically, as the team entered its sixth season, the attendance problem was reversed. Suddenly the Cotton Bowl was inadequate to hold the flood of spectators who wanted to see the Cowboys play.

The problem was not the number of seats but rather that most seats were bad. Those who sat on the upper decks were exposed to the blistering Texas sun in September and October and later to the fierce blue northers that swept through Dallas in December and January. From many of the splintery wooden seats in the stadium the view of the field was completely obstructed by large pillars supporting the upper decks. Spectators in end-zone seats in the oval-shaped bowl complained that they needed binoculars to see the ball, an exaggeration, but the point was made. Just as inadequate but in a different way were the private boxes and the press box, which the *Fort Worth Press* described as "a few semicircle cubicles of concrete."

In a city where temperatures during at least half the fall season reached into the 80s and 90s, there was no air-conditioning in the visiting team's locker-room. National sports writers dreaded working at the Cotton Bowl and took every opportunity in their stories to criticize the deplorable, outdated stadium. Most of the other NFL franchises boasted new, or relatively new, efficient stadiums.

Not only was the stadium itself woefully inadequate, but also it was located next to the city's worst black slums a few miles southeast of downtown. It was not a safe place to walk at night or even during the day, but because the stadium parking lot could hold only a small fraction of the spectators' cars, most fans had to park several blocks away.

Vandalism was so great that few fans were surprised when they returned to their cars after the game and found their hubcaps missing. Worse, there were numerous robberies and assaults. The city increased police protection in the area during games, but the ghetto was far too large to patrol adequately. Nor could the narrow residential streets surrounding Fair Park handle the thousands of cars before and after the game, with the result that there were massive traffic jams.

No one was more unhappy with the Cotton Bowl than Clint Murchison Jr. In fact, his dissatisfaction with the stadium had grown in direct proportion to the team's success. As early as 1963 Clint had begun dreaming about a first-rate football stadium with an adjoining performing arts center in downtown Dallas. A year later he informally presented his idea to a few members of the Dallas City Council. At the same time, he said he would be willing to remain in Fair Park if a new, larger stadium with sufficient parking could be constructed there, but that he preferred to be downtown.

Clint's desire for a downtown stadium was seconded by merchants and hotel operators and an overwhelming majority of Cowboys fans. But the Dallas City Council, under the iron rule of Mayor Erik Jonsson, was completely unresponsive to the idea. Nor did Robert Cullum, president of the State Fair Commission, which managed the Cotton Bowl, offer any support for Murchison's idea for a new facility at Fair Park, a surprising fact considering that the Cowboys were the Cotton Bowl's top tenant in terms of attendance and revenue. During a board of directors' meeting of the *Dallas Times-Herald* in

1965, Clint's plan for a downtown football stadium was brought up for discussion, but quickly shot down when one of the board members, a very powerful civic leader, said of Clint, "To hell with him. What have the Murchisons ever done for Dallas?"

As months passed, Clint complained that the cost of building a stadium was becoming increasingly expensive. Finally, in the spring of 1966, after more than three years of intermittent discussion, Murchison demanded an answer. Would the city of Dallas allow him to build a downtown stadium?

Mayor Jonsson insisted that the issue needed to be researched further. However, the city was willing to appropriate $2.6 million for major improvements to the Cotton Bowl. Theater-type seats would be installed, the visiting team's locker-room would be air-conditioned, and the private boxes and press box would be upgraded.

Clint described the proposal as "pouring money into a hopeless situation," and rejected any plan to improve the existing stadium. Instead, he began to push hard for a downtown stadium, and he called a private meeting with Mayor Jonsson. The meeting began at 4 P.M. and ended a half hour later. The following morning the *Dallas Morning News* reported that Jonsson had rejected Murchison's proposal for a downtown stadium. Clint was shocked at how quickly Jonsson killed his plan, and later recalled, "The verdict came as sure and swift as a Turk's scimitar."

Erik Jonsson enjoyed almost dictatorial power within the Dallas Establishment, not because he was one of the good ole boys whose families for generations had controlled the city's banks, stores, insurance, real estate, and cotton, but precisely because he was "new" and just the kind of new that was needed. As the city fathers began to realize that sooner or later the oil and gas that had made Dallas boom were going to play out, a handful of Yankees, led by Jonsson, came to town and started a business called Texas Instruments that manufactured computer chips.

The only chips Dallas business leaders knew were cow chips, but they recognized in Jonsson and his science-oriented associates the same inexhaustible energy that several decades earlier had built Dallas. The power structure was delighted to turn over to the son of Norwegian immigrants the responsibility to shape Dallas into something even richer in the upcoming twenty-first century. Jonsson had proven himself generous to the city with his money and his opinions on any and all subjects, so they made him mayor, stepped back, and waited for nothing less than a New Jerusalem.

But Clint did not like what he saw in Jonsson's handling of the downtown stadium, and he charged that the mayor had arbitrarily shot down his plan. Jonsson fought back, claiming that his decision was neither swift nor arbitrary, but simply that a great many public projects took precedence over building a football stadium and that downtown was the wrong location, anyway, because of the traffic problems it would cause. Clint explained repeatedly that traffic would come at nonbusiness hours, and that a stadium would revitalize downtown Dallas at times when it was desperately in need of activity—on Saturday nights and Saturday and Sunday afternoons. The stadium could be subsidized in part by weekday parking on adjacent lots.

From the very start it seemed that Jonsson and Cullum, who were close friends, were determined to ignore any and all ideas of Murchison's. It was no secret that Fair Park had always been a pet project of the Dallas Citizens Council.

Frustrated as he was, Clint publicly described his talks with the city of Dallas merely as "unrewarding." A man of action and not of words, he began to look for an alternate site for the stadium. In late 1966 he paid $1 million for ninety acres in the city of Irving, which borders Dallas seven miles north of downtown. A tear-shaped plot of land at the confluence of the three major freeways, its most attractive feature was accessibility.

A number of people insisted that this was "Clint's bluff." In fact, it proved to be his winning hole card, and he played it on January 28, 1967, when he announced that if the city of Irving could arrange financing for a new stadium, the Cowboys would play their games there in the future. He said his plans were to build "the finest football stadium to date in the world," at a cost that he believed could be held to $13 million.

The announcement did little to quiet the stadium controversy. Instead, it sparked the first real action from Dallas city leaders. The board of the State Fair immediately requested that the City Council place $29 million on the July bond ballot—$20 million for a brand-new Cotton Bowl, $9 million for additional parking.

But the State Fair's proposal was too little, too late. Murchison flatly rejected the Fair Park site, explaining that the results of a poll he had conducted and announced to deaf ears months earlier said the people of Dallas favored a stadium site other than Fair Park by a margin of four to one. "An overwhelming majority of the people of Dallas do not want a stadium at Fair Park at any price," he said. "The best thing you could build at Fair Park is a moat."

In August 1967 some 78,000 fans crammed into the Cotton Bowl for the Cowboys' game against the Green Bay Packers. But what remained in most people's minds after the game was not the battle on the field, but the crime spree that erupted afterward. More than a dozen fans, as they walked to their cars, were assaulted or robbed. One man was stabbed almost to death, and in another case a man was shot and his wife was severely beaten. From that point forward, many fans chose simply to stay away from the Cotton Bowl.

Just as he had closed his mind to the possibility of a stadium at Fair Park, Clint was also unwilling to continue his fight for a downtown Dallas stadium. By early 1967 he decided that his Cowboys stadium would be outside of town, and he was now ready to focus on a means of financing the stadium in Irving—one he believed would be the envy of every NFL owner and player in the country.

Despite his bold announcement, many businessmen and civic leaders still fatuously questioned whether Clint was serious in his plans to move the Cowboys, and many questioned his business judgment if he did so. Would the people of Dallas actually continue to support Murchison's team if he thumbed his nose at their city? Would they be willing to drive the few miles farther to Irving than they had to Fair Park? Would they get behind a team that might be renamed the Irving Cowboys?

Although in hindsight these questions seem ridiculous, at the time they were pressing concerns of many fans.

After Clint had announced his plans for Texas Stadium, he met one last time with Jonsson and a group of Dallas's city fathers. Jonsson, the powerful chairman of Texas Instruments, in a last attempt to keep Clint at the Cotton Bowl, asked, "If you take the Cowboys out of Fair Park, what are you suggesting we put there instead?"

Clint decided to have some fun with Jonsson and responded, "What about an electronics plant?"

"Now listen here, young man," Jonsson said, shaking his finger at Clint. After that, Clint just thumbed his nose at the city and in effect said, "I'm going to do what I want and you cannot stop me." The city proceeded to spend the commited $2.5 million to improve the existing Cotton Bowl. Not many years later Dallas spent an enormous amount of money improving the Dallas Museum at Fair Park before building a new museum downtown, and continued the trend more recently when it improved Symphony Hall at Fair Park at taxpayer expense only to build a new symphony hall a few years later downtown.

Jonsson won the battle, but Dallas lost the war. When in the 1970s and 1980s downtown real estate values plummeted, when dozens of retail stores and restaurants closed, when office buildings stood empty and hotel occupancy fell drastically, the city's planners and real estate magnates and business leaders who had been too frightened to contradict the prideful Jonsson now wrung their hands, thought of Clint, and said, "If only . . ."

Because Texas Stadium was not scheduled to open until the early seventies, in 1967 Clint was forced to sign contracts with the Cotton Bowl for the 1968, 1969, and 1970 seasons. The city fathers used the occasion to punish young Murchison one last time by peevishly stipulating that the Cowboys' share of proceeds from concessions during the next three seasons would be cut in half—from 50 percent to 25 percent.

But this move was small compensation for the billions of dollars the city lost in revenue simply because its leaders refused to play ball with a very determined and farsighted young man.

Murchison had far greater success with the leaders of Irving—a town of 46,000 in 1960—where city business was conducted publicly and by committee rather than by a few powerful businessmen behind closed doors, as it was in Dallas. Murchison and the Irving City Council quickly reached an agreement that made the stadium economically feasible. He deeded his optioned land to the city, and it, in turn, issued revenue bonds to finance construction of the stadium.

The story made news on Christmas Eve 1967. Bannered across the front of the *Dallas Morning News* in large type were the straightforward and relatively unexciting words: "Cowboys Carry the Ball to Irving." But behind the headlines was the story of one man's dream to build the finest football stadium in the world. With only minimal assistance from a few architects and engineers, Clint had almost single-handedly designed the space-age structure that would be called Texas Stadium.

"It will be the only stadium built primarily for football since World War II," he explained. In fact, it was far more than that. Clint had used the engineering and mathematical skills he learned at Duke and MIT to produce a dream stadium far ahead of any sports complex of its kind in the world.

"The problem with almost every modern stadium today," Clint explained, "is that they were designed to house both football and baseball. This is impossible. To accommodate baseball, the first row of seats must be so far from that portion of the field assigned for football that the last row is in the next county. Maybe that's the reason the name for the Astrodome is The Harris County Domed Stadium. And the Astrodome seats only 50,000 people; if it seated 65,000, as will Texas Stadium, the back row would be in Fort Bend County."

The most spectacular of the stadium's many features was a doughnut-shaped roof. Clint had mixed feelings about the enclosed roof at Houston's Astrodome. The dome had the advantage of shielding fans and players from Texas's wretched weather but the disadvantage of taking away the elements of nature that added measurably to the excitement of the game. Because he thought football should be played outdoors, he designed Texas Stadium with a roof that covered all but the playing field. The players would be rained on, snowed on, sleeted on, while the fans sat comfortably dry in their seats. He even placed the stadium so that the oppressive late summer and early autumn afternoon sun would fall on the playing field, but not on the fans.

At one point he considered adding a sliding, translucent plastic roof to the dome that could be closed during inclement weather, but he decided against it and then made certain it would never happen. Fearful that someone might someday try to tamper with his design, he made the roof so light it would collapse if it were enclosed.

The field was artificial turf, which was not in keeping with the natural setting Clint was trying to create but completely in line with the immaculate, almost sterile feel of the new stadium.

Keeping in mind that the big money in football came from television, not gate receipts, Clint designed Texas Stadium to look good on television. He wanted a large enough crowd in the stands to provide a lively studio audience for TV, but he wanted it small enough so that every seat seemed—both to the spectator in the stands and to the TV audience—relatively close to the field. He accomplished this by limiting the number of stadium seats to 58,000, some 20,000 less than at the Cotton Bowl, and by building the seats on a steep incline—up from rather than away from the field. Having complained that there were only 375 good seats in the Cotton Bowl, he was determined that every one at Texas Stadium have an unobstructed and relatively close view of the field.

Accessibility was another key. Not only would there be more than adequate parking, but once inside the stadium, the masses of spectators would flow swiftly through the infrastructure on fast-moving escalators and elevators. The model for the stadium looked like something out of a futuristic science fiction film.

For many of Dallas's rich, the stadium's greatest drawing card was its posh, luxurious "Circle Suites." Other stadiums had reserved boxes, but nothing on the scale of those 178, 16 × 16-foot "suites" (a word carefully chosen) that the do-it-yourself architect and founder of the Cowboys designed to circle the top of Texas Stadium.

The sales pitch for the private suites read like a satire of Texas big rich vulgarity—but it was real. "Your personalized penthouse at Texas Stadium . . . the ultimate in spectator luxury and comfort . . . similar to a second residence, like a lake home or a ranch." For the first time in their lives Dallas women became interested in attending Cowboys games.

A single suite cost $50,000, a purchase of two hundred $250 bonds; a double (16 × 32 feet) cost $100,000. And that was just for the bare, concrete box. Most fans would spend many thousands of dollars more, hiring professionals to decorate their suites, and nearly everyone would install the essential wet bar, refrigerator, automatic ice maker, telephone, and closed-circuit television set.

In addition, each suite owner was required to buy twelve tickets for each of the seven regular season games and two preseason games at $12 each, or $1,296 for the season. This obligation to pay thousands to the Texas Stadium Corporation was required each year for thirty-two of the next thirty-five years, when the bonds would come to maturity. At maturity, each $250 bond would pay its holder a meager $300.

Many in professional sports viewed Clint's bond plan as financial suicide. "People weren't buying the tickets as it was, and now he was asking them to buy bonds in addition," recalls a local sports editor. "It was like taking a tired horse that could barely walk and asking it to run another race."

While Dallas civic leaders were furious over the impending loss of the Cowboys to Irving, it was Dallas's blue-collar Cowboys fans who protested the loudest. The vehement objection was not the new location, a scant 100 yards beyond the Dallas city limits, but Murchison's plan for financing construction of the stadium. A single season ticket required a minimum purchase of a $250 stadium bond. The better seats in the stands, those between the 30-yard lines, required the purchase of four $250 bonds for each seat. For a family of four who wanted to sit between the 30-yard lines, the first season would cost an astounding $4,272 ($4,000 in bonds, $252 for four season tickets at $63 a ticket and $20 for parking). These fans too were required to buy four season tickets for thirty-two years or lose their option on the bond.

The September 1972, *Esquire* mocked the stadium's exclusivity with an article titled, "Wanta buy two seats for the Dallas Cowboys? Struck oil lately?"

If the title seemed exaggerated to some, it rang true to many ordinary sports fans who suddenly found themselves priced out of the market. Some said the Dallas Cowboys should be renamed "America's Sport of Kings." Other unhappy fans dubbed the stadium "Millionaires' Meadows," a distinction that could not have been more appealing to Dallas's nouveau riche who quickly snapped up the Circle Suites.

No one within the Cowboys organization could deny the fact that the seats were the most expensive in American sports. But while Clint had expected some criticism from spectators and the press, he believed it would be short-lived. When the criticism persisted, he tried to counteract it with an ad campaign detailing the "Trials of Stanley Mudge," the typical football fan who season after season had been cramped in his seat, kicked by passersby, rained on, and otherwise abused at the Cotton Bowl, but who at last would be able to watch his team perform from his comfortable, dry seat at Texas Stadium. Murchison even belatedly offered an economy plan for buying tickets: $6 down and $6 a month for 49 months.

When the criticism refused to die, Murchison shrugged. "What could be fairer than having the stadium financed by the fans who use it?"

He admitted, "I'd say we lost a whole group [of fans] in the $12,000-to-$20,000-a-year salary range who could afford season tickets at the Cotton Bowl but couldn't afford to buy bonds. If we discriminated against them, we discriminated against them, but no more than all America discriminates against people who don't have enough money to buy everything they want."

The *Dallas Times-Herald*, in an impassioned editorial, urged Murchison to reconsider his financing plan "on behalf of the tens of thousands of fans who dearly loved their Cowboys and now possibly can't afford them.''

But, typically, Murchison refused to budge. The MIT graduate was able, of course, to distinguish between a millionaire's income and the average workingman's. But because he cared so passionately about the sport, he misjudged the degree of desire in others, and their willingness to pay such a high price to watch a football game.

He was, however, practical enough not to begin construction on the mammoth project until he had sold $10 million in stadium bonds. Revisions to the original plan, as well as inflation and the cost of obtaining additional land for parking, had increased the cost of the stadium to $25 million.

With time, the criticism against his financing plan faded, and support for Texas Stadium grew more enthusiastic in direct correlation to the Cowboys' exciting performance on the field. Fans bought $18 million in bonds and Clint picked up the remaining $7 million.

The Cowboys ended the 1966 season with their best record yet, ten wins, three losses, and one tie, and fans were ready for a Texas-style shoot-out at the Cotton Bowl when the Green Bay Packers arrived to battle for the NFL championship title. The game was exciting from the moment it started, but the end was the team's most dramatic to that point in its six-year history. With five minutes and twenty seconds left in the game, and the Packers holding a commanding lead of 34–20, quarterback Don Meredith threw a long pass and the score became 34–27. In the final two minutes the Cowboys were trailing by seven points when Meredith threw another long pass into the end zone. But it was intercepted and the Cowboys lost the game.

One sportswriter claimed, "If ever a team attained tremendous stature in defeat, it was Dallas." Club emotion had soared, but the game left thousands of fans mourning the loss, heartbroken in defeat. Landry left the field with his head bowed. Schramm looked more dejected than the team had ever seen him.

Clint, never one to get emotional, smiled and with typical

good-natured aplomb, shrugged. "Oh, well, we didn't want to give 'em too much too soon."

Clint was a master at disarming a crisis with wry perspective. During the seventies, when the World Football League was founded, it attacked the NFL by signing veteran players. When word leaked that three Cowboys stars had signed future WFL contracts, reporters called Murchison to see if he planned a counterraid. "If the WFL succeeds," replied Murchison, "I don't want to sign their players. I want to sign their accountants."

Dallas had the look of a winner, but the NFL championship would continue to elude the Cowboys. In 1967 the team chalked up a respectable regular season record of nine wins and five losses, and won the Eastern Conference, but again lost the NFL championship to Green Bay. The game was played on a frozen Green Bay field where the temperature was 13 degrees below zero, the coldest December 31 in Green Bay history. One sportswriter wrote about the start of the game, "Dallas won the toss and elected to go home."

The Cowboys cared as much about fighting frostbite as fighting the Packers, and the warm-blooded Texans lost the game in its final seconds. They arrived back in relatively balmy Dallas the next day, but the effects of the loss lingered. The game shook the team's confidence for the next two seasons.

The 1968 and 1969 seasons looked like a repeat of the previous two years. Both times they made it as far as the Eastern Conference Championship game, but both times were soundly defeated by Cleveland.

Following the Conference Championship loss in 1969, coach Tom Landry was the most dejected he had been since he wept in the locker-room in 1965. "I don't know what the future holds," he said. "The team could quit or come back fighting next season. Why our offense doesn't produce in the big games is a mystery to me."

The team that had looked like a rising power in the NFL for the previous five seasons had failed to come up with the big wins, the major titles, and some sportswriters began to insist the team was jinxed. "The team doesn't need a coach," wrote a *Los Angeles Times* reporter. "It needs a witch."

Clint Murchison, completely unmoved by the criticism and the doubts of his own coach, confidently declared that the 1970s would be "The Decade of the Cowboys." Proving him right, the Cowboys finished the 1970 season as the NFC champions and won the right to face the Baltimore Colts in Super Bowl V. For most of the game the Cowboys appeared to be a better team than the Colts, but quarterback Craig Morton threw several interceptions, and the Cowboys lost Super Bowl V by just one field goal. The game ended 16–13.

The disappointing numbers on the scoreboard told only part of the story, however. Against some seemingly insurmountable odds, the Cowboys had made it to the Super Bowl within ten years of their founding. Instead of wondering why they could not win the Super Bowl, they suddenly realized they could not have lost it without having gotten there in the first place. They had played well against the Colts and knew they could play even better.

The welcome they received when they returned to Dallas the next day was like that of war heroes returning victorious from battle. Thousands of fans jammed the streets downtown for a confetti and ticker-tape parade. Secretaries and businessmen leaned out of their office windows as the players and coaches rode in covertibles down Main Street. The City Council, led by Mayor Erik Jonsson, proclaimed Monday "Cowboys' Day in Dallas" and recessed its meeting to come out and greet the players on the steps of City Hall.

The first championship was always the hardest to win, Landry said. But success would come, he added, and it would breed success. Amen, said the fans. They were believers. At the end of the 1970 season, Landry began thinking about using his second-string quarterback, Roger Staubach, the former naval officer whom the Cowboys drafted in 1965 but who had joined the team only after ending his four-year navy career in 1969. Staubach had thrown only 129 passes in his pro career, but Landry liked what he had seen.

The 1971 season would open a new era for the Dallas Cowboys. It would mark the beginning of the Staubach reign and the debut of the Cowboys in their new home, Texas Stadium.

Tex Schramm, Tom Landry, and Clint Murchison were determined it would mark yet another important milestone in the
Cowboys era, the final blossoming of the team into world
champions.

18

"... His informality, like his pursuit of money,
was not an attempt to prove anything,
save that he enjoyed it."

Big Clint was at his Athens ranch on Christmas Eve 1967
when the news flashed on the television screen that Clint Jr.
planned to build a $15 million football stadium in Irving. The
news report was the first he had heard of the idea, but he did
not hesitate to express his strong disapproval.

"That's going to break that boy," he said gravely.

"That was the only time I ever saw Clint worried or ever
heard him say anything about his sons' business judgment,"
says Virginia. "He never could see any financial gain in owning a professional football team."

Clint Sr.'s view of the Cowboys as a profit-making enterprise was colored even further as his health grew worse and he
was increasingly in the dark about nearly everything that was
happening at 1201 Main.

Not since the late fifties, when he suffered his first stroke,
had he taken an active role in Murchison Brothers. Even
though he moved back downtown in the late fifties, he went to
his office only two or three days a week, and then only for a few
hours. By 1961, when John and Clint Jr. were embroiled in the
battle for control of Allegheny, Clint Sr. was living almost full-
time at his Gladoaks ranch.

Clint Sr. felt he was coming home when he moved back to
his native East Texas. And this area where he grew up proved
to be not only home, but also a new canvas for his still active
and imaginative mind. He bought a dozen ranches and increased his East Texas land holdings from 3,000 acres to about
50,000. He still secretly yearned to own more cattle than anyone else in the world.

But as much as he loved rural East Texas where his roots were, he recognized that the area still consisted mostly of worn-out land and penny-pinching farmers. The oil had brought great wealth to some, but most of these men and women who made fortunes had moved to Dallas, so that East Texas was not unlike the English and French colonies in Africa, most of whose wealth flowed to London and Paris with very little remaining to improve the lives of the natives.

The chief problem unchanged by the oil that flowed from under the land was the same as it had been in Clint's grandfather's time: the land itself. The soil was still as much as forty feet deep in sand in places, producing poor, parched crops and fragile, sparse grass. In sandy spots the grass did not have roots long enough to reach the clay beneath.

But Clint found a way to change this when he learned about coastal Bermuda grass. Because its roots could reach down fourteen feet if necessary through the arid sand to the nutrients and water in the clay below, properly managed, it could grow where other grasses could not. Clint was excited about research on coastal Bermuda grass that was being done in Georgia, and he gutted one of his planes and sent a cattle partner to pick up a planeload of the sprigs. He planted them in the tilled sand, and in little time, the roots took hold and farmers from all around came to see the strong, emerald-green grass that could survive and even thrive in the sandy soil.

Within the next decade almost every rancher in Henderson and surrounding counties planted coastal Bermuda grass, transforming the area into superior grazing land. The grass that Murchison brought to East Texas was, in fact, so good for cattle that even many West Texas cattlemen, who thought of their herds as the best in the world, bought ranches in East Texas. This marked a significant change from earlier days when "East Texas cattle" was a derogatory term. Land prices rapidly escalated. An acre that sold for $25 in the mid-1960s increased to $800 in a decade.

While Clint was preparing his ranches, he was buying cattle, some 30,000 head. This was still far shy of the herds of Texas's biggest cattlemen, but Clint became bored quickly and, just as he had all his life, he began to diversify.

He bought a cattle trading company, a chain of supermarkets, a packing plant, and he got into dozens of livestock deals. Soon he was busier in Athens than he had been in his last years in Dallas. He owned a dozen ranches extending for hundreds of miles in several counties of East Texas, and he still owned many assets, companies, and properties around the United States, Mexico, and Canada.

He had merely switched his base of operations—from his office at 1201 Main to the oak card table at one end of his living room at Gladoaks. From this spot he placed as many as fifty phone calls a day to friends and business associates around the world. He never in his business career had found it necessary to visit a company or a ranch before buying it, so his apparent isolation in East Texas did not cramp his style in the least. He continued to wheel and deal.

In many ways he was even freer to operate without restriction when he was in East Texas than he had been in Dallas. A business associate recalls one time when Clint wanted to build a cattle feedlot in West Texas and took great pains to make sure that the chief comptroller at 1201 Main, Phil Bee, did not know about the deal.

"Before we got started, Mr. Murchison said, 'Look, let's don't tell Phil Bee about this.' He suspected that if Bee learned about the deal he would tell him he shouldn't do it," the friend recalls. "Mr. Murchison worked constantly to keep things from Bee because Bee clamped down on his freewheeling spending style."

Clint Sr. more often than not succeeded in circumventing his accountants. He merely telephoned any of a dozen banks that he or Murchison Brothers owned and took out a loan to finance the deal. By the time the boys at 1201 Main learned what he had done, it was too late to intervene.

With the First National Bank of Athens just down the road from Gladoaks, he could pull up to the front door, walk into the bank, come out a few minutes later with $10,000 in cash, and hand it to a cattle partner.

Clint had purchased 90 percent of the stock in the bank from the other Murchison heirs in the early 1930s. By the early 1960s, he was not only the bank's largest stockholder but its biggest borrower as well. But as his health grew worse through the 1960s, even the officers at the First National were loath to finance his wheeling and dealing. The stroke had left Clint mentally confused at times. John Rogers, who had joined the Murchison organization as an accountant, was brought to Athens by Clint Sr. to run the bank. Rogers remembers many times having to stop Clint when he was trying to get into a deal.

"One day he said to me, 'I'm going to borrow twenty thousand out of the bank.' I knew it was to finance a risky deal in Mexico, and I felt he would never see the money again. So I said, 'You can't. The bank examiner won't let you have it.' He was a little miffed, but not for long. He was too busy thinking of another way to get the money."

Few people who knew Clint suspected that he had created for himself a serene and peaceful retirement on a quiet ranch twenty-five miles from the nearest dusty town. Those who had visited Gladoaks knew that as much as he liked to talk about the "sounds of nature chirping in my ear," the screech of jet engines from airplanes taking off and landing at the ranch day and night was a far more familiar sound to him. Nor did they picture him sitting all day in a skiff on his lake with a cane pole hung over the side of the boat. They assumed correctly that he was still dealing in millions and playing host to many of the nation's top business executives, as well as state and national politicians. Instead of Clint traveling to Washington to meet with senators and congressmen, they now came to him.

The distinguished group of visitors, however, no longer included the nation's most powerful politician, President Lyndon Johnson. LBJ was repeatedly not invited to Gladoaks, and nothing he could do or say to Murchison would change that.

After Kennedy was assassinated and Johnson became President, LBJ tried to mend some bridges in Texas. Many of Texas's richest oilmen had supported Johnson for years with large contributions, but when he accepted the vice presidency under Kennedy, they felt betrayed. Johnson had enormous clout in the Senate, and much of this power was due to these Texas oilmen. During the fifties LBJ breakfasts at Clint's Preston Road home were commonplace. The Texas senator and ten or twelve of the state's richest oilmen would gather for coffee on the front porch, while Johnson gave an overview of what might happen in Congress affecting the oil industry and of the coming election. Johnson would announce which senators needed money and just how much they needed to defeat their opponents. Then Clint would assign the fund-raising job to one of the men gathered at the breakfast. The result was that Johnson again and again was able to deliver the marginal money that meant victory for these senators. In return, Johnson was expected to deliver the vote on the depletion allowance, and all other legislation of interest to the oilman. Those who did not know of the LBJ breakfasts at Clint's were puzzled when senators from a dozen states all across America, who were considered liberals and whose normal voting records were liberal, voted in favor of the depletion allowance. These Texas oilmen, after all they had done for Lyndon, were shocked that their man would join forces with the Yankee liberal Kennedy. Some supporters, including Murchison, were so disdainful of LBJ's decision that they cut their ties with Johnson.

But after the assassination, Johnson wanted to bring his old supporters back into his fold, and he was especially concerned with currying favor again with Murchison. But Clint was unforgiving. On Christmas Day 1963, a large group of friends and family had gathered at Gladoaks to be with Clint and Virginia. During the festivities Clint's butler, Warren Tilley, walked into the room and quietly announced that the President was on the phone.

"The president of what?" Clint asked.

"The President of the United States, sir," the butler responded gently.

"Tell him I'm asleep."

When LBJ was still a senator from Texas, Clint used to write to him suggesting things he wanted done in Washington. Johnson always responded to the letters in one sentence, "I hear you."

After he became vice president, he called Clint Sr. many times, but Clint would not take the calls. Finally, one day when Clint received a letter from Johnson, he promptly responded to it: "I can't hear you."

Johnson's reply to Clint's letters was a typically equivocal politician's answer, but there was nothing equivocal about Clint's. As was the case with J. P. Morgan when he was dealing with President Theodore Roosevelt, Clint had no doubt he was the equal of and probably superior to the President of the United States.

Clint continued to associate with dozens of other powerful politicians, including then-former Vice President Richard Nixon, who had been a regular guest at Del Charro, and when Nixon announced his quest for the presidency in 1960, Murchison was one of his chief financial backers. Then, as Clint Sr.'s health deteriorated during the sixties and he became less involved in politics, his sons stepped in. Just as their father rarely made a direct campaign contribution, the sons found a way to funnel as much money as they wanted to Nixon without leaving records of their gifts. When Nixon left the office of vice president in 1961, he bought a lot in the Murchison-owned Truesdale Estates, a residential development in Beverly Hills. Nixon paid only $35,000 for his lot, although most were selling for far more than that. Later, when Nixon became President, John Dabney served on a committee for the Preservation of the White House and was one of six Texans to donate $100,000 to refurbish three rooms in the President's mansion. The Murchison name surfaced during the Watergate investigation in 1974 when it was disclosed that John and Clint Jr. contributed $50,000 to Nixon's 1972 reelection campaign.

As much as Big Clint tried to keep up with the world, his failing health made it increasingly difficult. He had good days and bad, but the bad ones were becoming more frequent. Clint made regular trips to the Ochsner Clinic in New Orleans for tests and for what Dr. Alton Ochsner hoped would be extended periods of rest. Once there, however, Clint always found a way to continue making deals.

Clint had barely checked into the clinic for some tests when Dr. Ochsner introduced him to one of the clinic's board members. After making his acquaintance, Clint said, "I'd like to buy a bank in New Orleans. Can you tell me where I can get one?"

New Orleans was new ground for his fertile imagination, an area to be explored and exploited, and he began with the clinic itself. He devised a plan to operate a racetrack he owned in Maryland as a nonprofit institution whose proceeds would benefit the Ochsner Clinic. The idea was similar to that of the Del Mar Track benefiting Boys, Inc., but the Maryland racing syndicate strongly opposed the plan, as did the federal government. Rather than fight the inevitable adverse publicity, when he had the chance to sell the track at a $750,000 profit, he sold it and gave the money outright to the Ochsner Clinic.

Clint suffered a series of additional strokes in 1965 and took a dramatic turn for the worse. Out of desperation, one of his Dallas doctors suggested he visit a well-known clinic in Switzerland. The clinic outside of Montreaux had seemingly had some success revitalizing aged patients by injecting them with the cells of unborn sheep. This highly unusual practice was condemned by doctors in the United States, but many famous men and women from around the world had allegedly been successfully treated there, including Winston Churchill, Somerset Maugham, and Charlie Chaplin.

Clint spent two weeks at the clinic, and when he returned to Texas he felt much better. But within six months he suffered another series of setbacks. No longer able to get around on his own, he was forced to depend on a wheelchair. He and Virginia still made the trip to La Jolla during the summer and to the races at Del Mar each day from mid-July until Labor Day, but Clint no longer wanted to visit Acuña. It was too cold and damp much of the year. He wanted a place in Mexico but one where it was warm year-round, and he found it in Acapulco.

He bought the Las Brisas cliffside home overlooking Acapulco Bay that had belonged to Adam Gimbel, president of Saks Fifth Avenue, and his couturiere wife, Sophie. The already grand house was made even more magnificent when Virginia hired famed international architect and designer Arturo Pani to enlarge it. When the improvements were completed, Virginia invited some one hundred and fifty friends from around the country to come to Acapulco for a housewarming party to open the Quinta Gina. She thought that fewer than fifty friends would accept the invitation and could not have been more shocked when more than two hundred guests responded that they were coming. But Virginia did not panic, she merely instructed Pani to add a second level to the home and to build a temporary dance floor over the swimming pool.

Clint was in a wheelchair for the party and as always retired early, but not before watching a fabulous fireworks display. The Indians on the beach below had built a two-story scaffold out of bamboo, and when they lit the fuse the fireworks spelled out "Clint and Ginny," against a shimmering sky bright with stars and lights across the bay. The party did not break up until seven o'clock the next morning, and when Clint awakened it became all too clear to him just how successful the housewarming had been. Many of the two hundred guests stayed for more than a week, and even his large staff was hard put to handle such a crowd.

Because Virginia wanted to, Clint spent several months a year at Quinta Gina, but as time passed he was less willing to travel. When he was in Acapulco or Acuña or La Jolla, he called home several times a day. He finally insisted on staying in Athens.

Clint passed the days in East Texas riding in the front seat of an old station wagon driven by his butler, Warren Tilley. They would leave the house during the early morning and ride, never more than twenty miles an hour, to his different ranches, surveying work on the land but never getting out of the car. "Mr. Murchison would want Warren to drive out in the fields so he could get a closer look at trees being cleared," recalls John Rogers, who sometimes rode with them. "We warned him that if we got out there in the field, we'd get stuck in the sand, but there was no changing his mind. When we got stuck, he'd sit there quietly in the front seat of the car waiting for one of his foremen on a tractor to come pull the car out.

"One day Warren did something that made Clint mad and Clint said, 'Warren, you're fired.' Warren said, 'Mr. Murchison, you can't do that because I won't leave.' Clint got to thinking about it and started laughing.

"In later years he was very sentimental," Rogers continues, "especially about the bank in Athens because it had been in the family for so many years. I once told him that our deposits had increased from this much to that, and I looked up at him and tears had come to his eyes."

Another longtime Athens resident recalls that when Warren drove Clint to town and parked the old blue station wagon at the courthouse square in Athens, a large crowd would gather around. "All these old-timers would see Clint's car there on the square, and one by one each of them would go on over and speak to him and shake his hand."

Clint never lost his love of cattle and horse trading. He liked to attend the regular Friday afternoon cattle auction at one of the sale rings that he owned in Henderson County. "We'd stay at the auction about an hour or so," said cattle partner Carr Pritchett. "There might be sixty or seventy people in the room, and by the time we got up to leave, just about everyone had come over, and some would even be waiting in line to say hello to him."

Sadly, Clint saw much more of his friends than his family during the last years of his life. While his health was rapidly deteriorating, Virginia was still a very vibrant and attractive woman in her early fifties, and she looked ten years younger than that. She was as bright and cheerful and energetic as she had been when Clint married her. When she was not off traveling around the world, she often stayed in Dallas.

Clint Jr. hated East Texas, and only rarely visited his father there. The third-generation Murchisons also saw very little of their legendary grandfather and as a result have only the most superficial view of him. Clint Murchison III was a teenager when his grandfather became ill and retired to Athens, and says simply, "I really had no impressions of him at the time. I saw him maybe five or six times a year."

John and Lupe's eldest child, John Dabney Murchison Jr., has equally vague impressions of his grandfather. "He became sick when I was about twelve, and I just don't have much recollection of him one way or the other."

Surprisingly, Clint's youngest grandchild was the most observant of her grandfather. "When we would visit Gladoaks,

Pop would be sitting in a wheelchair and he usually had a long ash hanging on the end of his cigarette and when it got long enough it would fall off into his lap or onto the floor," recalls John and Lupe's daughter Barbara Jeanne. "He hated to have servants hanging around who reminded him he was helpless."

John Dabney and Lupe had their own house on one of the lakes at Gladoaks, and it was convenient for them to see Clint Sr. at least for a short time on weekends when they visited the ranch, but his butler Warren Tilley became his keeper. Warren, a frail, small man, was by his side at all hours during the day, and at night he slept on a cot outside the door to Clint's bedroom. Dallas doctors and specialists from around the country came and went, and each had a different prognosis and a different explanation about Clint's illness.

But it was Warren, who had worked for Clint for sixteen years, who shook his head and gave the simplest explanation: "Mr. Murchison's brain done wore out his body."

In early June 1969 Clint's health had deteriorated so markedly that Virginia moved her things to Athens and stayed with her husband. Then one day he contracted pneumonia, and Virginia and Warren took him to the hospital in Athens. They came back to the hospital the next day and stayed until early that evening, planning to return the following morning. But they would not see him again. At 4:35 A.M. on Friday, June 20, 1969, Clint Murchison died.

For the next two swelteringly hot days in late June, thousands of Murchison friends and business associates, as well as journalists from around the nation, focused on the tiny town of Athens, Texas. Telegrams poured into Athens and calls of condolence flooded the phone lines, including those from President Nixon in Washington and from former President Johnson at his ranch in South Texas. John Dabney and Clint Jr. dispatched Murchison airplanes to the faraway Mexican ranches to pick up friends and co-workers and bring them to Athens for the funeral that was scheduled for the next day. Most of the hundreds of people who came from out of town had heard the news on the radio and made it to Athens on their own in less than twenty-four hours.

Newspapers, from capitals around the world to the smallest hamlets and villages in Texas, carried the story of Murchison's death at the age of seventy-four. Many papers contained editorials that described his amazing life as one of the great American success stories of the twentieth century. The articles characterized him as a "college dropout" who became one of the world's wealthiest men by amassing a fortune of half a billion dollars using other people's money. He was described as one of the most colorful Texas oilmen, and the epitome of the Texas wheeler-dealer. It was a rare obituary that did not tell of his lifelong association with Sid Richardson and how the two had become legends long before their deaths.

The New York Times, in a lengthy front-page obituary, described Murchison as a "one-man conglomerate." But it was three short paragraphs in the *Times* that best summarized Murchison:

His entire life was devoted to making money—for himself, for his two sons, and for the thousands of people who were willing to lend him the money that under his Midas touch multiplied over and over and over.

What interested him was the challenge and excitement of making money grow—the details of the countinghouse concerned him little.

Although he was a Texan who started in a small town, made it big, and lived it up, he was a far cry from the caricature of the bragging, vulgar, big-rich Texan. Easygoing, shy, and relaxed, his informality, like his pursuit of money, was not an attempt to prove anything, save that he enjoyed it.

A few stories told of more than just his financial genius and idiosyncracies, and none was more poignant than that by *Dallas Morning News* columnist Frank Tolbert, who wrote of the tamale peddler Early Caldwell's reaction to the news of Murchison's death:

"Early went off into the woods to hide his sorrow," said Mrs. Early Caldwell of Athens at about 11 A.M. Friday.

"He couldn't stop his tears after he heard that Mister Clint died."

"By Mister Clint, Fairy Belle Caldwell meant Clinton Williams Murchison Sr.," wrote Tolbert, "a name which signifies a giant in the nation's financial circles but meant only a lifetime friend to Early Caldwell.

"Murchison and Caldwell were boyhood pals, hunted and fished and swam together. They were about the same age and their friendship endured."

That Clint saw no racial lines and had remained lifelong friends with many ordinary citizens of Athens long after he made his millions was obvious to the world during his funeral at Athens' First United Methodist Church. Services were scheduled for four o'clock in the afternoon of June 21. Before noon, lines were already beginning to form in front of the church, located just off the town square. Poor, struggling farmers in bib overalls stood in line next to some of the nation's most powerful businessmen dressed in dark gray pin-striped suits. Throngs of servants who had worked for the Murchisons, and old black men whom Clint had befriended as a boy, waited side by side with powerful senators and congressmen and governors from around the country.

When the service began, every one of the 850 seats in the church's pews was taken. Another 100 mourners stood at the rear of the church, and some 70 news reporters crowded into the doorways leading into the sanctuary. The church was virtually smothered with flowers, including large arrangements from the National Football League's Washington Redskins and Cleveland Browns.

Despite the commotion caused by the sheer size of the crowd, when the pastor began to speak the congregation fell silent. "He was a man of vision and integrity and daring who believed work was fun," the pastor said of Murchison. "He was a man known around the world for his great humility. He was a people-builder, not an empire-builder."

Clint was buried in Athens' City Cemetery next to his parents and only a dozen yards from the grave of Sid Richardson. But long after he was laid to rest, the town remained stricken with grief. The people of Athens had claimed for years that more millionaires, per capita, had come from their tiny East Texas town than from any other spot on earth, and among these many great successes Murchison was the most beloved. Not only had he amassed one of the greatest of the oil fortunes, but unlike many of the others who made millions, Clint never forgot his roots. Throughout his life he remained as devoted to Athens and as down-to-earth as he had been the day he left for the oil fields. Recognizing this devotion, the people of East Texas came to view Murchison as more than just a public hero. To some, he was immortal, a demigod. That the great man could fall, or had fallen, was almost incomprehensible.

Athens was not the only community crushed by the loss of Clint Murchison. When word of his death reached Acuña, a pall of sorrow fell over the ranch. The men and women and children whom Murchison had put to work, housed, and educated felt enormous gratitude to *el jefe*. While tending his cattle, building his home, running to retrieve his white wing dove, and serving his table, the Mexicans had come to know and admire the man who treated them so kindly. To express their grief and pay tribute to him, the Mexicans constructed a fifteen-foot solid ebony cross and hauled it up to the 3,500-foot summit of the tallest mountain at Acuña.

After erecting the cross and burying an old pair of Clint's boots at the foot of it, they bowed their heads in silent prayer. This quiet, simple ceremony at Acuña was as sharp a contrast from the media extravaganza at Athens' Methodist Church as the soft-spoken Clint Murchison was from most Texas oilmen. On the mountain at Acuña there was no throng of important mourners, no newspaper reporters, and no lengthy praise of the man. The group merely repeated the few simple words inscribed on the cross—his name, the dates of his birth and death, and, in Spanish, "We will never forget him."

19

"You can't tell me that guy couldn't have had more fun with ten broads than one painting."

When Clint Jr. leased the penthouse floor of the building on the southeast corner of Park Avenue and 57th Street in Manhattan, chasing women had become his chief obsession.

Just as he had with his homes in Dallas and Spanish Cay, Clint spent long hours designing the grand, five-bedroom apartment. "He hired and fired five different architects and ended up spending four million on the place," recalls a friend. "One day I came in and all the sofas were missing, so I said, 'Where are your couches?' He said, 'I sent them back. One of them was an eighth of an inch off.' "

Rather than decorate another home himself, this time he was assisted by a very talented New York designer by the name of Leonard Haber. Jane and Clint became personal friends of Leonard, as did the Murchison children, who called him Uncle Lennie. They had no idea just how prominently Leonard would figure in their lives.

Although Clint visited the apartment only two or three days a month, he hired a full-time butler, an Englishman named Harry Hughes, who had formerly worked for cartoonist Al Capp. Hughes, stately and aloof, was used to being treated with a certain amount of respect and was shocked at Clint's curt manner. Not only did he find Clint's abruptness degrading, but Hughes thought all of Clint's Texas friends lacked common courtesy. New Yorkers call their butlers by their last name, but the Texans always addressed him as Harry, a style he disdained.

These tense feelings were made worse by Clint's unwillingness to appreciate Hughes's skills in the kitchen. Although

Hughes repeatedly asked permission to prepare gourmet dishes, Clint refused and instead insisted he simply grill steaks or hamburgers on the balcony. Hughes came to hate Clint and to hate working for him, but the pay and the perquisites were too good to leave.

When Jane was in Dallas, the New York penthouse became a wild party place for Clint's drunken buddies and the young, attractive women whom they referred to as "light hookers." These women were not paid outright for their services, and many of them were one-nighters, but those who hung around long enough usually ended up with an airline ticket here or a necklace there.

It did not take long for an entirely new group of rapacious hangers-on to latch onto Clint in New York. Most of these men were no different from those who used him in Dallas, with the exception of Spencer Martin. "Spinny," as Clint called him, was well bred, well educated, and had the social graces that Clint so obviously lacked. Spencer's brother had been in the same class as Clint at Lawrenceville, and when Spencer and Clint met soon after World War II, they became fast friends. Spencer always had a witty comment and Clint a clever retort. They amused each other endlessly.

Spencer was not a sycophant, but he did often act as a cover for Clint, walking in step with one of Clint's women into or out of "21," while Clint walked a few paces behind.

After dinner the three often walked from "21" back to Clint's apartment. In front of the building Spencer departed, while Clint and his date rode an old, rickety elevator up to the penthouse. When they stepped off the elevator into the apartment, the butler was always there by the door to greet them.

When Jane was not with Clint in New York, someone else almost always was. "We'd be at the apartment and Clint would be there sitting in the living room and some woman would come out of the bedroom," recalls Spencer. "He never told us he had company, nor did he ever introduce the woman. She was just always sort of there."

Despite the times when one of his friends covered for him on a date, Clint far more often was indiscreet and made little if any pretense of hiding his infidelities. "He wasn't concerned if people saw him with other women," says a friend. "It just didn't seem to bother him. One time he was walking through an airport with a woman and one of Jane's friends in Dallas society saw him. When we told him he had been seen, he just said, 'Why don't you tell her to mind her own business?' "

"Clint's feeling was, 'So what if I'm screwing around—Jane ought to be able to accept that. After all, she has everything money can buy,' " says another Dallas friend. "Clint couldn't believe how much Jane spent on clothes. He once said, 'Jane has a black belt in shopping.' "

Jane had a $100,000 revolving account at Neiman-Marcus. As fast as Clint paid $10,000 on it, she spent another $20,000. One day in the early 1960s a Neiman-Marcus executive called Clint and told him that his bill totaled $168,000 and the store would be grateful for a partial payment of it. That afternoon Clint sent someone to the store to hand-deliver a check for the full $168,000.

After that, Clint lectured Jane. "I want you to realize that most of our money isn't liquid. It's very hard to come up with that kind of cash." He told her he intended to send one of Murchison Brothers' accountants out to the house to help her keep better track of her spending, but Jane said she would have no part of it.

She had some four hundred pairs of shoes, and it became a joke that she had more racks of clothes than the entire second floor at Neiman's. One friend recalls going with Jane to a trunk show of Norman Norell at Bonwit Teller in New York about 1965. "Jane walked right in and bought thirty-five thousand dollars' worth of Norell. I think she bought all but one dress in the entire collection."

Clint had hundreds of powder-blue suits, all exactly the same, and countless white short-sleeve shirts, but most of his clothes were very cheaply made and inexpensive. "One time he bought a pair of one-hundred-thirty-five-dollar shoes, and was feeling guilty about spending that much for a pair of shoes," recalls his secretary Jim Stroman. "He decided to return them. They sat in the office for a week and one night someone stole them. He was furious. He kept saying, 'I can't believe someone stole my shoes.' "

Clint was partly kidding around when he came home from work one day and dumped all of Jane's credit cards in the wastebasket. She later told one of his secretaries, "I'm sure if I'd have done that with his wallet I would have found a lot of numbers and addresses of his girlfriends."

Jane was a very attractive woman in her early forties, and Clint thought she was as cute as the day he met her. She wore her hair long and almost blond, and she maintained her shapely 110-pound figure from her wedding day. She was perky and fun and most of the time a good sport, willing to go along with her husband's crazy antics and pranks. His idiosyncracies that she could not change she merely ignored. Clint imitated his father in many obvious ways, and one was that he never carried any money. When he invited a large group of friends to dinner at the elegant Côte Basque in New York, his guests had no choice but to pick up the tab. Jane merely shook her head and said, "Oh, Cliiiiint." Clint figured that they could and would simply charge it to their expense accounts. Most of his buddies were business associates anyway.

In those days there were always hoards of employees, pals, and other dependents eager to ingratiate themselves with him. Once, as Clint was driving to an important meeting at Texas Stadium, his car broke down on the highway. He walked to the nearest phone, dialed his office, and minutes later a Murchison helicopter landed next to the highway and shuttled him off to the stadium.

Jane could laugh off her husband's pranks but not his friends. "Clint had so many strange people hanging around him. People who were just trash," she says. "I'd complain to him, 'Clint, I don't think they're good people,' but he just said, 'Oh, they're okay.'"

She had little choice but to go along with him if she wanted to stay with him, but Jane pursued her Dallas social life with increasing vigor. In 1965 she and two friends founded a Dallas fund-raising organization called TACA, which held an annual black-tie dinner and auction to raise money for Dallas arts groups. TACA was an immediate success, and is today one of the dozen largest society fund-raisers in the country.

Clint agreed to attend the annual TACA ball and a few

other society events during the year, but he did so grudgingly. At least one year, however, the auction turned out to be more fun than he anticipated. After eyeing an attractive American Airlines stewardess who was there to present airline tickets to the highest bidder, he motioned a friend over and whispered in his ear: "Use your Sherlock Holmes techniques and get me the name and phone number of that woman."

Large dinner parties were visibly painful for him. "At a party around 1965, I was seated on Clint's left," says Val Imm Bashour, then society editor of the *Dallas Times-Herald*. "He did not say one word to me or to the person on his right during the entire dinner. Finally I said to him, 'I'm glad to see you dress in keeping with your economic status—you know, your money-green pants.' This elicited a chuckle, but that was it."

Another acquaintance recalls sitting next to him at another dinner party during which he said a total of twelve words. "Isn't the lettuce delicious on the Braniff midday flight to New York?"

Rather than put her husband through the agony of attending large parties, Jane started entertaining more at home and without Clint at her side. She hosted regular after-show suppers for the large casts of the Dallas Theater Center, and its major donors. As the guests partied in the main part of the house, Clint spent the evening in another wing, quietly reading by himself.

Even in clubby restaurants, such as "21" in New York, Clint was socially ill at ease. "One night I was having dinner with him in the bar at '21' and Suzy the columnist was a few tables away," remembers one of Clint's girlfriends who dated him intermittently for three years. "She kept staring at Clint, and he couldn't figure out why. He was very impressed with seeing her, but it didn't occur to him that Suzy was just as impressed with seeing him.

"Clint once said to me, 'I think I'm so shy because I never had a mother. I know I wouldn't be this way if she had lived.'

"Sometimes when I was with him," recalls the girlfriend, "he would ask me to have dinner the following week. After he invited me, he looked away while I answered. I think he was looking away because he feared I might say no and he would feel horribly dejected."

Clint's shyness was not the only reason for his silent behavior. Like his father, he could not abide idle chatter, and if he found himself caught in it, he simply chose not to listen or contribute. Whether he was interested in what was going on around him or not, like Clint Sr. he was constantly spinning deals in his head, his mind always working, always preoccupied.

"When I was his guest at Spanish Cay," recalls a friend, "I remember passing him in the hallway and saying hello but he wouldn't respond. That was okay, though. I knew he was concentrating on something else.

"The only things he ever talked about voluntarily were technical ideas. He could explain the inner workings of the space shuttle or how a thousand bits of information fit onto a computer chip. He regularly read several scientific and mathematical journals, and he could talk for hours about what he had read, but you had to have an MIT doctorate in math to understand him."

Clint became bored by the inevitable similarities among the deals he engaged in. Murchison Brothers by the 1960s included more than 100 companies worth an estimated $1.25 billion. The partnership owned insurance firms, oil and gas properties, banks, hotels, country clubs, television stations, a publishing house, and one of the nation's largest residential builders. The companies ran themselves with very few problems that concerned Clint and John. Even the Dallas Cowboys, Clint's greatest passion, were the responsibility of President Tex Schramm and Coach Tom Landry.

But Clint increasingly yearned for new fields and new challenges. When Murchison Brothers decided to get into California real estate in a big way in the early 1960s, Clint was a victim waiting and ready to be caught.

The NFL was planning to hold its annual owners' meeting in Palm Springs, and Clint wanted to attend but with a woman other than Jane. "What am I going to do?" he asked one of his friends. "I can't be in the same hotel with the other owners and their wives. You got any pull out there in Palm Springs?"

"Hell, Clint," the friend replied, "you *own* the Racquet Club."

After a brief pause Clint replied, "Oh, that's right. I do."

The Murchisons had owned the famed Palm Springs Racquet Club since the 1940s when Clint Sr. bought it from actor Ralph Bellamy. Clint Sr. liked California so much that he then purchased the Del Mar Race Track and the Balboa Bay Beach Club and built Hotel Del Charro. Clint Sr. put his younger son on the board of Del Mar and tried to encourage him to handle these lucrative West Coast investments, especially the racetrack. But Clint Jr. was not in the least interested. Clint Jr. bet heavily on his own mind, his ideas and business deals. But he cared nothing about betting at the track, at cards, at casinos, or even at football games. Unlike his father, he never bet on anything he believed was more dependent on luck than on brains.

Still, Clint Jr. was intrigued with California, which was becoming the new America in the 1960s. The Beach Boys were a rock sensation, the hippie generation was about to explode on the scene, and flower children from New York to Miami were loading up their Volkswagens and heading for the West Coast. In the expression of the day, California was where it was at. Since the height of the 1940s baby boom, California had become the Promised Land. Its population increased by some 15 million people in the 1950s, and in 1964 it became the most populous state in the country.

John and Clint Jr. saw there was a great deal of money to be made in West Coast real estate, and Murchison Brothers' construction companies moved in aggressively. They built single-unit apartment complexes and posh residential developments up and down the coast.

Clint liked beautiful people, and he was wildly intrigued with the sexy, glamorous world of Hollywood. Just as in Dallas and New York, in California Clint quickly found himself surrounded chiefly by a court of unctuous flatterers whose livelihood depended on servicing his pleasures. But among his California cohorts was a likable and successful former advertising executive, Bill Dunagan. A Texan turned Californian, Dunagan became a major player in the Murchison saga. Twenty minutes after they met, Clint volunteered to invest $250,000 in a company of Dunagan's that imported football paraphernalia from Japan. During the meeting the figure $10 million came up, and Clint said, "Gee, Bill, that's a small fortune." Then and there, Dunagan says, "I decided I'd like to be friends with anyone who thought ten million was a *small* fortune."

Dunagan knew a lot of top actors and actresses and saw his chance to use this association to introduce Clint to the movie crowd whom he said he wanted to meet. Dunagan knew Hugh O'Brien and George Peppard, Clint Eastwood and Dennis Hopper, and he was able to swing an invitation for himself and Clint to their parties. Clint reciprocated by inviting these and other stars to ride on the Cowboys buses to and from the football games, and to sit in the visiting owner's box when Dallas played in Los Angeles.

Drugs were a new fad among the young and among the movie set as well. Clint did not join in when groups passed around joints at parties, and he was surprised that so many among the Hollywood crowd were so public and open about using an illegal drug. Clint used marijuana, but he was much more secretive about it. He kept a stash of marijuana in a bedroom closet of his apartment, and as he got into bed with a woman, he would roll a joint and ask her to share it.

But Clint was not one to criticize or stand in judgment of others. When a very popular Hollywood actor lit a joint on the back of one of the Cowboys' buses on the way to a game in Los Angeles, and some of Clint's Dallas friends at the front of the bus complained, Clint merely turned and stared out the window.

Young, beautiful women, who had come to Hollywood to be noticed by the movie executives, were in abundant supply, and Clint took advantage of many of them. There was one woman in particular who caught his attention. She was not an actress, but she was strikingly beautiful.

Clint liked good-looking, young vapid girls whom he treated as sex objects, then abandoned. But this woman was much more than just a great beauty. She was smart and very witty, and when she and Clint were introduced, he was immediately taken with her. Clint bought her a sleek Jaguar, and a few weeks later she totaled it. "Gosh, how could you have wrecked it?" Clint asked. She shot back, "Somebody ran a green light and hit me."

Clint began seeing her every time he was in Los Angeles, usually a few days a month. He had given other women gifts and money, but nothing on the order of what he would give her. The gifts became so frequent and so large that he started funneling them through a friend's account. Eventually, he bought her a house near Beverly Hills. He had a friend of his guarantee the $80,000 loan for the down payment (using Clint's signature) and put the house in her name. Clint then funneled the monthly mortgage payments through the same friend's bank account. One day an accountant asked the friend how he managed on a salary of $100,000 a year to have $3 million coming through his account. "I paid a lot of leases on a lot of cars and for a lot of other things for Clint's women," he replied.

Clint leased the penthouse apartment in the posh Century Park East, across the street from the Century Plaza Hotel. Just as his Park Avenue penthouse was the scene of wild parties, Century City became famous as the Texas millionaire's West Coast playground.

One afternoon Clint was alone in bed with a woman at the apartment when there was a rap at the door. "Clint, the phone's for you," came the voice. "It's the President."

"Tell him I'm coming," Clint laughed, and then made President Nixon hold the line for several minutes until he had finished making love. Nixon probably did not mind holding the line for his good friend Clint. The two spoke on the phone at least once a week, and Clint often visited Nixon at the White House. When Nixon described himself as the Dallas Cowboys' number-one fan, Clint smiled and merely took it in stride.

One morning Clint chuckled at a story in the *Los Angeles Times*. "Did you read this story on the front page about some guy who paid five million for a Rembrandt?" he asked one of his buddies. "The article says it's the most ever paid for a painting."

"Get me a pen and pad," Clint said.

He scribbled a few numbers on the pad, then said, "That same guy could have bought tax-free municipals, the earnings of which would have given him enough income to keep ten girls at a thousand a month. And that's without ever touching the principal.

"You can't tell me that guy couldn't have had more fun with ten broads than one painting."

When Clint was in California, and even when he was not, Dunagan made Clint's life easier by pursuing and tracking women for him. "Mr. Dunagan called Mr. Murchison practically every five minutes in Dallas with news of one girl or another," recalls one of Clint's secretaries.

One day Clint called and told Dunagan, "Karen's back in L.A.—find her for me." Dunagan telephoned Clint's friend Gordon McLendon, who owned two radio stations on the West Coast. "Help me find this girl that Clint's looking for."

Gordon put the word out to his broadcasters, "Every half hour make the announcement, 'If anyone knows how to locate this girl, contact the station.' " In less than an hour Dunagan called Clint with the girl's number. Clint's view of Dunagan escalated.

Not long after that, Clint was looking for another former girlfriend whom he had not seen in years. He asked Dunagan to find her, thinking it would take weeks to track her down. Clint was not even sure she was still living in California. But that day Dunagan happened to be visiting a movie actor friend in a Los Angeles hospital, and coincidentally he ran into the girl Clint was looking for. When Dunagan called Clint with the girl's phone number, there was a long silence on the phone. Finally Clint said, "Well, I'll be damned."

When Clint arrived in L.A., he expected to have his women lined up for him. He wanted a new girl each night, and most of the time got his wish.

In the 1960s, the Miss Teenage America Pageant was held in Dallas. Bedford Wynne owned part of the pageant, and he and Clint went to the rehearsal the night before the televised event. After the rehearsal Clint got the telephone number of one of the girls, and started dating her. She was eighteen and he was forty-five.

By the late sixties Clint and Dunagan had become almost inseparable. Dunagan leased a two-bedroom apartment a few blocks from Clint's home on Forest Lane, allegedly to have a place to stay when he was in Dallas. But it is likely that Clint and his fast-living, hard-drinking buddies used it more than Dunagan ever did. Clint's mass of courtiers continued to grow, and so did Clint's demands. What he increasingly demanded was not merely new women but women who had been pretested and rated.

John Dabney was disgusted by his brother's flagrant and constant womanizing. One of John's friends remembers being in a Dallas nightclub with John and Lupe and seeing a few tables away a man who was an executive in a company in which John owned a very large amount of stock. The man was making a scene with a floozy who was clearly not his wife. Leaving the nightclub, John said, "That guy was very irritating." Shortly after that, the man resigned under fire.

Dallas society sympathized entirely with Jane. Her husband's actions were clearly humiliating to her, and she seemed helpless to change him. It was embarrassing for her to attend parties alone, and know that all of Dallas society was snickering. "Wonder where Clint is?"

A few of Jane's friends suggested she threaten to divorce him unless he put an end to his constant philandering. But Jane, who had never had even the smallest degree of influence in the relationship—who did not even have a say in decorating her home—was ill-equipped to make such demands. From the start Clint had controlled the marriage and she merely went along. But Jane did begin spending more time in New York, establishing her own world apart from her husband. There she served on various social boards and became a part of New York society.

One day when Jane was in Dallas, she received a telephone call from a man in Chicago who told her that Clint had had a date with his girlfriend. The man was clearly angry and belligerent and looking for any means to seek revenge on his girlfriend. Jane wanted her own revenge. She finally filed for divorce, but not before first calling Clint's secretary, Jim Stroman, and asking him to meet her at a fashionable high-rise apartment building near the downtown area. She told him to say nothing to Clint about it. When Stroman arrived, Jane greeted him with two New Orleans attorneys by her side. "Mrs. Murchison is filing for divorce," one of the attorneys somberly announced. Then he added, "You've kept the wolves away from Mr. Murchison's door, and now Mrs. Murchison would like you to do the same for her. She would like you to come work for her in New York at a salary twice what Mr. Murchison is paying you."

Within minutes the reason for the job offer became very clear to Stroman. It seemed to him that the attorneys expected that in return he would reveal the secrets of his boss's extramarital sex life. Stroman refused to cooperate, and thanked Jane for the job offer but declined, saying he had no interest in living in New York.

Once Jane had gathered sufficient evidence elsewhere, she hit her husband with the news one day in the fall of 1972 when he came home from work. "I can understand a few women here and there, Clint," Jane said bitterly, "but thousands of women, no."

"Clint was totally surprised by it," recalls one of his closest friends. "He said later he had only one clue that she was leaving him. When he came home from work that day, she had taken his Phi Beta Kappa key, which she wore around her neck, and put it next to his bathroom sink."

Clint did not put up a fight. He agreed to give her a divorce and to work out a generous settlement. But he reminded her that because the bulk of his fortune was not liquid, the settlement could not be paid out overnight. In fact, it was paid out very quickly. When the divorce became final on January 3, 1973, Clint reportedly gave Jane $10 million cash and a five-story mansion on New York's Sutton Place.

The house that would become her permanent home had once belonged to Aristotle Onassis. Norman K. Winston, former United States Ambassador to England, lived there in the sixties, and when he ran into Clint one day and told him he wanted to sell the house, Clint immediately offered to buy it. The house, which is in a cul-de-sac overlooking New York's East River, was not only enormously valuable real estate; Jane was happy that at last she would have a home she could decorate to her taste. The house had old-world charm and elegance, the architectural detail and amenities that did not exist in Clint's ultramodern, exceedingly cold and bare home on Forest Lane. Leonard Haber got busy decorating it with elegant flourishes, and he and Jane began spending a lot of time together. Rumors spread quickly that they were going to marry, and a few years later they did.

Meanwhile, Clint seemed to have mellowed somewhat. His friends say he did not want his divorce, and that they noticed a big change in him after Jane left. "There was a very unusual softness in him, something very delicate about him that made us feel he missed her," says a Dallas friend. Another friend recalls, "Clint was furious when he learned that immediately following the divorce, another Dallas oilman sent her flowers."

And now that Clint was single he said his affairs were less fun. Clint had been divorced about a year when he and a friend met for lunch in New York. The friend mentioned that his attorney had just phoned him to tell him his own divorce, his second, was final.

"It'll hit you in a few weeks," Clint said dryly.

"What will?" the friend asked.

"That you don't have anyone to cheat on anymore."

Harry Hughes went to work for Jane, which did not bother Clint, who ate at "21" almost every day he was in New York. He even got owner Pete Kriendler to put chili on the menu. Clint's only serious complaint with New York was that he could not get a decent plate of barbecue. He first thought of air-expressing hickory-smoked beef and barbecue sauce to New York from Dallas, but opted instead to have a chef create barbecue right in midtown Manhattan—at 49th Street between Park and Madison. To no one's surprise, his plans for the restaurant received a flood of publicity. Charlotte Curtis wrote in *The New York Times* about the restaurant's menu and an interview with Clint Jr. "Tamale pie, Murchison noted, is chili, tomatoes, corn, and secret 'thangs' topped off with cheese and baked in the oven. He wouldn't reveal the recipe because Texans don't share recipes."

Clint named the restaurant the "Dallas Cowboy," but when his good friend and NFL commissioner Pete Rozelle went to dinner there and saw the name, he immediately called Clint. "Listen, this use of the name is against NFL rules," he said. "You've got to change it."

He reluctantly renamed it "The Cowboy," but the restaurant had more serious problems. The menu consisted of nachos, tamale pie, black bean soup, chili, barbecue, and steak, all things that Clint loved. But the Texas-style cuisine did not catch on in New York, and even most Texans found it underwhelming. Part of the problem was that Clint hired an Italian chef from a pool of unionized New York chefs, who was as ill-suited to the job as a French chef would have been running a barbecue pit in Dallas. The Cowboy was a long way from being the success he thought it would be. But Clint was just getting started. As with nearly everything he touched, he was about to make millions in the barbecue business.

Murchison Brothers outgrew its offices at 1201 Main Street and in the mid-sixties John and Clint sold the building, along with several other adjacent parcels of downtown real estate. These combined properties brought profits of many millions of dollars, which was precisely what their father had had in mind when he purchased the real estate with borrowed money twenty years earlier.

A new era began in 1965 when John and Clint signed a seventeen-year lease for the entire twenty-third floor of Dallas's tall and imposing First National Bank Building. The bank was the most desirable business address downtown, a considerable contrast to Murchison Brothers' former headquarters modestly tucked away between skyscrapers on Main Street. Friends and business associates who liked to snicker that John and Clint did not get along joked that because Clint's office was at one end of the floor and John's at the other, the brothers sometimes did not see each other for weeks at a time. In fact, when both were in town, they met several times a week to discuss new and existing investments. When John wanted to see Clint he walked to Clint's secretary's desk and politely asked if Clint could be disturbed. John need not have bothered. Clint was always available for his brother and expected the same in return. When he wanted to see John, he walked directly into John's office and began talking—whether John had visitors or not.

Some businessmen wondered whether the brothers' move into the elaborate bank building was a sign that they were going to take a more visible, high-profile role in the future. But no such plans were in the works. The telephone operators at Murchison Brothers' offices continued to answer the phone with the anonymous "Seven-four-one-six-oh-three-one," a symbol of the anonymity under which John and Clint Jr. planned always to operate.

When Clint was in his office in Dallas, he spent most of his time on the telephone, using it as a means to wheel and deal with people around the world. His two phones rang constantly, and no matter who was in his office at the time, he never told his secretary to hold his calls. He often took as many as one hundred calls a day, but most of them, like his business meetings, lasted less than five minutes. An associate remembers the first time he spoke with Clint on the telephone. "Mr. Murchison, I have three things to talk with you about," the man began. "Pick one," Clint interrupted.

First-time lawyers for Clint were often shocked at the brevity of their meetings with him. One of Clint's lawyers recalled that his first meeting with Murchison to draw an important real estate contract lasted four minutes. A few weeks later they met again and this time their meeting lasted three and a half minutes, after which the lawyer called one of Clint's associates aside and whispered, "My God. Doesn't he realize that lawyers charge by the hour?"

But Clint Jr., like his father, viewed business as a game, to be taken lightly and pursued energetically. "Make the deal and let the paperwork catch up later," he often said, repeating his father's words. Neither man really cared whether he made a large profit, or how the transaction was formalized. The thrill was in making the deal.

20

"God's coming to dinner."

On a Sunday afternoon in late October 1971, 65,708 obviously impatient men, women, and children ascended the escalators into Texas Stadium like thousands of ants coming to claim their new hill. Ticket holders who had paid thousands of dollars for stadium bonds and waited more than four years to get a look at their investment were excited and anxious. Would they move swiftly and easily into the super structure as its promoters promised? Would Texas Stadium, built at the astounding cost of $25 million, actually be a better place to watch the Dallas Cowboys than the Cotton Bowl?

The answers to these questions were overwhelmingly "yes." Few people who knew Clint well ever doubted that the stadium for which he had announced plans in 1967, would indeed be the finest stadium in the country built exclusively for football, and very likely the finest stadium of any kind in the world. But average fans had to experience Texas Stadium for themselves to be believers. And it did not take long. They had an unobstructed view of the field. They sank comfortably into theater-type seats, felt the luxurious legroom between rows, breathed the crisp fall air without having the sun in their eyes. The biggest surprise was the army of journalists who came to test the temperature of the fans.

The Dallas Morning News that day devoted ten pages to the event, in which it described every imaginable detail about the stadium, including such arcane facts as, "The scoreboard contains a total of 11,380 lamps and requires 400 KVA of 120/208 three phase, four wire electrical service." The story read as though Clint had written it himself.

Most of the articles reflected the overall feeling of the visitors, who were fascinated with Murchison's masterpiece. The traditionally immodest Texans had in this stadium, as in their oil and turkey and cotton production, the biggest and the best and the most. After all, this was Big D.

During the week before the game, many of this same overcapacity crowd of 65,708 had been calling their antiheroes the "Irving Cowboys" because of the team's loss the previous weekend to New Orleans. But any sour feelings disappeared as ticket holders found their seats and looked around at the magnitude and breadth of the structure. Because the vast majority of seats were so close to the field, visitors had the feeling they were sitting front and center in a theater. The opening-day crowd was a quieter, more polite crowd than most could ever recall at the Cotton Bowl.

Some spectators thought Clint's stadium was in fact too high-class, too sparkling, too sterile. But Clint wanted a place that outshone all other stadiums in the league. He forbade ticket holders to bring signs into the stadium because he "did not want anything cluttering up the place."

Above the stands were the 168 Circle Suites, more than half of which had already been sold by opening day. Many of them still had bare concrete walls, but that did not stop Dallas's social elite from bringing along their bartenders to serve hot and cold hors d'oeurves and carefully draping the mink coats over the folding chairs. Cameras covering the nationally televised game took every opportunity to pan the Circle Suites and to zoom in on the elaborately dressed Texas women, who came out for the game in jewelry that elsewhere would have been reserved for the opera or a ball.

Clint's 50-yard-line owner's box, which was more than twice as large as the other suites, was filled with oilmen and politicians, including former President Lyndon B. Johnson and Lady Bird. Clint Jr.'s view of LBJ was no more admiring than his father's had been. "LBJ is a guy who will do anything for his enemies and screw his friends," he once said, "because he's already got his friends and he needs his enemies."

But as television cameras panned the box, there sat LBJ for the world to see, munching on fried chicken served by black waiters in starched white jackets. Lady Bird ate half a dozen quartered sandwiches. "These are delicious, Clint," she said. "What are they?"

"I invented them," Clint said dryly. "You spread peanut butter on one slice of bread, grape jelly on the other, and stick them together."

Lost at times in the panoply of the stadium and the day's festivities was the fact that the fans had come to see a football game and hoped to witness their Cowboys trounce the New England Patriots. Landry was still using his famous two quarterback shuttle system. But a week before the game with the Patriots, the coach had decided that instead of starting Craig Morton, his seven-year veteran, he would start his substitute quarterback, Roger Staubach, the bright young naval officer whose ability far outweighed his experience in his third season with the Cowboys.

Just two minutes and sixteen seconds after the opening kickoff, Dallas ran the ball 56 yards to score the first touchdown in the Cowboys' new home. Staubach threw two touchdown passes, and the Cowboys defeated the Patriots 44–21, to begin an exciting era at Texas Stadium.

A few weeks later Landry announced he was doing away with the shuttle system for the remainder of the year and that Staubach would be his full-time quarterback. "I feel it's Roger's time to make his move if he's going to make it," the coach explained.

Many fans, as well as those within the Cowboy organization, wondered whether Roger had the ability to carry the ball club to the Super Bowl. But they did not wonder for long. Staubach led his team to nine straight victories, clinching the Cowboys' second National Football Conference title. With memories of their last year's loss to the Baltimore Colts in Super Bowl V still fresh in their minds, the team began preparing for their second Super Bowl. This time they faced the Miami Dolphins in the New Orleans Superdome.

Tacked on the bulletin board of the coaches' offices was a *Peanuts* cartoon. Linus, who is sitting at a table with his head in his hands, laments, "There's No Heavier Burden Than A Great Potential."

The players could not have agreed more with Linus, but from the moment Super Bowl VI began, the team never seemed burdened. It performed like a world champion. Staubach passed for two touchdowns and the Cowboys drowned the Dolphins 24–3. Not only was Staubach named the most valuable player in the game, he emerged as the number-one quarterback in the NFL. For years to come, his performance in Super Bowl VI would be remembered as the event that sparked the beginning of a decade-long, nationwide fascination with Dallas's seemingly invincible number "12."

Like the granite-faced coach Landry, even when his team played in the Super Bowl, Clint showed almost no emotion during the game. If a Cowboys player made a great catch or an important tackle, everyone else in his box would yell or applaud or jump up, but Clint did not move or make a sound. Only rarely, during the most dramatic points of a game, would a fleeting grin cross his face or a tightened fist jerk up from his lap. If the Cowboys won, Clint usually said nothing. But if they lost, he often had a lighthearted comment. "We'll get 'em next time," he might say, or "We just ran out of time."

Nor did John Murchison show any emotion when he watched the Cowboys play, from his box directly across the stadium from Clint's. The brothers were, in this, exactly like their father, who acted the same whether he was winning or losing. If Big Clint lost $5,000 on a horse race, he often said nonchalantly, "I'll pick that up next time around."

Clint Jr. had a statistician's mind and could recite the crucial plays and scoring, in sequence, through the team's history. He often displayed this extraordinary recall when he visited the Cowboys' locker-room after the game. "He would come up to you and comment on your best play of the game, and he would remember it exactly," recalls Lee Roy Jordan, one of the NFL's all-time great middle linebackers. "He might add, 'That reminded me of the time we were third and six and the Rams intercepted Meredith's pass right before the half in 1964 at the Cotton Bowl.'"

John did not go to the locker-room after the games, and he had very little association with anyone within the organization. But he had great fun in his stadium box, which was regu-

larly filled with some of the most talented and powerful people
in America. After one game, John was navigating his enormous Mercedes sedan through crowds of fans leaving the stadium on foot. Among those riding in the car was John's good
friend Democratic National Committee Chairman Robert
Strauss who, pretending to crouch down out of view, snapped,
"Get me the hell out of here, Murchison. You're ruining my
reputation as a Democrat." John did not share his brother's
passion for football or the team. Clint Jr. and John were both
strong believers in their father's philosophy that "You hire the
best and let them run it." John not only let others run the Cowboys; he viewed the team strictly as a business investment.

"Sentimental stocks were not a part of John's vocabulary,"
says a friend. Indeed, he was so placid, so unstirred by Cowboys hoopla that sportswriters, close friends, even many
within the organization had no idea he owned a single share of
the team. He was the ultimate silent partner.

Meanwhile, by 1971, Clint had become the city's number-
one public hero. In just one decade he had created a World
Championship football team and the finest facility built exclusively for football. Even more remarkable, he had accomplished these feats amid legions of doubters and doomsayers.
No top corporate executive in Dallas, no private philanthropist, no billionaire—including any member of the Hunt family—evoked the kind of admiration, even reverence, that Clint
Murchison Jr. did. Despite his protestations that the ball club
was run exclusive of him and that he did not interfere with
team business, Clint was viewed as the man behind the magic.

He was the man who had masterfully run Hunt's Texans
out of town, who refused to fire Landry when times were
tough, who took his team to Irving and convinced his fans to
follow. Without his wisdom and stubbornness, Dallas could
still be rattling around the Cotton Bowl watching amateur
Southwest Conference games.

The Murchison name alone conjured up mythic images of
vast oil wealth, and John, like Clint, carried the legend well,
using his brilliant mind and casual air of informality to carry
on the responsibilities and peculiarities that had made his father such a great man. John served on numerous civic, arts,

and corporate boards where he injected intelligent ideas and solutions as well as immense sophistication.

The Cowboys, however, put a great distance between the brothers' reputations—while John received none of the prestige connected with the team, Clint became a public idol. When people in New York and Los Angeles and London spoke of the Murchisons, they now were usually referring to "Clint Jr." When John bought a major company in San Diego or Washington, DC, or Nashville, the story often identified him as "John Murchison, whose brother Clint Jr. owns the Dallas Cowboys." Perhaps the best definition of John is that never once in nineteen years did he point out that he was an exactly equal owner of the team with Clint. But friends of Lupe say that she resented the much greater international publicity that now came to Clint Jr. One friend recalls being at her home on an afternoon in the early seventies as servants were scurrying around setting tables and preparing the house for a small dinner party. Late in the day Lupe said, "Well, I'd better get dressed now. God's coming to dinner."

When the friend raised her eyebrows questioningly, Lupe added, "Clint Jr."

While much of Dallas viewed Clint as a superman, he often acted more like a mischievous child. He spent inordinate amounts of time dreaming up pranks and schemes. On the eve of the Cowboys-Redskins game in Washington, Clint always hosted a big party in one of the city's best hotels. Senators and congressmen, lobbyists and Murchison business associates showed up for the affairs. The parties were wild, like the time one of Clint's group dressed as a cowboy and, firing blanks from two pistols, rode a horse into one of the city's fanciest ballrooms.

Trying to keep the rivalry going with his old nemesis George Preston Marshall, Clint once almost succeeded in releasing hundreds of chickens onto the field at RFK Stadium at halftime, having covertly scattered chicken feed on the field the night before. Another time the FAA at the last minute foiled Clint's plans for Murchison helicopters to hover over RFK stadium at halftime and release 10,000 silver and blue Ping-Pong balls.

Clint was great at acrobatics when he knew it would shock or surprise. Several times as he walked to his table in a fancy restaurant with a drink in his hand, he did a somersault without spilling a drop.

Once, when the *Flying Ginny* was lifting off the ground and making a steep climb, Clint stepped into the aisle and stood on his head. Hearing the roar of applause and laughter among the guests, the copilot turned and saw Clint somersaulting down the aisle to the rear of the plane. The pilot later came into the cabin and told Clint his joke was more dangerous than funny. The other guests tried to be straight-faced as Clint took the scolding like a bad little boy.

Another time, when Jane and Clint were spending the night at the White House, President Johnson was walking down the hall when he spotted Clint standing on his head in front of the Lincoln room. Taken aback, Johnson demanded, "Clint, what the hell you doin'?"

Remaining in his upside-down position, Clint answered coolly, "Ever since I was a kid, I wanted to stand on my head in the White House."

On another occasion John and a group of investors were gathered in the foyer of Murchison Brothers' offices admiring a new abstract work that John had just purchased. Clint walked out of his office, and saying nothing, he glided over to the sculpture and stood on his head to look at it. Then he got up, straightened his jacket, and walked out the door.

Clint loved to send shocking, one-sentence letters, such as the time a recently released mental patient was arrested for firing a bullet at Clint's friend Gordon McLendon, and the Dallas district attorney began looking into the case. Clint wrote to the D.A. suggesting that McLendon's would-be assassin was perhaps rendering a service to mankind.

Bob Thompson, Clint's longtime friend and associate in Tecon Corporation, was still a coconspirator in the many practical jokes Clint pulled on people, and the two often directed their pranks at one another. Once when Thompson was out of town, Clint used an enormous Tecon construction crane to place a 40-foot yacht in Thompson's 42-foot swimming pool. The boat displaced most of the water in the pool and when Thompson arrived home, he found his yard flooded and the yacht stuck in the pool.

Clint was a good friend of Democrat Robert Wagner when he was mayor of New York City. Clint and Thompson and another crony one day became very drunk at lunch at "21" and decided to visit Wagner at Gracie Mansion. They hired an ambulance and put Clint on the stretcher with a black wreath on his head, then sneaked him into the mayor's office in Gracie Mansion. When Wagner returned home late that afternoon, he found Clint passed out on a stretcher in front of his desk.

One of Clint's friends left his station wagon at Love Field, then took a plane on an overnight trip. When he returned the next day and went to his car, he found a very large and threatening black panther madly pacing the inside of his car. The man did not have to wonder which of his buddies would play such a prank.

There were times when Clint's fun backfired. His California friends gave him a forty-eighth birthday party at his Century City apartment, where, as always, he supplied the liquor. He agreed to let them dress him as a hippie, in a long-haired wig, peace sign medallion, and flowered bell-bottom pants. One of the guests took a picture of him, and, as a joke, sent it to a man in Houston with whom Clint was trying to do business. Clint later complained, "Those pictures almost blew a $40 million deal."

Sometime in the early seventies, a producer in the film division of the NFL was putting together an end-of-the-season highlight film for the Cowboys. In making the film, it occurred to the producer that there were Cowboys fans everywhere—in cities and towns across America, as well as around the world. GIs in Vietnam plastered Cowboys bumper stickers to their jeeps. Cabdrivers from San Francisco to Baltimore tacked Cowboys decals to their dashboards. Even in towns where the NFL had teams, there were large numbers of Cowboys fans. "You know," the NFL film producer said, "the Dallas Cowboys really are America's team."

The comment stuck. The team again and again was seen as a paradigm of Dallas—the fighting underdog that exploded almost out of nowhere. Along the way it acquired more than just heroic characteristics. It became the glamour team of the NFL. The Cowboys conjured images of adventure, great wealth, and as in all great American epochs, sexual intrigue.

The Cowboys added the element of sex in 1972, with the founding of a sideline attraction of eighteen young women, dressed in hotpants, halter tops with push-up bras, and white leather go-go boots. The wildly provocative new cheerleaders were as different from the team's original high school cheerleaders as the 1972 world champion Cowboys were from the expansion team of the early sixties. Gone were the chaste costumes and amateur rah-rahs and sis-boom-bahs. What replaced them were high-kicking dancers who provided spectators with a much more exciting, more adult form of entertainment. The new cheerleaders were college students or career women who were selected chiefly because they looked good in the skimpy cheerleaders' costume.

Although the idea of sexy cheerleaders was Schramm's, the Cowboys' owner was wildly excited by the idea. "Clint loved glamour and Hollywood and movie stars," recalls a friend, "and he liked the idea of a long row of cheerleaders doing a specific dance routine. He imagined the girls becoming the New York Rockettes of the sports world."

In the early 1970s no other team in the league had anything comparable to the sexy, organized, well-rehearsed Cowboys cheerleaders. Even so, while they were a big hit at Texas Stadium, they were not really recognized nationally until January 1976, at Super Bowl X in Miami. On that day, during a break in the action on the field, a television cameraman focused on the row of girls kicking and shaking their pom-poms. One cheerleader caught the cameraman's attention and winked, but during the rest of the game it was on the girls' partially exposed and undulating breasts, peekaboo navels, and bulging, bouncing buttocks where the camera mostly focused.

Seventy-five million viewers, one-third of the nation, had their television sets tuned in to Super Bowl X, and few of those watching missed the sideline thrills. Following the Super Bowl, the cheerleaders suddenly became wildly popular. New York talent agencies called offering auditions, and Hollywood producers inquired about making movies featuring the Dallas cheerleaders.

Clint, who had secretly dated a few of the early 1960s cheerleaders, now kept his distance from the girls. "When the cheerleaders became a big thing nationally, Clint was careful not to cause a scandal," says a close friend. "When he was seeing the earlier cheerleaders, he felt it was okay because most people didn't even know they existed. But by the seventies he stopped messing around with them. He didn't want anything, especially himself, to bring a bad name to his organization."

Despite Clint's prudence, with the cheerleaders' growth in popularity came the unauthorized commercial exploitation of their fame. Erotic posters were mass-produced of girls dressed in facsimiles of Cowboys cheerleaders' outfits, but, for instance, without the requisite halter tops or with their hotpants unzipped. In 1979 the cheerleaders' organization found itself mired in a complicated and embarrassing legal battle over a notorious X-rated film publicized as "an ex-Cowboys cheerleader" and her personal encounters of the sexual kind. Dallas Cowboys Cheerleaders, Inc. filed suit to stop the X-rated movie, *Debbie Does Dallas,* and eventually showings of the movie were halted in Dallas. But the enormous publicity generated by the fight clearly indicated the raw, sexual element the cheerleaders added to this great institution, America's Team.

Clint was always thinking of Schramm and Landry, and trying to find ways to make their jobs easier. One answer was to have his airplanes and his island at their disposal. During the Cowboys' off season, Landry and his coaches retreated to Spanish Cay for strategy sessions. Under tall palm trees by the crystal blue sea, they sat for hours with their playbooks. When the coaches put away their work, they went deep-sea fishing in *The Morning After,* an 85-foot teakwood former Coast Guard rescue boat that Clint had refurbished at a cost of $200,000 and later sold to Frank Sinatra. At lunchtime Clint's Bahamian majordomo and his staff of twenty sailed out to the boat with coconut rum drinks and a beautiful seafood salad served on bone china.

Clint loved lounging in the water at Spanish Cay. But he

was not a lazy man. He cared a great deal about his physique and did fifty push-ups, fifty knee-bends, and fifty sit-ups every day for most of his adult life. What he most enjoyed at Spanish Cay—other than a game of touch football on the beach—was taking underwater movies. He designed an advanced oxygen pump that allowed him to stay below the surface for hours at a time, and his cameras were always the latest and the best. Surprisingly, Clint easily became seasick on top of the water, and usually stayed behind when groups of friends went fishing.

Clint loved his Caribbean island as much as Clint Sr. had his island in the Gulf, and the son spared no expense in making it his most luxurious hideaway. When he took a group of friends to the island on the Murchison's Gulfstream jet, decorated by New York interior designer Ed Bennesch who installed carpeting of genuine zebra skin, one or two other Murchison planes carrying the luggage invariably followed. Upon landing, the guests were greeted on the tarmac by a platoon of servants carrying rum drinks. Clint even convinced the Bahamian Customs office to come to Spanish Cay, rather than burden his visitors with stopping at the customs office on another island.

Clint saw very little of Tom Landry or Tex Schramm socially or in business, but some thought that might change in 1966 when he built the ultramodern fifteen-floor office building five miles north of downtown that became the Dallas Cowboys' corporate headquarters. At the time, the building was the most expensively constructed in Dallas. The windows had state-of-the-art sun screens, and the air-conditioning and heating units all had backup systems.

Cowboys management moved into the eleventh floor, and Clint said he intended to have his offices on the fourteenth floor. He even built a private elevator that rose from his office to a 6,000-square-foot penthouse that not only included rooms for entertaining and sleeping, but a lavish terrace with beautiful trees and an elaborate garden sprinkler system, a sauna and weight room, and a very large projection room, all backed up with a vastly overabundant power generator. What amazed associates the most about the penthouse was that Clint never once used it.

In the early seventies Clint was still sharing the twenty-third floor of Dallas's First National Bank downtown with John and Murchison Brothers associates. He was clearly in no hurry to move out to the Cowboys Building. But he did spend some time out there, both on business and fun. After leasing space to a health club, Clint built a one-way mirror into the women's dressing room and invited his buddies to come by and watch the women undress.

The room on the fourteenth floor designated as his office for years contained only a desk. There was a secretary for another firm across the hall on the fourteenth floor who kept a careful eye out hoping to catch a glimpse of the owner of the Dallas Cowboys. But Clint's secretary, Jim Stroman, showed up more than Clint, and one day as Stroman was leaving the building, Anne Ferrell, the secretary across the hall, approached him.

"You work for Clint Murchison, don't you?" she asked.

When he said yes, she insisted on seeing Clint's office. He agreed, but when she saw it, she was clearly disappointed. "Kinda boring, isn't it?"

Anne may have been bored with the office, but she was not bored with the man. Not long after that, she found a way in to see him and positioned herself close to Murchison when she married Gil Brandt, the Cowboys' player personnel director.

Just about every business play Clint and John executed during the sixties turned into a touchdown. But by the early seventies Clint was becoming bored even with the touchdowns. He wanted excitement put back into the game of business, and he found it in complicated, risky real estate deals. About 1973 he met an Australian named Richard Baker, who became a key member of Clint's loosely put-together real estate organization. Baker was a great salesman, and Clint was immediately impressed with his big ideas. Not long after they met, Clint put him in charge of several of his biggest real estate deals. This period, remembered today by associates as the "Richard Baker Era," would mark the beginning of Clint's real estate troubles and his concomitant undoing.

Baker's game plan seemed to match Clint's exactly. As in

football, Clint preferred to skip the short yardage plays and go for the long pass. The riskier the deal, the more adrenaline it gave him. "According to Baker, every down was going to be a touchdown," recalls an associate. "He would give Clint a pro forma statement about what the deal was going to do and how Clint was going to make zillions on it. Clint would fall hook, line, and sinker."

Clint hated ordinary, mundane deals. If someone invited him to invest in a project that had a proposed compound growth rate of 15 percent, he would walk away from the table. His deals had to have romance. If he was told that the compound growth rate would be 500 times 15 percent, instead of making him dubious it excited his interest. "Because most deals were so boring to Clint," recalls a real estate partner, "he tried to make them more exciting by complicating them. If you were trying to get to four, everyone else in the deal figured you got there by adding two and two. Clint would try to make it more interesting by adding two and two, multiplying by three, dividing by six, and adding two. Clint was a genius, but he often managed to screw things up."

Clint's penchant for trying to do the most complicated, most difficult deals, which most businessmen thought impossible, amounted to standing on his head in business the way he stood on his head physically in his living room, on his plane, in his office, at the White House.

Part of Clint's troubles resulted from the infinite trust he had in his associates. One day Richard Baker informed him that the old Archibold estate in Washington, DC, was for sale. The property consisted of forty-six rolling acres in Georgetown, among the most beautiful parcels of untouched land on the East Coast. It had the added advantage of appearing isolated while in fact it was very accessible.

Clint thought he could make millions developing it with $275,000 to $500,000 homes, but the deal had major problems from the very beginning. Against the dire warnings of Murchison Brothers advisers, Baker paid too much for the land. A Washington business associate of Clint's recalls receiving a phone call from one of Washington's top developers. "About a week after Clint bought the property," recalls Tom Webb, "this developer called me and said, 'Has your boss lost his mind?' He paid four and a half million more for the property than I had agreed to pay for it, and we were about to close on my offer.' "

When Webb relayed the story to Clint, he merely brushed it off. "We'll make up for it down the road," was Murchison's typical reply.

But Clint was running an organization in which there were no checks and balances because no one—including Clint—knew what anyone else was doing. Although Clint was still making his real estate deals in the name of Murchison Brothers, family accountants at IMC, who had in the past put together the financing for the partnership's deals, were now left completely in the dark about what Clint was doing.

Just as Clint was turned on by Baker's salesmanship, he also became involved with another high roller by the name of Louis Farris Jr. "The only thing most people at IMC knew about Farris," recalls an IMC associate, "was that he had been in a lot of crazy deals and that he had gone bankrupt twice before he hit pay dirt with Clint."

No one, including Baker, had bigger plans for the Murchisons' millions than Lou Farris Jr. Before joining Clint in 1973, Farris had worked out of the office of Shreveport, Louisiana, banker Herman K. Beebe Sr., who operated a network of banks and savings institutions throughout the Southwest. In 1985 Beebe was convicted on a charge of fraud in connection with loans made to himself and several close associates through an investment company underwritten by the Small Business Administration. In 1988 Beebe was convicted and sentenced to a year in federal prison for bank fraud.

Farris had grown up in East Texas, well aware of the Murchison reputation, and when he was introduced to Clint, the two hit it off immediately. Soon after they met, Farris started working out of the conference room next to Clint's office. Although he was not given a title, in time he became Clint's closest and most trusted associate. Farris's charm, in Clint's view, was threefold. He was a master at providing Clint with out-of-the-ordinary deals and finding the financing for them. But the thing Clint like most about Lou was that the sky was always the limit with him. Anything was possible in Farris's view.

Clint desperately needed risky deals to keep his life exciting, and Farris inevitably provided them.

Farris says he helped arrange some of the financing on Baker's deals, but that he was against most of the deals Baker was doing because they provided no cash flow. "By the mid-seventies about eight out of ten of Clint's projects were failures," says Farris. "In the past Clint had paid for his failed projects by selling valuable real estate. He viewed his real estate as something that was always going to bail him out. In the beginning Clint didn't care that his real estate had no cash flow because real estate was going to continue to go up in his view, and he was going to make a killing years down the road.

"But Baker, instead of planning a development, would build a golf course and wait for people to build houses around it. Instead of creating a market, he expected the market to just appear out of nowhere."

At the same time that Baker and Farris were helping to run Clint's empire, Clint was busy experimenting with new hedonistic pleasures. Clint's life-style took a dramatic turn in the mid-1970s when he started using drugs other than just marijuana. "Some of the guys he was hanging around with on the West Coast lured him into a lot of bad things," says one of Clint's few longtime Dallas girlfriends who dated him when he was single. "One night in the early seventies he said to me, 'I trust you and so I'll let you in on a secret. Would you like some coke?' I thought he meant Coca-Cola, but then he went and got a vial of cocaine out of his closet and started snorting it.

"Many times he would call me right after he got back into town, and he'd say, 'Wait till you see what I got in California.' I always thought he had brought me jewels, but it turned out to be some fancy device for drugs. I didn't really worry about him, though, until he started calling me in the middle of the afternoon and I could tell he was on some drug or other. It got to the point where he needed drugs in order to perform in bed. Without cocaine, sex was impossible for him."

In the mid-seventies Anne and Gil Brandt divorced and

Clint started dating her. Anne, in her mid-thirties, was smart, dynamic, and there was nothing frivolous about her. Everything she did had a reason and a purpose, and she was always the initiator in a group. But because of her extremely high-strung manner, many of Clint's friends found it difficult to relax around her. Anne did not have the soft, sexy look of most of Clint's women. But she was handsome, with strongly chiseled features. Her dark brown hair was cut very short, and she wore simple clothes.

Anne had an in-depth, mathematical understanding of football, and she was a talented bridge player. But while she often had a logical approach to problems, she also believed in the mystical.

Anne's strongest feature, in Clint's view, may have been the deep emotional empathy she displayed toward him. A man who dated her in 1969 recalls, "She is the most empathetic woman I've ever known. I knew she was dating Gil Brandt at the same time she was dating me, but she made me feel like I was the only man in the world."

Anne was born in Norman, Oklahoma, the daughter of a traveling salesman who had witnessed the murder of his own father. Her mother was a depressed alcoholic. At sixteen, Anne left home and married a Marine with whom she had her first child at age seventeen. For eighteen months, while she was trying to take care of the baby and finish high school, she did not hear from her husband once. When he returned from the service, she became pregnant again, but they divorced shortly after the second child was born. Six months after her divorce, she married an engineer and they moved to Texas. At twenty-one, she divorced again and then took a series of jobs before becoming a legal secretary.

Anne worked hard, often sixty hours a week, and she played hard too. "I lived on the wild side of life for a number of years," she says. "Running, running, running." In 1970 she married for the third time, and this time it was to Gil Brandt. But four years later her third marriage ended bitterly when she and Brandt divorced.

It came as a shock in June 1975 when the owner of the Dallas Cowboys announced he was going to be married again and that the woman was the thrice-married, former Mrs. Gil Brandt.

Clint and Anne were married that same month in a small ceremony at his home. A reception for four hundred guests followed where Clint's cronies raised hell, beginning with auctioning off, page by page, Clint's personal address book. "He had a Xerox copy, of course," says a friend. Typically, Clint planned every detail of the reception. There was hard liquor and the finest vintage wines and champagnes, and each guest was given an individual picnic basket containing fried chicken and a peanut-butter-and-jelly sandwich.

Many within the Cowboys' organization felt sorry for Gil Brandt, but the only real change most Cowboys' personnel noticed was that for a full year after Clint and Anne married, the newlyweds stopped flying with the Cowboys on their chartered flights to games.

"That was the least Clint could do out of respect for Gil," says one of Clint's buddies.

It was not easy for Clint's friends and family to deal with the new Mrs. Clint Murchison Jr. She was jealous of his attention toward everything—football, business deals, his kids, his running buddies. And while Clint's sycophants were, of course, deferential to her, she was given a chilling welcome by Dallas society. The city's old and respected families had warmly embraced and admired the first Mrs. Clint Murchison Jr. And long after she divorced Clint, when Jane returned to Dallas periodically, they threw parties in her honor. She was, and is today, viewed as a lovely and gracious lady who worked hard for local charities, was kind to everyone she met, and never once boasted about her husband's wealth or the Murchisons' fabulous reputation throughout the country. These same men and women in Dallas society were at best civil to Anne, and most simply ignored her. Still, Anne publicly described her life as "a fairy-tale dream come true." She had struggled for years, and at last she had found her prince, she said.

But after they married, Clint had less time for her and was spending increasing amounts of time plunging into bigger and riskier business deals. With Farris's help, Clint was a magnet for the odd, out-of-the-mainstream venture. When a promoter asked him to invest in a project to convert cattle manure into the equivalent of natural gas and sell it to an Oklahoma pipeline company, Clint jumped at the opportunity. Clint loved acronyms and, ever the practical joker, named the company Calorific Reclamation Anaerobic Process (CRAP). But this was not the type of deal Clint Sr. was talking about when he suggested his sons treat money like manure. Clint poured at least $10 million into CRAP, but it proved economically unfeasible.

A major difference between Clint Sr. and his namesake was that Clint Sr. believed in the deals he invested in, while Clint Jr. seemed to invest in anything that sounded exciting. While the father calculated the risks and turned down many deals that seemed unlikely, the opposite was true of Clint Jr. The more a proposition appeared unlikely to succeed, the more it interested Clint.

"Clint would have a group of businessmen in his office, and one of the men in the meeting would say, 'Oh, Clint, that'll never work,' at which point a big grin would come across Clint's face and you could almost see the wheels turning in his head," recalls one of his secretaries. "Nine times out of ten he'd go ahead with a deal that everyone else said couldn't possibly work."

Clint gave a lot of money to a promoter who wanted to build a ski resort in Iran. "No one thought it would work," recalls a partner. "Who would go to Iran to ski? But if it worked, Clint thought, everyone would be amazed at his genius. Of course, the guy spent millions of Clint's money researching the project, but it never got off the ground. This was a familiar pattern."

An equally important difference between Clint Sr. and Clint Jr. was that Clint Sr. associated with men of high caliber. A business associate, in Clint Sr.'s eye, not only had to be smart and aggressive, he also had to possess honesty and integrity. In contrast, Clint Jr. sometimes put his sycophants in charge of his business dealings, or he turned certain deals over to people he barely knew. To make matters worse, Clint Jr. was undyingly loyal to these men, some of whom used him badly.

* * *

Nevertheless, Clint could still occasionally pick a winner. In 1975, when the Cowboys played Pittsburgh in Super Bowl X in Miami, Clint ate dinner one night in a barbecue joint called Tony Roma's. He thought the ribs and coleslaw were the best he had ever tasted. The next day he called Tony Roma and told him he wanted to buy the restaurant and turn it into a national franchise. "I'll provide all the capital and you run the restaurants."

The deal was sealed and a year later the first franchise opened in Beverly Hills. The opening party was spectacular. Among the large contingent of movie stars, football players, and sports announcers were Hugh Hefner and his twelve Playboy Playmates for the year. To top off the opening, Clint gleefully presented Anne with stock in the Beverly Hills restaurant. Tony Roma's was a huge success in California, and by 1981 the barbecue franchises had opened in thirty-five locations across the country, including the space formerly occupied by Clint's Cowboy restaurant in Manhattan.

21

*"I let Jesus handle even the little things.
Like I pray for parking spaces."*

"The thing you've got to remember about Dallas," John Murchison told a New Yorker who was considering moving to Dallas in 1973, "is that we're on a very steep improvement curve."

Indeed, Dallas was among the most popular of the Sunbelt cities that in the late 1970s and early 1980s would draw dozens of *Fortune* 500 companies, and thousands of yuppies, as well as jobless men and women, from cities in the Northeast. Dallas County's population had soared from 900,000 in 1960 to 1.3 million in 1970, and it was predicted that the population would exceed two million by 1985. John viewed the influx of Yankees as a great opportunity to make money.

John wanted to invest in North Dallas real estate, but he did not make the investment through Murchison Brothers. John had watched too many of Murchison Brothers' projects fail because Clint assigned them to incompetent people. Instead, John would enter the boom without Clint, marking the first time in the partnership's thirty-year history that one brother went into a deal without the other.

Long before most investors were fully aware of the rapid and apparently inexorable expansion of the city to the north, John began selling off parcels of the family homestead. In 1972 he and another Dallas developer began construction of a one-quarter-billion-dollar development on approximately two hundred acres of dry, parched earth that Big Clint had used for grazing land, as well as an additional newly purchased five hundred acres. John planned a development of office towers, retail space, apartments, and expensive homes, all centered around an 18-hole country club. He built much of the new development using Murchison Brothers construction companies, while selling other parcels of the land to his partners.

Five years later the area, named Bent Tree and located some fifteen miles north of downtown Dallas, had become a city all its own. Many people lived, worked, shopped, and played golf, all within a five-mile radius. With the rapid building boom came inevitable disadvantages, the most major being enormous traffic congestion. Although he was in large part responsible for the traffic, John complained that it now took him nearly an hour to drive the fourteen miles downtown to his office. He hated to waste time and considered trading in his Porsche for a helicopter.

But for him, at least, the inconveniences his Bent Tree development created were far outweighed by the millions he made. Having had success selling off parcels of his homestead, he began speculating in land in other areas of North Dallas the way his father had speculated on what was under the land—and to some degree John's was a self-fulfilling prophecy. Even though John bought in names other than his own or those of his companies, when it leaked out that the fabulous Murchison millions were being invested in North Dallas land, other speculators snapped up whatever was close in the same way that Clint Sr. and his fellow lease hounds had snapped up the subsoil rights near any farm where rumor said someone had smelled oil.

Because the speculators were competing fiercely to buy North Dallas real estate close to John's, land prices rose wildly. But soon John began to wonder how long the boom could continue. Cautiously, quietly, and effectively, he unloaded about 50 percent of his holdings at enormously inflated prices well before the North Dallas real estate bubble burst in 1974.

John had shrewd business insight, and he proved again and again that he was both forward-looking and very prudent. He invested tens of millions of dollars in a company or a parcel of land, then watched his investment increase as much as tenfold. He kept a close eye on his investments, reviewed his portfolios

with care, and what he did not understand he had an adviser
study and explain to him.

John was more of an overseer of the family fortune than either his father or his brother. His mind worked fast, but even
with this capacity, he gave slow, serious, and careful thought
to potential investments before he committed dollars.

With this reputation in the community, his were among the
most sought-after opinions in Dallas, not merely because he
might make an important financial contribution but also because he was a master at avoiding personal and political problems. He served on dozens of business, civic, and arts boards.
"John had the innate ability to see things clearly and put them
in perspective," recalls a civic board member. "Everyone de-
ferred to him because he had superb judgment. He would say
something at a park board meeting and suddenly everyone
would say, 'Yes. That's the answer. Why didn't I think of that?
It was so simple.' "

John was terribly shy, and public speaking was very difficult for him. He tried to keep a low profile, but there were
times when he simply could not get out of speaking in front of
a large group. There was nothing he dreaded more than talking to a crowd in the art museum's auditorium. Even when his
speech was very short, those who knew him well sympathized
with him during every second of it. He was at best uncomfortable, and often this tension, exacerbated by his chronic
asthma, made it very difficult for him to breathe.

John was devoted to the Dallas Museum of Art, served as its
chairman from 1972 to 1974 and as its president from 1974 to
1978, and became a major instigator in moving the museum
out of Fair Park and building a new home for it downtown.

But he was not nearly as free with his dollars as many civic
leaders thought he should be. When pressed to make a large financial contribution, John regularly gave excuses rather than
funds. One day a trustee of the Dallas Museum asked John
whether he could be counted on to give a large donation to the
proposed new museum.

The trustee knew that the price of the Murchisons' stock in
Centex, the real estate and development concern, had fallen
dramatically, and John used it as an excuse. "When the value

of one of your assets drops from $146 million to $22 million," he complained, "it puts a crimp in your ability to give."

By the mid-1970s John's business affairs had become secondary in his life. In addition to the time he spent on boards, he and Lupe were traveling extensively. The date book John kept at his office was marked off with trips for as much as a year in advance. There were certain mainstays: scribbled across the summer months was La Jolla; the fall, hunting at John and Lupe's plantation in Georgia; winter, skiing in Vail; spring, parties at their home in Sydney, Australia; and weekends in Texas were reserved for fishing and entertaining at Gladoaks.

In addition to these constants, there were always dozens of other trips. They cruised the Caribbean Islands and the Mediterranean, fished in Iceland, went on safari in Africa and stopped off in Paris to visit friends or throw a party at Maxim's.

"John and Lupe were the quintessential jet setters," recalls a friend. "No one in Texas could keep up with them. They would have dinner one night at the French Embassy in Washington and the next night a barbecue at their ranch in East Texas. And they were always on the cutting edge. Before it was chic in America to own a vineyard, Lupe and John bought the Château Greysac in the Loire Valley."

Lupe was as energetic as she had been as a little girl, but it often surprised friends that John agreed to keep up the pace she set. He had many responsibilities in Dallas, but increasingly he left them in the hands of others. Although this at times concerned Murchison Brothers' employees and some family members, it is precisely what many outsiders most admired about the Murchison men.

"What made the Murchisons far more interesting than most rich Texans was that they went out to see the world," says a longtime resident of Dallas. "Even with all the companies they had to look after, Clint Sr. and his sons always made time to enjoy their money."

Part of what made John Murchison such an intriguing person was his ability to be so many men at once. He gave the impression of being laid back and cool, while at the same time strong and powerful. He was both a rugged Texan and the ultimate sophisticate, who enjoyed camping in a sleeping bag on the Australian outback as much as sipping champagne and listening to Bobby Short on the piano at the Carlyle in New York.

John looked like a cowboy and fit in well at Dallas's Petroleum Club, but in many other ways he was the opposite of the oil-rich Texas deal maker. When Mortimer Adler came to Dallas to speak, John went to hear him. Few of his crowd, if any, had ever heard of Adler. In 1975 John went to London to hear the then-president of Yale University, Kingman Brewster Jr., give the Churchill Lecture to the English-speaking Union of the Commonwealth.

John loved to entertain elegantly, and before dinner parties at home in Dallas he looked over the tables to be sure they were set properly. He could spot an out-of-place fish knife in an instant, but even his sophisticated eye could not always guarantee a perfect party. Before one dinner for twelve, Lupe instructed her cook to take a salmon out of the freezer, decorate and serve it. That evening during the fish course, John whispered to Lupe, "This isn't salmon," to which Lupe replied, "Hush. It is too."

Some time before dessert, it occurred to John what had happened. Instead of serving the salmon John caught in Iceland, the cook had accidentally thawed and decorated a prize ten-pound bass he had caught in Athens. John was keeping the bass frozen until he could have it mounted for the game room, but it was too late now.

John and Lupe's friends still talk about the fabulous pigeon shoot one fall at Gladoaks. The Kleebergs came up from the King Ranch for the shoot, and a hundred other friends flew in from their ranches around Oklahoma and Texas. On the day of the shoot, private jets, of varying sizes and logos, began descending on Gladoaks just after sunrise. The deplaning guests, dressed in the latest hunting clothes from Abercrombie & Fitch and carrying expensive English guns, had to walk only a few hundred yards to enormous tents where they were served a lavish spread of East Texas food and drink, with whiskey as the main beverage.

The real excitement began when the hunters divided into groups and walked to different locations of the ranch. At each site there were professional pigeon throwers who released the birds into the air, while the hunters took turns shooting. Those who were not shooting were busy placing bets on who would kill the most pigeons. The hunting and whiskey drinking continued unabated throughout the day, with time out only for a hearty luncheon of fried bass, corn bread, string beans, and peach cobbler. Lupe had a large staff to take care of all the details, and she brought an interior designer from Dallas to decorate a dozen portable toilets for the shooting party.

At dusk the hunters devoured another feast, and the party lasted well into the morning hours. At dawn the hunters climbed back onto their planes and headed home. The planes were barely off the ground before their passengers were counting their bets. Whether they won or lost money at the shoot, the guests looked forward to returning another year.

John and Lupe gave many small dinner parties for powerful politicians, United States ambassadors, even princes and princesses. It was not unusual to see New York Senator Jacob Javits sitting on Lupe's right at her parties, or Texas Senator Lloyd Bentsen's long legs draped over an ottoman in John's library. Nor were any of the Murchisons' friends surprised that Gerald Ford, when he was President, took time from skiing to stop by John's home in Vail.

When Lupe was named Nepal's consul to the United States in 1983, she was well prepared for the job. One of her chief responsibilities in the role was to host a dinner party for the king and queen of Nepal, a rather ordinary task considering her experience in the area. She and John had given dozens of parties for European royalty through the years. Friends recall the time she served sausage for dinner to the German chancellor. And few could forget the stories of a small dinner at Lupe's home where Princess Michael of Kent first met Lupe's nephew Ward Hunt, with whom the world's tabloids would later link the married Princess romantically.

Lupe's parties were unarguably lavish and important in the annals of high society. But what made her one of the best hostesses in Texas was that her parties were always fun. Lupe was as loquacious as John was laconic. She shot around her parties, flailing her arms, hugging her guests, laughing and shouting gleefully. She was never still a moment, with the result that first-time guests relaxed immediately. Lupe had an extraordinary knack for putting her guests at ease and making them feel wanted. During dinner she was the first one to jump up from her chair and make a toast, and at small dinner parties she made an individual toast to everyone at the table. Lupe's guests felt appreciated, as though they individually played an important role in the success of the party. Dallas had much more than its share of extravagant hosts and hostesses, men and women who spent tens of thousands of dollars on a single dinner. But there was no social invitation in Texas that was more sought after than one from John and Lupe Murchison.

While Lupe entertained the international set, by 1976 the new Mrs. Clint Murchison Jr. had established quite a different set of friends for herself and her husband—different from John's friends, as well as from what Clint was used to. Liquor, drugs, even many of Clint's longtime buddies were off limits under Anne's stringent new house rules. Anne had found a new purpose to her life, and she was determined that Clint share in it.

Not many months after she married Clint, Anne recognized there were problems in this, her fourth marriage. Although she entered the marriage thinking all her troubles were over, she now experienced an entirely new set of difficulties and anxieties. Chief among these was being looked down on by Dallas society. Before she attended a party with Clint she worried endlessly, "what to wear, do I have the correct shoes and purse, what will I say, can I possibly be smart enough to fit into this crowd, can I possibly be chic enough to fit into that crowd, how can I make myself acceptable?"

Her deep insecurity manifested itself in a violent temper, as she went into tirades that lasted for as long as three days. "I wouldn't even let Clint sleep," she said. "I would kick, scream, bite." At times she wished she could just give up and die.

But then a friend took her to a meeting of the Dallas Christian Women's Club, which gave her the impulse to be born again. She finally found a place, she says, "to put those failures, guilts, and despairs, and that place was in the very big hands of Jesus Christ." Nine months of formal counseling followed, and once she found the way herself, she began speaking to large groups of Christians, and on the side, to any friend or stranger who would listen. Her proselytizing became a full-time profession.

When she gave her testimony, it sounded like something out of the television show *Dallas*. "We have our own private island in the Bahamas, a beautiful penthouse in New York, and an absolutely gorgeous home right here in Dallas in the middle of twenty-five acres of perfectly manicured grounds, all staffed with lots and lots of servants," she said. But, she added, somehow all those luxuries, and even the Dallas Cowboys, were not enough—without God.

Clint's friends tried to dodge her one-on-one sermons, but she was a model of perseverance, as well as amateurishness. "She made the whole born-again thing sound like such a joke," recalls the wife of one of Clint's business associates in New York. "It was very hard to take Anne seriously."

Indeed, many of Clint's friends, as well as Dallas society, got a laugh out of a 1979 *People* magazine article, in which Anne explained, "I let Jesus handle even the little things. Like I pray for parking spaces."

Clint, however, clearly did not think his wife's evangelism was a laughing matter. On the contrary, whether or not he believed in or approved of her preaching, he went along with many of her demands. By the late 1970s the mainstays in his life during the previous two decades—his wild friends, his ever-present vodka on crushed ice, his marijuana and cocaine—were no longer to be seen.

He had even agreed to attend the Bible sessions Anne hosted each Wednesday evening in their home. Members of Anne's church sat on the six large sofas in the living room, surrounded by a dozen servants. The home had a state-of-the-art stereo system, but the meetings always ended on a simple note, when Anne picked up her guitar and sang "Amazing Grace."

Anne's interest in the Cowboys had decreased, but the team managed to thrive nevertheless. The 1977 season had the best start ever. The Cowboys won their first eight games, and rolled to a 12–2 record, marking their twelfth consecutive winning season. They went on to win their fourth National Football Conference crown and the right to meet the Denver Broncos in Super Bowl XII at the New Orleans Superdome.

This was the second time in six years that Clint and his entourage would make the trip to the Superdome, and Clint expected to return to many more Super Bowls in New Orleans. Murchison Brothers owned a 36,000-acre parcel of property, which comprised slightly less than one-third of the land within the city limits of New Orleans. Despite its enormous size, the land had the disadvantage of being located in a racially mixed, poor section of town and in the flood plain right on the Gulf Coast.

Because the land was very marshy, and pure swamp in areas, the brothers had done nothing with it, after acquiring it in the late 1950s. Sometime in the seventies, however, Clint decided to develop it into a "second city" for New Orleans, with stores, hotels, homes, offices, and lavishly landscaped parks and lakes. Murchison Brothers' construction companies would build the boulevards and bridges, as well as a major multimillion-dollar levee system. Under Clint's plan, the project would be the most ambitious Murchison Brothers had undertaken, more ambitious even than the widening of the Panama Canal many years earlier. Before construction could begin, Clint would need major financing, and he began looking for it.

Between Super Bowls and business, Clint was spending so much time in New Orleans that he decided to buy a house in the French Quarter. This time it did not take him long to find what he wanted. He bought an elegant, old three-bedroom house with a beautiful garden and courtyard and three separate guest houses all hidden behind a high brick wall. Like his other homes around the country, the New Orleans estate became a wild party place, and, to no one's surprise, there soon developed a New Orleans contingent of Clint hangers-on.

Clint loved country-and-western music and became a fan and friend of Willie Nelson and Waylon Jennings. He invited the country-and-western singers to be his guests in the visiting owner's box at the New Orleans Superdome for Super Bowl XII. Before the game started, Clint realized that there were more guests for the box than seats to go around, so he left and sat in the stands with some other friends. The guests in the box had just settled into their seats when Willie and Waylon straggled in. A few were convinced that the seedy-looking strangers were bums who had wandered in off the street, and could not have been more surprised when Clint returned at halftime with news reporters and photographers. As the cameras clicked rapidly, the five-foot-six Cowboys owner, with his trademark burr haircut and white cotton short-sleeve shirt, stood grinning between the two unshaven, long-haired, jeans-clad country-and-western singers.

Meanwhile in the stands the crowd was wild with excitement and at times it seemed the fans on both sides would lift the roof off the Superdome. On the Cowboys' first offensive play Landry called a double reverse. The play failed, but it was typical of the coach's daring style. One of the reasons Dallas had become so popular was its flair for excitement. Win or lose, the Cowboys were thrilling to watch.

Dallas created drama by throwing the ball a lot—more than twice as often as most NFL teams did. And because Staubach was so adept at hitting his pass receivers, the Cowboys almost always put a lot of points on the board. In addition, Landry introduced new techniques, including the shotgun formation and putting players in motion, which were not only effective but also exciting.

Super Bowl XII was a classic Cowboys game. Staubach was nothing less than mesmerizing, completing 19 of 28 passes with no interceptions, as he skillfully led the team to a sound 27–10 victory. After the game Clint invited hoards of fans, players, and Cowboys personnel back to the French Quarter for a huge victory party that began at 1 A.M. and lasted until well after sunrise. Jennings, Nelson, and Charley Pride provided the entertainment, and, as always, Clint picked up the tab for the entire party, which numbered several hundred.

Clint's projection that the 1970s would be the decade of the Cowboys had come true. This, the team's fourth Super Bowl appearance, tied them with Minnesota for the most Super

Bowl appearances ever. Dallas was now also tied with Green Bay, Miami, and Pittsburgh for the most Super Bowl victories.

"The most efficient organization in the National Football League," wrote the *San Francisco Chronicle* about the Cowboys. "Their front office runs with military precision—and the team they put on the field reflects it."

"Franchises in the National Football League count up to twenty-eight," wrote *Sporting News,* "but the team most of America seems to respect as no other is one that has a star on its helmets . . . the Dallas Cowboys are fast becoming an American institution."

Friends, business associates, and those within the Cowboys organization (including players) praised Clint's nonmeddling management style as key to the Cowboys' long-running success. Clint viewed his way as the only way. "When you try to second-guess your associates, they'll quit. I don't picture myself as a football genius. I have people who I think are. The wisest thing for me to do is let them perform to the best of their abilities without hindrances from me."

His refusal to meddle was in no way an indication of lack of interest. During the twenty-four years he owned the team, Clint missed only two games.

Again in 1978 the Cowboys won the National Football Conference title and advanced to the Super Bowl for the fifth time, achieving the most Super Bowl appearances by any team, ever. Although they lost to Pittsburgh, the Cowboys were undaunted. They were on a decade-long high, and it seemed nothing could bring them down. Roger Staubach would retire at the end of the 1979 season, but even without "Captain America," the team was confident that its success on the field would continue. They proved to be wrong in this prediction, but at least for the next few years, in terms of glitz, glamour, and glory, no other team could compete with the Dallas Cowboys. There was little doubt that the ball club Clint Murchison Jr. founded in 1960 had come to deserve its name, "America's Team."

In fact, just how exalted the team was in Clint's view was

obvious when a society woman asked him at a dinner party, "Why did you leave that great big hole in the roof of your stadium?"

Clint grinned. "So that God can see His team play."

22

"Borrow all the money you can. That's the way to make it to the top."

As venture capitalists, John and Clint for decades were a high-powered team with a clear and similar mission—taking risks that other businessmen would not, channeling funds into areas of the economy where they believed demand would expand, with profit as their goal and their measure of success. They were optimists by instinct, always ready to take a chance on American growth and their own shrewd business judgment. The brothers liked to describe themselves as speculators who justified their business existence by spreading money around. Because their business interests were different—Clint cared about real estate, John was involved in finance—they were able to study and do more deals than if their interests had been the same. With an almost Calvinistic compulsion they drove themselves to work, work, work—even after they had made much more money than they could ever spend.

But by the mid-1970s Clint and John were beginning to look less like the lethal business combination that had catapulted them onto the cover of *Time* magazine and more like strangers with two very different ideas about how to invest their money and their lives. Clint remembered a story he heard about his father borrowing money in the early 1940s from Chase National Bank in New York. Clint Sr. had borrowed more than $100 million, making him the largest individual debtor the Chase had ever had. When the bank's chairman, John McCloy, was shown the loan receipt, he was so impressed that anyone could finagle such a large loan that he asked to be introduced to the Texas wheeler-dealer. McCloy never stopped being impressed with Clint Sr.'s financial savvy, and the two men became lifelong friends.

The younger Clint proved he was his father's son. He had inherited his father's love of leveraging, but carried the practice to a fatally exaggerated degree. No matter how highly leveraged he was, it never seemed high enough. "Clint Sr. and Clint Jr. were nervous with cash," recalls a longtime family attorney. "But Clint Jr. made borrowing money a full-time preoccupation."

When John and Clint Jr.'s friends asked Big Clint for advice on how to become rich, he invariably replied, "Borrow all the money you can. That's the way to make it to the top."

Like his brother, John also had learned the use of leverage from his father and practiced it, but his loans were much smaller and only rarely did he give his personal guarantee. For a Murchison, John was "a paragon of fiscal restraint." While Clint spurred the partnership into one new deal after another, John tried to hold the reins that would keep his brother from risking too much. Even when he did not agree with Clint's plunging, John stuck by him. "Clint Jr. always supported John in whatever John said at a meeting, and vice versa," recalls a longtime employee of Investments Management Corporation, the operating company for Murchison Brothers. "Although to people outside the company the brothers did not appear very close, the bond between them was very strong."

Many years earlier Clint Sr. had asked John to keep an eye on his younger brother in business, to make sure there were limits on how much of the partnership the brothers would risk. Clint Sr. often repeated this request, and John promised to do so. But by the mid-seventies it was evident that John was having virtually no success restraining Clint, and consequently that there was trouble ahead.

As John spent more and more time traveling in the early seventies, Clint had taken a much larger role in selecting Murchison Brothers' investments. Worse, Clint operated independently of the two dozen accountants and advisers who had for years maintained reasonable business procedures and precautions at Murchison Brothers. At the same time these associates were left in the dark, Clint gave carte blanche to his other associates who operated for him on the side.

"Clint Jr. just threw money at people he perceived to be his friends," says Henry Gilchrist, who had been one of the family's chief attorneys since the 1950s. "He was doing this out of sight of his family and family advisers and there was no way of stopping him."

A longtime family accountant remembers the enormous expenses some of Clint's associates charged to Murchison Brothers. "Those guys would turn in requests, that were not itemized, for hundreds of thousands of dollars with no explanation of even what the deal was. Nor did Clint tell us what the expenses were for. He simply wrote across them, 'Pay.' "

Foremost among the potential problems was the enormous debt the partnership was incurring. With Clint at the helm and John absent, the partnership's debt was constantly reaching new heights, and at a period when interest rates were climbing. "Borrowing money was a game and a challenge to Clint," recalls an associate. "He was trying always to see how much he could borrow. Most businessmen would get an idea for a deal and then go out and get the financing for it. Clint did the opposite. He'd pledge a Murchison Brothers asset, get a twenty-million-dollar loan for it, and then he'd look for a place to put the twenty million. Most people thought it was ludicrous, but it worked for him for years."

Clint owned four undeveloped acres of land adjacent to his Palm Springs Racquet Club. One day in the late seventies Clint and one of his friends had lunch with the head of a Beverly Hills, California, bank. Twenty minutes into the lunch Clint asked the banker whether he would give him a $2.5 million loan to develop the four acres. The banker immediately agreed, and Clint turned to his friend. "Okay, what are you gonna do with the property?" The friend, who knew absolutely nothing about land development, was completely surprised to learn Clint wanted him to carry out the deal.

This lack of judiciousness on Clint's part was not new. What John and many IMC associates had feared three and four years earlier was coming true. Many of Clint's major real estate projects were headed for failure. Not only were the projects mismanaged, but they also were stung by bad timing. Several of his real estate projects had been expected to start showing profits in the tens of millions of dollars by the end of the seventies. Instead, because of skyrocketing interest rates, and in many cases poor construction, a number of the projects were stalled for lack of funds.

Credit and inflation were the twin spurs that drove the Murchison empire for decades. Clint Sr. had taught his sons that as long as they invested other people's money in Murchison properties, and the purchasing value of the dollar continued to fall, they would get richer and richer. But Clint Sr. built the bulk of his fortune when interest rates were 2 percent or 3 percent and inflation was rampant. By 1978 interest rates had hit 18 percent, a much higher rate than inflation. Houses stopped selling because potential buyers could not afford the mortgage interest, and land values plummeted.

While the long-planned-for cash flow on their projects was not forthcoming, Murchison Brothers' bank notes kept arriving. Suddenly employees and associates were scrambling for ways to pay off loans that were coming due. Because the partnership had invested so much money in noncash-flow real estate and in Clint's crazy deals, there was very little steady and dependable income. Sometimes money came in from deals that had miraculously beat incredible odds. But usually the cash came only when John and Clint called on bankers to lend them more money—a process that did not reduce the debt but did raise the interest on the debt.

Although John's involvement in the North Dallas real estate boom in the early seventies was made separately and not through the partnership, the majority of his investments with Clint were joint and several, which put John's fortune in the same precarious position as Clint's. "John's lawyers and business associates started warning him to get out of the partnership, but John was reluctant," recalls a close associate of the family. "At one point his chief counsel said, 'John, give me one good reason why you won't break it up.' John just said, 'Well, he *is* my brother.' "

Secretly, however, John had been warning Clint for months that if he pledged any more assets without first consulting him, or Murchison Brothers advisers, he would immediately terminate the partnership. John was more worried than he had ever before been in business, even more than he had been during the Allegheny fight. He started smoking again, and he was no longer able to put business concerns aside when he left the office.

Clint either did not believe John's threats or he simply did not have the willpower to abstain from secretly pledging more assets on more risky, highly leveraged deals. When John learned that Clint had continued his freewheeling, he finally told Clint he wanted out. John sent letters to several of Clint's business associates saying he would not be signing any more Murchison Brothers notes. "In essence he was saying, 'I'm no longer liable for what Clint does,' " recalls a New York business partner of Clint. "When I told Clint about the letter, he just said, 'Oh, don't worry. I'll handle it with John."

Clint thought he could change his brother's mind. "He pleaded with John to stay with him," recalls a longtime employee of IMC. "Clint would say, 'John, just give me a little more time. We're going to have a Hail Mary pass. If this next deal works, it will clean up all the bad deals of the whole year."

But John refused to listen any longer to his brother's pleas. A major rift in their relationship was caused by Optimum Systems Inc. (OSI), the computer company Clint started in the 1960s to assist the Dallas Cowboys in ranking and drafting college football players. The company later expanded into devising programs for health-care institutions and other businesses, and Clint believed it would someday put Ross Perot's EDS out of business. In truth, even OSI's most successful ventures were rarely a threat to the much-better-managed EDS.

John had stood by for years while Clint poured more than $50 million into OSI. By the mid-1970s Clint was still determined the company would eventually make money, but John now looked at the investment, and his brother's handling of it, with contempt. He finally refused to allow another cent of the partnership to be put into OSI.

But John was soon to be rid of OSI, and the complicated unraveling of the intricately bound Murchison Brothers was about to begin. Ironically, the partnership that was formed in

1942 without a written agreement would begin to be dissolved thirty-six years later, with the first agreement between them that the brothers had ever had in writing. The dissolution agreement, signed in 1978, stated that Clint and John would begin working to remove John from the OSI debt, and it stated in broad, unspecific terms that the brothers would work to dissolve the partnership by no later than October 1981. Clint agreed to remove from the partnership several of his riskiest, most controversial assets, which carried huge liabilities, and allowed John to take many of the more conservative, more valuable investments. But the dissolution of a partnership that had taken thirty-six years to build proved extraordinarily difficult.

Murchison Brothers, which included hundreds of different assets when Clint Sr. turned it over to his sons in 1950, had in the last three decades become even more compartmentalized. The result of years of complicated, tax-avoiding deals by the father and sons was a tremendously complex infrastructure of legal relationships among entities, intricate debt arrangements, stock holdings, holding companies, corporations, and subsidiary corporations. So while the brothers agreed to a division on paper, the actual legal untangling of their assets, with the help of an army of advisers and attorneys, was inevitably years away.

Meanwhile, John still harbored enormous guilt about dividing Murchison Brothers. But he was being torn apart by two irreconcilable commitments: one to his father to keep his younger brother in check and continue building the empire; the other to protect his own family from the increasing possibility of bankruptcy. John not only worried that Clint was now in greater danger of losing his fortune; he knew that in destroying the partnership he was destroying his father's proudest creation. These thoughts haunted him through unhappy days and sleepless nights.

Like John, Clint was ambivalent about the agreement to dissolve Murchison Brothers. Clint's feelings, however, had less to do with honor and commitment than with simple business practicality. The bright side for Clint was that he would be free of John's restraints, but the gloomy side was that his borrowing power would be greatly diminished. Since the early fifties, all of the partnership's assets had been at his disposal, but once Murchison Brothers was divided he would have only half as many assets to borrow against. Complicating matters even more for Clint was the fact that many of the assets he would receive in the distribution were already leveraged to the hilt. And while leveraging was initially used as a method for getting richer, by 1979 Clint's borrowing was becoming a necessity for survival.

The dissolution agreement did more than merely sever Clint and John's business ties. There was a persistent feeling among Clint and John's children that simply dividing the partnership was not enough. Once the brothers had acknowledged publicly that they could not get along, it paved the way for the children to voice their worries and grievances as well.

Primary among the children's complaints was John and Clint's handling of the trust funds that Clint Sr. had set up for his grandchildren beginning in 1949. Clint Sr. had established three groups of trusts for seven of his eight grandchildren. The first were the Murchison Trusts, one each for John's two eldest children, John Jr. and Ginger, and Clint's two eldest children, Clint III and Burk. The next group, called the Marco Trusts, were established for John's third child, Mary Noel, and Clint's third child, Coke Ann. The last trust, called the Robert Trust, was for Clint's youngest child, Robert. After that, Clint and John changed the family's estate planning, and when John's youngest child, Barbara Jeanne, was born, she did not get a trust.

By the mid-seventies the seven Murchison, Marco, Robert (MMR) trusts were together valued at more than $150 million. About 80 percent of the assets in them was stock in the real estate and development company Centex, a subsidiary of Tecon, which Clint Jr. started in 1955. Over the years the brothers placed all of Centex's shares in their children's trusts, and in 1969, when Centex went public, its stock skyrocketed. By then, all of the assets in Murchison Brothers had been pledged as collateral on loans.

Anxious to get their hands on the MMR trusts' assets, Clint

and John in 1971 had their children sign an agreement called ROTAG, which permitted the brothers to use the trusts' assets as collateral and to move marketable securities out of the trusts and into their partnership. Clint and John moved swiftly to pledge the trusts' assets as collateral, sometimes on loans for companies related to the MMR trusts but more often for their own companies in Murchison Brothers. As long as the children were in high school and college, the ROTAG arrangement worked well. The children were unaware of how the assets were being used, and it provided Clint and John with enormous leverage to keep operating through bad times as well as good.

The brothers, however, had not planned for the problems that would arise later, when their children began expecting distribution of the assets. The trusts were designed to vest in the beneficiaries when they reached age twenty-five. But when Clint Murchison III turned twenty-five in 1971, the brothers made no attempt to pay out his trust. And it surprised no one that when John Dabney Jr. reached twenty-five in 1973, he received not a cent from his trust. By 1977 six of the seven beneficiaries were scheduled to have received their assets, but still not a single distribution had been made.

Clint III, in 1977, urged his father to take the debt off the trusts and pay them out, but he received no response. A similar request by John Jr. to his father met with the same fate when he approached John in his office. "I appreciate all that you have done to make our trusts grow and all the money you've put into them," John Jr. said, "but I don't think that makes it right for you to pledge them and lose money that's in them."

John did not respond. He merely got up and walked out of his own office. That was the first and last direct confrontation between the father and his only son on the subject. "Dad couldn't talk about hard subjects. He hated to discuss anything controversial," says John Jr. "He wanted to keep peace within the family and at the office even if it meant completely ignoring major problems."

But John Jr., who was now working at IMC, was becoming very bitter, not only because he did not have his trust, but also because his father offered him no business help whatsoever. He felt that he had been left to fend for himself as a child, but John Jr. was amazed that his father would continue to ignore him when he went to work at IMC.

John Jr. had attended college in Colorado and was living in Denver in 1973 when he turned twenty-five. His birthday came and went with no mention of the trust which was to have become his, according to his grandfather's wishes. Two years later, in 1975, John Jr. returned to Dallas to live, in large part to convince his father to distribute his trust that was by then two years overdue. While working at IMC, in its twenty-third-floor offices downtown, John Jr. held a series of jobs, but he had only a very superficial understanding of the family businesses.

"Basically John put his son in a room and said, 'Here, look over these files and see what businesses we're involved in,'" recalls a longtime attorney of the family. "That was about all the business instruction John Jr. ever got, and he deeply resented it."

What John Jr. resented most of all was the feeling that his father did not love him or even like him. "When my parents were home, which was seldom, they never wanted to be alone with us. They always had to have a lot of friends and famous people around, people who would entertain them constantly.

"I had only two serious discussions with my father in my life. One was when I told him I was getting a divorce and he said, 'You need to be careful with the assets in your trust,' and the other was during the Vietnam draft, and he told me he wanted me to go to officer's training school."

John and Lupe's youngest child, Barbara Jeanne, also had long-standing doubts that her father loved her. Of his four children, Barbara seemed to please her father the most. She was very competitive as a child, especially at horseback riding. She enjoyed riding so much that John brought an English riding instructor to Dallas from Virginia. With the instructor's help, Barbara won several state championships in riding and jumping.

Barbara seemed to excel in whatever she tried. At Madeira preparatory school in Virginia, she made straight As and became president of the school. From there, she went to Yale, her father's alma mater. But for all her acomplishments, Barbara never had the feeling her parents were proud of her. She assumed her father was delighted when she got into Yale, but he never told her so.

"I took my junior year off from Yale, because I was having some difficult times emotionally, and came home to live. I really needed some support from my father, some feeling that he cared about me, but he had a terrible time expressing himself. I finally confronted him and said, 'I have no idea whether you love me or not, and I want some answers. You can't act this way to your children, refusing to show any sort of caring or emotion.' We had a long and serious talk about it, and after that we became very close."

Sadly for John Jr., he was unable to form an emotional bond with his father. But friends say they are surprised that even one of John's children became close with him. "John had a very Victorian view of his children," says a family friend. "He thought of them as the absolute and complete responsibility of governesses and he did not want his life disturbed in any way by them."

Nor were John's feelings toward his son and his nephews helped by the third-generation's demands for their trusts. "John and Clint felt that their children were greedy in wanting their trust assets," says an IMC associate. "Their feeling was, 'We've put millions of dollars into those trusts through the years, and the children ought to be grateful.' Sure the children wanted their trust assets, but the mid-seventies were hard times for Murchison Brothers, and the brothers felt it just wasn't a good time to let go of all that collateral.

"Clint and John had forked over money to their father for years and they didn't mind doing so. After all, he had made their fortune possible. John and Clint expected the same thing from their children. In their view, those trust assets were there to be used, to be borrowed against with the purpose of increasing not only Murchison Brothers' worth but the trusts' value as well."

But there was a major difference between the way Clint Sr. borrowed from his sons and the way John and Clint borrowed from their children. Clint Sr. was borrowing from his sons' partnership, and they approved of it, in part because Clint Sr. made many more good deals than bad. What Clint and John were doing was quite different. In borrowing money against the MMR trusts, they were in danger of violating their fiduciary responsibilities. There were major questions about whether what John and Clint were doing was not only unethical but also illegal. When the trusts' three eldest beneficiaries—Clint III, Burk, and Dabney—began in business, they saw that their assets were being pledged whenever Clint and John needed money for deals, and often very risky deals.

"When Clint and John needed money, it was pretty simple for them to get it," recalls an IMC associate. "They would say, 'Take some stock out of the trusts and pledge it for a loan.' "

Many advisers and attorneys warned Clint and John that what they were doing with the trusts could very likely result in major legal problems. Amid the warnings and after years of serving as primary trustee, one of John and Clint's lead attorneys signed off the trusteeship in 1977. At that point, a corporation called the Bankers Trust Company of Texas was established for the purpose of assuming trustee powers. But the formation of Bankers Trust was little more than window dressing, for although Clint III was named president of the corporation, he was unable to touch the assets in his and his siblings' and cousins' trusts because the assets were pledged.

Clint Sr. had made his millions in Texas in the first half of the twentieth century when what few laws existed could be evaded or circumvented. When Clint Sr. was running hot oil, he gave not a damn that it was illegal, and, in fact, he was proud that it was patriotic. Trained by their father, John and Clint Jr. were not overly concerned with the sanctity of the law.

But the law of trusts was different. It had developed and grown in England for centuries before Texas was known to anyone except a few Indians. The idea that widows, orphans, and other helpless persons should be protected from the rapaciousness of their relatives and friends was well expressed in all civilizations.

Perhaps the best expression of this was that by Justice Benjamin Nathan Cardozo of the United States Supreme Court: "A trustee is held to something stricter than the morals of the marketplace. Not honesty alone, but the punctilio of an honor the most sensitive is then the standard of behavior."

The punctiliousness of which Cardozo writes was not a characteristic of either brother, so that despite persistent warnings to do otherwise, John and Clint continued to pledge the assets of the MMR trusts. As late as the spring of 1979 the brothers had extraordinary control of the situation. Although Clint and John were going their separate ways, they remained a united front against their children. As long as Clint and John held control not only of Murchison Brothers stock, but also had full use of the trusts' assets, they could continue business as usual, albeit separately.

Whether the brothers would have vested the trusts even if times were good is doubtful. "I don't think John and Clint had any immediate plans to take the debt off the trusts' assets," says an IMC accountant. "That was always going to happen somewhere down the road. It was clear that they were not looking after their kids' best interests."

Many associates say that John and Clint totally lacked any sort of dynastic feelings. They were both very forward thinking in a business sense, but not in terms of their children's futures. Clint Sr. had hired several very smart businessmen to teach John and Clint Jr. the business ropes, but the brothers left their children to fend for themselves. Because John and Clint's children knew so little about the family empire, when it ran into serious problems in the 1980s, they were forced to turn to outside advisers for help.

Despite the third generations' numbers and the fact that they had a legitimate complaint, they were no match for the second-generation brothers. "The kids had an incredibly starry-eyed view of John and Clint," says an IMC associate. "For years people had been telling these kids about the dozens of fabulous deals John and Clint had masterminded. There was this unbelievable aura around the Murchison name, and when the kids started in business and saw the strings the name pulled they were amazed. They probably had a reason to be angry at John and Clint, but they were not about to go up against that kind of power."

Clint III, Burk, and Dabney were each considered a long way from ready to shoulder the family's vast business responsibilities, and no one was more aware of this than Clint and John. But the notion that the brothers, now both in their late fifties, had full and absolute control of the empire was not always a comforting one.

A distant relative remembers chatting briefly with Clint at a small party at his home in the late seventies. "Clint adored his children, and he knew they were smart and well-educated, but he did not think they had nearly the intelligence or maturity to fill either his shoes or John's if the need arose. It was unlike him to reveal his feelings, but that night he said, 'If anything happened to John or me, this whole thing would go down like the *Titanic*.' "

PART
FOUR

23

"If we're not careful, we may find out we're suing ourselves."

It was a hot afternoon on June 14, 1979, when John and Lupe landed in Dallas from Europe. They had spent an exhausting week at the Paris Air Show, and John would have preferred to go home to bed. But he had returned to Dallas only for the purpose of speaking that night at a fund-raising dinner for the Boy Scouts of America at the home of Texas Governor William Clements. Having been elected president of the national Boy Scouts organization just a week earlier, John felt obligated to attend the dinner, and he dropped Lupe at home before driving to the governor's home in Highland Park.

At the end of the dinner John stood to say a few words to the group. He hated public speaking, even at informal dinners such as this—a fact that was obvious to many of the Dallas businessmen who sat on the governor's terrace. They had watched John struggle through speeches before, but this night was different. He seemed especially nervous and tired, and not long into his speech, his asthma flared up. He began coughing and choking and had to excuse himself. A few minutes later he stepped inside the house, where the governor and his aides assisted him. When John continued to gasp for air, Governor Clements quietly helped John into the squad car of a highway patrolman assigned to the governor's staff, who volunteered to drive John to a local hospital.

On the way to the hospital John's condition grew worse, and he lay down on the back seat. At just that moment the squad car, running a red light, was hit broadside by another car. On impact, John suffered a heart attack and fell unconscious. A few minutes later a fire department ambulance arrived at the scene of the accident, but it was already too late. John was rushed to a nearby hospital, where he died an hour later.

In the weeks preceding his death, John had been taking instructions to convert to Catholicism. His family doctor knew about the classes, and when the doctor arrived at the hospital minutes before John died, he found a priest and had him baptize John a Catholic. Lupe's strong Catholicism had helped her through difficult years, beginning with her father's death when she was only sixteen. She wished John had had the comfort of her religion all his life, but there was consolation in knowing that he finally found it, however late.

"The morning after John died, we all went out to Lupe's house to be with her," recalls a close friend. "But, typically, she seemed more concerned that all the guests were handling it okay than she was with her own grief."

But another friend recalls that, in fact, "Lupe took John's death very hard. She was sad and even bitter that he had spent so much of his life looking after everyone else, especially Clint. She had wanted him to break off the partnership with Clint years earlier, and to go about his own life."

Indeed, John had spent his entire adult life bound with responsibilities that he probably would not have chosen for himself. Although Clint Sr. had good intentions when he created Murchison Brothers, the partnership was a great burden.

Barbara Jeanne Murchison Coffman recalls her father's relief when she told him she decided not to go into business. "For several years I was a very driven person. My cousin Robert Murchison and I used to ride back and forth on the plane to Yale, and we'd talk about how we were going to carry the Murchison empire into the third generation," Barbara Jeanne says. "But then one day I decided that a business career really wasn't what I wanted in life. One morning at breakfast I told my father, 'I really don't have to try to be the success grandfather was and you are. What I really want to do is be married and breed good children.' My father put down his fork and closed his eyes, and when he opened them, he was the most relieved and peaceful I had ever seen him. I think he felt unbelievably comforted that I was not going to spend my life saddled with the tremendous business pressures he had had.

"I know that the one thing my father hoped for his children more than anything else was that they would be just regular people with ordinary lives," says Barbara Jeanne. "He did not want his children to suffer under the public spotlight the way he had for most of his life."

John had known since he was twenty that stepping out of his father's shadow would be very difficult. Although he made an attempt at becoming his own man when he won the largest corporate proxy fight in history, John slowed down later in life and seemed content to maintain the family's economic position. In fact, because of his brother's risky deals, near the end of his life he was having to struggle just to maintain the status quo.

John was eulogized in a Roman Catholic service in Dallas, attended by some one thousand grieving friends, relatives, and business associates. He was buried next to his father in Athens' City Cemetery.

That his reputation was not as great as either his father's or his brother's was apparent in dozens of stories of his death at age fifty-seven. Obituaries that appeared in newspapers around the world described how John had inherited his father's oil fortune and followed his father's dictum to spread money like manure. As was almost always the case, he was repeatedly identified as the brother of the owner of the Dallas Cowboys.

What was universally unnoticed by the obituary writers was John's quintessential role as the Murchison ship's keel. Clint Sr. and Clint Jr. had the imagination to sail where no other ships had gone before, but John had kept the ship from capsizing. It would be years before outsiders realized just how important John's role had been. But within the organization that fact was already painfully obvious. Any hope that the family might remain united through the third generation disintegrated with John's passing.

In its obituary *Time* magazine explained that the Murchisons' holdings were so complex that John joked, "If we're not careful, we may find out we're suing ourselves." Those words proved prophetic, but in quite a different way than John had in mind. The internecine lawsuits that erupted following his death came not out of carelessness. They were fought for important reasons and usually with knowledge of their ramifications.

First to voice his grievance was John Jr., who was thirty-one at the time of his father's death. John Jr. had been working for four years at Investments Management Corporation, but he seemed to be getting nowhere. His futile attempts to convince his father and uncle to take the debt off the grandchildren's trusts so that they could vest had become increasingly frustrating. At the same time, he was living on an annual salary of $18,000 and growing very bitter about his financial situation.

This bitterness was intensified by the scars of an unhappy childhood. While outsiders must have thought little Dabney Murchison, as he had been known since birth, was lucky to be born into such a great family, he often felt like an orphan. He strongly resented the fact that his father and mother had left him and his sisters almost exclusively in the care of governesses while they traveled the globe. This long-standing feeling exacerbated his attitude toward what he believed was his father's and uncle's flagrant misuse of his trust's assets. "John had a full head of steam, and the only thing that was capping it was his father," recalls an IMC employee, "but the day his father died, the cap blew off."

John Jr. was so angry he did not hesitate a moment to wage a full-scale frontal attack to get his trust. Following his father's death, Dabney moved quickly to take command. Within two weeks he moved into his father's large and imposing corner office and fired off a memo to his uncle: "I want Murchison Brothers dissolved quickly, and I want the trusts delivered."

Clint tossed the memo into the wastebasket and said, "We'll just call that the Dabney file." When an employee told John Jr. about the incident, he responded, "Well, you can by God put out the word around here that from now on, I'm not Dabney, I'll be called John."

John saw that for the first time he was able to exercise power at IMC. His father's will accomplished this by appointing him coexecutor of the estate, along with his mother, Lupe. As an independent coexecutor, John was able to disrupt business at

IMC simply by refusing to sign papers that required signatures of both sides of the partnership. At the same time, he sent dozens of memos to his uncle, questioning what Clint was doing and demanding answers.

Clint paid no attention to his nephew's memos, recalls an IMC employee. "Clint's reaction to John was, 'He's just a stupid kid, what does he know?' "

In fact, as early as 1975, John could see that his uncle was heading downward. "He was pledging everything in sight with no plan for when or how he was going to pay it off," says John. "This huge debt was growing by the day."

Very few assets had been legally and physically removed from Murchison Brothers by this time, and John was desperately afraid that if Clint went bankrupt, he would drag John's side of the family down with him. As coexecutor, and as a beneficiary of his father's estate—then estimated to be not much under a quarter of a billion dollars—John had a keen interest in seeing the partnership divided quickly. Still, John's chief focus was on his trust, and he decided the only way to get it was to bring a lawsuit against Clint. John was ready and anxious to bring an intrafamily suit, but he was completely unprepared for the difficulty he would have trying to enlist a top Dallas law firm to represent him. He first looked for legal representation at the Dallas firm of Robert Strauss, former chairman of the Democratic National Committee and a longtime friend of both Clint and John Sr. But Strauss's law firm was not willing to become embroiled in this kind of messy family fight.

Some of the firms John approached declined to take the case, claiming it was a conflict of interest because they represented various other Murchison enterprises. Others candidly admitted that suing Clint Murchison Jr., mythic millionaire and owner of America's Team, would be like suing George Washington—they just were not interested. After months of being rejected by Dallas's biggest firms, John finally enlisted a country attorney from tiny Georgetown, Texas.

In the meantime Lupe was also increasingly anxious for an expeditious liquidation of Murchison Brothers, and she began to threaten her brother-in-law with a suit if he did not increase the pace of doing so. Under Texas law, at the time of a partner's death, the other partner is legally required to pay off all debts and collect the assets, but there is no time limit on how long the dissolving partner may take to divide it. In effect, Clint could take as long as he wanted to divide the assets of the partnership, and it was in his interest to do so. Only as long as he had access to Murchison Brothers' assets could he continue his freewheeling business activities. His excuse to Lupe and his nephew John was simply, "I'm working as fast as I can to get it dissolved. These things don't happen overnight."

While John was frustrated with Clint's excuses, Lupe listened to her brother-in-law, and not only in this matter. John was a thorn in Clint's side, a constant roadblock as he tried to pledge Murchison Brothers' collateral to make deals, and Clint was quick to wage his own counterattack. He began telling Lupe about the trouble her son John was causing at the office, and his right-hand men sent out the word to everyone at IMC to stonewall John, telling him nothing and discrediting virtually everything he did and said.

"In meetings John would say, 'Let's have a plan and strategy for how we're going to pay off these loans,' " a former associate explains. "But Clint and his kids, who thought their father could do anything, including work his way out of this growing debt, would ridicule John and call him a stick-in-the-mud. They would goad John until his face got redder and redder and he would finally explode.

"One day I was in John's office, and one of Clint Jr.'s right-hand men walked by and saw me in there. When I came out, he said, 'If we ever see you speaking to John again, we'll move you out of this building so fast you won't know what happened to you.' "

At the time of John's death there were two conflicting factions. One consisted of a half dozen of Clint's wheeler-dealer intimates; the other was five times larger—some thirty loyal and trusted family advisers, many of whom had been with the organization since the days at 1201 Main Street and who now operated IMC at Murchison Brothers' twenty-third-floor downtown offices. Both groups were unhappy with the way John Jr. acted after his father died.

Clint's high-roller friends, who now controlled his business life, were infuriated that "this punk," as they referred to John Jr., was threatening to put brakes on his uncle's spending. The second group was equally upset, but for a different reason. "Most of the people at IMC were deeply devoted to the Murchisons," recalls an employee who had worked at IMC since the 1950s. "We felt the family was going to take care of us for the rest of our lives. When John Jr. came in and started causing problems, he was threatening to upset the cocoon we had all been living under for years."

Clint began complaining to Lupe that John was so anxious for his inheritance from his father's estate that he would do anything to get it. He insisted that John had gone berserk and that she must step in and stop him. He told Lupe that many problems could be avoided in distributing the partnership if her son was simply removed as coexecutor.

In the fall of 1980, little more than a year after John's death, Lupe and her three daughters filed suit to have John Jr. removed as coexecutor of the estate. John was shocked by the action his mother had taken, but this time he did not waste time looking for a Dallas attorney to represent him. He flew to Houston and hired a famous criminal lawyer, Richard "Race-horse" Haynes.

Lupe had been talking to top Dallas lawyers who were intimately acquainted with Murchison financial matters. She hired a tough trial lawyer who convinced her that, however embarrassing and unpleasant for her, she must expect and prepare herself for a public confrontation with her son in the courtroom.

Lupe's suit to remove John from his position as coexecutor was scheduled to come to trial in April 1981. Just a few weeks before the court date, Lupe got the scare of her life. When she and her escort returned to her mansion late one evening after dinner, they were confronted by two masked men, armed with revolvers. They blindfolded and bound Lupe's escort and threw him in the back seat of one of her Mercedes. The gunmen then locked Lupe in the trunk of the car. When Lupe's youngest child, Barbara Jeanne, arrived later with two friends, they were ordered into the living room where they were bound and gagged. Lupe and her escort were brought into the mansion as well.

Four hours later the gunmen left, and no one was harmed. Oddly, in this mansion full of millions of dollars in art, jewelry, silver, furs, the men took only a few coins and several pieces of Lupe's jewelry. The gunmen were white, in their thirties, and carried a two-way radio on which they communicated with a third party, who apparently was watching the house and may have been monitoring police channels. The robbery was well-planned and well-executed, but the gunmen walked away with very little.

Lupe was terrified through the ordeal and later said she had felt certain the intruders were going to kill her. But the rumors that unfolded in the coming days were almost as frightening as the incident itself.

Some people suspected that Clint staged the robbery, hoping Lupe would think that John did it. "Lupe had been weakening as the trial date with her son drew near," recalls an attorney who later joined John's fight against his uncle. "Clint wanted Lupe to have the impression that John was so crazy he would do anything, and that she must not back down in her suit against him. This was the kind of secret prank Clint would have loved to stage."

Lupe went into seclusion and was visibly shaken, but she moved forward with her suit. On the heels of the robbery came the trial. But on the first day of jury selection, in front of a packed courtroom, Lupe's attorney described to prospective jurors the way in which John would be portrayed in the trial. He gave a description of John that was "more scathing and more shocking" than John had ever imagined possible.

Before the trial John was prepared for his mother's attorney to paint a picture of him as "a stupid kid who lacked business acumen," but he was completely taken aback when, instead, he was portrayed as a vicious and ungrateful son.

Horrified at the thought of such a courtroom battle, John settled the case that night. He resigned as coexecutor, and in exchange, Lupe agreed to make him a ten-year $3 million loan at an interest rate of 18 percent to be adjusted annually. Since that was the current commercial interest rate, the loan was not

a suitable *quid pro quo*. But John, who at that point did not
have the funds to bring a serious lawsuit, viewed the settlement as a minor victory, for the $3 million gave him the means
to wage a major attack against his uncle. If John had faced his
mother in the courtroom, he would have been in the position
of having to defend himself, when all he really wanted was to
get the money that was rightfully his. In his capacity as coexecutor, he had tried to get his assets by attrition, by throwing
up roadblocks to Clint's freewheeling. Now he was free to
leave IMC and set up his own office, where he would plan his
attack.

A few months earlier, in February 1981 he finally did what
many in the Dallas business community thought unthinkable—he filed suit against Clint and Clint's four children. The
children were included in the suit because they were directors
of an organization purportedly set up to manage the trusts,
which were in fact run by Clint. The suit claimed that Clint
had used funds from John's $30 million trust fund, and it de-
manded $30 million in exemplary damages and a temporary
injunction forcing Clint to segregate John's assets from the
family trusts.

Almost from the time of his father's death, John became estranged from his family, and when he resigned as coexecutor
he began communicating with his mother strictly through letters to her attorneys. He was surprised to find, however, that
he was ostracized by Dallas society and by the Dallas business
community as well. "When John showed up one night at
Brook Hollow Golf Club, people ran the other way to get away
from him," recalls a friend. "They parted like the Red Sea to
let him through."

After several such experiences John decided briefly to live
up to this vilification. When he brought a Texas State Fair
sideshow stripper, barely clothed in a black leather string bi-
kini with tassels, to the Memorial Day opening of Brook Hollow's swimming pool, it caused precisely the shock he had
intended.

John was not only bitter toward his family, but he also felt a
certain amount of guilt toward his father. He doubted his father would have approved of his resignation as coexecutor,

and he wondered whether he should have at least fought it in the courtroom. John believed that his father had specific reasons for appointing him coexecutor. For, while his own knowledge of IMC and Murchison Brothers was limited, Lupe knew next to nothing about the family businesses. Was she prepared to take on the complex role of sole executor of an estate that was fraught with internecine problems, enormous debts, and legal difficulties?

"When John died, Lupe was completely in the dark about business," recalls her son-in-law Bill Lamont. "She had never even balanced her own checkbook."

John was hurt and bitter about his mother's suit against him, but he tried to block out of his memory the scathing attacks by his mother's attorneys. He wanted to free his mind of the past and turn his attention to his claim against Clint. However, six months after filing, the suit was going nowhere. John felt that his lawyer might have had a certain degree of disdain for him suing the famous and seemingly impregnable Clint Murchison Jr. Dissatisfied, he began to look for legal help elsewhere. He finally got some serious help when he hired Taz Speer to become his chief adviser. Speer, a very bright young attorney who had worked at the Internal Revenue Service and in the attorney general's office of Texas, felt challenged both at the prospect of rectifying an injustice against John and at taking on Goliath.

Speer knew John needed a top Dallas attorney to represent him, but he discovered the same attitude that John had. No one wanted to represent the young rebellious Murchison. Just as Jane had gone to New Orleans to get legal representation when divorcing Clint, John saw he would have to get counsel from elsewhere. "The business community viewed John as real scum for even considering suing his uncle," Speer recalls, "At this time, Clint's name was still as good as gold, and I, too, realized we had to go out of Dallas for a lawyer."

Speer finally called in his own brother, a probate lawyer in El Paso, Texas. When Clint and his associates learned that Speer had to resort to bringing his brother onto the case, they laughed out loud. But John and the Speer brothers paid no attention and got busy working on the suit.

*   *   *

Lupe had suffered through three hellish years of grieving over her husband's death and fighting to keep her family's fortune intact. The deep sorrow caused by the drastic changes in her life, however, put her in the right frame of mind when Betty Marcus came to her home one day with a model of a Claes Oldenburg sculpture. Despite the fact that John had for years served as president and chairman of the Dallas Museum of Art, he never became one of the museum's most generous donors. Betty Marcus, the then president of the museum and a close friend of Lupe's, was convinced that the time was now or never to get a major contribution from the Murchison clan.

Betty told Lupe that the museum's directors would like her to commission the Oldenburg sculpture at a cost of $250,000. The sculpture, Betty explained, would become the focal point of the soon-to-open new museum that John had been instrumental in planning. Called "Stake Hitch," the work would be an eighteen-foot-high metal stake in the museum's floor, attached to a forty-foot-high rope hanging from a three-story, vaulted ceiling.

Lupe was immediately excited by the chance to donate and dedicate the work in memory of John, who had been an admirer and collector of Oldenburg since the 1960s when he brought the "Oldenburg Happening," to Dallas. Lupe could see that "Stake Hitch," with its suggestions of Texas cowboys and tent stakes, would make a dramatic statement in the museum's cavernous barrel-vaulted main gallery. John loved art that was powerful and in the vanguard of the modern art movement. "Stake Hitch," was both these things, but it also signified permanence and stability at a time when Lupe's life was in turmoil. She agreed to make the gift. "I love 'Stake Hitch' because it's so John," she said recently. "It's strong and powerful, and it's like having his hand right there at the museum staking it down."

Lupe's troubles, while far from over, were nothing compared to those of her brother-in-law Clint, and John Jr.'s suit was but one of Clint's many problems. Far more serious for the moment was the dramatic drop in value of his oil and real estate properties in 1980 and an ever-increasing flood of bank loans coming due. Murchison Brothers had been the major shareholder in Kirby Exploration, which Clint Sr. created decades earlier. In 1981 Kirby's stock price peaked at $45 when the company began drilling deep gas wells. But when the project failed, Kirby's stock plummeted to $13 and continued to fall. Clint had been borrowing against the Kirby holdings when the stock was at $45. When the price fell, Murchison Brothers took a paper loss in the neighborhood of $100 million, and the lender wanted more collateral or payment of the debt.

"All the assets were mortgaged to the hilt and interest rates in 1980 and 1981 went up to twenty percent or more," says Truman Kemper, an accountant at IMC for twenty-five years. "So it got to where they couldn't pay the interest on the debt.

"I remember looking at the books and records of the various Murchison companies as far back as the sixties and thinking, *how could you do it?*" says Kemper. "There was all this debt coming in and no steady source of income you could depend on. . . . I thought that's the difference between the wealthy and the poor. It worked for over twenty years. It worked as long as they could borrow money and [the value of] the assets they'd pledged went up faster than the interest costs."

Even worse than the fall in oil prices, in Clint's view, were climbing interest rates. He had borrowed $7 million in 1979 to build expensive homes in a fancy Beverly Hills development called the Summit. After getting the loan, he had the land zoned and platted for his project. But construction was very slow getting started, while his subordinates spent hundreds of thousands of dollars advertising the posh development. Two years after construction began on a few houses, Clint was scrambling for cash to pay the interest on the $7 million. He was finally forced to borrow $3 million more to pay the interest, but this provided only temporary relief and all construction was brought to a halt. "The problem was he never had any cash," says his partner in the Summit. "When he put a second mortgage on the Summit in 1982, I knew that was it. His debt was growing so fast I knew he would never catch up. The bank finally foreclosed on the development in 1984."

By this time Clint was taking water from one fire to put out another. Many assets were cross-collateralized, which greatly complicated his financial picture. Clint, himself, became confused about what he owed and owned. "The only way we knew a loan had come due was a banker would call," recalls an IMC employee. "Then all hell would break loose, trying to find a way to pay it."

Many associates believe that Clint's greatest fault was his enormous arrogance and absolute refusal to listen to advice when times got tough. "When what few honorable and intelligent associates he had warned him to get out of bad deals, he would just stare blankly at them," recalls a family associate who had watched Clint from the day the bright young MIT graduate began working at Murchison Brothers. "He would stay in bad deals notwithstanding the objections of his family, friends, attorneys, business advisers at Murchison Brothers, even some of his longtime 'yes men'."

A classic example of this was his Hillandale development of town houses in Georgetown, in Washington, DC. On top of paying too much for the land, Clint built and sold only about thirty of the two hundred planned dwellings in the Hillandale development. The early buyers became some of the project's worst advertisements. They warned their friends not to buy the townhouses, claiming that construction was far below standard. The roofs leaked and doors did not open. Not only was it difficult to sell the homes, but also, because they were not selling, it was nearly impossible to get new financing to pay for more construction.

"Clint could have sold the Georgetown project when it was half finished and gotten his money out of it," recalls his partner in the deal. "He was warned to pull out, but no matter how bad things got, he refused. All of this was against the better judgment of many people who saw him headed for the ashcan."

If Clint was ever afraid during those hard times, it never showed. In fact, his unrelenting confidence in himself seemed to increase with his problems. He believed that he was too smart and too rich to worry about things most people worried about. And he still believed as late as 1982 that interest rates would eventually come down and that he could turn his economic troubles around.

But Clint's problems were peculiar in many ways. His snowballing debt was even more serious than it appeared on the surface because he owed far more than his assets were worth. Where the Murchisons were concerned, the banks went along with a much lower than normal collateral-to-loan ratio because for more than half a century the family had always paid back every penny it borrowed.

A Fort Worth banker recalls when Clint sent a subordinate to Fort Worth in July 1981 to borrow $1.5 million with Clint's personal guarantee. "I was chairman of the large loan committee, and I thought it was funny that Clint Jr. was coming to Fort Worth to borrow money when there were plenty of banks in Dallas," recalls the banker. "But it was always the case that if Clint Jr. or his daddy wanted to borrow money, you didn't think about it or look at a balance sheet. You just went ahead and loaned the money."

Clint elevated the act of borrowing money to a new art form. In Texas and in New York he relied on the stellar reputation of the Murchison name. In parts of the world where he was less well known, he merely presented a pro-forma statement that listed the total of his assets at $1 billion. Because he did not use an outside auditor and because he personally guaranteed his loans, he did not have to list the debts on his financial statements, only the assets.

Each time Clint made a deal he established a corporation for it. Had these corporations borrowed the money strictly on their own credit, even by the extraordinary elastic standards of Murchison, the debt would have had to show in the balance sheet of the company. But when he assumed the debt personally, it enabled him to pretend that there was no debt against the corporation but only against him, which made the debt position of the company look much healthier.

His personal guarantee gave him almost unlimited borrowing power, a kind of leverage that far exceeded what he could have borrowed against only his assets. In signing his C.W. Murchison Jr. to loans, he put his entire fortune at risk, but he signed it with reckless abandon, giving no thought to the proc-

ess. In addition to guaranteeing personally his loans, Clint Jr.
guaranteed notes of virtually any friend or associate who
asked. There was a common saying that, "You could paper the
walls of the entire twenty-third floor of Murchison Brothers
with the signatures Clint was passing out."

Clint not only borrowed, he made loans—and usually on a
handshake. "We could be in the john," recalls a friend, "and
I'd start telling him about a deal. By the time we walked out,
he'd have agreed to loan me a million bucks."

Clint's family and associates worried about the many loans
he made to his friends on a handshake. "If Clint's plane ever
goes down," they said, "we'll never see that money again."

Part of the reason he passed out his personal guarantee so
freely was an undying loyalty he felt toward his associates. He
went to great lengths to show his appreciation for and repay
favors to those who had worked for him. In 1976, at the height
of the Cowboys' success, Tex Schramm purchased a small marina in Key West, Florida, then asked Clint if he would participate in a deal to build a 200-acre resort in Key West with 597
luxury condominiums surrounding an 18-hole championship
golf course. Out of gratitude to Schramm for all that he had
done for the Cowboys, Clint agreed to supply $21 million to
Schramm's Key West project and to furnish additional capital
when needed. But when Clint was late on interest payments
and the creditors of the project learned of his illness, they
called in the note and there was not enough financing to finish
construction. As were so many other projects in which Clint
was involved, the Key West development was stalled for lack
of funds, and finally foreclosed.

Clint's abiding loyalty to associates had other negative side
effects. Just as he refused to get out of bad deals, he also refused
to cut his ties with bad associates. Despite repeated warnings
and clear evidence that one "friend" or another was using him,
or even stealing from him, he repeatedly refused to do anything about it. The only exception came when he broke off a
thirty-year relationship with one of his chief skirt-chasing
playboy friends. The two were such close friends that Clint
had included him in many deals and, typically, had given him
carte blanche to act on his behalf in several interrelated

multimillion-dollar deals around the world. Everyone around Clint warned him that this intimate was losing and wasting enormous sums of Clint's money. But only when Clint looked at the books did he finally cut his ties with the man.

"Clint hated to hear bad things about people, especially his friends and associates, even if the things being said were true," recalls a partner.

Delegating responsibility was a Murchison trademark that worked well for Clint Sr. and John—several of their most successful ventures were companies they had never seen but for which they had chosen first-rate managers. But because Clint Jr.—too often—chose fourth-rate people to run his enterprises, many of his projects were doomed from the start. Too many of the men Clint put in charge of his real estate projects were in over their heads.

For nearly a decade, Clint had depended on Lou Farris to supply him with bigger and riskier deals, and that attitude did not change when times got tough. Although Clint's family pleaded with him to stop his wheeling and dealing, Farris kept the wheels turning, kept the deals coming. Clint did not have the willpower to refuse a deal, even if he had the desire.

But because respectable lenders were growing wary of providing Murchison with the money he needed to stay afloat, he depended increasingly on others. The most notorious of these was Lou Farris's former associate Herman K. Beebe Sr., who counted among his borrowers the reputed boss of New Orleans organized crime, Carlos Marcello. Farris had apparently kept in contact with Beebe, for between 1977 and 1983 Beebe institutions reportedly lent tens of millions of dollars to Murchison.

But even Beebe's help was not enough. By now the new loans that Farris got for Clint went immediately to pay interest due on earlier loans, leaving no capital for new deals or paying down debt. Farris's and Clint's solution was to purchase several banks around the country, which would provide an immediate cash flow. Beebe provided the loans that helped Murchison purchase the Dallas/Fort Worth Airport Bank. Clint also bought a majority interest in six other banks—three others in Texas, one in Chicago, one in Reno, Nevada, and one in Minneapolis. Together, the assets of these banks totaled more than a billion dollars.

In addition to borrowing from these banks, Clint had in mind the long-anticipated arrival of interstate banking. He planned later to sell the banks at a large profit to a major banking chain. But the purchases were too highly leveraged to make a profit for Clint when he sold them.

Farris had been successful for years in getting loans in large part because of his promise of a C. W. Murchison Jr. signature on the note. But the purchase of the banks provided only a very thin wall from Murchison's creditors. With interest rates at 20 percent, Clint was required to pay $80 million annually just to service the interest on his debt. And he was capable of paying only a small fraction of that amount.

Many longtime Murchison associates could see that Clint was headed for bankruptcy, but virtually no one would have predicted that his own family would put the wheels in motion that would bring him down. Leading the way was Clint's nephew John, who by now was beginning to be taken seriously. John reached a major breakthrough more than two years earlier, in October 1981, when he forced Clint and his children to release his assets from all debt connected with the OSI computer firm that John's father had so disliked. But while those now-released assets amounted to $6 million, another $24 million in assets in John's trust were still encumbered with debt.

John dealt his most severe blow to his uncle when his attorney obtained a temporary injunction prohibiting Clint or his children from refinancing any debt on assets in the trusts. Under this injunction, Clint needed court-ordered approval to do anything that affected the trusts in any way. This injunction tied the hands of a man who had never had to do more than sign his signature to get a loan.

John also began threatening to expose his uncle publicly. "John essentially said, 'If you don't release my assets, I'll expose your financial mess, and your creditors will bankrupt you,' " says Taz Speer, John's chief adviser in his fight against his uncle.

In December 1981 John offered to settle the suit, which asked for his $30 million trust, as well as $30 million in damages. He said he would relinquish his one-seventh interest in two companies in his trust whose assets were worth approximately $4 million (but were also heavily leveraged) and would forget the damages if Clint would pay out the remainder of his trust. Clint and several of his close associates reportedly laughed at the proposed settlement. But one of Clint's attorneys took the offer very seriously. He believed that John was like a "kamikaze pilot" who was so angry he would risk anything, including bringing down the entire family empire, to get his trust. He advised Clint, "Unless we quiet this kid, he'll publicize your financial problems, and there will be a tremendous run on the trusts and Murchison Brothers."

At this point, liabilities against the trusts (either through guaranteed loans or direct obligations) totaled $178 million, roughly $28 million more than the trusts' minimum estimated worth. Liabilities against Murchison Brothers' assets were even greater. As fearless as Clint appeared, he must have known that the publicity alone resulting from a court battle could destroy him. His attorneys also pointed out that John was legally entitled to his trust and that if the case went to trial a jury would almost certainly find that Clint had greatly abused his fiduciary responsibility.

"Clint really had no defense," says Jim Speer, John's attorney in the case. "He must have known that he would lose in court, and when you're in the ball park Clint was playing in, a judgment can kill your ability to do business."

There were two other reasons advisers thought Clint should settle with John. Chief among these was that the other six beneficiaries were becoming increasingly anxious for their assets. They too were by now worried that Clint was in serious danger of losing his fortune and their trusts. Even Clint's four children were being advised to bring a lawsuit against their father. Clint was increasingly aware that his children and two of his nieces were unhappy and were threatening to follow John to the courthouse.

"Clint could not afford to pay out all six of the trusts as well as damages from all six," says Jim Speer, "He was better off paying out John's trust and giving the other kids the impression theirs would be paid soon as well."

Another problem was a lawsuit that was pending by the H.B. Zachary Company of San Antonio, which had participated with Clint in a deal to build sewers in Saudi Arabia. Zachary claimed that mismanagement caused the deal to lose about $80 million. What Zachary did not know was that while Clint personally was the lead defendant in the case, the trusts had also been used as collateral against the loan. Clint wanted to keep this fact from Zachary, which would have been difficult if John exposed the family's financial mess in a courtroom battle. Clint settled with Zachary for at least $22 million.

Finally in April 1983 Clint removed all the debt from John's assets and delivered the remainder of his $30 million trust. This victory for John was followed by demands from two of his sisters for their assets, and by new demands by Lupe. "Soon after this, Lupe began listening more closely to what John was saying, and she was looking more closely at what Clint Jr. was doing," says attorney Jim Speer. "I think at this point she was beginning to see some things she didn't like."

The family finally met together with dozens of accountants, advisers, and attorneys to force the liquidation of Murchison Brothers. "These meetings painted a very sad picture of a very unhappy family," recalls an insider. "Everyone was threatening to sue everyone else. It didn't matter that these people were family." At this time, a massive settlement was reached between the accounts of Clint, the estate of John Sr., and the trusts—and it cost Clint dearly.

With Lupe taking numerous Murchison Brothers assets, and her children taking their trusts and leaving Clint with the debt, Clint found himself financially strapped.

Just how serious things had become was obvious in early 1983 when Jenkens & Gilchrist, the law firm that was built and thrived on Murchison business for more than thirty years, and as a result became one of the biggest, most prestigious firms in Dallas, announced it would no longer represent the family. The Dallas legal community was shocked to see a major law firm repudiate the family that had made the firm what it was.

"We backed off when the intrafamily lawsuits began," says

senior partner Henry Gilchrist, "Our firm really didn't feel we could represent one family member against another."

But insiders say another and perhaps more important reason the firm stopped representing Clint Jr. was its uncollected fees in the millions of dollars. Although the family had always been "slow pay," many of the firm's younger partners complained that, in not demanding payment, they were financing Clint Jr. What the new, young partners could not feel was the extraordinary loyalty most senior partners had toward the family. For the first fifteen years of the firm's existence, the Murchisons were, with a few minor exceptions, Jenkens & Gilchrist's only client. Although the firm took other clients in the late 1960s and grew to include 150 lawyers, as late as the 1980s the Murchison family alone still comprised more than 20 percent of the firm's business. One of the younger lawyers recalls happier days for the Murchisons in the 1970s when only the firm's brightest minds were allowed to come into contact with the family. Murchison matters, says a former partner, "were protected like the crown jewels." But eventually, when Murchison's legal bill went unpaid month after month, the younger partners won out. "Let's flush him," they said. And the firm did.

By early 1983 Clint's once shining reputation was becoming tarnished in the Dallas banking community as well. Most Dallas bankers found that their requests for repayment on loans were simply ignored. And while the majority was not angry yet, they were growing restless. As is often the case, the bankers who were pushy got paid, while those who politely requested their money were passed over. One banker recalls filing suit against Clint immediately upon hearing that he was in trouble and that he had been late with payments on the loan. "Our families had been friends for years, but I was looking out for the interests of the bank. I gave him until December thirty-first of the year to pay us the two million two hundred thousand he owed us. He wired in the money at noon that day."

Clint had some valuable assets other than oil and real estate, but most Dallas bankers knew that the Murchisons had lived their lives short on cash. Bankers in other parts of the country, however, were not nearly as knowledgeable about Clint's financial position. Most lenders, whether in St. Louis or Memphis or Milwaukee, knew Clint as the owner of the Dallas Cowboys, and long after Texas banks had refused to make new loans, the team still worked magic for him in other cities.

"Most of the meetings with out-of-state bankers began with talk about the Cowboys," recalls Clint's right-hand man Lou Farris. "Usually we'd spend more time talking about the team than the terms of the money we were trying to borrow."

Even when rumors of Clint's financial troubles started hitting the newspapers, the Cowboys were the calming factor. "Don't worry," Clint's associates would tell the bankers. "The Cowboys are our ace in the hole."

But this, too, was about to change.

24

"Selling the Cowboys would be like selling one of my kids."

As if Clint's desperately weakened financial position was not enough to bring him down, his health was now failing as well. As early as 1980 his friends noticed that his walk was unsteady and his speech was slightly slurred, making him appear drunk even though he was no longer drinking. In the last several years, Clint had often drunk as many as five or six straight vodkas on crushed ice a day, and in 1974 he confided to a girl-friend that he was worried he drank too much. He quit drinking about 1976 to please his born-again wife.

Clint always had a witty comment for friends who now, be-cause of his uneven walk, suspected he was sneaking drinks be-hind Anne's back. In early 1982, on a chartered Braniff flight returning from a victorious Cowboys playoff game, Clint am-bled to the back of the plane to talk with the players about their great performance. Walking down the aisle, he fell against the arm of a seat and cracked two ribs. Suffering from intense pain, he turned to a friend and said with difficulty, "Di-di-did you notice this wobbling started after I quit drinking?"

Clint joked about his illness, and his friends joked too, sometimes hiding his cane that he now depended on for sup-port. But by late 1983 his illness was becoming more acute and less of a laughing matter. When Laurence Rockefeller, a major benefactor of New York's Memorial Sloan-Kettering Cancer Center, learned that Clint was suffering from a disease of the nervous system, Rockefeller asked the Center's chairman of neurology, Jerome B. Posner, to take Clint as a patient. Clint was diagnosed as suffering from olivopontine cerebellar atro-phy, an extremely rare degenerative nerve disease. The disease would not affect his mental abilities, Posner said, but it would continue to inhibit his mobility and his speech, and it would become progressively worse.

For all his problems, as late as the winter of 1983 Clint did not project the image of a sick man or a man in financial trouble. He still was famous for his lighthearted quips, and he went to work each day at the Cowboys Building, where he had finally moved his corporate office in 1982. "He always wore a slight grin on his face, as if to say, 'I've got a secret and I'm not letting any of ya'll in on it,' " recalls a friend. "He always maintained the look of a man on top of the world."

Several people who were closest to Clint during the last years of his life insist that the enormous strength and optimism he displayed at this difficult time was due to a deep faith he had recently found in God. Indeed, by all appearances, he had become a religious man. He began going to church every Sunday with Anne, and participating in the Bible sessions she held at their home. He even attended a businessman's Bible class with his youngest son. But whether or not he actually found God and actually became a born-again Christian—as it appears on the surface he did—is still a mystery.

Anne Murchison had been holding Bible studies at the home on Forest Lane since 1978, and Clint usually attended the meetings, sitting on the edge of the group, without asking questions or contributing to the discussion. But by the early eighties, he seemed to be growing more interested in what was being discussed.

During the spring of 1980, before Clint learned of his illness, he and Anne invited the pastor of Anne's church and his wife to Spanish Cay for a weekend. Pastor Olen Griffing was so impressed with the luxurious island that one morning when he and Clint were having breakfast alone on the patio, he could not contain his delight and gratitude. "I could never have afforded a trip such as this," the pastor told Clint. "How can I ever repay you?"

Without hesitating, Clint responded, "You can teach me how to get through the eye of a needle." Clint was referring to the passage in the Bible that states, "It is easier for a camel to go through the eye of a needle than for a rich man to enter into the Kingdom of God."

Clint's interest did not end there. He started moving in closer at Bible study meetings at his home, and he began conversing with Griffing about the meanings underlying many passages in the Bible. According to Griffing, a few months after the trip to Spanish Cay, Clint was growing interested in the practice and concept of "being saved." Griffing says Clint said to him, "How do you know when you can hear God's voice?"

Clint now regularly attended Sunday services at the Shady Grove Church in Irving, Texas, a thirty-minute drive from his home. The church, on the outside, resembles a high school gymansium. On the inside it looks like a television evangelist's set. The structure, however, was the least of its extraordinary features.

The church Clint entered was nondenominational and relentlessly fundamentalist. Its working-class members were mostly "charismatic Christians" who sang and danced and clapped their hands, spoke in tongues, and were thoroughly washed in the blood of the lamb. It was not a church for the undecided or questioning, but only for "people who have been saved, who have given their lives to Christ."

Griffing says he felt Clint was interested in becoming born-again, but that he wanted to be sure Clint's interest was genuine. "When he came to me and said he wanted to give his life to Christ," Griffing recalls, "I said, 'Are you being pressured into this?'

"Clint looked me in the eye and said, 'Do you think anyone has ever pressured me into anything?' "

Griffing was convinced, and in the fall of 1981 he went to 6200 Forest Lane and was met at the door by Clint in his swimming trunks. The pastor changed into a bathing suit and waded into one of Clint's swimming pools. Once the two were waist deep in the water, Griffing baptized Clint.

Clint was later baptized in a public ceremony on December 16, 1981, at Shady Grove Church. During the ceremony Clint and Anne came to the altar at the front and, as a group of parishioners gathered around, Clint experienced the laying on of hands. One of the leaders of the church, who was purportedly speaking words directly inspired by God, said, "I am going to cause you to understand the ways of the Lord, the way you understand the ways of business." Clint must have wondered whether God had seen the financial pages of newspapers in recent months.

About this time, Clint was asked by the director of the Boys' Clubs of Dallas if he would allow a Dallas Boys' Club building to be named in his honor. Clint had founded a recreational facility for low-income youths in 1965, and in the years since, he had given millions of dollars to the local organization, as well as hundreds of hours of his time. The Boys' Clubs of California had been the principal charity of his father and Sid Richardson's foundation, Boys, Inc., and there were, and still are, chapters around the country. Clint Jr. was carrying on his father's legacy to help underprivileged boys.

But like his father, Clint Jr. insisted that his charitable gifts be absolutely anonymous. Still, the director of Boys' Clubs of Dallas knew that Clint was sick and he wanted to put his name on one of the club's buildings. Clint usually responded to such requests by saying, "No, I'm too shy for that," but this time he gave a different reason for saying no. "I don't need thanks here on earth. I'll get my rewards when I get to heaven."

The comment seemed totally out of character. In his long association with Clint, this was the first indication the director ever had that Clint was a religious man.

Because Anne had become something of a religious fanatic, many of Clint's running buddies, girlfriends, and several family members suspected he had been pressured into becoming born-again, that he just "went along to please Anne." Others questioned whether he had not simply taken an interest in a higher calling because he knew the end of his life was near. This charge is often refuted because although he did not experience the "baptism" until after he learned he was sick, his sudden interest in God took place months before he learned he was ill.

Clint's youngest son, Robert Murchison, says, "Other people, including my older brothers, will tell you that Dad didn't become born again, but I feel absolutely certain he did."

Robert says that when his father became ill, "He never complained or expressed sorrow or pity for himself. I think this was attributable to his faith in Jesus Christ."

Robert recalled a Bible session at his father's house in the early 1980s when one of the members of the group asked Clint, "What do you think caused your illness?"

"I think it's because of my past sins," Robert says his father replied.

"But now that you have given yourself to Christ and He has forgiven your sins, why are you still ill?"

"It's like a woman becoming pregnant out of wedlock," Clint replied. "She may repent and give her life to Christ, but she's still pregnant."

Clint, everyone knew, was not a man likely to repent. Did he have misgivings about any phase of the fast life he had led? Were there things he would have done differently in retrospect? Most people doubted it. If ever there was a man with no regrets, it would seem to be Clint Murchison Jr.

Despite his stubborness and unwillingness to give in on any score, because he was desperately pinched for funds and becoming physically weaker each day, Clint did the unthinkable—he toyed with the idea of selling his beloved Cowboys. At first he rationalized the idea of a sale by committing to nothing but merely asking one of his friends to "find out what the team would sell for." When the friend called Clint a few weeks later and said he had worked out a deal to sell the team for $40 million, Clint seemed totally uninterested. He knew that the Denver Broncos of the National Football League had been sold three years earlier for $30 million. But regardless of price, he simply could not bring himself to sell. "Thanks," he told the friend. "But you know, selling the Cowboys would be like selling one of my kids."

In early 1983, however, word that Clint was interested in selling the team leaked to the press. Clint and the Cowboys organization staunchly denied the reports, but the media nevertheless pursued the rumors. Sources close to the family at the time insisted that Clint needed to sell the team in order to settle the estate of his late brother, John. Word also circulated that because he was in ill health, Clint no longer wanted ownership responsibility.

Despite the clear signs that he was a sick man, and despite his obligation to settle his brother's estate, the idea that Clint would sell his greatest creation was difficult to believe. Even those who knew him only casually understood that the team was his primary passion. What only a small group of people knew was that he was mired in a cash crisis and the only asset he could quickly and easily convert to cash was his Dallas Cowboys. He had no choice but to sell.

On a Saturday afternoon during the spring of 1983, he called Tex Schramm and invited him to his home. Clint rarely called Tex to a meeting on a Saturday unless it was urgent. Tex had witnessed Clint's uneven walk and slurred speech, but had resisted the temptation to confront Clint about it. Tex now suspected the worst. When he arrived at the house, he was met at the door by a butler who showed him to the library. Clint, who usually got right to the point, this time talked slowly and with great difficulty. "He began by explaining that during the early evolutionary process, animals had in the back of their heads very small brains which controlled their gait and equilibrium," recalls Schramm. "He said that, as the animal grew increasingly intelligent and became man, the brain grew larger, but that the small part in the back of the head remained. He told me that he had problems with that particular part of his brain, and he didn't know if there was a cure for the problem, but that he thought it would not be fatal." Clint told Schramm that because of his health, he wanted to sell the Dallas Cowboys and he wanted Schramm to be in charge of finding a proper buyer. Schramm was crushed when he left the house that day, but—much as he hated to—he agreed to carry out Clint's request.

The news that "America's Team" was for sale reverberated through the sports world, where the most common reaction was disbelief. Why would the Murchisons sell the football team that had won two Super Bowls, had completed the last seventeen seasons with winning records, and was tied that year with the Washington Redskins and Pittsburgh Steelers as best in the NFL? The Cowboys were the glamour team of professional football. What could possibly be more prestigious or more exciting than owning America's Team?

The Cowboys received a flood of offers from businessmen around the country. The first serious bid came from a Florida real estate developer, but neither Schramm nor Clint wanted an absentee owner. Other local bids were forthcoming, but most of the serious proposals involved heavy financing using the team as collateral. Schramm wanted a buyer who resembled Clint, someone he believed was so strong financially that the future stability of the team would not be in jeopardy when economic hard times came and went.

When Clint founded the team in 1960, he had given both Schramm and Tom Landry stock options, and each had sold his stock back to the team in the 1970s at a great profit. Now, before the club was sold, he again took care of his loyal employees. He raised Schramm's salary to $400,000 per year and gave him a $2.5 million bonus. He also gave Landry a $2 million bonus, and a bonus of $500,000 to player personel director Gil Brandt, ex-husband of Clint's wife Anne. Schramm then raised Landry's salary to $650,000 and Brandt's to $225,000.

Murchison gave the bonuses to show his gratitude for his employees' long years of service but also as an enticement for them to stay with the team when it changed ownership. "Whether he owned the team or not, the Cowboys would always be Clint's most prized accomplishment," recalls a close friend. "It was his baby that he had nurtured and fed from infancy. He was damn well going to look out for its future."

Many businessmen when they sell an enterprise fire as many executives and employees as possible (or outline to the potential buyers how this can be done) in order to show how much more profitable the enterprise can be, and therefore, how much more the buyer should pay for it. Clint, as typically loyal in adversity as in success, did the opposite—the generous thing.

The Cowboys meant everything to Clint—more than his millions, more than his business deals, more than his women, possibly even more than his family. Selling the team was the most emotionally wrenching experience in his life. But the decision to sell was one that Clint had to make and one that was made no less difficult by his family.

The Cowboys sale was a classic in Murchison family chronicles, erupting into family fights with threats of lawsuits and intense hostility from all sides. Arguments arose in trying to determine the value of two assets that were being sold at the same time. Texas Stadium Corporation, the company that owns the lease to operate the stadium until the year 2008, had been removed from the partnership and was now owned entirely by Clint. But the franchise, which was still in the partnership, was owned jointly by Clint and John's estate (each with 45 percent) and by two other investors who together held 10 percent.

In late 1983 Schramm had found a buyer, an eleven-member limited partnership headed by Dallas businessman H. R. "Bum" Bright. The asking price was roughly $65 million for the Cowboys and $25 million for the stadium lease.

Lupe, who was now sole executor of John's estate, was being warned by her son, John Jr., to be aware that Clint Jr. was looking out solely for himself in the deal and that he was trying to get a higher price for the Stadium Corporation, which lowered the price that could be asked for the team. Lupe, who loved the Cowboys and at one point had considered buying the team herself, again was caught between her son and her brother-in-law.

After months of intense negotiations and threats of intra-family lawsuits, the Cowboys finally sold. The negotiated price was $20 million for the stadium, and $60 million for the team. The franchise price was the largest amount ever paid for a professional sports team. (When the Cowboys were sold again in February 1989, for $140 million, it was again the largest amount ever paid for a professional sports franchise.)

The day Clint closed his deal to sell the Cowboys was one of the lowest days in his life. He did not attend the formal closing at RepublicBank in downtown Dallas, and he said not one word about it to his friends who came to the house the next day with a T-shirt that read, "Clint Murchison Jr., the only ex-owner the Cowboys ever had."

Despite the fights for money among family members and increasing public suspicions that he was in deep financial trouble, Clint still had the trappings of a public hero. The lead editorial in the *Dallas Morning News* the day after the sale typified the high esteem in which he was still held:

> There are thousands of businessmen who could learn some very important lessons from studying the methods of the man who bought a franchise and a few players for $600,000 in 1960 and sold the team Monday for about $60 million.
>
> It's not just in the buy-low, sell-high aspect that Murchison has earned high regard—though we like to see somebody who knows how to play a good game of free enterprise, too. No, Murchison has won respect for the way that he brought wisdom and self-discipline, as well as capital, to the task so well performed. He had the intelligence, common sense, and commercial savvy to hire good people and let them do their jobs.

Lots of people would have traded places with Clint when he sold his football dynasty for $80 million on March 19. An apparent profit of $45 million ($20 million for the stadium and about $25 million for his portion of the team) would have to be appreciated by anyone, even a high roller whose assets were estimated a few months earlier by *Forbes* magazine to be more than $350 million. But what observers still did not know was the truth behind why the team was sold. Only the family and a dozen lawyers and accountants knew that large portions of the proceeds from the sale were used to quiet a handful of Clint's most anxious creditors.

Since John's death in 1979, Clint's empire had grown more on myth than reality. With his magical C. W. Murchison Jr. guarantee, he had finagled millions of dollars in unsecured loans long after he was unable to repay his outstanding debts. Even when things began to sour for Clint, his lenders could not ignore the tremendous asset he still had in the Dallas Cowboys franchise.

But once the team was sold, there was nothing substantial to fall back on. Suddenly Clint's creditors, not only in Dallas, but everywhere, panicked.

25

"People wanted to celebrate something that was lasting, that was solid."

At eight o'clock on a late April evening in 1984, Lupe rushed across the slate terrace in front of her house, then down a few steps to an enormous pink-and-blue tent. "Won-er-ful!" she squealed when she saw that a dance floor had been constructed over the fountain at the center of the circular drive.

A bright moon glistened against the sapphire sky, and from the trees came the shrill echoing sound of cicadas. The sound became louder and softer and then louder again, replacing the familiar afternoon roar of bulldozers and trucks spewing concrete a few miles away. Tomorrow the trucks would be back again, creating more noise and more office towers. The sweeping Texas sky, which once bent down to touch Clint Sr.'s land on all sides, was now divided by skyscrapers amid one of the largest building booms in the nation.

In recent years the Murchisons had sold all but seventy acres of the original family estate. What remained had served two purposes: it was Lupe Murchison's home and it helped to keep alive the myth of the quintessential Texas rich family. This was the place where, despite falling oil and real estate prices, Texans could still get together and act as rich as they once were. Parties at the house on Keller Springs Road, even without John, were as lavish as always. In fact, tonight's ball, celebrating the tenth wedding anniversary of Lupe's daughter and son-in-law, Mary Noel and Bill Lamont, promised to be even more spectacular than the wedding itself. Four hundred guests had said they were coming, and not only from Dallas. More than fifty friends of Lupe's and Mary Noel's were jetting in for the party from around the world.

Moving vans had come by the house earlier that afternoon to haul off large, cumbersome furniture to make room inside for dozens of dining tables. In a game room once described as the size of a "high-school gymnasium," a long banquet table was being secured. Salmon-colored roses were flown in on one of the Murchisons' private jets from their ranch in East Texas, and cherished bottles of wine from the Murchisons' French vineyard were brought up from the cellar.

In her dressing room the hostess slipped into a sinuous Mary McFadden gown, a rich shade of garnet that complemented Lupe's short, brown hair. The gown clung to her body and revealed a figure that was attractively voluptuous but that Lupe was forever struggling to make thinner.

She fastened on a pair of large diamond and emerald, drop earrings, and a necklace consisting of one shockingly large emerald surrounded by diamonds. Lastly, she slipped on the contemporary-cut 29-karat diamond ring that surrealist Salvador Dali had designed for her. Lupe had safes full of extraordinary jewels, but when friends spoke of "the ring," there was no doubt which one they were talking about.

In fact, this was the second such ring Dali had created for her. The first was taken in a robbery—unrelated to the break-in at the time of her scheduled trial with her son—in her own living room, where she was held at gunpoint. "When the robber looked the other way, I slipped the ring off my finger and down the front of my dress," Lupe explains. "Not until it hit the floor with a loud *clink* did I remember I wasn't wearing a bra."

Lupe had become the embodiment of what the rest of the world perceives a Texas matriarch to be—fiesty and headstrong as Luz Benedict in Edna Ferber's *Giant;* as authoritative but compassionate as Miss Ellie on television's *Dallas.* Producers of *Dallas* insist that the fictional Ewings were modeled after a combination of Texas families, but there are great similarities between the late John Murchison and the fictional Jock Ewing, between the real-life Lupe and the fictional Miss Ellie. Barbara Bel Geddes, who plays the role, even looks like Lupe—the weatherbeaten skin and brown hair; the squinting eyes and broad smile. At night Lupe may attend a party in a

McFadden gown, but during the day she often wears work shirts, jeans skirts, and boots. She is a Texan's Texan.

Of Lupe's four children, her third, named Mary Noel because she was born the day after Christmas, had become the most like her mother, always smiling and contagiously effervescent. "She's Lupe's clone," friends say.

Moments before nine, the hour on the invitation, Lupe surveyed the house, beginning in a large gallery near the front foyer where spotlights illuminated major works of abstract art. The once bare walls of the mansion were now filled with fabulous works of dozens of famous artists, among them Nancy Graves, Morris Louis, Kenneth Noland, Robert Rauschenberg, Frank Stella. Lupe and John loved moving and changing the collection in the house, and once, when a Stella did not fit on the wall Lupe chose for it, she merely instructed her staff to turn it sideways. Later, a friend pointed out that the work was hung improperly. "How do you like that?" Lupe teased. "And Stella came out here and hung it himself."

Tonight a dozen cooks moved about easily in the industrial-size kitchen, preparing silver trays of caviar. Two dozen waiters lingered in the main pantry, straightening their white jackets and shuffling around, eager as the hostess was for the party to begin. She was careful not to leak to the kitchen the name of the evening's entertainers, but the help knew that big-name musicians were coming.

At just after nine a stream of headlights appeared at the foot of the drive. A few hundred yards up the drive each car was stopped at the gatekeeper's house where one of the Murchisons' round-the-clock security guards checked each invitation. Security was especially tight at the Murchison estate following the recent robbery, and at large parties guests were politely asked to present their invitations before entering.

The cars came gliding toward the house, a sparkling flotilla of jet-black, burnished silver, or gold Cadillacs, Mercedes and Rolls-Royces. Bumper to bumper, the cars kept coming—up the mile-long, tree-lined, stone-paved drive, past the works of contemporary sculpture that rose like dinosaurs on the rolling lawn. At the top of the drive, security guards on either side of the car checked invitations once more. Beyond this second checkpoint, a squadron of uniformed valet parkers, under the direction of Lonnie Webb, were on hand to relieve the guests of their cars. It was a cliché in Dallas that you could count your social standing by the number of times each week you saw the white-haired Mr. Webb.

When Webb and his attendants opened their car doors, well-coiffed Texas women, dressed in expensive beaded and sequined gowns, flashed their jewels and their bright flirtatious smiles. The men wore black tie and shouted to each other, "Har y'all?"

Lupe spotted Nancy Lemmon across the room and rushed to greet her. Nancy, herself a great Texas heiress, had remained one of Lupe's closest friends from their grade school days at Dallas's exclusive Hockaday School.

"You look more beautiful tonight than I've ever seen you," Nancy whispered in Lupe's diamond-and-emerald-draped ear. With Nancy was her husband, Mark, who also had a professional eye for beauty. The favorite plastic surgeon of Dallas society, Mark had held a knife to many of the most beautiful cheekbones at tonight's party.

The evening's honorees stood near the door and greeted guests, who in turn offered congratulations on the ten-year milestone and admired Mary Noel's necklace of large, graduated diamond baguettes. Even in Dallas society where big jewels are the norm, the necklace, which she wore with a strapless gown, was an eye-catcher.

"This is my anniversary present from Bill," she barked in a throaty voice just like her mother's. "That's what ten years will get you."

Many of Mary Noel's friends had been divorced, some of them more than once, and she considered her happy marriage a proud accomplishment. Others agreed. "Ten years of marriage among your crowd is like fifty years in my generation," snapped one of Lupe's friends.

The party was flowing through the house and onto the front terrace. There, the guests' attention was focused on the dance floor a few yards from the terrace, where a group of twenty young black teenagers from New York—dressed in black pants, white turtleneck shirts, and black hats—introduced Dallas society to the rock generation's newest fad, break dancing.

Around the stark dance floor, soft lights in the trees glinted off a sea of sequined, shimmering dresses and diamonds. To the rear of the dance floor was a large wooden stage, with eight-foot speakers at either end. For now the stage was dark. The women eyed each other's diamonds, emeralds, rubies, and—in the words of one local wit—"other assorted Texas fruit salad jewelry."

Collecting expensive jewels was one of the great passions of rich Texas women; in fact, some viewed the owning of jewels as a birthright. The competition for the largest emerald among friends was second only to having the largest diamond. In another city Lupe might have outshone everyone else with her hen-egg-size stones. But in Dallas there were many women with jewels as large as or even larger than hers. At the top of this list was one of Lupe's close friends, Nancy Hamon, whose husband Jake had made hundreds of millions of dollars in the oil fields. She turned out for the party in full regalia. "Now that limes cost forty cents each, some hostesses have started cutting them into tiny pieces," Nancy once complained, peering into her gin and tonic. She added, "Hell, I've got emeralds bigger than these."

Lavish trays of caviar were passed, but even so, some of the Texans were beginning to grumble about the lateness of the dinner hour. Then one of the servants announced that there were oysters in the bar. When the help began shucking oysters on a large metal counter, the black-tied guests quickly swept forward, picked up just-opened half shells, stabbed the slippery oysters with forks, and drenched them in fiery Mexican *picante* sauce before swallowing them.

Lupe always had a large contingent of good ole boys at her parties, and tonight was no exception. Several of the men smoked cigars, drank a good deal, and spoke in a heavy Texas drawl, and most of them still could not fathom Lupe's taste in art.

"Ah'm the last fella in the world to talk about art, but what the hell's *that?*" asked a banker, pointing to a Morris Louis painting consisting of different shades of green paint dripping down a canvas. The banker might have been more impressed with the work had he realized its estimated worth of $300,000.

Oilmen and bankers aside, by the late seventies, many of the Murchisons' more sophisticated Dallas friends had come to accept their taste in art, and some tried to imitate it. But even after contemporary art had become acceptable in Dallas, Lupe still had a marvelous knack for collecting works that shocked or surprised.

"Have you seen that black marble thing in one corner of the living room that looks like a bird nesting?" one male guest hoarsely snickered to another. "In fact, it's not a bird at all, it's a female vulva."

Lupe loved the reaction of guests when she explained of the work, "People can't believe we have it right here under a spotlight in the living room."

The house was buzzing with whispers, and not only about the art.

"Who do you think the entertainment is?"

"I've heard it's Lester Lanin's orchestra," someone said.

"No, it's some new-wave rock group from London," said another, "Look at all that sound equipment."

The name of the performers had been a carefully guarded secret, but everyone knew the entertainment was going to be spectacular. Rumors had circulated all week about who it could be, but few of the guesses were even close.

Early in the evening the powder room was becoming crowded, despite its two stalls intended to keep traffic moving. The room has a large sitting area, hanging chandeliers and gilded sconces, a vanity table and tufted benches where groups of guests can sit down together to touch up lipstick, puff cigarettes, and exchange gossip. "Lupe once considered having an attendant on hand, but decided against it," says a friend. "She felt too much business was already being conducted at her parties without adding powder-room tipping to the list." Doyennes held court there, lingering on the circular settee. "Everyone was talking about the fact John Dabney Jr. wasn't at the party," recalls one of the guests. "All the rumors were that he and his mother hadn't spoken a word ever since he brought that terrible lawsuit against her. He may have been invited to the party but had the good sense not to show his face."

Most of the truth about John's legal fight with his mother was lost in endlessly embellished gossip. John never sued his mother, she sued him, but several of Lupe's friends nevertheless complained endlessly about what a tragedy it was that "any child would sue his own mother."

John did not receive an invitation to the party, but Lupe was still trying desperately to give the impression that this was a happy family. And, although Lupe and her children's financial future was far from certain, she conveyed the idea in public that things downtown at Murchison Brothers were, in her expression, "just won-er-ful."

Few people were fooled. While the Murchisons had for years been masters at keeping their personal lives private, the curtain of secrecy that had for so long been impenetrable now had holes in it. Reports of Lupe's suit against her son, followed by John's against his uncle, had appeared in both Dallas newspapers. The court records were sealed, but that did not stop the gossip. There was not a business lunch at the Petroleum Club downtown or a cocktail party in Highland Park where there was not at least a new detail—real or fictional—about the latest Murchison fight.

By now the same questions were being asked again and again: Is Clint in serious financial trouble? If he is bankrupt, will Lupe and her children be brought down too, or did John manage to separate Murchison Brothers before he died?

John Jr. was nowhere to be seen tonight, but his ex-wife was there, as was their six-year-old son, John Dabney III, who spent most of the evening on the dance floor trying to imitate the break dancers. Although Lupe was estranged from her son, she had remained close friends with her former daughter-in-law.

Also at the party was Lupe's second child, Virginia Lucille "Ginger" Murchison, then thirty-six. Ginger was living in Athens, Texas, and had recently bought Clint Jr.'s stock in the First National Bank, making her the majority owner and fifth-generation Murchison at the helm.

Lupe's youngest, Barbara Jeanne Murchison, then twenty-eight, flew in for the party from Los Angeles. Blond, ebullient, Barbara Jeanne was an aspiring actress, though without work at the time.

Several of Mary Noel's cousins came to the party, including Judy and Clint Murchison III. Judy had been telling her husband for months that during the property division of Murchison Brothers, insiders warned her John's side of the family was going to end up with the more valuable assets, while Clint Jr. and his children would be left with "the junk." Judy had been urging Clint III to confront his father about the property division and to demand that his father deliver his trust fund, but Clint III had repeatedly refused.

Shortly after ten, an English feast was laid on the long table in the game room. There were silver trays of decorated salmon and bouquets of vegetables. Large crystal goblets held chocolate mousse and strawberry Napoleons in a *coulis* of kiwi fruit. Vases of flowers and lighted candlesticks filled the table. On either end of the spread was a baby boar stuffed with venison. Mary Noel exclaimed excitedly, as she made her way around the party, "We shot the pig and the venison on our lease in South Texas."

Conversation at dinner, both inside and outdoors, was the usual: the women spoke about clothes and parties, the men about business. "There's a rumor that Hermès is going to open a boutique in the Village," a guest revealed excitedly. Someone else changed the subject to the Dallas Museum's upcoming Beaux-Arts Ball, "It's going to be a sellout this year. The decorations are being done by some famous designer from New York, and cost is no object."

The men were equally passionate on their favorite subject. "Heard BancTexas's earnings fell something like fifty percent," an oilman exclaimed. "They're being eaten up by bad loans."

There was a pause before someone else mumbled, "Who ain't?"

During dessert a slight but chilly wind came up, rustling tree branches and causing women in strapless gowns to rub their shoulders. At just the same time, three stretch limousines were turning into the estate. The limousines, with dark-tinted windows, moved slowly up the drive, then pulled up behind the stage, out of view of the guests.

Then suddenly the tranquillity of the night was interrupted when enormous speakers boomed, "Ladies and gentlemen, the Pointer Sisters."

The guests swung around in their seats as the three-member black rock group burst onto the stage, singing their latest hit single, "Jump."

"Within seconds everyone was on the dance floor," recalls Mary Noel. "Even my mother's most conservative friends were dancing. People were swinging each other around like it was the last dance at a high-school prom. The Pointer Sisters did one great song right after another, keeping everyone out there dancing like crazy. It's a miracle that no one fell down or got hurt."

Most of the guests stopped dancing only long enough to take a breath or cool themselves with more champagne. Waiters stepped to the lively beat and somehow managed to balance top-heavy trays of tall, fluted glasses filled with champagne, as they maneuvered cautiously through and around the mass of twirling and embracing socialites. The kitchen help, in starched white uniforms, took turns sneaking to the front of the house to get a glimpse of the entertainers.

The music stopped only once during the show, long enough for one of the sisters to announce, "Happy anniversary, Mary and Bill Noel." The guests roared at the gaffe, but not Bill Lamont. "I'm glad they know the names of the honorees," Lamont sneered sarcastically.

But Mary Noel was jubilant, as always, and made her way around the party, explaining, "When Bill and I got engaged, the Pointer Sisters were our favorite group."

That was in 1973, and that same year, Bonnie, Anita, Ruth, and June Pointer had just produced their first hit single, "Yes We Can Can." In the last year the Pointer Sisters—minus sister Bonnie—had become wildly popular again with their hit album "Break Out." Released just a few weeks before the party, the songs electrified the musicians as well as the guests.

Shortly after midnight the stage fell dark again, and the Pointer Sisters left as abruptly as they had arrived. The guests clapped and shouted for an encore, but the limousines were already speeding down the drive and out of the estate.

The party, which continued until 3 A.M., was written about and talked about for weeks, not only in Dallas but also in New York, Los Angeles, and London. When Mary Noel was asked why it was such a big story, she insisted it was not because of the international guest list or the Pointer Sisters.

"It worked," she said, "because we had been married for ten years and that's a long time for my generation. People wanted to celebrate something that was lasting, that was solid."

Her marriage continued to prove lasting and solid, but little else at Lupe's ball has. The Murchison family fabric had already begun to unravel into recriminations and lawsuits, and a large part of its fortune was about to disappear in bankruptcy.

For most of the rich Texans at the ball, their world of mythic wealth and the unembarrassed spending of it had already begun to vanish. In the coming months and years, as oil and real estate prices continued to plummet, many Texas millionaires lost the fortunes founded on what had erupted from the earth only fifty years earlier. In small towns and large across the state there were intrafamily lawsuits and bankruptcies, but most of them on a less monumental scale than the Murchisons'.

It was the end of a flamboyant era in America. This wealth was vanishing as certainly as had the wealth of the pre-Civil War plantation owners. Lupe's party symbolized the high point and the end of the Texas oil phenomenon. Nowhere else in America had so much money been made so fast by so many people with so little experience. And nowhere else in America in this next decade would so much personal wealth disappear.

Debutante parties at the country club continued. Charity balls in hotel ballrooms, paid for by anyone who had the price of tickets, continued. But Lupe's kind of elegant and extravagant party, put on by a Dallas oil family in its own home, has never been seen again.

26

"S-s-sue me. E-e-everybody else is."

"Clint, now that you can barely talk, aren't you sorry you didn't speak more when you could?" a friend asked. For once the words came easily for Clint. He rounded his lips and uttered, "No."

Clint never gave up. He was as determined at the age of sixty as he had been at twenty-six when he started work at 1201 Main. He was Clinton W. Murchison Jr., smartest boy at Lawrenceville, founder of the Dallas Cowboys, multimillionaire real estate magnate. His empire was crumbling around him, but he still conducted himself as he had through years of triumphs. The same impishness and imperturbable calm that had characterized him in his years of success never left him in defeat.

The sale of the Cowboys was intended to buttress Clint against mounting claims on long-overdue debts, but it had the opposite effect. Newspaper reports that the owner of the Dallas Cowboys had received $45 million in cash in the transaction suddenly triggered courtroom demands for Texas-sized blocs of money as private gentlemanly requests for repayment on loans continued to go unanswered.

There had been much publicity during the Cowboys sale that there was brutal fighting among family members for assets and that Clint's worsening health was making it increasingly difficult for him to settle his brother's estate. In addition to the dozens of attorneys and advisers now working to aid Clint, the family had brought in a longtime, trusted associate of Clint Sr. to serve as the first nonfamily, codirector of Murchison Brothers to help the family solve its growing financial mess.

Clint continued to go to work each day at the Cowboys Building, but—by now confined to a wheelchair—he rarely went downtown to lunch. Many Dallas businessmen had not seen him in months but had heard that he was ailing and growing worse by the day. Several of his close friends said he suffered from the same illness his father had. Although this was untrue, many longtime businessmen remembered that Clint Sr. became so ill in the last years of his life that he was forced to rely entirely on others to handle his business dealings.

The critical blow to Clint's reputation came on the eve of the Cowboys sale, at the Boys' Clubs of America dinner in his honor. "Practically the next day, his creditors who were at that dinner called their attorneys and said, 'Let's sue Murchison,'" recalls one of Clint's associates. "Each creditor knew that he was not Clint's only lender, but that Clint had lenders all around the world. It was a fight to see who could get to the courthouse first."

In fact, a few impatient lenders had already sued Murchison four months before he sold the Cowboys. As early as November 8, 1983, a Cleveland-based bank filed suit charging that Murchison owed $2 million on a $4 million loan. Eight days later the Paris-based Saudi-European Bank filed suit in connection with a $4.5 million loan, of which the bank charged Murchison owed the $4.4 million balance. These claims, which Clint had great difficulty paying, were as nothing compared to what lay ahead.

In March, just days before the sale of the Cowboys, an Arkansas savings and loan association hit him with a $20 million suit. This was followed by a number of smaller suits, and then by another large suit by a second Arkansas financial institution for $25.5 million. By the end of May 1984—just two months after parting with his Cowboys in order to protect himself from lenders—he faced claims totaling $75.7 million.

The majority of these loans had been made in connection with real estate deals gone sour. But in the face of these enormous lawsuits, Clint insisted that his tardy loan payments were strictly the result of a general slowdown in the oil and housing industries and that his creditors would eventually be paid in full. He described his cash flow problems as merely "transitory" and explained that he would be able to resolve his problems within a few months.

But by now Clint was increasingly weak and incapable of helping himself. By the summer of 1984, he had stopped going to his office. Instead, a growing number of attorneys and advisers now came to the house to help him try to untangle his massively complicated financial web. About once a week a group of Clint's friends drove out to his house, loaded him and his wheelchair in their car, and took him to lunch. They always let Clint pick where he wanted to go, and he almost always chose a greasy little hamburger shack nearby that he thought had the best burgers in the world.

On one occasion he and his buddies went to a Murchison-owned Tony Roma's restaurant. One of the men ordered turkey and dressing, then complained about his choice. "Goddamn it, Clint," he said, "the turkey's cold and the dressing tastes funny. This is terrible!"

Clint, struggling to form the words, said, "S-s-sue me. E-e-everybody else is."

But Clint did more than simply take the blows, one after another, from his bankers. He fought back. Faced with prospective loss of his oil and real estate empire, he began a counteroffensive against some of his creditors. He demanded more than $34 million from the Cayman Island branch of a French lender, Banque de l'Union Européenne, blaming the bank for some of his legal difficulties. The bank had sued Clint and a business associate for $4.6 million, but Clint took the offensive, contending that the bank reneged on a 1982 promise to lend him $7.8 million for the purchase of stock in Reno-based Nevada National Bancorporation. Only $4 million was provided by the French bank and the $3.8 million shortfall created problems that, Clint and his associate claimed, forced them to default on other loans and sparked "numerous lawsuits."

Nevada National Bank—a subsidiary of the holding company in which Clint owned 419,742 shares of stock valued at $15 million in 1983—was one of the banks Clint purchased in

1982 with the hope of putting his escalating debt in friendly hands. Ironically, this bank was anything but friendly when, in 1984, it sued him for $3 million, which the bank charged was owed on a loan.

Clint's creditors knew that even a man as rich as Clint Murchison seemed still to be could not afford to pay all his debts at one time. And while each was scrambling to gain a portion of Clint's assets, they knew that those same efforts could potentially force Clint into bankruptcy, which would further hamper their ability to collect what was owed. But by now the creditors were tired of waiting for him to make good on loan repayments that he had promised for months, sometimes for years.

The president of a large Dallas bank sat outside Clint's office and insisted he would wait there until he got a check from Clint for the amount owed him. Clint had his associates ask the man to leave, but the banker did not budge. "I'm going to sit here until I get my money." And he did.

For a long time, Dallas bankers were reticent to demand repayment on loans for fear of endangering a future business relationship. But by the fall of 1984 Clint's problems seemed so enormous that most observers doubted he would be able to work his way out of trouble. Bankers were willing to gamble that demanding their money now and offending Clint in the process was worth the risks that they would lose his future business. Moreover, Texas banks had so many bad oil and real estate loan problems of their own that they could not afford to be either generous now or concerned with future relationships. With huge delinquent oil and real estate loans, virtually every Dallas banker felt the economic noose tightening around his own throat.

Not only was Clint being charged massive legal fees to fight these lawsuits, but he was losing them. By early fall of 1984 he had been ordered to pay more than $20 million to his lenders, which included a judgment of $17 million awarded to New York-based Citicorp Real Estate Inc.

Still, many bankers suspected Clint was down but not out. *Forbes* magazine, in its October 1, 1984, list of the richest people in America, estimated Clint's worth to be "at least $250 million." That figure was down $100 million from the previous year, but even so, the 1984 estimate seemed to be more than enough to cover his claims. At least outsiders thought so.

But only two days after the *Forbes* article appeared, Clint was sued again, this time for $25.8 million. The lender, New York-based Merrill Lynch Private Capital, charged that Murchison refused to pay the principal, interest, and expenses on a loan made in 1982. Interest alone, the bank claimed, was accruing at a daily rate of $8,998.

The number of lawsuits continued to escalate through November. By December the suits had reached an astounding $100 million and were still climbing. Not all of the suits came from outside creditors. Just a week before Christmas, Lupe's two eldest daughters—Ginger Murchison and Mary Noel Lamont—sued their uncle Clint seeking repayment of $500,000. The sisters, through their trust firm, charged that $250,000 was borrowed from each woman's trust in 1982 and that half of the principal was due in May 1985 with the remainder to be paid by May 1986. Clint had guaranteed the payment, the trust firm charged, but interest payments were missed in May of 1984, and Clint's nieces declared the loans to be in default. Clint immediately filed a response in court, denying the allegations contained in his nieces' suit.

Just how desperate Clint's problems were became clear in early December when a Fort Worth bank threatened to hold a courthouse auction of the twenty-four acres surrounding his home that Clint had foolishly pledged as collateral. The Fort Worth bank, which was attempting to force the sale of the property to collect $9.7 million in loans, was one of sixteen banks that now held liens to the property.

At Clint's request, a Dallas judge issued a restraining order at 10:55 P.M. on the eve of the scheduled auction of Clint's acreage. Clint would face a similar predicament two months later when an El Paso creditor would try to auction the land around the mansion to collect a $475,000 debt. But for now, it appeared he would celebrate Christmas at home on Forest Lane. His family breathed a sigh of relief.

But Clint's advisers and attorneys saw little to rejoice in as they often worked through the night, scrambling to keep him afloat. Part of the problem was the extraordinary secrecy under which he had operated his entire life. Because Clint put each of his deals into a separate company, his empire was unbelievably compartmentalized.

He owned 100 percent of 140 corporations and smaller interests in another 110. Like his father, Clint built and operated his empire out of his hip pocket. He had saved very little correspondence. Most of the files he had were stacks of papers on his desk pertaining to current deals. Clint was bored by lengthy, complicated financial statements. So, while there were the cursory financial statements in his filing cabinets, he used these more as a fictional formality for bankers than as a true picture of his assets and liabilities. He thought he knew what he owned and owed, and saw no reason to put it on paper for others to study. As a result, he was now the only person with a clear understanding of the full extent of his financial position.

But this longtime secrecy would prove devastating. By early 1985, he had lost his ability to write. His signature was reduced to a shaky *C*, and only with great difficulty could he speak a few coherent words. He still had the brilliant mind that MIT had wanted to keep, and he was still mentally alert; his brain had not been affected by the disease. But because he could no longer communicate, the answers to many of his problems were locked inside of him, presumably adding to his torment. One of Clint's doctors provided him with a computer-run synthesizer that would allow him to generate sounds with the blink of his eyes, but friends say he was too stubborn to learn how to use it.

A few friends contended that were it not for his illness, he would have been able to extricate himself from his financial quagmire. But most of his closest associates and a few family members insist that while his illness may have contributed to the speed of his descent, he could not have, even if he had been well, overcome the huge debt and the run on his assets.

Clint's doctors were bombarded with calls from anxious creditors asking for a prognosis on their delinquent account from Dallas, and Posner, of Sloan-Kettering in New York, gave an affidavit on Clint's health.

Finally, Clint hired Philip I. Palmer, one of Texas's top specialists in solvency problems, to try to keep the creditors from stampeding him into bankruptcy. In mid-January 1985 Palmer asserted that on paper Clint's assets comfortably exceeded his liabilities, but he added, "If you go over and sell his assets at a sheriff's sale, you aren't going to get enough to cover the liabilities."

No one at this point, however, seemed willing to wait for an orderly liquidation of his assets and subsequent repayment on their loans. The only chance Clint had at cooperation from his creditors, whose claims now totaled $175 million, was to call a meeting and candidly explain his precarious position. Despite his troubles, Clint still cast a very big shadow in the financial world, and he believed there was not a banker in the United States who, in a face-to-face confrontation with him, would have the courage to force him into bankruptcy. Palmer sent a letter to lawyers and representatives for some thirty of the major lenders inviting them to a meeting at 6200 Forest Lane.

Everyone accepted the invitation for Friday, February 1. Typically, Clint had left his money lenders in suspense about the nature of the gathering. Had he called the meeting to announce a payout plan? Was he planning to declare bankruptcy? The meeting, creditors thought, would come none too soon.

But when the day finally arrived, there was concern about whether the meeting would actually take place. Dallasites woke to find their city covered in snow and ice. A massive storm had hit during the night, knocking down power lines and destroying trees throughout the city. By morning many roads and bridges were impassable, and motorists were warned not to travel except in an emergency.

Despite the warnings, Clint did not cancel the meeting at his house. Because of the treacherous weather, most of the men and women invited did not go in to work that day, but instead drove directly from their homes to 6200 Forest Lane. As they made their way down the long private drive from Clint's front gate to his house, the visitors saw for themselves the secluded estate that most had only heard or read about. "Pulling in the drive you had the impression that this was an incredibly rich man who had come to a devastating end," said one attorney. "It was almost eerie."

The visitors saw the ice-covered outline of years of work by the owner. Even after Clint planted the initial hundreds of trees and bushes on the property, he never lost interest in adding to and perfecting his design. He imported flowers from around the world and planted banks of thousands of tulips, his favorite, along the curving drive.

But now many trees were destroyed and the two-mile-long rows of azaleas that were a breathtakingly brilliant fuchsia in the spring were covered with ice. It was doubtful the azaleas would survive the storm and bloom again. If Clint thought about it, he probably would have viewed his own life the same way.

Still, he planned to make a last valiant effort on this day. Once inside the mansion, the attorneys and representatives for Clint's main creditors were directed to the living room, where they greeted the beleaguered but still mythic millionaire. Clint did not try to speak, but sat hunched over in his wheelchair while his right-hand man, Lou Farris, and his solvency attorney, Philip Palmer, spoke for him. They explained that Clint had plans to resolve his debts with a cash infusion from a member of the Fort Worth Bass family. The proposal called for Ameribass, a company owned by Fort Worth's Robert M. Bass, to enter into joint ventures with Murchison's major lenders to develop or sell eight of Clint's real estate projects across the country.

The group discussed the idea, and at first there was some expression of hope from the lenders, in large part because Robert Bass was a young man with enormous resources and because of the generational ties between the two families. Robert, whom Clint's representatives described as "something of a white knight" in this financial epic, was one of the billionaire Bass brothers who had inherited millions from their great uncle Sid Richardson, then multiplied the fortune many times over. One of the great tragedies of the Murchison saga was that during the years when Sid's heirs were increasing their fortune, Clint Sr.'s were losing theirs.

By the mid-1980s Clint Jr. had carelessly gambled away much of the Murchison fortune in bad deals he selected merely because they sounded exciting. Conversely, the Basses, in buying valuable, profitable assets, had carefully become one of the most, if not *the* most, successful family investment groups in America. They shrewdly triumphed in financial fields as disparate as Walt Disney Productions, Alexander's stores, and Munsingwear underwear while retaining their vast oil reserves. Like Sid Richardson, the Basses were in business to get richer; their exclusive goal was profit and more profit.

But for Clint Sr. and his sons there was more to business than just making money. In fact, profit was always secondary to having fun. Texans recognized Big Clint's style in Clint Jr., and in the Bass brothers no one could mistake the old wildcatter's affinity for turning millions into billions. But few people could have predicted the opposite direction in which the two fortunes would travel.

While Clint's representative called Bass a "white knight," top bankruptcy attorney D.M. Lynn, who later became the plan trustee for Clint's creditors, was one of several attorneys at the meeting on that frigid February day who soon saw that the Bass's interest was very tentative. "A representative from Robert Bass's office was saying, 'Well, we might be interested in looking at some of the property that Murchison owns,' " recalls Lynn.

This left Clint's attorney Philip Palmer in the position of having to plead with the creditors. He asked that they give Murchison additional time to obtain sufficient cash to begin an orderly repayment of loans. One of the attorneys at the meeting recalls that even on that brutal winter day there was still an incredible aura to Murchison. "Clint was sitting in a wheelchair, appearing almost comatose. He could not speak or move. He had a list of judgments against him a mile long. Yet just about everyone in the room was still in awe of him. He still had unbelievable mystique."

During the meeting, different groups of creditors left the room to confer privately. In one of these smaller meetings, in other parts of the mansion, attorney Lynn argued fervently in favor of forcing Clint into involuntary bankruptcy, but his pleas met with strong opposition. Although several of the creditors that day held unpaid Murchison notes of between $20 million and $25 million, they were still fearful of the Murchison magic. "He could pull out of this and rise again," one lender said.

In fact, most of the creditors wanted to see Clint in bankruptcy, but no one wanted to be among the three creditors needed to file a petition that would accomplish this. Just as Clint predicted, the creditors left the house assuring him that they would seriously consider his associates's pleas. But six days after the meeting, three creditors finally summoned up their courage—an Atlanta bank, a Dallas real estate corporation, and Citicorp Real Estate Inc., New York, which was seeking $17 million—filed a petition forcing Clint into Chapter 7 involuntary bankruptcy proceedings.

Lou Farris, who was still scrambling to keep Murchison afloat, was furious when he learned of the creditors' petition. Farris still insists that had the bankers not called in their notes, Clint could easily have pulled out of his troubles. "When the group of creditors left that day, they were all so polite to Clint and so agreeable to what we said," says Farris. "Clint was totally surprised when they turned around and forced him into bankruptcy. If the creditors hadn't gotten so anxious, Clint would have been riding high to the end of his life."

On February 22 Murchison exercised his legal right in responding to the creditors by asking that their petition be converted to Chapter 11 voluntary bankruptcy in order to prevent a forced liquidation of his assets.

Although Clint's problems had been widely publicized for months, when he officially filed for bankruptcy, the family was suddenly inundated with hundreds of letters and telephone calls of condolence. "People would call and say, 'We're so terribly sorry about this great tragedy,' recalls a family member. "There was a great deal of sadness. Each morning you opened the newspaper and saw another story about our family's downfall. We kept wondering, when is all this going to end?"

The last two years were seen by Clint's family as a tragic epilogue to a once proud life, but the trauma was far from over. In fact, the creditors' work was just beginning. Two weeks after the filing, lawyers for a score of banks and corporations gathered in the Federal Building in Dallas to begin the process of determining just what he owed and owned. The court-appointed accountant for Clint's estate described the task as "absolutely enormous." The accountant added that Clint was "attempting with all his power to maximize the estate in hopes that everybody will get what is owed to him."

It took almost five months for the accountants to get a picture of Clint's debts and assets. Finally, the task was completed on June 17, 1985. The enormity of the debt was even more astounding than predicted. According to documents filed with the U.S. bankruptcy clerk's office, Clint personally owed $396,693,827.89. His assets totaled $70,767,295.88.

Just as astounding was the fact that more than 60 percent of his debts were unsecured. In effect, he had borrowed $281 million, merely by putting his signature on a slip of paper. The secured debts, totaling $115 million, could be collected in part, but the assets he pledged were almost inevitably worth less than the amount of the loan.

At this point, Murchison's assets included: approximately $45 million in interests in corporations and companies; some $10 million in partnerships; his island in the Bahamas, valued at $8.5 million, and the Forest Lane home that, oddly, was listed at a very deflated $5 million. This was a small fraction of what it had cost to build. The most telling and most predictable item in the court documents was the amount of cash he had on hand. His total cash deposits in Dallas banks came to $4,876.66.

But still more creditors stepped forward, and their demands began cascading into state and federal courts. The tab on his personal debts finally increased to $560 million. Claims against his corporations exceeded $600 million.

For the next year Clint struggled to help his attorneys organize a liquidation of his estate. In June 1986, one day short of a year after Clint filed Chapter 11, a U.S. bankruptcy judge approved Clint's plan for providing the distribution of most of his remaining assets. By selling his half-completed real estate projects, Clint had already raised some $300 million, which was then paid to creditors. Clint's attorney Philip Palmer estimated that the sale of his remaining assets would produce between $20 million and $60 million, or between 10 cents and 30 cents for each dollar sought. Palmer explained, "Clint is through (with bankruptcy proceedings). He is discharged. He can go about his life."

"The big question for Clint at this point was, 'What's left to enjoy in life?' " recalls a girlfriend who later became a lifelong friend. "He no longer owned the Cowboys, he didn't have the money to make any more deals, he was too sick for sex. What was there? Nothing. He lost his will to live."

Although some of Clint's friends continued to see him after he became ill and bankrupt, many of his longtime buddies were now nowhere to be seen. Some of the men who had used him for years no longer had time for him. Others of Clint's friends were cut off from him by Anne. One of Clint's closest friends had made it a practice to drop by each week with video tapes of old classic movies. "Each time I went to the house, Anne met me at the door and looked over each tape closely to make sure it wasn't pornographic. She said she didn't want anything in the house that wasn't allowed in God's eyes."

One day a friend returned from California and told him that he had seen many of Clint's friends in Los Angeles, and that they all expressed their sadness about his financial and physical state. Among those sending their best wishes to him was one of Clint's longtime girlfriends.

Anne overheard the conversation and became angry with the friend. Although Clint listened to the argument, he was too helpless to try to break it up. Clint hated confrontation, but the man who had once commanded every ear in some of the most important boardrooms in America was now powerless to affect even the tiny world around him.

In the fall of 1986 Clint decided the time had come to leave the home that he had spent so many years building and perfecting. The house was becoming run-down and with his now relatively meager worth of $2 million, he was unable to afford the upkeep. To raise money, Clint and Anne held a garage sale—of everything from furniture and electronic equipment to Cowboys paraphernalia—a few weeks before Clint and

Anne left the home. "Clint was back in his bedroom, and I went in and showed him some coasters with the Spanish Cay insignia that I bought," recalls a friend. "He just grinned as if to say, 'Yeah, wasn't life grand?' It was obvious that he had resigned himself to the fact his life was over. Leaving the house must have been sad for him, but it was nothing compared to what he had already been through."

Clint and his wheelchair were carried out of the house in November 1986. He and Anne moved almost directly across Forest Lane, a major thoroughfare, into an ordinary middle-class development home. Clint spent the last few months of his life in a tiny room, much of the time alone, relying on his wife and a nurse to help him when he rang a small bell.

His health deteriorated rapidly, and in mid-March 1987 he contracted pneumonia and was admitted to a Dallas hospital. A few days later, Clint's ex-wife, Jane, was in town from New York for a meeting with her children, and after the meeting, all the children and Jane went to the hospital to see him.

Even stranger than seeing Clint's ex-wife at his bedside was a visit to the hospital by his longtime nemesis John Jr. It was a Sunday afternoon when John received a call from one of Clint's close associates telling him that his uncle was near death. That night John walked into Clint's room and found Clint's associate Lou Farris standing by his bed. John walked up to the bed, took his uncle's hand in his, and said he was sorry about everything that had come between them and that he held no grudges against his uncle. Farris had been with Clint enough to read his eyes. "He is still conscious," Farris told John, "and he understood you."

Whether Clint still held a grudge against his nephew will never be known. What is known is that the thirty-eight-year-old nephew, who stood by his dying uncle's bed, had played a major role in bringing Clint down. In filing suit against him and eventually putting an end to Clint's free use of the MMR trusts, John had helped trigger his uncle's long fall. Before going to the hospital, John told his closest business associate that he was making the visit in order "to pay his last respects" to a man for whom he still felt admiration, respect, and even some amount of envy. But, in many ways, John was the man to envy now. He was the conqueror and Clint the defeated.

The following day Clint became unconscious, and that evening, Monday, March 30, 1987, at 10:40 P.M. the sixty-three-year-old founder of the Dallas Cowboys died.

Many months before his death, Clint's children told their mother, Jane, that they were worried that when their father died no one would come to his funeral. So many of his longtime friends had not been around in years. But Clint's children need not have worried.

Some 1,600 of his friends and acquaintances from around the nation, his fellow church members, and curiosity seekers from throughout the city packed into the Shady Grove Church on April 2, 1987, to witness the last memorial to a man who had risen higher and fallen farther than most men. Obituaries throughout the world explained that Clint Murchison Jr. had suffered one of the largest personal bankruptcies in history, but the enigma of the man himself was perhaps the most fascinating aspect of his life.

Clint had so many unexplainable idiosyncracies that most people simply did not understand him. Few realized that the man who once commanded business respect around the world was, inside, a shy, sensitive, and sad little boy. Why did he refuse to speak to people in the same elevator or boardroom? Why did he need so many sexual partners? Why did he continue on his downward course when he could have pulled out of his financial troubles in time to save much of his fortune?

Even at his death his actions were puzzling. It was said that he planned every detail of his funeral, from the blanket of yellow roses that covered his coffin at the private graveside service to the peculiar religious antics at the church memorial that followed. But many friends who attended the funeral could not believe their eyes and ears, and doubted that what appeared to be a religious revival was actually what Clint intended for his memorial. Even more perplexing was the question of whether Clint had been born again.

The service began with the congregation singing "Amazing Grace" and ended with what the pastor said was Clint's favor-

ite song, "Jesus Loves You." In between, there were four eulo-
gies, including one by Cowboys coach Tom Landry, music
played by a ten-piece orchestra, and a guitar solo, dancing by
young women dressed in togas, and "witnessing" by the
woman piano player, who told the congregation that she had a
message from God to play a certain song. All of this took place
on a large lighted stage whose backdrop was a giant video
screen. As the words to "Amazing Grace" flashed on the
screen, the congregation sang along and at times clapped their
hands.

Pastor Olen Griffing, who had baptized Clint in his swimming pool five and a half years earlier, was dressed in a white
suit and spoke from a plexiglass pulpit. He referred to Clint as
"Brother Clint," and when he spoke of "the joy Brother Clint
received when he found the Lord," church members responded with, "Amen." At one point the pastor said, "I
wouldn't be surprised if Brother Clint's not up there right
now, dancing before the throne and singing hallelujahs and
shouting, 'Great is the Lord.' "

Many of Clint's friends were appalled at the memorial service; others were merely confused. Clint was portrayed as being
a born-again Christian, but many of his closest friends, even
family members, strongly doubted that he had made a religious conversion. The pastor referred to Murchison as
"Brother Clint" in the fundamentalist tradition that all of us,
alike, are brothers and sisters under the fatherhood of God.
But, except for his mortality, it would be difficult to think of
what Clint W. Murchison Jr. had in common with the other
members of Pastor Griffing's congregation. In fact, Clint's extraordinary, extravagant, exciting life, filled with the highest
highs and lowest lows, was far removed from the experiences
of virtually all other Americans of the twentieth century.

While some of his family and friends were embarrassed by
the service, others were able to laugh it off as a fitting farewell
to an odd and puzzling life. "His memorial service was Clint's
last prank," insists one of his closest friends. "It was his last
big joke on the world."

*   *   *

Only a year or two after John and Clint started working at 1201 Main, Clint Sr. proudly confided to his brother Frank, "You know, those boys of mine made two million dollars last year—all by themselves."

"What do those boys need all that money for?" Frank asked. "They've got millions of their own already."

"My God," Clint replied, "What else is there for them to do?"

Clint Sr. had a very dynastic feeling about the Murchison empire and of what his sons should accomplish. To this end, he began mapping their futures in business when they were still in prep school. But in many respects, Clint's sons were ill-suited for the lives their father prepared for them. Both John and Clint Jr. might well have been happier had they never gone to work at Murchison Brothers.

John and Lupe were just becoming accustomed to the serene and relaxed atmosphere of Santa Fe when Clint Sr. insisted John return to Dallas. Dutifully following his father's orders, John was immediately thrust into a business climate that frightened him. Although he tried to please his father, John was never comfortable in the role of an aggressor.

While he tried to put up a courageous front during the Allegheny fight, he secretly and desperately yearned to hide from his corporate responsibilities. Although he tried to give the impression that he was in charge of his business life, from the beginning until the end of it he was often afraid of what lay ahead with each new day. John's greatest dilemma was that while he hated excessive risk, he was surrounded by big risk-takers, chief among them his father and brother.

Business associates insist that he would have been much happier managing a small investment portfolio, primarily of insurance companies, a field in which he had over the years gained considerable knowledge and expertise. Instead, John spent his entire business life bound to a partnership that was a tremendous burden and to a partner who was his opposite.

Clint Jr. might also have been happier had his career taken another path. Although he gave the impression of a man on top of the world, especially as founder and owner of the Dallas Cowboys, he was, in fact, often just as unhappy as John in the role his father established for them. Clint spent most of his adult life trying to be as great a success as his father had been.

"Clint tried to emulate his father in so many ways," recalls his ex-wife Jane Murchison Haber. "He started the Cowboys, but he still wanted to do so much more to be the success his father was."

Not only was Clint Jr. unfulfilled in the role of businessman, matching his father's success was a virtually unattainable goal. He lacked so many of the traits that were essential to Clint Sr.'s success—shrewd judgment and common sense, as well as an ability to adapt to changing circumstances and to pick capable partners and subordinates.

But with his brilliant mathematical mind, if Clint Jr. had remained in Cambridge and pursued a career in teaching, as he had planned and hoped to before his father called him back to Dallas, his success might very likely have been greater than it was. And his life might well have been happier.

To outward appearances, each brother at the end of his life embraced a religion he had never held before. Perhaps after fifty-seven years John had come not only to accept but to believe in Roman Catholicism and perhaps after sixty years of wine and women, Clint Jr. had been reborn. Whatever the depth and sincerity of their religious convictions, both men were searching for an inner peace and happiness that neither found during his lifetime.

27

"The most important thing is family."

The questions are still asked in Dallas today, "How well did Lupe and her children survive Clint's bankruptcy? Did Clint's own children end up with anything?"

Lupe and her children, by rescuing valuable assets before the ship went down, survived the trauma with most of their assets intact. Ironically, the once rebellious and socially shunned John Murchison Jr. is finally given enormous credit for saving his family's half of the ship. "If John Jr. hadn't started raising hell, they all would have gone down with Clint Jr.," says a longtime family associate. "No one thought so at the time, but what is very clear now is that John Jr.'s lawsuit paid off for his side of the family."

The assets in John's and his sisters' trusts were paid out almost in their entirety. As a result, he got his $30 million trust and his eldest sister, Ginger, survived the family wars with trust assets reportedly in excess of $20 million. Their sister, Mary Noel Murchison Lamont, also received most of her assets, estimated at more than $10 million.

Not only were their trusts paid out, but John Sr.'s estate also survived the creditor's rush. Lupe's attorneys, working fast, were able to remove from the deck hundreds of valuable assets before Clint's lenders capsized the ship. John's estate was valued at $145 million, and each of his four children reportedly received $17.5 million, for a total of $68 million. Lupe reportedly received the other $77 million.

The first two generation Murchisons were never known for squirreling away their millions, and the same can be said for the third generation. Once the trust and estate distributions were made, each of Lupe's children got busy building himself or herself a new home or ranch.

Taking a lesson from her grandfather, Lupe's eldest daughter, Ginger, bought a large ranch outside of Athens and oversaw construction of stocked lakes and winding roads, caretakers' homes, her own fabulous home, swimming pool, and tennis courts. Ginger, now thirty-eight years old, has lived in Athens since attending the local junior college there and today owns 90 percent of the stock in the First National Bank, founded by her great, great grandfather in 1890. Like her grandfather, Ginger has been a student of livestock and nature her entire life. She has no interest in society and attends parties in Dallas only when there is no way out of it. Of Clint's eight grandchildren, Ginger also looks the most like him. She has his nose and eyes, his small mouth and slow, shy smile.

Barbara Jeanne, Yale-educated, thirty-three years old, and married with two young sons, also has made her home in East Texas. With her inheritance from her father, she acquired two ranches that once belonged to Clint Sr. She and her husband, John Coffman, renovated and live in an old farmhouse on one of the ranches and have already begun raising their children in East Texas, happily far from socialites and city life in Big D. "I like the country because I want my children to grow up in wide open spaces," says Barbara Jeanne, echoing her grandfather's wish for his sons.

But Barbara Jeanne, who still has very vivid recollections of her father's relief when she told him she would not enter the family business, is quick to insist, "I don't want my children to feel they have to continue some long-ago legacy, that they have to live up to their great-grandfather's successes the way my generation tried to. That's just too much to ask of anyone."

Although Barbara Jeanne never received a trust from her grandfather, Lupe has reportedly promised to make up for the discrepancy in her will.

Mary Noel Lamont, now thirty-six, is the only child of Lupe and John who has an interest in Dallas society. But even Mary Noel insists that, she puts her children first. "I'm not in a lot of organizations because I want to be here for my children when they need me." Nor does Mary Noel travel very often without her children the way her parents did when she was a child. When the Lamonts visit Australia or the house in Vail that Mary received from her father's estate, they take their children with them.

In other ways, however, Mary Noel has copied her parents precisely. Although as a child she was embarrassed by her parents' contemporary art collection, she is today building her own collection of abstract works, using one of the same dealers her parents did years ago. And she recently spent part of her inheritance building a major addition to her already large home in North Dallas.

Forty-one-year-old John Murchison Jr. married for the third time in 1988 and began constructing a lavish, multimillion-dollar Frank Welch home on Lakeside Drive, the most prestigious address in Dallas. The house, which sits on a hill overlooking Exall Lake in Highland Park, is next door to the rambling Spanish-style mansion of a grandson of H. L. Hunt. Although Dallas society, the business community, and John's own family for years regarded John as sharper than a serpent's tooth in his disloyalty to his family, he is now viewed either with admiration or envy or both. His magnificent Lakeside Drive home has ended any remaining doubt about who won the Murchison family wars.

John owns a series of oil exploration properties in several oil-producing states, and he views it as a proud accomplishment that his multimillion-dollar company, Murchison Oil and Gas, is free of debt. With his ten-year fight with his family now ended, his oil company doing well, and his new wife, John is just beginning to make a happy life for himself, attempting to put behind him the deep resentments of being abandoned by his parents as a child and ostracized by his family as an adult. He believes one way to overcome this is through his relationship with his son, John Dabney Murchison III.

"Some members of my family say I went about fighting Clint in the wrong way," says John. "But I couldn't just sit back and take the abuse and injustice. I had to throw up roadblocks at Murchison Brothers just to get Clint's attention. I did the very best I knew how."

In fact, several longtime family friends recognize Clint Sr.'s character in John Jr. "John took a huge shellacking in the community when he was fighting for his trust," recalls a friend of Clint Sr. "But a few of us who remembered Big Clint's battles with proration could see a lot of the courage of the old wildcatter in his grandson. They both fought hard for what they thought was right."

Lupe's attorneys managed to separate her husband John's assets from Clint's before Clint took bankruptcy, and Lupe's children's trusts were also delivered before Clint's creditors began devouring the family fortune. Even so, Lupe and her children bought what was essentially an insurance policy against any potential future claims by creditors. In December 1987 they paid Clint's creditors $2 million in exchange for a release stating that the creditors could not come after Lupe and her children for any debts in connection with Clint or Murchison Brothers.

While John and Lupe's children are now out of the woods and very rich, Clint's children are neither. Just how much of the Murchison millions Clint Murchison III, Burk, Coke Ann, and Robert will end up with is still far from certain. The bulk of their trusts were never delivered, but instead were entangled with their father's assets, many of which went to repay Clint's creditors. Nor did the children receive an inheritance at their father's death. Even what their father had given them earlier is still at risk.

The petitioning committee for Clint's creditors, which includes some two hundred lenders who still have claims against Clint for more than $175 million, is currently fighting fiercely for assets belonging to Clint's children. In July 1988 the petitioning committee filed two major lawsuits and amended another earlier suit against Clint's children seeking to recover various properties that the creditors claim were fraudulently transferred from Clint to his children. Chief among these properties is the children's stock in the nationally franchised Tony Roma's restaurants, reportedly their most valuable asset. According to the creditors' suit, Tony Roma's stock was transferred to Clint's children from their father in exchange for worthless stock of the children's. The suit charges that the transfer was made a year and eighteen days before Clint filed for bankruptcy.

The children are hotly contesting the creditors' suit involving Tony Roma's. But this, as well as other legal battles for what remains of their assets, could continue for many years and could result in their retaining next to nothing of what was once one of the great American fortunes.

Perhaps even more tragic than the millions they lost and the money they could still lose is the emotional turmoil Clint's children suffered. "Clint's kids had an incredibly lofty opinion of their father," says a family member. "But in the end, when Clint Jr. repeatedly promised to deliver their trusts and then was unable to, they felt betrayed. It wasn't just the money they lost. They were heartbroken that this great figure, whom they held in such awe, had let them down."

No one appeared more devastated than Clint Murchison III, the forty-two-year-old namesake and eldest grandchild of Clint Murchison Sr. After graduating from Lawrenceville, and then cum laude from Washington and Lee University in the mid-1960s, Clint went to work for a Murchison-owned company in Dallas during the height of Murchison Brothers' fame. He was long regarded as the bright and serious heir apparent to the Murchison empire. In business, he was far more like his uncle than his father. "Going to work for the family was an eye-opener," says Clint III. "I was saddled with a lot of responsibility, and it was very frightening."

Clint was especially frightened of his father's freewheeling business habits, and he several times in the mid-1980s made his objections known in the uncharacteristic form of shouting at his father. But his complaints came too late, at a time when the family fortune had begun its irreversible decline. The terrible trauma of the family's downfall also contributed to the breakup in 1986 of his marriage to his first wife Judy, the mother of his two sons.

Clint III ended up with some oil and gas properties, a few small companies that were once part of Murchison Brothers, and, for the moment, part ownership (with his brothers and sister) in Tony Roma's restaurants.

The bright spot in his life seems to be his new wife, Shannon, a beautiful and effervescent blonde from Athens, whom he married in 1987. While Clint III shares his father's painful shyness, some friends suspect that might be changing. According to a friend, "If anyone can bring Clint out of his shell, Shannon will."

Clint Jr. thought his second son, Burk, now forty, was the best-looking of his four children. As a boy growing up, Burk not only had Tom Sawyer good looks, but also he was an all-American kid, athletic, popular, and smart. Burk attended Lawrenceville, then Trinity College, before returning to Dallas to work at a Murchison-owned company. Not long after that, Burk struck out on his own with various food ventures. A few of them failed, but he learned enough about the business to open a popular chili and hamburger restaurant in downtown Dallas.

Burk, who was the apple of Clint Jr.'s eye, was in turn the most loyal to his father. When attorneys advised Clint Jr.'s children to bring a lawsuit against their father, Burk would not even consider it. One close associate of the family was utterly surprised by his independence in this matter: "One reason Clint Jr. always favored Burk was that Burk would go along with whatever his dad told him to do. Clint Jr. could always count on the fact that Burk was incredibly easy to sway."

Burk and his first wife, with whom he had two sons, were divorced, and he has since remarried.

Thirty-seven-year-old Coke Ann Murchison Saunders, Clint Jr.'s only daughter, now married and with two young children, is thought to be the smartest of the third-generation Murchisons. Educated at the Madiera preparatory school and Princeton, Coke Ann received a degree in architecture and joined a large New York architectural firm. When she saw her father declining fast in 1980, she flew to Dallas, withdrew all of her personal financial assets she could from her father's control, and brought them back to New York. Of Clint Jr.'s children, Coke Ann appears to be the most in command of her life, as well as the richest. She owns a large Fifth Avenue apartment where she lives, and works as an independent architect, and raises her two young children.

Robert, thirty-five, now married and the father of a one-year-old girl, is probably the least affected emotionally by the family misfortunes, largely because he suffered through fewer traumatic years than the others. When the older grandchildren were pleading for their trusts, Robert was still in college at Yale and not yet due to receive his. By the time he returned to Dallas in the late seventies and began to ask for his assets, the other children were already exhausted in their futile efforts. Clint Jr. and his associates were so busy trying to keep the empire afloat that there was no time to spend teaching Robert the business. "Robert was pretty much in the dark about what was going on," says a family associate. "He just arrived on the scene too late."

Today Robert manages his investment in Tony Roma's.

From the very start, Clint's children had trouble accepting their stepmother Anne, and after their father's death they saw very little of her. "She's not one of my favorite people," says Robert. "She cut off Dad's friends, which was a really cruel thing to do to him when he was sick and dying."

Anne, who received from her husband a $1 million insurance policy and the house she and Clint last lived in, continues to support the Shady Grove Church in Irving and individually to shepherd new lambs for the flock of Jesus Christ. But she has never been seen again in Dallas society.

The great house on Forest Lane, on which Clint had lavished a decade of thought and planning before even moving in, stood vacant from the time he and Anne left it in early 1987. During the next two years, it was badly vandalized, and hundreds of trees and shrubs were left to die.

"I can't drive by the house," Robert Murchison said in the fall of 1988. "It's so run-down that it makes me too sad."

But the news about the once-fabulous Forest Lane estate became even worse. When it finally sold in March 1989, for a much-deflated $6 million to a residential real estate developer, friends and family were crushed to learn that the twenty-five acres on which Clint had spent years of effort and millions of dollars will be subdivided into one-third-acre residential lots and that the home will be demolished.

Although Clint Jr.'s children will each probably receive a welcome inheritance from their mother, their last hope of receiving a large inheritance rests with Clint Sr.'s widow, Virginia Murchison Linthicum. Now in her seventies, "Ginny," as the third generation calls her, was not affected by the family wars and simply kept up her social pace through it all. "Nothing slows her down," marvels a friend. Even the death of her second husband, Ed Linthicum, in 1987, did not restrain her jet-set style. With homes in Dallas, Athens, La Jolla, Acapulco, and the Acuña ranch in Central Mexico, Virginia keeps herself busy hopping from home to home on her elegantly appointed nine-passenger jet.

She is still an avid sportswoman and enjoys shooting wild turkey at Acuña as much as bass fishing on one of her lakes at Gladoaks in Athens. Early in the evening of a stultifyingly hot June day in 1988, Virginia and one of her guides climb into a boat and motor out into the middle of the lake looking for bass. She waits to see the fish jump, then, pointing to a spot, she instructs the guide, "Let's go on over there." Wearing a large brimmed straw hat and white cotton gloves as protection from the sun, Virginia sits as the guide baits her hook. She casts, reels in her line, and casts again. Virginia keeps casting and reeling in fish long after the sun goes down. She finally agrees to return to the dock only when it is too dark to see. "Clint was happier here, on this lake, than anywhere else in the world," says Virginia, who is still beautiful.

Clint Sr. would be proud that two of his grandchildren have made East Texas their home, and four others own property there and visit regularly. The third generation has, in fact, carried on many of the Murchison traditions. A few of the children are ranchers, a few others have oil properties. Coke Ann shares her father's and grandfather's architectural talent. John Jr. inherited his grandfather's courage, to become David against Goliath in his fight to win his trust.

The third-generation Murchisons are generally smart, and all of Clint Jr.'s children are well educated. But they all lack the drive and ambition that characterized the first two generations. None of Clint Sr.'s grandchildren shows promise of becoming a leading figure in the city or state, let alone the country. Their pictures may well appear in the society sections of their local newspapers, but almost surely not on the cover of *Time* magazine.

Lupe's jet-setting life-style slowed during the eighties, as serious business meetings with Clint Jr. and her children, her attorneys and advisers, repeatedly forced her to put off travel. But by 1986 she was back at her full-time occupation of racing around the world. After John's death, she acquired a new set of traveling companions, in particular one Bill Lee, who seemed as eager as John was to drop his business dealings and jet with Lupe to Paris, or charter a yacht in the Carribean on a moment's notice.

While other oilmen watched their fortunes disappear with the drop in oil prices in the early eighties, Lee's oil company became richer and richer. Not only does he have the cash to keep up with Lupe, but he also has the style—apartments in New York and Paris, memberships in such exclusive international clubs as Paris' Golf de Saint Cloud, a multimillion dollar collection of pre-Columbian art. Like John Murchison, Lee comes across both as the ultimate Texas good ole boy and as a smart man of the world. He chews a cigar, refers to himself as "Billy Boy," and speaks with a heavy Texas drawl, but he also speaks French and listens to classical music. "Lupe's having a great time with Bill," says a friend, "but whether they will marry is anyone's guess."

There seems little doubt that Lupe will continue to maintain the life John gave her. She surfaced from the Murchison family wars with a worth in the neighborhood of $100 million. Although she has continued John's practice of selling small parcels of the old homestead, she now vows that she will not part with the home and immediate grounds that her father-in-law built fifty years ago. "I'll never sell it," insists the woman who was reluctant to move there in 1960. "Ever."

Lupe has seen her life turned upside down by forces beyond her control, beginning with her husband's death. But she also stepped forward and, in matters not beyond her control, she refused to let her world be destroyed. She knew very little about business, but she surrounded herself with able advisers who helped her save her fortune.

Publicly, Lupe had been the leading Murchison woman ever since the early seventies. During the multiple family lawsuits, she tried hard to preserve the Murchison image. But once the intrafamily fights ceased, as matriarch she had an even greater challenge—to bring the family back together again.

On her sixtieth birthday in November 1985, Lupe's friends gave her a surprise party. Clint Jr. had filed bankruptcy just eight months earlier and family hostilities were still deep, but Lupe wasted no time trying to rise above the unhappy stories of family fights that had filled the newspapers for four years. Following an elegant five-course dinner, she stood with a glass of champagne in her hand to make a toast in front of the one hundred guests. All of her children and three of Clint Jr.'s children were there, as was Clint Jr.'s ex-wife Jane Haber and her husband, Leonard. John Jr. was seated next to his mother.

"I just love y'all for coming, and y'know this is what it's all about," Lupe said gleefully. In a serious tone, she explained, "Our family's had some bad times and we've had good times, and I guess everyone has had some problems along the way.

"But this is really what it comes down to," she said, her voice growing faster and louder. "The most important thing is family."

EPILOGUE

Almost since the days when Clint Jr.'s great-grandfather T. F. Murchison came to Texas before the Civil War, Texans had considered themselves a race apart. Their state was the largest in the Union, their Alamo was greater than Greece's Thermopylae. For many years Texas produced more oil than any other place on earth, as well as more cotton, more turkeys, and more tall tales. Sitting on top of an ocean of oil and endowed with many other rich resources, Texas had provided its bravest and most aggressive citizens with tremendous fortunes.

Then an event halfway around the world, for which Texans could take no credit at all, made them many times richer still. The Arab states, acting in concert, embargoed the export of their oil and drove the price sky-high. The fact that this made Texas millionaires into megamillionaires did not decrease their delusion that they were smarter than other folks and somehow invulnerable to economic misfortunes. There was a pervasive attitude that what goes up must go up still further. Oilmen believed it, land speculators believed it, and bankers believed it. All empires, political and personal, have suffered from the same delusion that they were somehow specially blessed with endless success. But all empires fall—the only differences are how, and how quickly.

As the price of oil soared through the seventies, Texas banks reacted by shoveling out money as though it were manure. This careless cash resulted in frantic growth throughout Texas where new skylines sprouted almost overnight. Any aggressive entrepreneur could leverage himself to the hilt based on projected earnings that could only keep rising. The new wealth was so intoxicating that professional men—lawyers, accountants, and doctors—who knew nothing about real estate but wanted desperately to be part of the boom, borrowed huge sums and built millions of dollars' worth of unnecessary and uneconomic apartment buildings, office towers, and shopping centers.

Texas was the last place where men and women could get away with borrowing huge sums without full financial disclosure. Clint Murchison Jr. used and abused this practice to the fullest extent he could, but so did thousands of other Texans. A million-dollar line of credit at the bank was almost as easy to come by as a leased Mercedes or rented tuxedo. These thousands of loans were smaller than Clint's, but their total was many times larger.

When the Arabs fell out among themselves and oil prices began a downward spiral in 1982, thousands of oil operators and real estate speculators were caught short. The downturn continued from 1982, when the price of a barrel of oil was $40, until 1986, when it sold for a meager $10 (the inflation-adjusted equivalent of $3 a barrel in the early 1970s). Foreclosures began to dot the North Texas landscape, and in 1988 in Dallas, business and personal bankruptcies reached an all-time-high of 8,024. Both Dallas newspapers devoted several pages each day to stories of failed businesses and failed dreams. By the end of 1987 nearly 40 million square feet of Dallas office space stood vacant.

The biggest bank in Texas, Dallas's First Republic Bank, the most lavish pusher of this careless cash, met its own demise in 1988. It was forced to seek a $4 billion federal bailout, the second largest in history. In 1988 alone, 113 banks failed in Texas, accounting for more than half of the 200 bank failures throughout the country. The federal government also merged or sold 88 savings and loan institutions in Texas and 220 in the nation, committing a total of nearly $37 billion to the bailouts, $25 billion of that in Texas alone.

The trauma of falling oil and real estate prices marked the most pernicious economic downturn in Texas since the Great Depression. Texans watched as some of the state's richest and most famous men and women were destroyed by debt they could not repay.

Clint Murchison Jr. was only the first of the state's mythic multimillionaires to fall. In 1986 the Hunt brothers—William Herbert, Nelson Bunker, and Lamar—put their Placid Oil Company into bankruptcy. The Hunts had continued to feel the effects of the silver collapse in 1980, in which they reportedly sustained a loss of $1 billion in one day. In 1988 Nelson Bunker Hunt and William Herbert Hunt filed for personal bankruptcy.

Just as doctors and lawyers and shopkeepers helped to fuel the boom, they were among those to come crashing down with the bust. World-famous Houston heart surgeon Denton Cooley, who reported more than $9 million in income from his medical practice in 1987, listed his debts at $99 million when he filed for Chapter 11 in 1988. Cooley had borrowed heavily and invested most of his millions in Houston real estate.

Former Texas Governor John Connally also bet heavily on Texas real estate and lost the great bulk of his fortune in Chapter 11.

Robert Sakowitz, Houston's high fashion storekeeper, had built additional stores thoroughout the Southwest, betting that the oil-stimulated boom would continue. But, like so many others, he bet wrong. In 1985 his family-owned Sakowitz, Incorporated, was forced to file Chapter 11.

Many of Texas's greatest families trace their decades-long successes and their later financial reversals either directly, like the Hunts, or indirectly, like the Sakowitzes, to the powerful black gold that erupted out of the Texas earth during the Great Depression. In fact, when the boom ended, almost everyone in the state, at every economic level, was affected.

But no family better exemplifies the Texas myth than the Murchisons—from the time Clint Sr. arrived in Wichita Falls with nothing but a rabbit's foot in his pocket, until that dark day more than fifty years later when Clint Murchison Jr. was pushed into one of the largest personal bankruptcies in history.

The Murchison family is, in fact, a paradigm of Texas. What helped build Clint Sr.'s oil fortune in the twenties and thirties and destroyed Clint Murchison Jr. in the eighties was the same attitude that built and then badly damaged Texas— an unlimited optimism that the economy would always grow richer, that prices would always go higher, that spending would always increase, that the direction was inevitably upward. The casual, freewheeling, free-spending attitude that characterized many of the great wildcatters of the thirties and forties and fifties never ended, even when oil prices began to sink and interest rates rose.

Clint Sr. always believed that the easiest way to get rich was to borrow all the money he could and watch his assets climb before selling them at a large profit. Many of the state's greatest oil fortunes were built the same way. What neither the Murchisons nor Texas could conceive of was the fall.

Afterword

My interest in writing this book began in the fall of 1984. I had just resigned after three years as a city desk reporter at the *Dallas Morning News* when I decided to write a biography of three generations of the Murchisons, the quintessential Texas rich family.

Only a few months later I was surprised to learn that the great American success story I was hoping to write had taken a different turn. From the start, I had heard rumors that Clint Murchison Jr. was ill and in financial trouble, but his troubles were usually described as "a temporary setback." As the months passed, the seriousness of his problems became public, and in February 1985 he filed for bankruptcy.

But even then I had no idea of the enormity of Clint Jr.'s troubles. Nor did I have any knowledge at all of the bitter fights that had been taking place within the family since John Murchison's death in 1979. Many other oil and real estate operators in Dallas took bankruptcy at about the same time as Clint Jr. The practice, in fact, provided a means for rich men to keep much of their fortunes when their deals turned sour. Unlikely as it seems in retrospect, there was still some talk that Murchison could rise from his bankruptcy ashes.

As I first learned the facts about Clint Jr.'s downfall, I became concerned that readers would be turned off by such a sad tale of failure. But I was not concerned for long. For all the terrible pain it caused the family and many close friends, business associates, and creditors, the saga of the Murchisons in three generations was made vastly more interesting precisely because of its unpredictable ending.

From the moment I began researching and writing this biography, I have viewed it as more than just a saga of one family's rise to great fame and riches and its subsequent fall. The Murchison story is an important part of American history. From Clint Murchison Sr.'s early play in the great Texas oil boom to his son John's powerful takeover of the giant Allegheny Corporation and Clint Jr.'s founding of the Dallas Cowboys, the Murchisons serve as a paradigm of Texas and America. The family rose with the oil boom and with the country, and fell with the oil bust and the national economic decline.

It also seemed to me that the Murchisons were, to use an apt cliché, larger than life. No other Texas family during the glory days of oil—in the half century from the 1920s through the 1970s—was more flamboyant or extravagant. No oilman exemplifies better than Clint Sr. the true spirit of the Texas wildcatter, a man of incredible energy who relished trading oil leases even more than advising Dwight Eisenhower or hunting wild turkey with the Duke of Windsor. Clint Sr.'s sons and their wives furthered the Texas myth of bigger and better and more expensive, jetting around the world in private planes and spending millions on their homes and hobbies and wardrobes. They were an exciting clan, who went out to see the world and enjoy life's experiences.

Researching the lives of the Murchisons was a thrilling, as well as educational, experience for me. To my great surprise, not once during the three years I worked on this book was I bored with the subject. What interested me most about the Murchisons was not Clint Sr.'s fantastic ability to parlay a string of oil leases into one of the largest fortunes in America, nor Clint Jr.'s creation of the Dallas Cowboys, nor even the family's glamorous and extravagant life-style, but that the Murchisons had such fun with their money. Unlike so many other families with new or old money who are eccentrically parsimonious, the Murchisons did not squirrel away their millions. This, perhaps more than any other aspect of their lives, made them the most exciting of the Texas rich.

Notes and References

The abbreviations used in these notes are:

Int. Interview by Jane Wolfe
EVB Ernestine Van Buren
VML Virginia Murchison Linthicum
DMN *The Dallas Morning News*
DTH *The Dallas Times-Herald*
NYT *The New York Times*

The aphorisms for which Clint Sr. was famous (i.e. "Cash makes a man careless," "Money is like manure . . .", "After the first hundred million . . .", "I figure a man is worth about twice what he owes.") were told to me by many friends and relatives and appeared in dozens of periodicals.

Part One

PAGE   CHAPTER 1

3   courthouse auction: "Murchison acreage scheduled for auction by El Paso creditor," *DMN,* Feb. 5, 1985.
4   directed the planting: Int. Henry Lambert, whose landscape firm handled the project.
4   "could float the Queen Mary,": "High Finance. Texans on Wall Street," *Time,* June 16, 1961, pp. 80–84.
5   "a coup that outdealt," Ibid.
6   pledged the acreage: *DMN,* December 5, 1984.
7   "Because he cares about.": Int. Jim Clark Jr.
7   "I still sin . . .": *People,* Oct. 29, 1979, p. 104.
7   ten-year contract: Int. Tom Landry.
7   "There were very few,": Int. Jane Murchison Haber.
10   "That's when people really,": Int. Spencer Martin.
10   final effort to plead: Int. Lou Farris.
11   In 1981 he sold: Ibid.

12   In 1981 he filed: In Dallas District Court, on Feb. 2, 1981, Case No. 8101082F against Bankers Trust Co. et al.; Burk Y. Murchison et al.; Clint W. Murchison et al.; Clint W. Murchison, Jr.; Robert F. Murchison et al.; Coke Ann M. Saunders et al. The suit was later sealed.

12–13   ashamed of their past: Int. D. M. (Michael) Lynn.

13   "It was like a death . . .": Int. Judy Rice Murchison.

CHAPTER 2

14–15   Murchison genealogical details: See Van Buren, Ernestine, *Clint:* Eakin Press, Austin, Texas, 1986, pp. 19–32. Also see Genealogy of the Family of Clinton Williams Murchison prepared by Ernestine Van Buren, 1977.

15–16   Description of East Texas land: See Owens, William A., *This Stubborn Soil: A Frontier Boyhood,* Nick Lyons Books, New York, 1966; see also, McDonald, Archie, *Eastern Texas History,* Jenkins Publishing Co., Austin, Texas, 1978.

16   T. F. Murchison built: Int. Mary Ann Perryman.

17   T. F. offered credit: Int. Frank LaRue.

17   took the title "Colonel Murchison": Int. Ibid.

18   three black men were hanged: McDonald, *Dallas Rediscovered,* pp. 15–16.

19   Hubbard was so elated: *The Southland* newspaper, Waco, Texas, February 1903. Also see Van Buren, *Clint,* p. 30.

20   top of this list of villains: Current, Freidel, Williams, *A History of the United States, Since 1865,* Alfred A. Knopf, New York, 1964, p. 170.

CHAPTER 3

22–23   Description of Murchison home, 407 Tyler Street: Int. Broughton Gauntt, Mrs. A. M. Barnes, longtime Athenians who played at the house as children.

24   His first trade: Tolbert, Frank X., "Athens Tamale Man Mourns Death of Mr. Clint," *DMN,* June 21, 1969.

24   named their son for Sid Williams: Harris, Eleanor, "The Case of the Billionaire Bachelor," *Look,* Nov. 30, 1954, p. 86.

24   "My daddy taught me . . .": Ibid.

24   "Doc Bass had to remove . . .": letter to the Henderson County Historical Society from Perry R. Bass, Fort Worth.

25   "I cheat my boys . . .": Josephson, Matthew, *The Robber Barons,* A Harvest Book, Harcourt, Brace & World, Inc., 1934, 1962, p. 46.

26   Description of First National Bank, and of John Murchison and his brother D.R.: Int. Mrs. Louis Carroll, who worked at the bank from 1919 to 1969.

31   barefoot Clint would meet: Int. Frank LaRue.

32   "The dean told me . . .": Van Buren, *Clint,* p. 10.

32   Nearly every day he balanced: Int. Louis Carroll.

33 "I was out drumming up . . .": Ibid.

36 "I got out my pocket . . .": *Look,* Nov. 30, 1954, p. 87.

37 "I swung around that dusty . . .": Ibid, p. 86.

CHAPTER 4

38 "No, if you wear . . .": *Time,* May 24, 1954, p. 93.

39–41 For description of early boomtowns see Boatright, *Tales From the Derrick Floor.* Doubleday & Company, Inc. Garden City, New York, 1970, pp. 59–81.

42 threatened to evict: Van Buren, *Clint,* p. 41.

42 Late one night in 1919: Pirtle, "Lucky a last time," *DTH,* Dec. 26, 1982.

43 "To some extent . . .": *Time,* June 12, 1947.

44 a terrible blow fell: *Time,* May 24, 1954, p. 93.

44 accepted the invitation: Int. EVB.

45–47 Anne was born in Tyler: description of Dabney White, Burk Yarbrough White, and Clint's courtship with Anne Morris comes from interviews with the late Lucy Morris Runge, Anne Morris Murchison's older sister.

50 Clint began to grow restless: Van Buren, *Clint,* pp. 45–46.

50 Clint walked away: "Tycoons, The New Athenians," *Time,* May 24, 1954, p. 93.

50–51 "Saving Is the Secret of Success,": *The Athens Review,* March 12, 1925.

CHAPTER 5

52–55 Clint planned a business trip: Description of trip to New York, Anne's sickness and death: Int. Lucy Morris Runge.

54 Shattered and inconsolable: Int. Mrs. A. M. Barnes, Int. Mary Ann Perryman.

55 the Bible from cover to cover: Int. VML.

55 "Please let the children . . .": Int. Lucy Morris Runge.

55 "people said I stayed drunk for a year.": Int. EVB.

56 Clint decided to re-engineer his pipe: the story of his beginnings in pipeline transport and subsequent formation of the Southern Union Company is told in Chestnutt, N.P. *Southern Union,* Mangan Books, El Paso, Texas, 1979.

58 There was no good reason: Harris, *Merchant Princes,* p. 149.

59 determined to find a means: Ibid., p. 150.

60 "We don't have that kind of money . . .": Chestnutt, *Southern Union,* p. 25.

61 "Just covering a few overdrafts,". Int. John E. Kilgore Jr.

62 "A gigantic banner: *The Santa Fe New Mexican,* October 21, 1930.

65 "I'm just the shyest little boy . . ." Int. EVB.

65 Burk was the opposite of John Dabney: Int. VML.

65   late picking the boys up: Ibid.
66   Clint W. had a double mastoidectomy: Int. Jane Murchison Haber.
66   Instead, he preferred to close: Int. Carr Pritchett.
67   placed bets on whether: Int. EVB.
68   sold John Dabney a calf: *Time,* June 16, 1961, p. 81.
68   "I was shooting craps . . .": Van Buren, *Clint,* p. 127.

CHAPTER 6

71–77   The Daisy Bradford No. 3's: the discovery, as well as description of H. L. Hunt and his dealings with Dad Joiner: See Clark, James A., *The Last Boom,* Shearer Publishing, Texas, 1972, 1984; and Hurt, Harry III, *Texas Rich,* W. W. Norton & Co., New York, 1982, pp. 75–103.
77   construction of a pipeline: Int. Albert Oldham.
79   too much of a gamble: Van Buren, *Clint,* p. 84.
79–80   half million barrels: Presley, James A., *Saga of Wealth,* G.P. Putnam's Sons, New York, 1978, p. 139.
79–80   twice the size of Manhattan: Ibid., p. 138.
81   Pennsylvania Supreme Court: Clark, *The Last Boom,* p. 145.
81   On August 17 Sterling: Ibid. p. 140.
84   Clint would switch that property: Van Buren, *Clint,* p. 88.
85   Jake Louis Hamon Jr.: Presley, *Saga of Wealth,* pp. 151–152.
86   "Your reputation in hot . . .": Presley, *Saga of Wealth,* p. 148.
87   "Inch by inch and step . . .": *ULTRA* magazine, Feb. 1986, p. 87.
87   wore his pants: Int. Frank LaRue.
90   Rattlesnake meat was frequently served: Int. Carr Pritchett.
91   five or six suitcases: Tolbert, Frank X., "Country Boy Sid Knew His Trading," *DMN,* September 31, 1959.
92   When oil was selling at 10: Van Buren, *Clint,* p. 87.
93   occasionally advanced $50,000: Int. Marcus Ginsburg, nephew of Sol Brachman.
93   variation of the reversionary: Int. Phil Bee.
93   sense of future trends: Ibid.
93   "He sold a producing . . .": Lincoln, Freeman, "Big Wheeler-Dealer from Dallas, *Fortune,* January, 1953, p. 132.
94   "Murchison, in 1938 . . .": Ibid.
95   integrity and reputation mattered: Int. Phil Bee.
96   "Fields that everyone else . . .": Int. Albert Oldham.
96   "Clint was lucky, but he made . . .": Int. Darrell Hamric.
98   Southern Union had grown: Int. Phil Bee.
98   "I'll stay with you . . .": Int. Carr Pritchett.

CHAPTER 7

100–101   he had a high fever: explanation of Burk's death comes from Int. VML and Int. Lucy Morris Runge.
101   kitchen at the Waldorf-Astoria: Int. VML.

104   nine domestics lived at the farm: Ibid.

105   These boys fit in: Int. Leon Harris.

105   "I drove a La Salle . . .": Int. John Black.

105   Often they were penniless: Ibid.

105   "My daddy gave my mother . . .": Int. Bernard Fulton.

106   Clint Murchison was the opposite: Ibid.

106   "Mr. Murchison, this sure is . . .": Int. Carr Pritchett.

106   "Clint was so smart . . .": Int. Bernard Fulton.

107   "finest residential area . . .": McDonald, *Dallas Rediscovered,* p. 204. Armstrong's sons-in-law, Hugh Prather and Edgar Flippen, were the foremost developers of Highland Park.

108   "Many a Texan was puzzled . . .": "Texas: Mr. De," *Time,* Dec. 24, 1956.

109   Dallas's retail stores: For anecdotes about Neiman-Marcus, see Harris, Leon, *Merchant Princes,* Berkley Books, New York, 1980, pp. 149–189; Marcus, Stanley, *Minding The Store,* Little, Brown and Company, Boston-Toronto, 1974; Tolbert, Frank, *Neiman-Marcus, Texas,* Henry Holt and Company, New York, 1953.

110   Clint greatly admired: Int. VML.

112   Hunt found time to: More on Hunt's right-wing enterprises may be found in Chapter 11 of this book, and in Harry Hurt's book *Texas Rich.*

112   Hunt's antiblack: Not only was Clint Sr. free of prejudice against minorities, but he successfully taught his children the same principle.

112   "the customers would go elsewhere,": Wright, Lawrence, *In the New World,* Alfred A. Knopf, New York, 1988, p. 5.

114   Matagorda Island was still: Description of Virginia Long's courtship with Clint Murchison, including visits to Matagorda, come from interviews by the author with her.

114   "My mother said I jumped . . .": Int. VML.

117   Clint lent him: Van Buren, *Clint,* p. 106.

118   "Murchison didn't get upset . . .": Int. Albert Oldham, chief geologist for American Liberty Oil Company from 1937 to 1952.

120   Clint Jr.'s solid A-plus: Int. Bernard Fulton.

120   "I'm going to MIT . . .": Int. Carr Pritchett.

121   "It's a great shock . . .": *Time,* June 16, 1961, p. 81.

CHAPTER 8

123   Fascinated by his brother's: Int. Jane Murchison Haber.

124   "Clint was very ingratiating . . .": Int. Jane Murchison Haber.

124   "Before you marry her . . .": Ibid.

125   "We were driving along . . ." Int. Carr Pritchett.

125   wrote Jane many letters: Int. Jane Murchison Haber.

126   In mid-1944: Explanation of Clint's split with Toddle Lee Wynne comes from several sources, including Frank Schultz, Frank LaRue, and Robert F. Murchison.

127   Lieutenant Murchison flew in: Int. Lupe Gannon Murchison.

127 Born Lucille Hughes Gannon: During several interviews Lupe
     Murchison gave me the details of her childhood and put me in contact
     with classmates who also had clear recollections.
128 "Mrs. Gannon had a beautiful . . ." Int. Mary Lynn Aldredge
     McEntire.
128 "Lupe was always jumping . . .": Ibid.
129 "John was like no one . . .": Int. Lupe Murchison.
130 hard on him, both physically: Int. VML.
130 "If you go partners . . .": *Time,* May 24, 1954, p. 90.
131 most of his deals on a handshake: Int. Henry Gilchrist, who joined
     Holman Jenkens' firm (now Jenkens & Gilchrist) in 1950.
131 Clint usually wanted nothing more to do: Ibid.
132 "When word got out . . .": Ibid.
132 "My wife and I figured . . .": Int. Frank Schultz.
132 "The waiter passed . . ." Int. Estelle Pritchett.
133 planning for the enormous business expansion: Int. Phil Bee.
133 "We are starting on a course . . .": Presley, *Saga of Wealth,* p. 217.
133 American Mail Line of Seattle: Van Buren, *Clint,* pp. 261–62.
135 "I was utterly amazed . . .": Int. Phil Bee.
135 "Mr. Murchison put me in charge . . .": Int. Truman Kemper.
135 "There's no finer heritage . . .": This, as well as most of what is writ-
     ten about the Murchisons' involvement with Henry Holt & Co., is doc-
     umented in the Dec. 1959 *Fortune* article titled "Henry Holt and the
     Man from Koon Kreek."
138 Clint never paid any attention: Int. Jim Clark Jr.
139 His step was so light: Ibid.
139 never raised his voice to her: Int. EVB.

CHAPTER 9

141 a 300,000-acre ranch that he owned: Int. Roy Reed.
142 Hacienda Acuña, a group of six ranches: description of Acuña
     comes from author's visit to the ranch as well as numerous interviews.
142 Leaving Virginia behind: Int. VML.
142 "I have found . . .": Int. VML.
143 "necklace of cabochon . . .": Int. Jim Clark Jr.
143 What attracted Clint most to Mexico: Int. Roy Reed.
144 wanted to house and educate: Ibid.
144 slept in an old, crumbling adobe: Int. VML.
145 "Goddamit, Clint," Ibid.
145 architect of the main house: The architect (and builder) was an Eng-
     lishman named Horace Rich.
145 "It sounds presumptuous . . .": Int. Roy Reed.
146 Clint also brought in dairy cows: Int. Howard Reed.
146 increased his Acuña land holdings: Int. Carr Pritchett.
146 "I told the Duke and Duchess . . .": Int. VML.
147 "It would be nice if you had some . . .": Int. VML.

149   arrived with some 150 pieces of luggage: Int. VML.
149   "They're marvelous,": Ibid.
149   "After dinner we were all still . . .": Ibid.
149   the duchess wanted her hair done: Ibid.
151   "What's in that suitcase?": Int. VML.
151   the battery went dead on the boat: the story of what happened when
       the group was stranded off El Toro is from recollections VML.
151   "We'd have paid thirty thousand . . .": Int. VML.
152   increasingly disgruntled with the government regulation: For more
       on the government regulation of Southern Union, see Chestnutt, *South-
       ern Union,* pp. 50–51.
152–153 "If you tried hard and produced . . .": Int. Frank Schultz.
153   "If a good drilling or pipeline . . .": Int. Phil Bee.
154   "So long as you add value,": Ibid.
154   Clint brilliantly maneuvered: Lincoln, *Fortune,* Jan. 1953, p. 136.
156   "Though they lived in one of the coldest . . .": Kilbourn, William,
       Pipeline, Clark, Irwin & Company Limited, Toronto, Vancouver, 1970,
       p. 18.
156   Murchison's plan had touched a patriotic nerve: Bill Carey, who
       joined Delhi Oil in 1950, wrote a speech to the Canadian Legislature,
       the last line of which was, "Canadian gas for Canadian consumption
       through an all-Canadian line." This became Canadian Delhi's slogan in
       fighting to win the pipeline permit.
157   "Mr. Murchison, have you ever traveled . . .": Ibid, p. 27.
157   Howe had been a guest at Acuña: Gray, *The Great Canadian Oil
       Patch,* p. 180.
158   "You Canadians don't know the value of gas,": Kilbourn, *Pipeline,*
       p. 27.
158   By 1955 Clint had spent $10 million: Int. Frank Schultz.
159   The criticism bothered Clint: Int. Frank Schultz. Clint at one point
       considered hiring a publicity man to combat the criticism.
159   "We went through seven years . . .": Int. Frank Schultz.
159   Clint Sr. was worried about: Int. VML.
160   "John seems to be over . . .": Ibid.
160   "You can come back . . .": Int. Lupe Murchison.
160   John and Lupe loved the relaxed: Ibid.
161   Jane went along with what Clint wanted: Int. Jane Murchison
       Haber.
161   "When Clint was getting his master's . . .": Ibid.
162   "Have at it,": Int. Jim Clark Jr.

Part Two

CHAPTER 10

165   James H. Clark, who was from an old-line: Ibid.
165   "You're not going to Texas and get in . . .": Ibid.

166   "All you need is eatin' money.": Int. Steve Rooth.
166   "Clint Jr. loved everything . . .": Ibid.
167   "Because Clint Jr. had married . . .": Int. VML.
169   "This is so risky,": Int. Jim Clark Jr.
169–170   Carter, a savvy and aggressive: Int. Steve Rooth.
171   family's investment in Henry Holt & Co.: much of the information about the Murchisons' involvement with Holt is contained in a lengthy article in *Fortune* (Dec. 1959), titled "Henry Holt and the Man from Koon Kreek."
172   He treated Jim Clark and the other advisers: Int. Jim Clark Jr.
173   A flip of the coin was an index: Int. EVB.
173   "If you'd be more careful: Int. Jim Clark Jr.
173   "What am I supposed to do?": Int. Steve Rooth.
174   Clint believed in the concept: Ibid.
175   "You can have five percent . . .": Ibid.
176   "Give me thirty days,": Int. Darrell Hamric.
177   "I wouldn't have had the nerve,": Int. Howard Reed.
178   "Well, would you like to buy it?: Int. Phil Bee.
180   "Dear Stanley, Virginia's got a diamond." Ibid.
182   "Holman worshiped the ground . . .": Int. Walter Spradley.
183   Clint Sr. continued to borrow: Int. Gerald Mann.

CHAPTER 11

185   "Ah, the Texans . . .": Bainbridge, *The Super-Americans,* p. 38.
185   "Clint loved to pick horses . . .": Int. VML.
186   actors and actresses mingled with Texas's richest: all information about the rich and famous at Del Charro from VML.
187   "That swingin' walk of mine . . .": Harris, *Look,* Nov. 30, 1954, p. 84.
188–189   Sid was so deeply in debt: Ibid.
189   "I'd have to rate it second . . .": Int. VML.
189   Like Clint, Sid placed big money: information about betting at Del Mar from VML.
190   he had been electrified by his spectacular: Murphy, Charles, J.V., *Fortune,* "Texas Business and McCarthy," May 1954, p. 210.
191–192   nowhere had that system reached: Murphy, *Fortune,* May 1954, p. 101.
193   there had as yet been no Hiss trial: Ibid., p. 100.
193   a strong and devoted friend of oil: information on the "Big Four" from Texas who backed McCarthy comes from Cook, Fred J., *The Nightmare Decade,* Random House, New York, 1971, pp. 201–207, *Fortune,* May 1954.
196   "McCarthyism" as synonymous with "Americanism.": Gerald Mann, Clint's right-hand man, told the author, "McCarthyism seemed such an *un*-American thing to believe in. But a lot of these oilmen had a lot of money and a lot to lose if Communism took over."

196 Murchison printed and distributed: Cook, *The Nightmare Decade*, p. 294.

197 "I'm with you, Joe . . .": Bainbridge, *The Super Americans*, p. 235.

197 Richardson traveled to Paris: *Fortune*, May 24, 1954, p. 208.

201 "After Joe came out . . .": *Fortune*, May 1954, p. 208.

201 Lillian, refused to attend: Int. Jim Clark Jr.

201 the final blow to his relationship: Int. Gerald Mann.

203 his spirit, if not his name: author's information on Dallas's right wing comes from numerous interviews with Dallas citizens, as well as Leslie, Warren, *Dallas Public and Private*, Grossman Publishers, New York, 1964, pp. 124–132.

CHAPTER 12

206 ". . . had the money that's spent . . .": "Murchison Suing U.S. on Taxing Charity That Runs a Race Track," *NYT*, Jan. 1, 1964.

207 Clint and Sid acquired 7,000: Ibid.

207 Clint began planning a much larger venture: "2 Texans Seeking Race Tracks to Support Foundation for Boys," *NYT*, July 13, 1954.

209 "This is no tax dodge.": *NYT*, Jan. 1, 1964.

209 "Theoretically, a good end . . .": *NYT*, July 20, 1954.

210 In 1954 Sid Richardson claimed: *Time*, May 24, 1954, p. 96.

210 "As long as there is oil . . .": Ibid.

211 "Let's drill that up.": Int. Steve Rooth.

211 Clint began to think that Henry Luce: Int. Phil Bee.

212 the U.S. could assure itself: Int. Phil Bee.

212 He wrote a number of articles: Ibid.

214 "Those two don't lay out . . .": "Fight for New York Central," *Business Week*, Mar. 6, 1954, p. 27.

215 "About five, six or, seven . . .": "Railroads: Rumor in Texas," *Newsweek*, Nov. 7, 1955.

215–216 Dun & Bradstreet, according: "Tycoons: The Bachelor," *Time*, Oct. 12, 1959, p. 106.

216 Clint was very fond of Bob: Information on Bob and Anita Young and the Murchisons' visits at Young's homes come from interviews VML.

220 "If they would take a page out of my book,": "Murchisons on TV Interview Show," *DTH*, Mar. 26, 1955.

221 *The New York Times* named Murchison: "List of 76 Said to Hold Above 75 Million, *NYT*, Oct. 28, 1957.

CHAPTER 13

224 "Once you get over . . .": Markel, Helen, "A Business of Brim," *Sports Illustrated*, May 21, 1956 p. 69.

224 Clint drilled on the lease: Ibid.

225 The blind was number 11: Int. Frank LaRue.

225 "They put the spitoon...": Ibid.

226 Teddy's cousin Franklin: Markel, *Sports Illustrated*, p. 66.

226 amusing visitors was Pete Kriendler: information on his visit to Koon Kreek comes from the author's interview with Kriendler.

228 Richardson did not become a member: "Koon Kreek Klub Fabulous Millionaires' Playground," *DTH*, April 17, 1957.

228 "Murk, why do you want...": Int. Frank LaRue.

231 "The unhappiest time...": Int. Jim Clark Jr.

232 "*I* don't. I work for fun.": *Fortune*, Jan. 1953, p. 120.

233 Clint suffered a stroke: Int. VML.

234 Clint overheard a workman: Int. EVB.

Part Three

CHAPTER 14

240 "Oh, no," came the swift: The comment was made by Ed Pauley, one of three owners of the Rams at the time.

240 Clint would never forget: Int. VML.

241 he was also unbalanced: Ibid.

241 he was lured by the buy-low: Int. Tex Schramm

241 Clint believed that Hunt: "Cowboys' Owner Explains Offer," *NYT*, March 22, 1962.

242 He was indeed under the impression: Ibid. Hunt was not the only person under that impression. *Dallas Morning News* sports columnist Blackie Sherrod (who was then sports editor of *The Dallas Times-Herald*) says, "I strongly doubt the NFL would have granted Clint a franchise when they did if it hadn't been for the AFL starting a team in Dallas. Clint might have eventually gotten the franchise, but it was probably several years down the road."

243 "Lamar, if you want to own...": *NYT*, March 22, 1962.

243 calling the move into Dallas: Chipman, Donald, *The Dallas Cowboys and the NFL*, University of Oklahoma Press, Norman, Oklahoma, 1970, p. 26.

243 "the only person the players...": Int. Tex Schramm.

244 "personally obnoxious.": Luksa, Frank, "Cowboy birth a bit of harmony, *DTH*, Dec. 4, 1982.

246 "We thought and thought...": *DMN*, Nov. 10, 1985.

249 Clint felt confident that crowds: Ibid.

251 Clint believed his team: Int. Blackie Sherrod.

252 the crowd booed him so loudly: Int. Lee Roy Jordan.

254 "Dear Blackie,": Int. Blackie Sherrod.

254 Schramm each day used a ruler: Int. Blackie Sherrod.

254 refused to give their loyalties: Ibid.

257 "I had become a born-again...": Int. Tom Landry.

258 showed up at training camp: "The History of the Dallas Cowboys," *DMN*, Aug. 17, 1986.

CHAPTER 15

261 the prize Clint's eyes were on: Int. Steve Rooth, who was put in charge of running the Murchisons' fight for Allegheny. "No one really cared about the New York Central Railroad," says Rooth. "IDS was the carrot."

261 In a series of eleven joint: *Business Week,* Oct. 1, 1960.

263 Kirby kicked the brothers,: Int. Steve Rooth, who adds, "One weekend when I was in Nantucket, John and Clint called me and said, 'You've got to come to New York. They've kicked us off the board (of Allegheny).'"

263 John Connally to try to settle: Int. Steve Rooth.

264 "Kirby was an odd man,": Int. VML.

265 "Brought Wall Street . . .": Int. Steve Rooth.

266 extraordinarily cautious, burning: Ibid.

267 "John never discussed business . . .": Int. Lupe Murchison.

268 "Women adored John,": Ibid.

268 ". . . the most difficult in our marriage,": Ibid.

268–269 "two great American economic . . .": "The Murchisons and Allan Kirby," *Life,* April 28, 1961, pp. 74–79.

270 "We lost our shirts . . .": *NYT,* May 24, 1961.

271 "We're going to pay a six-cent . . .": *DMN,* May 24, 1961.

271 "He should do what he used . . .": *Time,* June 2, 1961.

272 "John remembered his boarding . . .": Int. Lupe Murchison.

273 after the vote count in Baltimore: *NYT,* Dec. 22, 1963.

273 "war-like moves": *NYT,* Jan. 17, 1962.

273 he had promised to recapitalize: *NYT,* May 23, 1961.

275 Chairman John J. McCloy: *Time,* June 2, 1961.

275 moving Allegheny's offices: *NYT,* Oct. 10, 1962.

275 "It was worth it." *DMN,* May 24, 1961.

275 The clear answer: Int. Steve Rooth, who adds, "We won the battle but we lost the war."

275 discussing a sale: *NYT,* Sept. 25, 1962.

275 ". . . sold down the river . . .": *NYT,* Nov. 8, 1962.

276 set up a spate of rumors: *DMN,* Nov. 9, 1962.

276 troubles false but shrewdly explained: Ibid.

276 "Pride. Family pride.": *NYT,* July 5, 1963.

CHAPTER 16

278 But the financial profit: Int. George Caulkins.

278 called Caulkins and apologized: Ibid.

279 "Our house is always . . .": "American Action, The Ski Life in Colorado," *Town & Country,* February, 1964.

279 John often piloted: Int. Enslie Oglesby.

279 Following John's lead: Ibid. Caulkins says, "Among the people I know at Vail, 90 percent came directly or indirectly because of John

Murchison. He was a strong drawing card, both for investors and people who came later and built houses."

280   "Maybe we should try . . .": Ibid.
282   "where the sand was pure white . . .": Int. Enslie Oglesby.
282   "Clint Jr. wanted our input . . .": Ibid.
282   "We looked and looked . . .": Int. Jane Murchison Haber.
283   whom Clint named Robert: Int. Robert F. Murchison.
284   "Clint would debate for hours . . .": Int. Jane Murchison Haber.
284   by 1960 she began to wonder: Ibid.
285   "Other women were totally . . .": Ibid.
286   Jane wanted the same type: Ibid.
287   ". . . stopped flying on his private planes . . .": Int. Jim Stroman.
287   much to be gained in attending graduation ceremonies: Ibid.
287   Art Modell stopped by Clint's house: St. John, Bob, *Tex! The Man Who Built the Dallas Cowboys,* Prentice-Hall, Englewood Cliffs, New Jersey, 1988, pp. 80–81.
288   opposite impression at 1201 Main: Int. Jim Stroman.
290   "We had very little furniture . . .": Int. Lupe Murchison.
291   "John had a very good eye.": Int. Andre Emmerich.
291   "The thing that impressed me . . .": Int. Kenneth Noland.
293–294 ". . . must have thought he had flipped.": Int. Harry S. Parker III.
295   "My mother did not speak . . .": Int. Lupe Murchison.
295   "When I was born,": Int. Barbara Jeanne Murchison Coffman.
295   Mrs. Hale was in complete charge: Int. Golden Hale.

CHAPTER 17

300   spectacular 45.3 percent increase: See Chipman's book *The Dallas Cowboys and the NFL* for many more statistics on early attendance figures.
302   "To hell with him.": Int. Blackie Sherrod.
302   "The verdict came as sure . . .": *DMN,* Oct. 10, 1970. In an Oct. 23, 1970, letter "To the Dallas News," Clint wrote about the meeting, "within this eight-hour period if not, in fact within the thirty minutes of our discussion, the mayor made up his mind, stated his position, and refused to discuss the matter further."
303   he paid $1 million for ninety-acres: "Clint Tosses Stadium Pass," *DMN,* Jan. 29, 1967.
303   "Clint's bluff.": Chipman, *The Dallas Cowboys and the NFL,* p. 146.
305   to punish young Murchison: Ibid., pp. 148–49.
306   almost single-handedly designed: Int. Enslie Oglesby, an architect who designed many of the family's homes. "He'd call me occasionally, but he didn't really have an architect on the stadium."
307   he made the roof so light: Int. Enslie Oglesby.
307   designed Texas Stadium to look good on television: Ibid.
308   Clint's bond plan: Int. Blackie Sherrod.

309 "Wanta buy two seats . . .": Lukas, J. Anthony, "Wanta Buy Two Seats for the Dallas Cowboys?", *Esquire*, Sept. 1972.

309 "I'd say we lost a whole group . . .": Ibid., p. 122.

310 Fans bought $18 million: Int. Tex Schramm.

311 ". . . to give 'em too much too soon.": Ibid.

311 "Dallas won the toss . . .": Blair, Sam, *Dallas Cowboys: Pro or Con?*, Doubleday & Company, 1970, p. 273.

311 The game shook: Int. Lee Roy Jordan.

CHAPTER 18

314 "That's going to break . . .": Int. VML.

316 "Before we got started . . ." Int. Carr Pritchett.

318 LBJ breakfasts at Clint's: Int. Jim Clark Jr.

318 "I can't hear you." Int. EVB.

319 Nixon paid only $35,000: *NYT*, June 25, 1973. The $35,000 was $7,000 less than the mortgage (which the Murchisons paid). The lot next door was offered at $99,000.

319 contributed $50,000 to Nixon's 1972: *NYT*, Sept. 29, 1973.

319–320 "I'd like to buy a bank . . .: Van Buren, *Clint*, pp. 341–42.

320 a well-known clinic in Switzerland: Int. Dr. John Jenkins, who suggested the visit and traveled there with Murchison.

322 "In later years he was very . . .": Int. John Rogers.

322 ". . . no impressions . . .": Int. Clint Murchison III.

322–323 ". . . don't have much recollection . . .": Int. John Dabney Murchison Jr.

323 "Mr. Murchison's brain done . . .": Int. VML.

324 "His entire life was devoted . . .": Whitman, Alden "Oilman Enjoyed Making Money Grow," *NYT*, June 21, 1969.

325 "Early went off into the woods . . .": Tolbert, Frank X., "Athens Tamale Man Mourns Death of Mister Clint," *DMN*, June 21, 1969.

326 "We will never forget . . .": Van Buren, *Clint*, p. 357.

CHAPTER 19

327 "He hired and fired five . . .": Int. Spencer Martin.

327 who called him "Uncle Lennie.": Int. Jim Stroman.

327 These tense feelings: Int. Spencer Martin.

328 "We'd be at the apartment . . .": Ibid.

329 ". . . saw him with other women,": Int. Walter Hagan.

329 'Jane has a black belt . . .": Int. Bill Dunagan.

329 "Jane walked right in . . .": Int. Buffy Martin.

329 'I can't believe someone . . .": Int. Jim Stroman.

330 Murchison helicopter: Int. Robert F. Murchison.

330 "Clint had so many strange . . .": Int. Jane Murchison Haber.

332 "He did not say one word . . .": Int. Val Imm Bashour.

333 "When I was his guest . . .": Int. Steve Schneider.

334   "Gee, Bill, that's a small fortune.": Int. Bill Dunagan.

339   going to marry: Int. Jane Murchison Haber. Her marriage to Leonard Haber took place in 1976.

339   "There was a very unusual softness . . .": Int. Steve Schneider.

CHAPTER 20

344   "These are delicious, Clint,": Int. Bill Dunagan.

344   "I feel it's Roger's . . .": "And Then There Was One," *DMN,* Nov. 4,
1971.

345   Tacked on the bulletin board: Blair, *Dallas Cowboys: Pro or Con?* p.
420.

345   displayed this extraordinary recall: Int. Lee Roy Jordan.

346   "Get me the hell out of here . . .": Int. Enslie Oglesby.

346   strictly as a business investment: Int. John Murchison Jr.

347   On the eve of the Cowboys-Redskins: Int. Tom Webb.

348   great at acrobatics: Int. Bill Dunagan.

348   Clint stepped into the aisle: Int. VML.

348   "Clint, what the hell . . . ?": Int. Robert F. Murchison.

348   stood on his head to: Int. Enslie Oglesby.

349   ". . . almost blew a $40 million . . .": Int. Bill Dunagan.

350   "Clint loved glamour and Hollywood . . .": Int. Bill Dunagan.

350–351   Following the Super Bowl: Int. Suzanne Mitchell, director of
the Dallas Cowboys Cheerleaders.

352   Clint easily became seasick: Int. VML.

352   6,000-square-foot penthouse: the author toured the never-used
penthouse and Clint's former offices on Oct. 8, 1985.

353   "Kinda boring, isn't it?": Int. Jim Stroman.

353   Baker was a great salesman: Int. Lou Farris.

354   "He would give Clint a pro-forma . . .": Int. Spencer Martin.

354   compound growth rate of 15 percent: Bruck, Connie, *The American
Lawyer,* July/Aug. 1985, p. 76.

354   "Because most deals were so boring . . .": Int. Spencer Martin.

354   Archibold estate in Washington: Explanation of Clint's involvement with Archibold Estate comes from Spencer Martin and Tom
Webb.

355   Before joining Clint in 1973: "Beebe's Network Cast Long Shadow
in Thrift Industry," *DMN,* Dec. 23, 1988.

355   In 1985 Beebe was convicted: Ibid.

356   ". . . eight out of ten of Clint's projects . . .": Int. Lou Farris.

356   nothing frivolous about her: Int. John Taylor.

357   believed in the mystical: Int. Bobby Goldman, whom she dated before marrying Gil Brandt.

357   "She is the most empathetic . . .": Ibid.

357   "I lived on the wild side . . .": Murchison, Anne, *Milk for Babes:
Using the Bible to Find the Answers to Life's Questions,* Word Books,
Waco, Texas, 1979, p.22.

358 newlyweds stopped flying: Int. Bill Dunagan.
358 "a fairy-tale dream . . .": "Anne Murchison's Wealth 'Worth Nothing Without God'," *DTH,* March 25, 1978.
359 "Clint would have a group . . .": Int. Ruth Woodard.
359 the guy spent millions: Int. Lou Farris.
360 "I'll provide all the capital . . .": Int. Bill Dunagan.

CHAPTER 21

361 ". . . you've got to remember . . .": Int. Harry S. Parker III.
363 "John had the innate ability . . .": Int. Sid Stahl.
363 sympathized with him: Ibid.
364 "No one in Texas could . . ." Int. Nancy Overton Lemmon.
364 ". . . they went out to see," Int. Enslie Oglesby.
366 Senator Jacob Javits sitting: Int. John D. Murchison Jr.
367 knack for putting her guests: Int. Mary Noel Murchison Lamont.
367 "what to wear, do I have . . ." Murchison, *Milk for Babes,* p. 27.
367 "I wouldn't even let Clint sleep,": "ANNE MURCHISON FOUND CLINT, OIL MONEY, AND THE COWBOYS WEREN'T ENOUGH—WITHOUT GOD," *People,* Oct. 29, 1979, p. 104.
368 "We have our own private island . . .": "Anne Murchison's wealth 'worth nothing without god,' " *DTH,* March 25, 1978.
368 "She made the whole born-again thing . . .": Int. Buffy Martin.
368 "I let Jesus handle . . .": *People,* Oct. 29, 1979, p. 104.
370 Willie and Waylon straggled in: Int. Bill Dunagan.
372 "Why did you leave that great big hole . . .": Int. Robert Dedman.

CHAPTER 22

374 "Clint Sr. and Clint Jr. were nervous . . .": Int. Henry Gilchrist.
374 "a paragon of fiscal restraint.": Bruck, *The American Lawyer,* p. 70.
374 "Clint Jr. always supported John . . .": Int. Truman Kemper, longtime accountant for IMC and the family.
374 asked John to keep an eye: Int. John D. Murchison Jr.
375 Clint operated independently: Int. Truman Kemper.
375 "Those guys would turn in requests . . .": Ibid.
375 "Borrowing money was a game . . .": Int. Spencer Martin.
375 "Okay, what are you going to do . . .": Int. Bill Dunagan. It was Dunagan of whom Clint asked the question.
375 This lack of judiciousness: although this was typical of Clint's putting friends rather than qualified people in charge of his investments, Dunagan successfully planned the nineteen-condo project, Sundance Villas, and quickly sold all the condos (several to Hollywood stars). The project was such a success that Clint (with another associate) tried, but failed, to duplicate the concept of the development on another parcel of land nearby.
376 scrambling for ways to pay off loans: Int. Taz Speer, who was

brought in by Clint Jr. in 1980, to oversee the New Orleans East project, and who later joined John Jr.'s legal fight against his uncle.

377   'I'm no longer liable . . .' ": Int. Spencer Martin.

378   The dissolution agreement: Int. Taz Speer.

378   These thoughts haunted: Int. John D. Murchison Jr.

380   an agreement called ROTAG: Int. Taz Speer.

380   "I appreciate all that you . . .": Int. John D. Murchison Jr.

380   "Dad couldn't talk . . .": Ibid.

381   "When my parents were home,": Int. John D. Murchison Jr.

383   "When Clint and John needed money . . .": Int. Truman Kemper.

383   lead attorneys signed off the trusteeship: Henry Gilchrist had been the primary trustee for the MMR trusts from 1974 until he resigned in 1977.

384   "That was always going to happen somewhere . . .": Int. Truman Kemper.

384   "The kids had an incredibly starry-eyed: Int. Taz Speer.

Part Four

CHAPTER 23

389   His family doctor: Int. Dr. Raymond Thomasson, who had been Lupe's doctor since her childhood. In the last few years of his life John had asthma attacks and was taken to St. Paul Hospital about once a month. Lupe was grateful when Thomasson told her he had had John baptized a Catholic.

389   "The morning after John . . .": Int. Nancy Overton Lemmon.

389–390   ". . . I was a very driven person.": Int. Barbara Jeanne Murchison Coffman.

390   "If we're not careful, we . . .": *Time,* June 25, 1979, p. 55.

391   "John had a full head of steam . . .:" Int. Taz Speer.

391   "We'll just call that the Dabney file." Ibid.

392   "He was pledging everything . . .": Int. John D. Murchison Jr.

392   to threaten her brother-in-law: Bruck, *The American Lawyer,* p. 70.

393   "I'm working as fast as I can . . .": Int. Taz Speer.

393   ". . . 'Let's have a plan . . .' ": Ibid.

393–394   "Most of the people at IMC . . .": Int. Truman Kemper.

394   however embarrassing and unpleasant: Bruck, *The American Lawyer,* p. 73.

394–395   confronted by two masked men: "Murchison Widow Robbed by 2 Bandits," *DMN,* April 4, 1981.

395   "Lupe had been weakening . . .": Int. Taz Speer.

395   "more scathing and more": Int. James Speer.

395   "a stupid kid who lacked . . ." Int. John D. Murchison Jr.

396   $30 million in exemplary damages: John later agreed to drop the damages he had demanded in his original suit.

396–397   guilt toward his father: Int. James Speer.

397   ". . . Lupe was completely in the dark . . .": Bill Lamont told this to the author at a party at Lupe's home honoring Princess Michael of Kent.

397   ". . . viewed John as real scum . . .": Int. Taz Speer.

398   told Lupe that the museum's directors: Int. Harry Parker III.

398   "I love 'Stake Hitch' . . .": Int. Lupe Murchison.

399   took a paper loss: Bruck, Connie, *The American Lawyer*, July/Aug. 1985, p. 73.

399   "All the assets were mortgaged . . .": Ibid.

399   "I remember looking at the . . .": Ibid, p. 75.

399   He had borrowed $7 million: Int. Spencer Martin, Clint's partner in the Summit.

400   "When what few honorable . . .": Int. Phil Bee.

400   ". . . headed for the ashcan." Int. Spencer Martin.

400   he still believed as late as 1982: Int. Lou Farris.

401   "I was chairman of the large loan . . .": Int. Marcus Ginsburg.

401–402   "We could be in the john . . .": Int. Bill Dunagan.

402   Schramm purchased a small marina: St. John, *Tex! The Man Who Built the Dallas Cowboys*, p. 332. Note: "This was really Schramm's deal. Dad just got involved in this out of gratitude to Schramm," says Robert F. Murchison.

403   The most notorious of these: "Beebe's Network Cast Long Shadow in Thrift Industry," *DMN*, Dec. 23, 1988.

403   Beebe institutions reportedly lent: Ibid.

403   arrival of interstate banking: Bruck, *The American Lawyer*, p. 75.

404   October 1981, when he forced Clint: Int. Taz Speer who says Clint Jr. was forced into this, in part, because he was trying to sell one of OSI's divisions and he had to state there was no pending litigation. Also, John Jr. refused to sign his name to a petition that would allow an extension on the OSI debt.

404   John dealt his most severe blow: Int. James Speer.

404   'If you don't release my assets . . .": Int. Taz Speer.

405   "Clint really had no defense.": Int. James Speer.

406   "Soon after this Lupe began . . .": Ibid.

406   "We backed off when the intrafamily . . .": Int. Henry Gilchrist.

407   "were protected like the crown . . .": Bruck, *The American Lawyer*, p. 79.

407   "Let's flush him.": Ibid.

407   One banker recalls filing: The banker was Marcus Ginsburg, whose uncle, Sol Brachman, provided Clint Sr. with much of the credit that helped build his oil fortune in the 1930s.

408   "Most of the meetings with . . .": Int. Lou Farris.

408   "Don't worry,": Bruck, *The American Lawyer*, p. 80.

CHAPTER 24

409   Rockefeller asked: Int. Spencer Martin.
411   seemed to be growing more interested: Int. Rev. Olen Griffing.
411   "I could never have afforded . . .": Ibid.
411   'Are you being pressured . . .': Ibid.
411   Griffing baptized Clint: Ibid.
412   "I don't need thanks here . . .": Int. Ralph Pahel, executive director, Boys' Clubs of Dallas.
412   "Other people, including my older brothers . . .": Int. Robert F. Murchison.
413   a Bible session at his father's house: Int. Robert F. Murchison.
413   "find out what the team . . .": Int. Bill Dunagan.
414   "He began by explaining that during . . .": Int. Tex Schramm.
414–415 Schramm was crushed: Ibid. During the interview with the author, as Schramm talked about Clint's illness and selling the team, he could barely hold back his tears.
415   he had given both Schramm and Tom Landry stock options: St. John, Tex!, The Man Who Built the Dallas Cowboys, pp. 324–25.
416   at one point had considered buying the team herself: Int. Steve Rooth.
417   "There are thousands of businessmen . . .": DMN, March 21, 1984.

CHAPTER 25

418   Four hundred guests: much of the description of the party and its guests comes from an interview with Mary Noel Lamont at her home in 1985.
420   "How do you like that?": Int. Annette Besser.
422   "Now that limes cost . . .": overheard by the author at a party.
423   "People can't believe we have it . . .": Int. Lupe Murchison.
423   John did not receive an invitation: Int. John D. Murchison Jr.
426   "When Bill and I got engaged . . .": Ibid.
427   "It worked,": Ibid.
427   Charity balls in hotel ballrooms: the author, as Society Editor of the Dallas Morning News, witnessed at first hand this end of an era.

CHAPTER 26

428   "Clint, now that you can barely . . .": Int. Steve Schneider.
429   longtime, trusted associate of Clint Sr.: this was Steve Rooth, who says, "The family asked me to step in and help, and I felt I owed the Murchisons that much."
429   "Practically the next day . . .": Int. Spencer Martin.
429   In fact, a few impatient lenders: Information on which lenders sued Clint, when, and for how much comes from dozens of newspaper articles, as well as the author's study of the actual legal documents.

430 problems as merely "transitory,": Lou Farris, Clint's righthand man, insists that Clint at this time truly believed he could work his way out of his financial problems within a few months.

430 "Goddamn it, Clint,": Woolley, Bryan, "The Rise and Fall of the Murchison Empire," *DTH,* April 14, 1985.

430 he began a counteroffensive: "Murchison Fights $100 Million in Creditor Claims," *DMN,* Sept. 9, 1984.

431 this bank was anything but friendly: Ibid.

431 president of a large Dallas bank: Int. Taz Speer.

431 Dallas bankers were reticent: Int. D. M. Lynn, who became the Plan Trustee representing Murchison's creditors.

431 *Forbes* magazine: Oct. 1, 1984, It wrote, "Despite cash flow, creditors' problems, worth at least $250 million."

432 Lupe's two eldest daughters: the lawsuit was filed in Dallas District Court on Nov. 13, 1984, Case No. 8414932F.

432 Just how desperate Clint's: "Auction of Murchison Properties Blocked," *DMN,* Dec. 5, 1984;

432–433 would try to auction the land: "Murchison Blocks Land Auction," *DMN,* Feb. 6, 1985.

433 He had saved very little correspondence: Int. Ruth Woodard.

433 a few family members insist: Int. Robert F. Murchison. "His problems were really complex, and I'm not even sure that 'Pop' [Clint Sr.] could have pulled out of the troubles that came with high interest rates. Also Dad was dealing with a lot of bad people in his businesses. These guys really hurt his ability to operate."

434 ". . . sell his assets at a sheriff's sale . . .": "Rich Man, Poor Man: Murchison Confronts Texas-Size Problems," *Wall Street Journal,* Jan. 22, 1985.

435 "Pulling in the drive . . .": Int. Gerald Urbach

437 Lou Farris, who was still scrambling: Int. Lou Farris.

438 he had borrowed $281 million: "Murchison Debt Meeting," *NYT,* June 19, 1985.

438 Murchison's assets included: "Murchison's Debts Total $396,693,827," *DMN,* June 18, 1985.

438 Clint had already raised some $300 million: "Judge OKs Murchison Debt Plan," *DMN,* June 17, 1986.

438–439 30 cents for each dollar sought: Ibid.

439 "Each time I went to the house . . .": Int. Bill Dunagan.

439 meager worth of $2 million: Int. D.M. Lynn.

439–440 "Clint was back in his bedroom,": Int. John Taylor.

440 the children and Jane went to the hospital: Int. Robert F. Murchison.

440 John walked into Clint's room: Int. John D. Murchison Jr.

441 Clint's children told their mother: Int. Jane Murchison Haber.

441 he planned every detail of his funeral: Int. Ruth Woodard.

441 what Clint intended for his memorial: the service was videotaped.

442 ". . . was Clint's last prank.": Int. Bill Dunagan.

CHAPTER 27

445 "If John Jr. hadn't . . .": Int. Truman Kemper.

445 The assets in John's: Int. John Murchison Jr.

445 John's estate was valued at $145 million: Lists of inventory filed in the Probate Court of Dallas County.

446 "I like the country . . .": Int. Barbara Jeanne Murchison Coffman.

446 "I'm not in a lot of organizations . . .": Int. Mary Noel Murchison Lamont.

447 abstract works, using one of the same dealers: The dealer is Janie C. Lee of Houston, Texas.

447 is free of debt: Int. Taz Speer.

448 "Some members . . .": Int. John D. Murchison Jr.

448 an insurance policy against: Int. D.M. Lynn.

448 filed two major lawsuits: Case No. 385-31014-A-11, charging that money was fraudulently transferred in connection with a company called CBCR, Inc., was filed July 22, 1988, in the Dallas Division of the U.S. Bankruptcy Court; Case No. 385-30266-HCA-11, charging that the children and their trusts gave themselves priority in insuring that Clint Jr.'s financial difficulties were diverted from them, filed on July 24, 1988 in the Dallas Division of the U.S. Bankruptcy Court.

448 and amended another: Case No. CA3-88-0929-T, charging— among other things—that Tony Roma's stock was transferred to Clint Jr.'s children in exchange for worthless stock, was originally filed in 1986 and amended July 21, 1988, in the Dallas Division of U.S. Bankruptcy Court.

449 "Going to work for the family . . .": Int. Clint Murchison III.

450 withdrew all her personal financial: Int. Truman Kemper.

451 "She's not one of my favorite people.": Int. Robert F. Murchison.

451 "I can't drive by the house,": Int. Robert Murchison

451 "Clint was happier here . . .": Int. VML.

453 "I'll never sell it . . .": Int. Lupe Murchison.

454 "I just love y'all,": the author attended the party.

EPILOGUE

456 business and personal bankruptcies: Statistical Report prepared by the U.S. Bankruptcy Court Northern District of Texas, Dallas Division, Dec. 1988, p. 3.

457 put their Placid Oil: *Wall Street Journal,* Sept. 2, 1986, p. 3:1.

457 sustained a loss of $1 billion: "HUNTS ARE RULED PART OF SCHEME TO CONTROL SILVER," *NYT,* Aug. 21, 1988.

457 heart surgeon Denton Cooley: "Bankruptcies Elevate Failure to a New Level," *DMN,* Jan. 22, 1988.

457 Former Texas Governor John Connally: "Bringing Down the Gavel on the Life of a Texan," *NYT,* Jan. 24, 1988.

457 Robert Sakowitz, Houston's high: Cook, Alison, "The Fraying Empire of Bobby Sakowitz," *Texas Monthly,* Dec. 1985.

Bibliography

Newspapers and magazines are identified in the Notes.

Acheson, Sam, *35,000 Days in Texas: A History of the Dallas News and Its Forebears,* The Macmillan Company, New York, 1938

Ambrose, Stephen E., *Nixon: The Education of a Politician, 1913–1962,* Simon and Schuster, New York, 1987

Amory, Cleveland, *Who Killed Society?: The Warfare of Celebrity with Aristocracy in America—from the "First Families" to the "Four Hundred" to "Publi-ciety,"* Harper & Brothers, Publishers, New York, 1960

Anderson, Patrick, *Lords of the Earth,* Doubleday & Company, Inc., Garden City, New York, 1984

Askins, Col. Charles, *Texas, Guns & History,* Winchester Press, New York, 1970

Bainbridge, John, *The Super Americans: A Picture of Life in the United States, as Brought into Focus, Bigger than Life, in the Land of the Millionaires—Texas,* Holt, Rinehart and Winston, New York, Chicago, San Francisco, 1972

Blair, John M., *The Control of Oil,* Pantheon Books, New York, 1976

Blair, Sam, *Dallas Cowboys: Pro or Con?,* Doubleday & Company, New York, 1970

Boatright, Mody C., and Owens, William A., *Tales from the Derrick Floor: A People's History of the Oil Industry,* Doubleday & Company, Inc., Garden City, New York, 1970

Boorstin, Daniel J., *The Americans: The Democratic Experience,* Random House, New York, 1973

———, *The Americans: The National Experience,* Vintage Books, New York, 1965

Breen, Divine, and Fredrickson, Williams, *America: Past and Present,* 2nd Edition, Scott, Foresman and Company, Glenview, Illinois; London, England, 1987

Bryan, J., III, and Murphy, Charles J.V., *The Windsor Story,* William Morrow & Company, Inc., New York, 1979

Carleton, Don E., *Red Scare: Right Wing Hysteria, Fifties Fanaticism and Their Legacy in Texas,* Texas Monthly Press, Inc., Austin, Texas, 1985

Caro, Robert A., *The Path To Power: The Years of Lyndon Johnson,* Alfred A. Knopf, Inc., New York, 1982

Chesnutt, N. P., *Southern Union,* Mangan Books, El Paso, Texas, 1979

Chipman, Donald, Randolph Campbell, and Robert Calvert, *The Dallas Cowboys and the NFL,* University of Oklahoma Press, Norman, Oklahoma, 1970

Clark, James A., *An Oilman's Oilman,* Gulf Publishing Company, Houston, Texas, 1979

Clark, James A., and Halbouty, Michel, *The Last Boom: The Exciting Saga of the Discovery of the Greatest Oil Field in America,* Shearer Publishing, Texas, 1972, 1984

Clark, Joseph L., and Linder, Dorothy A., *The Story of Texas,* Heath and Company, 1955

Conaway, James, *The Texans,* Alfred A. Knopf, New York, 1976

Cook, Fred J., *The Nightmare Decade: The Life and Times of Senator Joe McCarthy,* Random House, New York, 1971

Curran, Bob, *The $400,000 Quarterback: or The League That Came in from the Cold,* The Macmillan Company, New York, 1965

Current, Freidel, Williams, *A History of The United States, Since 1865,* Alfred A. Knopf, New York, 1964

Elder, Jack, and Pirtle, Caleb, III, *The Glory Days,* Nortex Press, Austin, Texas, 1986

Engler, Robert, *The Politics of Oil: A Study of Private Power and Democratic Directions,* The Macmillan Company, New York, 1961

Fehrenbach, T. R., *Lone Star: A History of Texas and the Texans,* The Macmillan Company, New York, 1968

————, *Seven Keys to Texas,* Texas Western Press, The University of Texas at El Paso, 1983

Ferber, Edna, *Giant,* Doubleday and Company, Inc., New York, 1952

Gent, Peter, *North Dallas Forty,* William Morrow and Company, Inc., New York, 1973

Gray, Earle, *The Great Canadian Oil Patch,* Maclean–Hunter Limited, Toronto, Canada, 1970

Greene, A. C., *Dallas: The Deciding Years—A Historical Portrait,* Encino Press, Austin, Texas, 1973

Griffith, Robert, *The Politics of Fear: Joseph R. McCarthy and the Senate,* The University Press of Kentucky, Lexington, Kentucky, 1970

Hand, Jack, *Heroes of the NFL,* Random House, Inc., New York, 1965

Harris, Leon, *Merchant Princes: An Intimate History of Jewish Families Who Built Great Department Stores,* Berkley Books, New York, 1980

Hellman, Lillian, *Scoundrel Time,* Bantam, New York, 1976

Higdon, Hal, *PRO FOOTBALL U.S.A.,* G. P. Putnam's Sons, New York, 1968

Hurt, Harry, III, *Texas Rich: The Hunt Dynasty from the Early Oil Days Through the Silver Crash,* W.W. Norton & Co., New York, 1982

Johnson, Arthur Menzies, *The Development of American Petroleum Pipelines,* Cornell University Press, Ithaca, New York, 1956

Josephson, Matthew, *The Robber Barons: The Great American Capitalists,* A Harvest Book, Harcourt, Brace & World, Inc., 1934, 1962

Kilbourn, William, *Pipeline,* Clarke, Irwin & Company Limited, Toronto, Vancouver, 1970

LaRue, Frank, *Have I Told You This One?* Frank LaRue, Athens, Texas, 1980

Leslie, Warren, *Dallas Public and Private,* Grossman Publishers, New York, 1964

Lisle, Laurie, *Portrait of an Artist: A Biography of Georgia O'Keeffe,* University of New Mexico Press, Albuquerque, 1986

Marcus, Stanley, *Minding the Store: A Memoir,* Little, Brown and Company, Boston, Toronto, 1974

McDonald, Archie, ed., *Eastern Texas History: Selections from the East Texas Historical Journal,* Jenkins Publishing Co., Austin, Texas, 1978

McDonald, William L., *Dallas Rediscovered: A Photographic Chronicle of Urban Expansion 1870–1925,* The Dallas Historical Society, Dallas, Texas, 1978

Meyers, Jeff, *Dallas Cowboys,* Macmillan Publishing Co., Inc., New York, 1974

Murchison, Anne Ferrell, *Milk for Babes: Using the Bible to Find the Answers to Life's Questions,* Word Books, Waco, Texas, 1979

Nevin, David, *The Texans: What They Are–and Why,* Bonanza Books, New York, 1968

O'Connor, Harvey, *The Empire of Oil,* Monthly Review Press, New York, 1955

O'Connor, Richard, *The Oil Barons: Men of Greed and Grandeur,* Little, Brown and Company, Boston, Toronto, 1971

Owens, William A., *This Stubborn Soil: A Frontier Boyhood,* Nick Lyons Books, New York, 1966

Pearson, Preston, *Hearing the Noise: My Life in the NFL,* William Morrow and Company, Inc., New York, 1985

Presley, James, *A Saga of Wealth: The Rise of the Texas Oilman,* G. P. Putnam's Son's, New York, 1978

Reeves, Thomas C., *The Life and Times of Joe McCarthy,* Stein and Day, New York, 1982

Rogers, John William, *The Lusty Texans of Dallas,* E. P. Dutton and Company, Inc., New York, 1951

Rosenberg, Leon Joseph, *Sangers': Pioneer Texas Merchants,* Texas State Historical Association, Austin, 1978

St. John, Bob, *We Love You Cowboys,* Sport Magazine Press, New York, 1972

St. John, Bob, *Tex!: The Man Who Built the Dallas Cowboys,* Prentice-Hall, Englewood Cliffs, New Jersey, 1988

Terry, Marshall, *Dallas Stories,* Southern Methodist University Press, Dallas, 1987

St. John, Bob, *Tex!: The Man Who Built the Dallas Cowboys,* Prentice-Hall, Englewood Cliffs, New Jersey, 1988

Terry, Marshall, *Dallas Stories,* Southern Methodist University Press, Dallas, 1987

Tolbert, Frank X., *Neiman-Marcus, Texas,* Henry Holt and Company, New York, 1953

Van Buren, Ernestine, *Clint: Clinton Williams Murchison—A Biography,* Eakin Press, Austin, Texas, 1986

Wright, Lawrence, *In the New World: Growing Up with America, 1960–1984,* Alfred A. Knopf, New York, 1988

Unpublished Manuscript:

Murchison, Robert, *Clint Murchison, The Texas Entrepreneur* (written April, 19, 1976)

Index